BRIEF SIXTH EDITION

# THE INFORMED ARGUMENT

## ROBERT P. YAGELSKI
State University of New York at Albany

## ROBERT K. MILLER
University of St. Thomas

## with AMY J. CROUSE-POWERS
State University of New York at Oneonta

THOMSON

WADSWORTH

Australia • Canada • Mexico • Singapore • Spain • United Kingdom • United States

BRIEF EDITION

# THE INFORMED ARGUMENT

**ROBERT P. YAGELSKI**

State University of New York at Albany

**ROBERT K. MILLER**

University of St. Thomas

with **AMY J. CROUSE-POWERS**

State University of New York at Oneonta

**THOMSON**
™
**WADSWORTH**

Australia • Canada • Mexico • Singapore • Spain • United Kingdom • United States

**THOMSON**
™
**WADSWORTH**

**The Informed Argument, Brief Sixth Edition**
Yagelski/Miller

**Publisher:** *Michael Rosenberg*

**Acquisitions Editor:** *Dickson Musslewhite*

**Senior Development Editor:** *Michell Phifer*

**Editorial Assistants:** *Marita Sermolins, Stephen Marsi*

**Senior Production Editor:** *Sally Cogliano*

**Director of Marketing:** *Lisa Kimball*

**Marketing Manager:** *Carrie Brandon*

**Senior Print Buyer:** *Mary Beth Hennebury*

**Compositor:** *ATLIS Graphics & Design*

**Project Manager:** *Hearthside Publishing Services*

**Photography Manager:** *Sheri Blaney*

**Photo Researcher:** *Kathleen Olson*

**Cover/Text Designer:** *Linda Beaupré/Stone House Art*

**Printer:** *Quebecor World*

For permission to use material from this text or product submit a request online at: http://www.thomsonrights.com

Any additional questions about permissions can be submitted by email to thomsonrights@thomson.com

ISBN: 0-8384-5709-6
(Brief Sixth Edition with Infotrac® College Edition)

Library of Congress Control Number: 2003106822

Cover Image: © 2003 Getty Images

Inside Front Cover Image: Oil on canvas mural from the U.N. Security Council Chamber, by Per Kogh. UN/DPI Photo.

*The Informed Argument,* Brief Sixth Edition, represents a significant revision and redesign of *The Informed Argument,* fifth edition. Like the previous editions, this new edition of *The Informed Argument* grows out of the belief that argumentation can be a powerful vehicle for learning. The book is intended to encourage students to read, reflect, and write arguments about serious issues in an informed way. But although our focus in this new edition is squarely on argumentation, our more ambitious goal is to contribute to the development of students as literate citizens in a complex and changing society.

Accordingly, this new edition builds on an idea that was introduced in the fifth edition: that argumentation should be a means of negotiating differences in an effort to address serious problems that we face as citizens, consumers, and members of various communities and cultures. Our hope is that as students inquire into argumentation, develop an understanding of its complexities, and gain the competence to engage effectively in argumentation, they will also acquire a sense of the possibilities for argument to serve social and ethical purposes.

This new edition of *The Informed Argument,* Brief Sixth Edition incorporates recent scholarly thinking into a traditional framework for argumentation based on the principles of classical rhetoric. Specifically, our presentation of argument reflects a contemporary understanding of the ways in which cultural context shapes arguments. In addition, our approach to argument draws on recent theories of language and discourse to provide students with a sophisticated lens through which to view the arguments they read and develop their written arguments.

## KEY FEATURES OF THIS EDITION

### A CONTEMPORARY PERSPECTIVE ON TRADITIONAL ARGUMENTATION

Throughout this book, we present argument as an activity that always occurs within specific contexts and is intended to serve a wide range of social and political purposes. Chapter 1, "The Purposes of Argument," will help students appreciate how argumentation occurs in various situations for a variety of ends. Chapter 3, "The Contexts for Argument," explores the different aspects of context, including culture, influence argumentation. Chapter 4, "The Media for Argument," examines how various media shape argumentation and can be powerful tools for argument in their own right. These chapters all include substantial new material. However, we have retained from the previous edition the discussions of traditional elements of argumentation that will be familiar to writing teachers, especially in Chapter 2, "Strategies for Argument." There you will find treatment of various approaches to logic in argument, including the Toulmin model for argumentation, as well as logical fallacies. You will also find expanded discussions of *ethos* and *pathos* in argument. Similarly, Chapter 5, "Constructing Effective Arguments" includes the same straightforward advice to student writers that has characterized the previous editions of *The Informed Argument.* But it also includes an expanded treatment of the writing process as an integral part of inquiry into the topics about which students compose their arguments. As in previous editions, student essays are included here as

## RESEARCH AS AN INTEGRAL PART OF ARGUMENT

Like all previous editions, *The Informed Argument Brief,* sixth edition, includes substantial treatment of research — from exploring a topic to finding and documenting sources. We believe that effective argumentation is informed argumentation; consequently, we pre-sent research as an integral part of the process of writing an effective argument. In Chapter 6, "Doing Research" and Chapter 7, "Documenting Your Sources," students will find useful advice for becoming informed about their subjects in ways that will enhance their arguments.

## DIVERSE READINGS THAT FOCUS ON NEGOTIATING DIFFERENCES

The reading selections in this edition reflect the book's focus on argumentation as a way to negotiate differences and solve problems. The readings are organized around six main themes. The organizing scheme grows out of our view that arguments that follow familiar pro/con patterns tend to oversimplify important issues and thus work against problem solving. Accordingly, we have resisted presenting examples of arguments that fall easily into pro or con categories.

The themes of the six reading chapters reflect traditional issues — education, the environment, free enterprise, and so on — that are being transformed by recent social, political, cultural, and technological developments. The writers represent a range of interests, professions, perspectives, and cultural backgrounds. Moreover, the majority of readings are recent, reflecting contemporary points of view; they also reflect a diversity of media: there are selections from traditional print publications, such as the *New York Times,* newer publications such as *Z Magazine,* and online journals. Some classic arguments, such as Martin Luther King, Jr.'s "Letter From a Birmingham Jail," have been retained from previous editions, which helps provide historical context for contemporary arguments and also gives students traditional examples of argumentation.

## NEW TO THIS EDITION

The new features of *The Informed Argument Brief,* sixth edition, can be grouped into three main categories: (1) expanded discussion of key elements of argumentation, including new sections on context and media; (2) new and re-organized readings selections; and (3) innovative new pedagogical features — all in a completely redesigned text.

## SIGNIFICANTLY EXPANDED TREATMENT OF KEY ELEMENTS OF ARGUMENTATION

- A new chapter on context includes discussion of the role of culture in argumentation.

- A new chapter on the media for argument, which includes in-depth treatment of electronic media such as the Internet.

- Expanded discussion of visual rhetoric, including issues of design and layout.

■ Expanded discussion of the uses of evidence in argumentation.

■ New student essays that provide models of different approaches to argument.

## NEW READING SELECTIONS ORGANIZED AROUND SIX MAIN THEMES

■ A "cluster" of readings on related topics in each chapter: ownership, education, environments, national identity, free enterprise, and globalization.

■ New reading selections that reflect diverse viewpoints and cultural backgrounds.

■ Readings from a variety of traditional and online publications.

■ "Con-Texts" that include important documents to provide historical and cultural background and reinforce the importance of understanding argument in context.

## INNOVATIVE NEW PEDAGOGICAL FEATURES

■ Lively introductions to each cluster to provide background for the cluster topic.

■ Four kinds of supplementary boxes for each reading selection to help students better understand the argument and to highlight argumentative strategies:
   ■ *Gloss:* Information on specific people, events, or concepts in the reading. Glosses are linked to the text with asterisk and dagger symbols.
   ■ *Context:* Background on issues, ideas, events, or persons in the reading.
   ■ *Sidebar:* Excerpts from texts referred to in the reading.
   ■ *Complication:* Information that complicates the argument made in the reading.
   ■ Context, Sidebar, and Complication boxes are color keyed to the text.

■ *Questions for Discussion* for each reading that include three main kinds of questions:
   ■ Questions to help students understand the argument,
   ■ Questions that focus attention on argumentative strategies and context, and
   ■ Questions that encourage students to be self-reflective about their views.

■ *Negotiating Differences* assignments at the end of each cluster that engage students in argumentation as way to solve a problem related to the cluster topic.

## ACKNOWLEDGMENTS

The debts we have incurred in writing this new edition are too great to repay in words. Many people have helped us put this project together and have seen it through to publication. In particular, several terrific people at Heinle have been instrumental in producing this new edition. Most importantly, Dickson Musslewhite provided guidance, leadership, insight, savvy, and good humor throughout; we are deeply grateful to him and appreciate his efforts and friendship. Michell Phifer was an extremely dependable and consistent editor whose knowledge of the editorial process and attention to detail kept the project moving in the face of many unexpected obstacles; we are sincerely thankful for her good humor and seemingly infinite patience. Also, Steve Marsi deserves our gratitude for putting up with endless requests and complaints in handling paperwork, answering questions, and getting materials where they needed to go. Linda Beaupré expertly created the innovative design of this edition. Laura Horowitz and Karyn Morrison were also instrumental in keeping the project on track. The many other Heinle staff members involved in this project were always professional and efficient and ultimately helped make the work go smoothly and successfully. We are very grateful to all of them.

We owe an enormous debt to Amy Crouse-Powers, of the State University of New York at Oneonta, who served as research assistant and sometime writer for this project. As reliable as she is efficient, Amy's excellent work was crucial for this project, which would never have been completed without her. We cannot thank her enough.

Sincere thanks also go to Cheryl Glenn, of Pennsylvania State University, who offered advice and moral support at key moments in the writing of this edition, and Maria Markiewicz, of the State University of New York at Albany, who never failed to get manuscripts in the mail on time, even when they were dropped on her desk at the last minute.

We also wish to thank Kristen Brubaker, Rachel Guetter, and Kristen Montgomery Szala, all of whom contributed essays to this edition and who displayed patience and commitment throughout the process of responding to our comments on their writing. Their hard work and dependability made our work easier, and their essays have made this a better book.

In addition, we are grateful to the reviewers who examined parts of the manuscript for this edition as we developed it: Brenda Brueggemann, Ohio State University; Jim Crosswhite, University of Oregon; John Fleming, Southern New Hampshire University; Julie Foust, Utah State University; Debbie Hawhee, University of Illinois; Andrea Herrmann, University of Arkansas, Little Rock; Elizabeth Johnston, Indiana University of Pennsylvania; Thomas Mitchell, Texas A&M International University; John Orozco, Los Angeles Mission College, Mission; Phil Stucky, Harold Washington College; Theresa Thompson, Valdosta State University; and Mark Wiley, California State University, Long Beach. Their careful and thoughtful comments gave us much needed guidance as well as affirmation for the project. We also wish to thank the many instructors and students who have used earlier editions of this book and helped us to understand what to retain and what to revise.

Finally, special thanks must go to Adam and Aaron Yagelski, and especially to Cheryl Hafich Yagelski, who provided space, support, love, and confidence as this book was being completed.

**Bob Yagelski**
**Robert K. Miller**

# CONTENTS

## Part I
### AN INTRODUCTION TO ARGUMENT 1

What Is an Argument? 4
Why Learn to Write Effective Arguments? 6

## CHAPTER 1 | THE PURPOSES OF ARGUMENT 8

**Arguments to Assert 11**
**Arguments to Inquire 13**
**Arguments to Dominate 16**
**Arguments to Negotiate and Reconcile 18**

## CHAPTER 2 | STRATEGIES FOR ARGUMENT 22

**Logical Arguments 24**
   Reasoning Inductively 25
   Reasoning Deductively 26
      *The Syllogism 28* | *The Enthymeme 29* | *Cultural Differences in Logical Arguments 30*
   The Toulmin Model of Argumentation 31
      *Understanding Claims and Warrants 32* | *Evaluating Claims and Warrants 33*
**Fallacies 35**
   Appealing to Pity 36
   Appealing to Prejudice 36
   Appealing to Tradition 37
   Arguing by Analogy 37
   Attacking the Character of Opponents 37
   Attributing False Causes 38
   Attributing Guilt by Association 38
   Begging the Question 38
   Equivocating 39
   Ignoring the Question 39
   Jumping to Conclusions 39
   Opposing a Straw Man 39
   Presenting a False Dilemma 40
   Reasoning That Does Not Follow 40
   Sliding Down a Slippery Slope 40
**Emotional Arguments 41**
**Character-Based Arguments 43**

## CHAPTER 3 | THE CONTEXTS OF ARGUMENT 52

**The Rhetorical Situation 54**
Analyzing Your Audience 55
Imagining Your Audience 56
**Cultural Context 58**
Understanding Culture 58
Considering Culture in Argument 60
Considering Gender 61
Considering Age 63
Considering Sexual Orientation 64
**Historical Context 65**

## CHAPTER 4 | THE MEDIA FOR ARGUMENT 68

**Analyzing Arguments in Print 70**
Reading Arguments Critically 70
Evaluating Ethos 73
Appraising Evidence 76
*Facts as Evidence 76 | Personal Experience as Evidence 78 | Authority as Evidence 79 | Values as Evidence 80*
*Presenting Evidence in Visual Form 81*
**Analyzing Arguments in Visual Media 82**
Design and Color 86
Art as Visual Argument 88
Integrating Visual Elements and Text 93
**Analyzing Arguments in Electronic Media 97**
The Internet 97
Web Sites 99
*Online Versions of Print Arguments 99 | Hypertextual Web Sites 99 | Web Sites as Arguments 103*
Online Discussion Forums 105
Radio and Television 110

## CHAPTER 5 | CONSTRUCTING ARGUMENTS 112

**Managing the Composing Process 114**
Understanding Composing as Inquiry 114
Defining Your Topic 115
Considering Audience 117
Identifying Your Audience 117 | Making Concessions 118 | Understanding Audience Expectations 119
How One Student Addresses Her Audience 119
Defining Your Terms 124
**Structuring an Argument 125**
Classical Arrangement 126
Rogerian Argument 127
Logical Arrangements 132
Inductive Reasoning 132 | Deductive Reasoning 134 | Using the Toulmin Model 138
**Supporting Claims and Presenting Evidence 144**
**Using Language Effectively 145**

# Part II
## WORKING WITH SOURCES

## CHAPTER 6 | DOING RESEARCH 150

**Reading Critically 152**
Previewing 153
Annotating 154
Summarizing 155
Synthesizing 157
**Taking Notes 159**
**Avoiding Plagiarism 161**
**Finding Relevant Material 163**
Getting Started 163
Avoiding Selective Research 164
Using the Internet 164
Searching for Magazine and Journal Articles 167
Searching for Newspaper Articles 170
Using Abstracting Services 173
Looking for Books 173
**Conducting Interviews and Surveys 175**

## CHAPTER 7 | DOCUMENTING YOUR SOURCES 178

**Compiling a Preliminary Bibliography 180**
**Organizing a Research Paper 180**
**Integrating Source Material into Your Paper 181**
**Citing Sources 182**
  Footnotes and Content Notes 184
  Parenthetical (In-Text) Documentation 185
    *The MLA Author/Work Style 186* | *The APA Author/Year Style 188*
  Organizing a Bibliography 190
    *Works Cited in MLA Style 191* | *References in APA Style 199*
**Preparing Your Final Draft 207**

# Part III
## NEGOTIATING DIFFERENCES

## CHAPTER 8 | OWNERSHIP 210

**Cluster: Who Owns Music? 212**
  *Con-Text: The Importance of Music 213*
  1. Janis Ian, "Free Downloads Play Sweet Music" 214
  2. Richard Taruskin, "Music Dangers and the Case for Control" 219
  3. Jeffrey O.G. Ogbar and Vijay Prashad, "Black Is Back" 227
  4. Jenny Toomey, "Empire of the Air" 232

## CHAPTER 9 | EDUCATION 238

**Cluster: How Should We Determine What Our Children Learn? 240**
  *Con-Text: The Report of the Committee of Ten, 1892 241*
  1. Eleanor Martin, " 'No' Is the Right Answer" 242
  2. Patricia Williams, "Tests, Tracking, and Derailment" 246
  3. Gregory Cizek, "Unintended Consequences of High Stakes Testing" 250
  4. Bertell Ollman, "Why So Many Exams? A Marxist Response" 262

## CHAPTER 10 | ENVIRONMENTS 270

### Cluster: How Do We Design Communities? 272

*Con-Text: "A Beautiful Place Made Ugly"* 273

1. David Plotz, "A Suburb Grown Up and All Paved Over" 274
2. Virginia Postrel, "Misplacing the Blame for Our Troubles on 'Flat, Not Tall' Spaces" 278
3. Donella Meadows, "So What Can We Do — Really Do — About Sprawl?" 282
4. Robert Wilson, "Enough Snickering. Suburbia Is More Complicated and Varied Than We Think" 288

## CHAPTER 11 | AMERICAN NATIONAL IDENTITY 294

### Cluster: What Kind of Power Should We Give Our Government? 296

*Con-Text: "The Declaration of Independence"* 297

1. Martin Luther King, Jr., "Letter From a Birmingham Jail" 298
2. Michael Kelly, "Liberties Are a Real Casualty of War" 311
3. Heather Green, "Databases and Security vs. Privacy" 314
4. Alan M. Dershowitz, "Why Fear National ID Cards?" 318

## CHAPTER 12 | FREE ENTERPRISE 322

### Cluster: What Does It Mean to Be a Consumer? 324

*Con-Text: "Conspicuous Consumption"* 325

1. Ian Frazier, "All-Consuming Patriotism: American Flag: $19.95. New Yacht: $75,000. True Patriotism: Priceless" 326
2. James Deacon, "The Joys of Excess" 331
3. Norman Solomon, "Mixed Messages Call for Healthy Skepticism" 336
4. Peter Singer, "The Singer Solution to World Poverty" 340

## CHAPTER 13 | GLOBALIZATION 348

### Cluster: Is Globalization Progress? 350

*Con-Text: The Marshall Plan* 351

1. Daniel Yergin, "Giving Aid to World Trade" 352
2. Helena Norberg-Hodge, "The March of the Monoculture" 356
3. Vandana Shiva, "The Living Democracy Movement: Alternatives to the Bankruptcy of Globalisation" 365
4. Bjorn Skorpen Claeson, "Singing for the Global Community" 374

**Text Credits 378**

**Photo Credits 384**

**Index 386**

# PART I

# AN INTRODUCTION TO ARGUMENT

1 | The Purposes of Argument

2 | Strategies for Argument

3 | The Contexts of Argument

4 | The Media for Argument

5 | Constructing Arguments

Argument is a means of discovering truth, negotiating differences, and solving problems. Although argumentation focuses on problems, argument itself is a solution. You routinely engage in argumentation in all aspects of your life. When you ask your teacher to extend the deadline for an assignment or seek admission to a study-abroad program or a graduate school, you are putting yourself in a position that requires effective argumentation. You might also have occasion to argue seriously about political and ethical concerns. Someone you love might be considering an important step such as opening a business, a large corporation might try to bury its chemical waste on property that adjoins your own, or you might suddenly be deprived of a benefit to which you feel entitled. Such situations require you to organize, articulate, and support your beliefs so that others will take them seriously. In doing so, you are engaging in a social interaction about important matters that can deeply affect your life and the lives of others.

One of the most common misconceptions about argument is that it is about winning. Look again at the examples in the preceding paragraph. Each case involves people trying to address a complicated situation and solve a problem satisfactorily. The need to ask a teacher for a deadline extension, for example, might have arisen from a complicated set of circumstances involving, say, an illness or a schedule conflict. Perhaps you caught the flu a few days before the assignment is due and are therefore unable to complete it on time. Consider some of the many other factors that complicate that apparently simple situation. For one thing, the deadline itself results from your teacher's effort to organize the course, anticipate the time it takes for grading, and perhaps accommodate a school holiday that required a class to be canceled. For another thing, you probably have other responsibilities to fulfill — a work schedule, assignments for other classes, maybe meetings for a club you belong to — all of which are also affected by your illness. All these factors complicate the problem created by your illness. In asking for a deadline extension, you are attempting to solve that problem. So you make an argument to justify an extension.

But the matter doesn't end there, because extending your deadline might create problems for your teacher. She might, for instance, have a tight deadline of her own for reading her students' essays. She might also worry about being fair to other students whose requests she denied or to the students who handed their work in on time. So your argument in this case is not just a matter of convincing your teacher that you need an extension. Rather, your argument is an attempt to solve your problem in a way that also takes into account the potential problems your teacher faces. Ideally, a successful argument in this case would mean that both you and your teacher "win." In this sense, you can think of argumentation as an intellectual effort that is intended to solve a problem by drawing people together.

As this hypothetical example suggests, argument requires you to look beyond the surface. When you address a more difficult or controversial issue, argument might also involve moral or ethical choices. Imagine a situation in which you are trying to decide on a course of medical treatment for a family member who is in a coma. You might feel strongly that your relative would not want to remain on artificial life support systems, and you might even have ethical misgivings about such medical treatments. In trying to articulate your position to your family members, who might wish to continue artificial life support, you will probably address several deeply complicated and difficult moral and ethical issues. For instance, you might believe that artificial life support is unethical if it diminishes the quality of life for both the patient and his or her family. You might argue, too, that the costs — financial and emotional — of such life support outweigh the potential benefits. You might even invoke probability, noting that the doctors cannot guarantee a full recovery for your relative. And you would certainly discuss these matters in the context of your love — and the love of your family members — for your relative, perhaps arguing that your love requires you to make a choice that is best for the patient, no matter how difficult it is for the family. Moreover, you would want to listen carefully to what other members of your family have to say and consider what doctors and nurses have said. You could not argue in a vacuum, as if only your opinion matters. It would be irresponsible to try only to prevail in such a case. Rather, you would want to recognize what others think and try to draw people together. You would use argument to build consensus so that your family will be able to live with its decision.

Fortunately, most argumentation that you will be involved in will not address such weighty matters. But if you consider the many different kinds of arguments you may encounter or make in your daily life, you quickly begin to see that argument is not just an important skill that will serve you well as a college student or as an employee. Argument is also an important part of how you live your life with others. It is a central feature of the way our communities, social networks, and institutions function.

Written argumentation in particular, which can take many forms, is a way for you to work out your ideas and positions on an issue. It is also a way to consider carefully the situation in which you are making your argument and addressing the positions and needs of others involved. Constructing an effective written argument requires you to think clearly about an issue or problem without letting your feelings dominate what you say, which can be difficult at times. It encourages careful inquiry that can lead to a deeper understanding of the issue or problem. In addition, it can be tremendously satisfying to succeed in making other people understand what you mean and to engage with them in a genuine effort to address a problem. You might not always convert others to your point of view, but you can earn their respect and perhaps enhance understanding of an important issue on all sides. This, in the end, is what argument is all about: engaging with others to address problems.

This book is intended to help you learn to solve problems through argument. It rests on the conviction that effective argumentation requires an ability to understand differences, for you cannot solve a problem or resolve a conflict that you don't understand. When writing an argument, you must often give consideration to beliefs that might differ from your own, recognizing what makes those beliefs appealing in a given situation. Indeed, the fact that many arguments involve deeply held beliefs is one reason that argumentation can be so challenging. Becoming familiar with diverse points of view will help you write arguments that address the concerns of people who might disagree with you. In the process, you might learn more about your own beliefs. Ideally, such learning not only will enable you to develop your own thinking and be more persuasive in your arguments, but might also enable you to negotiate differences with others and thus solve problems to everyone's advantage.

The situations we have described so far — and the examples we discuss throughout this book — reflect the complexity of the problems and conflicts that we routinely face in a diverse and increasingly technological world. The more informed you are about such issues, the more effectively you can write about them. But remember that controversial subjects are controversial in part because they are so complex and because so much can be said about them — much more than you might realize at first. You do not need to become an expert on a topic before you can write a thoughtful argument about it, but you do need to be able to support the claims you make, and that requires adequately understanding the issues involved.

As you'll see, arguments that are made without adequate support for their claims can be persuasive in many cases, depending on the issues and the audiences involved. But being persuasive might not actually lead to a solution to the problem you are trying to address in an argument. You might, for example, persuade your teacher that you do need that deadline extension, yet she might decide against granting it because it would create too many problems for her. Or you might persuade your brother to support your wish to end life support for another relative. But if your brother is not truly at ease with the position you persuaded him to adopt, your relationship with him could become troubled. This complexity is part of our view that argument is more than persuasion: Argument seeks to clarify thought, not obscure it; argument relies on evidence or widely accepted truths and does not necessarily dictate any particular course of action. The truly effective argument would have well-supported claims that ultimately lead to a satisfactory resolution of the problem at hand. While such a goal may not be realistic in every situation that calls for argumentation, it is the ideal toward which we hope you will strive when you write an informed argument.

## WHAT IS AN ARGUMENT?

That question is not as simple as it might seem, and we can begin to answer it by first examining what is *not* an argument. In the first place, a quarrel is not an argument. Typically, when we use the term *argument* in casual conversation, we mean a quarrel or a disagreement. But there are significant differences between a quarrel and the kind of argument addressed in this book. Quarrels rarely involve any genuine effort to engage in a dialogue for the sake of understanding an issue, and very often quarrels have nothing to do with trying to resolve a conflict. If you find yourself arguing with your roommate over which kind of music to play on your stereo, for instance, you are not likely to be engaged in a reasoned attempt to make a decision on the basis of claims or evidence. Nor are you likely to be very concerned about understanding your roommate's reasons for choosing a particular CD. Rather, you probably want to hear a certain kind of music and are interested primarily in getting your way. It is perhaps conceivable that you will try to persuade your roommate to let you have your way rather than simply insisting on your choice of music, and in doing so, you may actually employ some of the strategies for argument discussed in this book. But even so, the point in such a situation is not to present a convincing argument in order to address the conflict; the point is simply to state your demand and oppose your roommate's choice.

This example might seem trite or even silly, but if you look closely at popular discussions in our culture, you will notice that many such discussions are not too different from arguing with a roommate about music. Consider the following exchange, which was taken from an online discussion forum at the *New York Times* Web site. In this case the participants were discussing an editorial written by columnist Bob Herbert in which

Herbert argued that we must address the problem of global warming very soon if we are to avoid disasters caused by the melting of the polar ice sheets:

> "The public is wonderfully tolerant. It forgives everything except genius." — Oscar Wilde

> Your most "well reasoned post." Incredible!

> Recent reports indicate that the planet Mars is warming up. What a coincidence. Is it possible that something outside the atmosphere is warming both Earth and Mars? No, let's not let any contradictory evidence upset our political agenda.

> 1. How much will the earth warm up in the next century if we do nothing, Bob?
> 2. We can build atomic power plants for electricity. Are you for that, Bob?
> 3. Our caves will keep us cool & cut air conditioning costs.
> 4. Do you want to compare your use of power & energy annually with my usage Bob? Perhaps you can cut back.

Such an exchange amounts to little more than a quarrel, despite the seemingly sophisticated ideas that several participants present. The first post, which quotes Oscar Wilde, a well-known British playwright from the 19th century, can be read as either a compliment or a criticism of Herbert's editorial, but it makes no argument itself. The second post is a thinly veiled insult directed at the writer who posted the Oscar Wilde quote. The third post is characterized by a sarcasm that reflects that participant's disdain for Herbert's argument (and perhaps for Herbert himself). And although the fourth post does present some potentially effective counterarguments to Herbert's position, it too is marked by sarcasm and doesn't lend itself to reasoned debate. In many ways, then, this exchange might be an "argument" in the popular sense of the term, but it is not an argument of the kind discussed in this book. And notice here that what makes a genuine argument is not the nature of the topic being argued about. Obviously, these participants are discussing a serious matter. But to engage in genuine argument requires an effort to address the issue at hand in a substantive way, not just to criticize or oppose another's position.

Given the adversarial nature of so much public debate today, especially with the proliferation of various kinds of radio and television talk shows, electronic discussion forums on the Internet and e-mail lists, it is easy to mistake such quarreling for argument. Often, in popular media, the primary purpose is to entertain — not to inform, address a problem, or resolve a conflict. As a result, people with deep differences and even intractable positions on controversial issues are selected to participate. Nor surprisingly, their discussions rarely move beyond staking out their positions or criticizing one another. Such discussions are not very different from an argument between two roommates or family members about what kind of music to play on the stereo.

Some scholars believe that genuine argument is not a conflict between adversaries but an effort to find truth (see the sidebar). This notion that arguments involve truth can help

## ARE ARGUMENTS ADVERSARIAL?

Although arguments often involve people with divergent and even opposing views, they are not inherently adversarial. In fact, British philosopher Ralph Johnson believes that "the adversarial approach is inimical to argumentation" (*Manifest Rationality*, 2000). Johnson believes that what separates genuine argumentation from quarrels, debates, legal argumentation, and even conflict negotiation, such as in a divorce or a worker's compensation case, is the role of truth. He asserts that a genuine argument invokes truth not only as a way to evaluate claims, but also as a standard by which to judge the effectiveness of an argument. In other words, when we consider an argument, we try to determine whether or not it is true.

us distinguish argument from other kinds of discourse in which participants seek to win or persuade without concern for the truth of their claims or positions. Let's return to our earlier example of a student asking a teacher to extend an assignment deadline. In that case the ideal goal was to solve the problem created by the student's illness to the satisfaction of both student and teacher. That goal assumes good intentions on all sides. But the student cared only about getting the extension to solve *his* problem of not being able to meet the original deadline, and he might make claims without concern for their truth value. He might not have taken the teacher's concerns into account, or if he did, it was only for the purpose of getting the extension. By our definition he would be engaged in something other than genuine argumentation, no matter how persuasive he might be. Genuine argumentation should be an ethical endeavor.

This example reveals how difficult it can be to distinguish between argument as a genuine effort to negotiate differences or solve a problem and argument as a way to get what you want. In some ways two such arguments might seem very much the same — with the same kinds of claims and evidence, even the same strategies. You might even say that the distinction is irrelevant because it emphasizes a kind of argument that is unrealistic in our complicated day-to-day lives. But if argument were only about getting your way — about winning — then it would not be an effective tool for living our complicated lives with each other. In fact, it is precisely because our lives are complicated — and because we must live among others with their own complicated needs and opinions — that a view of argument as a way to solve problems and negotiate differences is so important.

## WHY LEARN TO WRITE EFFECTIVE ARGUMENTS?

There are at least two important reasons to learn how to write effective arguments:

1. **To be able to engage with others, through language, to solve problems and negotiate differences satisfactorily.** Your daily life presents you with numerous opportunities to engage in argumentation, and the more effectively you can do so, the more successfully you can fulfill your own responsibilities as a member of the communities to which you belong. You might, for example, find yourself writing a letter to the editor of your local newspaper about a controversial construction project that may affect traffic in your neighborhood. Or you might file a petition with your local school board to oppose a property tax increase. Writing such arguments is an important kind of participation in your community. It is part of the means by which we address issues and solve problems together. Given the increasing diversity of our communities and the way in which media such as the Internet have made our world smaller, learning to argue in these ways may be more important than ever. As citizens, we now encounter diversity perhaps more readily than we did in the past, and diversity and change can lead to conflict. Being able to engage in argument as a way to negotiate differences may be a step toward resolving such conflict.

2. **To succeed as a writer in college as well as in other contexts, such as your workplace or community.** This is perhaps a more practical reason to learn to write effective arguments. Indeed, writing various kinds of arguments is one of

the most common tasks you will be assigned in your college courses. To write effective arguments about important issues within an academic discipline, such as history and economics, is to engage in substantive inquiry about those issues and learn about the central ideas of that discipline. When you write an essay for your history course arguing against, say, the decision by the United States to drop atomic bombs on Japan during World War II, you are not only participating in an ongoing debate about a pivotal moment in history, but also learning about that event — and about history more generally — in a sophisticated way. In this sense, writing arguments is an important kind of thinking.

In addition, we must regularly evaluate arguments made by others to make appropriate decisions about an issue or problem. When someone approaches you asking you to sign a petition opposing, say, the building of a prison in your community, you will almost certainly be presented with an argument to justify the petition. Politicians, of course, not only make arguments in favor of the positions they take on specific issues, such as gun control or tax reform, but also make arguments to persuade you to vote for them. Television, radio, print, and Internet advertisements can be considered arguments whose purpose is to persuade you to purchase an item or service. Your ability to understand what argument is and how arguments work will enable you to evaluate the merits of the argument before deciding how you will act.

There is no better way to understand argument than to write arguments. Writing engages you in an issue or topic as no other intellectual activity can. In addition, writing an argument involves important thinking and language skills that can serve you well in other contexts. In working through an argument, you will have to read critically, think carefully and in sophisticated ways about complex issues, and use language effectively to articulate your position. In short, writing effective arguments can make you a better writer, a more careful thinker, and a more informed person.

# 1

## THE PURPOSES OF
## ARGUMENT

THE PURPOSES

**A**lmost anything can be argued, but not everything *should* be argued. The decision about what to argue and how to make an argument is not just a practical one (What topic should I argue about for the essay due in my English class next week?) but can also be an ethical one (What position should I take in a debate banning smoking from public places? What are the potential consequences of opposing a local ordinance prohibiting pesticides on private lawns?). To make an argument is to engage in a social activity that can have consequences for you and others, and it's part of your task as a writer to consider those consequences as you decide what to argue, how to do so, and even whether to make an argument. To make such a decision, it is helpful to consider *why* we engage in argument.

O F   A R G U M E N T

We engage in argumentation in all kinds of circumstances. Consider the following situations:

A local school board has been asked by the parents of a first-grade girl to adopt a policy that would allow their daughter to say a prayer before her lunch each day in school. When the girl tried to pray in school, her teacher stopped her. The teacher subsequently explained to the parents that vocal prayer in school is illegal. At the public school board meeting, debate among school board members focuses on the legal problems and expenses the school district could face if the parents of the girl take the case to court. They are sympathetic to the parents but worried about legal complications. In view of these concerns, the board eventually decides, by a 4–1 vote, on a policy that allows the girl to pray before lunch but not in the presence of her classmates. The school board member who voted against the policy expresses concern after the vote that the new policy will not hold up in court and emphasizes the necessity of maintaining the constitutional separation of church and state. After the meeting, he decides that his concerns should be heard by members of the community who did not attend the board meeting, and he writes an article for the monthly school district newsletter explaining his opposition to the new policy.

A young couple has decided to buy a car, but they disagree on which kind of car to purchase. Both are concerned about the environmental impact of their driving, and both wish to keep expenses low. But one partner will use the car primarily for commuting eleven miles to work on city streets and therefore sees fuel efficiency as a primary concern. This partner advocates buying one of the new hybrid cars, which are very small but have high fuel efficiency. The other partner shares the concern for fuel efficiency but sees a need for more space than the hybrid cars offer, primarily to deliver the vegetables that the couple raise for the local farm market. Neither partner feels knowledgeable about the technical details of the hybrid cars or about the potential environmental impact they have compared to conventional cars. After exploring these issues at local car dealers, reading about them on the Internet, and consulting with knowledgeable friends, the couple decides to write a letter to the editor of their local paper in which they discuss their decision to purchase a new hybrid car and advocate the purchase of these cars as a way to address problems of air pollution, global warming, and dependency on foreign oil.

A state legislator delivers a stinging speech after the legislature has voted against the reform of the state's laws regarding criminal penalties for drug offenses. He attacks his colleagues who voted against the reforms, charging that they care more for their political careers than for the lives of people who have been treated unfairly under the state's drug laws. Although those laws were implemented in the 1980s in an effort to combat large-scale drug dealers, the laws are regularly used to imprison individual drug users for relatively minor offenses. As a result, many citizens and legal experts consider the laws too harsh and unfair. A proposal to reform the laws to ensure that they target drug dealers rather than users moved through the legislature but was opposed by the governor, who feared that it would make the state appear soft on drug-related crimes. At the last minute, legislators in the governor's party have mustered enough votes to defeat the reform bill. The legislator knows that his speech will not change the outcome of the vote, but he delivers an angry attack on his colleagues nevertheless, arguing that they have voted in a way that undermines the principles of fairness and justice on which the legal system rests. His speech, which will later be published in the legislature's proceedings, is carried on television.

For several years a union has been trying to organize workers at a large hospital without success, but recent job cuts at the hospital have made unionization more popular among the workers. One of their complaints involves benefits, including the retirement plan, which the union claims is less lucrative for workers than its own plan would be. As the vote on whether to accept the union draws near, the administrator in charge of retirement benefits is asked by her boss to write a memo describing the potentially negative impact on the hospital's retirement plan if the workers vote in favor of the union. The retirement plan administrator believes that the union has not fairly represented the hospital's retirement plan, but she also believes that the union's plan has some advantages. However, if she describes those advantages in her memo, she could help convince some workers to vote in favor of unionization, which the hospital opposes. In her memo, she explains the advantages of the hospital's retirement plan for workers — advantages that would be lost to the workers if they voted for the union. But she also acknowledges some of the advantages of the union's retirement plan, and she argues in her memo that the hospital should consider altering its plan to include some of the features of the union's plan. Doing so, she believes, would serve the workers' interests without compromising the hospital's budget.

As these four examples show, people engage in argument for many reasons, and the complexity of arguments can make it difficult to categorize different kinds of arguments. Moreover, all arguments contain certain essential elements, such as an identifiable position on a subject, specific claims, and supporting evidence, and many arguments address several purposes at once. But to understand argumentation better, we can identify at least four broad purposes for argument:

- To inquire
- To assert
- To dominate
- To negotiate differences

The preceding examples illustrate each of these purposes, which we will examine in this chapter.

## ARGUMENTS TO ASSERT

In the first example the school board member who opposed the district's new policy on school prayer saw a need to publicize his view. He wished to assert his position as part of the ongoing discussions about prayer in his district's schools. You can probably imagine many situations in which your primary goal is to assert a position on an issue about which there may be disagreement or controversy:

- In a class discussion about teaching evolution in science classes in public schools
- In a meeting of a student organization that is deciding whether to boycott products in the school's bookstore that are produced in sweatshops

■ In your place of employment as your coworkers decide how to respond to a new overtime policy

In such situations many voices may be heard, and each one asserts a position on the issue. To do so effectively not only can contribute to resolution of an issue, but can also help you gain credibility as a participant in the discussion of the issue.

In some ways, all arguments are arguments to assert. Even advertisements whose primary purpose is to persuade people to purchase a product often assert a position or perspective (see Figure 1-1). Traditionally, argument has been understood as a formal attempt to state a position on an issue (your thesis), offer acceptable reasons for that position, provide evidence in support of those reasons, and anticipate objections. Indeed, to write an effective argument of any kind requires you to make a clear assertion and support it

**FIGURE 1-1**

**Advertising as Arguing to Assert**

This advertisement for a climbing rope manufacturer might be seen as an argument to assert a particular point of view about women. It plays off cultural stereotypes about women as passive and presents a different view of women as aggressive and athletic.

adequately. But what counts as "adequate" evidence isn't always obvious, and different readers can bring different assumptions and expectations to an argument. (We'll address the issue of evidence in Chapter 4.) Moreover, in argument writers are usually dealing with probabilities rather than certainties. So part of the challenge in writing an effective argument is managing probability in a way that readers will find acceptable. In other words, we rarely can know something for sure (Will allowing prayer in schools result in legal problems? Will driving hybrid cars reduce global warming?), so we must proceed as best we can by working with what we do know (the Supreme Court has banned school prayer in the past; all cars emit carbon dioxide, which is a greenhouse gas) and then taking probability into account. Learning how to do so is an important component of writing effective arguments.

## ARGUMENTS TO INQUIRE

In the second example described previously, the letter written by the couple does argue in favor of a position — that consumers should buy fuel-efficient cars — and their argument might be seen as an effort to convince others to do the same. But its primary purpose is to explore the complexities of their decision as well as its environmental and economic implications. In other words, the couple is just as interested in examining some of the complexities of the issue as they are in asserting their position that purchasing a new hybrid car is an environmentally responsible act (see Figures 1-2 and 1-3). You probably engage in similar kinds of arguments. Perhaps the best example is class discussion. In a sociology class, for instance, you might find yourself discussing welfare reform. As a student in the class, you are not considered an expert on welfare reform, nor do your arguments or your classmates' arguments have consequences outside your class (unlike, say, a

**FIGURE 1-2**

**A Prototype Hybrid Car**

The couple in the example on page 10 are making an argument as part of an effort to inquire into the consequences of buying such a car. This photo might also be seen as an argument to assert: It portrays a sleek, almost sporty car that seems to suggest not only fuel efficiency but also sexiness and speed.

FIGURE 1-3

**A Page from the Web
Site of the Institute for
Lifecycle Energy
Analysis (ILEA)**

In its mission statement, ILEA
states that its goal is to "provide United States consumers
with the education and tools
necessary to make purchasing
and lifestyle choices that work
toward a sustainable global
economy." This Web page can
be seen as an argument to inquire: it is part of ILEA's effort
to examine the environmental
impact of purchasing a hybrid
car as compared to a conventional car.

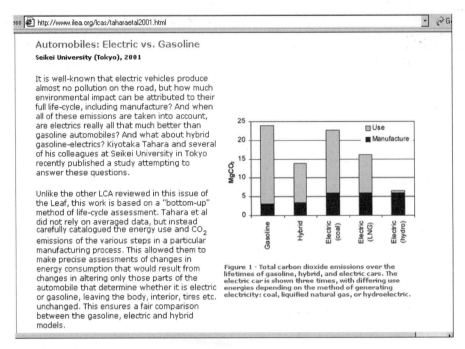

http://www.ilea.org/lcas/taharaetal2001.html

**Automobiles: Electric vs. Gasoline**
**Seikei University (Tokyo), 2001**

It is well-known that electric vehicles produce
almost no pollution on the road, but how much
environmental impact can be attributed to their
full life-cycle, including manufacture? And when
all of these emissions are taken into account,
are electrics really all that much better than
gasoline automobiles? And what about hybrid
gasoline-electrics? Kiyotaka Tahara and several
of his colleagues at Seikei University in Tokyo
recently published a study attempting to
answer these questions.

Unlike the other LCA reviewed in this issue of
the Leaf, this work is based on a "bottom-up"
method of life-cycle assessment. Tahara et al
did not rely on averaged data, but instead
carefully catalogued the energy use and $CO_2$
emissions of the various steps in a particular
manufacturing process. This allowed them to
make precise assessments of changes in
energy consumption that would result from
changes in altering only those parts of the
automobile that determine whether it is electric
or gasoline, leaving the body, interior, tires etc.
unchanged. This ensures a fair comparison
between the gasoline, electric and hybrid
models.

Figure 1 - Total carbon dioxide emissions over the
lifetimes of gasoline, hybrid, and electric cars. The
electric car is shown three times, with differing use
energies depending on the method of generating
electricity: coal, liquified natural gas, or hydroelectric.

SOURCE: ILEA *Leaf,* Institute for Lifecycle Energy Analysis (Seattle, WA), summer 2002.
www.ilea.org/lcas/taharaetal2001.html.

social worker's arguments to a family court judge about a specific case). Most important,
your arguments in this situation are not necessarily intended to convince your classmates
to support or oppose a particular position about welfare reform; rather, in making your
arguments and listening to those of your classmates, you are engaged in a collective
inquiry into the sociological issues surrounding welfare reform. You are arguing to learn
and to understand.

Arguments to inquire imply a special kind of dialogue between writers and readers.
Although all arguments to some extent imply a dialogue, in arguments to inquire, the author's goal is to open up an issue for careful inquiry, to convince readers that the issue is
worth their attention, and to encourage them to consider the writer's perspective on the
issue. Indeed, in such an argument the writer's primary goal might be to persuade readers that a particular kind of problem even exists.

As a college student, you will probably be asked to write arguments to inquire more
often than other kinds of arguments. Indeed, much academic writing can be characterized as arguments to inquire. The author will perhaps argue for a position on an issue, but
the argument is exploratory and even informative, implicitly inviting readers to join the
inquiry into the issue at hand. Consider this excerpt from the opening chapter of *Writing
Space,* a book by Jay David Bolter about how new computer technologies are changing
the nature of writing. As the following excerpt suggests, Bolter believes that computers are
fostering dramatic changes in how and what we write. His position is not universally
shared among scholars interested in literacy and technology, however. Bolter knows this,

of course. He isn't concerned about convincing other scholars that he's right and they're wrong; rather, he wishes to examine a very complex issue that other scholars want to understand better.

In Victor Hugo's novel *Notre-Dame de Paris, 1482,* the priest remarked "Ceci tuera cela": this book will destroy that building. He meant not only that printing and literacy would undermine the authority of the church but also that "human thought . . . would change its mode of expression, that the principal idea of each generation would no longer write itself with the same material and in the same way, that the book of stone, so solid and durable, would give place to the book made of paper, yet more solid and durable" (p. 199). The medieval cathedral crowded with statues and stained glass was both a symbol of Christian authority and a repository of medieval knowledge (moral knowledge about the world and the human condition). The cathedral was a library to be read by the religious, who walked through its aisles looking up at the scenes of the Bible, the images of saints, allegorical figures of virtue and vice, visions of heaven and hell. . . . Of course, the printed book did not eradicate the encyclopedia in stone; it did not even eradicate the medieval art of writing by hand. People continued to contemplate their religious tradition in cathedrals, and they continued to communicate with pen and paper for many purposes. But printing did displace handwriting: the printed book became the most valued form of handwriting. And printing certainly helped to displace the medieval organization and expression of knowledge. As Elizabeth Eisenstein has shown, the modern printing press has been perhaps the most important tool of the modern scientist. (See *The Printing Press as an Agent of Change* by Elizabeth Eisenstein, 1979, especially vol. 2, pp. 520ff.)

Hugo himself lived in the heyday of printing, when the technology had just developed to allow mass publication of novels, newspapers, and journals. Hugo's own popularity in France (like Dickens' in England) was evidence that printed books were reaching and defining a new mass audience. Today we are living in the late age of print. The evidence of senescence, if not senility, is all around us. And as we look up from our computer keyboards to the books on our shelves, we must ask ourselves whether "this will destroy that." Computer technology (in the form of word processing, databases, electronic bulletin boards and mail) is beginning to displace the printed book. . . .

The printed book, therefore, seems destined to move to the margin of our literate culture. . . . The shift to the computer will make writing more flexible, but it will also threaten the definitions of good writing and careful reading that have been fostered by the technique of printing. The printing press encouraged us to think of a written text as an unchanging artifact, a monument to its author and its age. . . . Electronic writing emphasizes the impermanence and changeability of text, and it tends to reduce the distance between author and reader by turning the reader into an author. It is changing the cultural status of writing as well as the method of producing books. It is changing the relationship of the author to the text and of both the author and text to the reader.

To write an effective argument of inquiry requires researching the topic and examining the issues surrounding it. It might require using evidence, but the evidence might be used as a means to *illustrate* a point rather than to support it. For example, in the excerpt above, Bolter refers to historian Elizabeth Eisenstein to help him develop his point about the important impact of the printing press. He doesn't do this as a way to say, "I'm right," but as a way to lend credibility to his main point about writing and technology.

What is especially noteworthy about an argument to inquire is that your own position might very well change or evolve as you examine the topic and go through the process of planning, writing, and revising your argument. In fact, you might begin the process of writing this kind of argument without a clear position on the topic. Your position will emerge through the process of writing. These arguments, then, are exploratory in two ways: (1) They encourage the writer to explore a topic in order to arrive at a reasonable position, and (2) they invite writers to engage in exploring that topic as well.

## ARGUMENTS TO DOMINATE

Perhaps when most people think of formal arguments, they think of arguments whose primary purpose is to dominate. The most common example is an argument made in a legal case. A lawyer might be arguing before a judge to grant bail to her client — let's say a young man accused of stealing a car — so that the client will not have to remain in jail while waiting for the trial to begin. In such a case the lawyer has one main goal: to win. She wishes only to convince the judge that the client should be free on bail. Her opponent, the prosecutor, will try to counter the defense lawyer's argument so that the young man remains imprisoned. In most such cases the arguments tend to be adversarial and the opponents easily identified. The writer of an argument in such a case will try to muster any available evidence and employ any available strategy to win. We encounter other such arguments to dominate — for example, protests against a particular law or corporation (see Figure 1-4).

But as the example of the state legislator suggests, you can make an argument whose purpose is to dominate, even when winning is not likely. The state legislator understood that the vote on the bill would go against his position, yet he argued vigorously for his position anyway. In that instance winning the argument wasn't necessarily the goal. A closer look reveals that the legislator might lose the immediate argument — because the vote goes against reforming the drug laws — but his speech might win the larger battle for public opinion about the state's drug laws. In other words, he can use his defeat in the vote on the reform bill as part of his effort to change the public's attitude about drug laws and perhaps win a later vote to change the drug laws.

We noted above that legal arguments often seem to be concerned only with winning and not with truth. For the lawyer trying to gain a legal victory for her client, getting at the truth of the situation (Did her client in fact steal the car?) is not the goal. She may therefore argue to win even if her client is guilty. But such situations are not always so clear-cut. Consider a different example of a young man pulled over for drunk driving:

A man in his twenties with no criminal record and a clean driving record is driving home late at night from a party celebrating his company's recent increase in sales. On the way home he realizes that he has had too much to drink and that it is dangerous for him to be driving. So he pulls onto the shoulder of the road, puts the car in park, and then falls asleep with the car still idling. Later, a police officer stops to investigate and, realizing that the young man has been drinking, arrests him for drunk driving.

According to the laws in that state, the young man is technically guilty of driving while intoxicated, because he was seated behind the wheel of the car while the car was still running. In the eyes of the law it doesn't matter that the car was parked and not moving at the time the officer found the man. In his summary argument to the jury, the defense lawyer points out that his client is indeed technically guilty but that convicting him would amount to penalizing him for realizing that he shouldn't have been driving; a conviction would punish him for making the safe and responsible decision to stop his car and wait until he sobered up before continuing to drive home. In other words, the lawyer argued that his client did the right thing, even though he was legally guilty of driving while intoxicated. Why, he asked, should this young man, with no prior offenses, be punished for making the right decision?

In this case the lawyer's purpose was to win — to dominate his opponent, the prosecutor, by convincing the jury that they should find the defendant not guilty. And his argument that his client did the "right" thing — if not the legal thing — can be seen as a strategy to win the jury's sympathy and appeal to their sense of justice. But if you consider the argument in the larger context of the state's efforts to impose laws that will reduce drunk driving accidents, then the lawyer is arguing in a way that contributes to that larger purpose. He tries to persuade the jury that what his client did — pulling over his car so that he would avoid an accident — was really what the drunk driving laws are all

**The People's Strike:**

WE ARE THE CITY    WE CAN    SHUT IT DOWN!

**A Day of Non-Compliance and Resistance**

*September 27th, 2002*

Direct Action Against the World Bank and IMF. The day before their Fall Meetings protest the effects of capitalism in DC and around the world!

Convergence on DC - Skillshares, Spokescouncils and Orientation - September 25 - 26

**Direct Action September 27th!**

http://www.abolishthebank.org

SOURCE: www.abolishthebank.org.

**FIGURE 1-4**

**A Flyer from the Washington, D.C., Anti-Capitalist Convergence**

Although the purpose of this flyer is to announce an event sponsored by this organization, the flyer also reflects an argument to dominate. Notice the illustration, the bold lettering, and the exclamation points. It argues forcefully for a point of view opposing capitalism.

about. Punishing the young man for his decision therefore makes no sense. In short, the social and ethical considerations of the case go beyond the immediate goal of winning the argument and the case.

You will at some point very likely find yourself in a situation in which winning an argument is extremely important to you. Understanding arguments to dominate can help you to construct an effective argument in that situation. In the same way, being able to recognize the complexity of such situations will help you identify arguments to dominate so that you can make informed decisions about them. Even then, you might find that your position evolves as you develop and revise your piece.

## ARGUMENTS TO NEGOTIATE AND RECONCILE

Glance through your morning newspaper, and you will quickly find examples of situations in which people have seemingly irreconcilable or even intractable differences about an issue or occupy such divergent perspectives that no option seems to exist except for one side defeating or silencing the other. At the same time communications technologies have brought people into more frequent contact with one another, so we now routinely confront all kinds of differences — social, cultural, religious, political, ethnic, regional. Such diversity enriches our lives, but it also challenges us to learn how to live together peacefully. In this sense, one of the main purposes of argument is to confront the complexity that arises from diversity in order to negotiate and, ideally, to reconcile differences. This might be the most difficult kind of argument of all.

In the hospital unionization example on page 11, the administrator of the hospital's retirement plan must consider a number of factors as she drafts her memo. As a hospital administrator she is responsible for managing the retirement plan in a way that serves the hospital's interests as well as the interests of the employees. It isn't hard to see that those interests can diverge. For example, to keep the hospital running efficiently in tough economic times, the hospital might find it necessary to reduce some of the retirement plan benefits, such as how much money the hospital contributes to each employee's retirement account. Reducing that contribution might serve the hospital's financial interests, but it might compromise the employees' financial well-being by giving them less money just when they need it most. Each side seems to be protecting its interests in reasonable ways. So it wouldn't seem wrong for the administrator of the retirement plan to make a strong argument against the union's proposal for the retirement plan. It would make sense, furthermore, for her to argue so that the hospital wins (by encouraging the employees to vote against the union). But it also seems to make sense for the union to argue as aggressively as possible for its own plan, which seems to protect the employees. If both sides proceed in that way, one will win, and presumably, the other will lose.

The administrator of the hospital's retirement plan, however, recognized that both sides could benefit by some changes to the hospital's plan. In a sense, she argued for a win-win outcome: Both the hospital and its employees would gain some benefits, and neither would really lose. Her argument was an effort to negotiate a complicated situation and reconcile the differences between the two sides.

Such an outcome might sound idealistic, but in fact many situations are argued in this way. Return for a moment to our examples of the two legal cases. In such situations it is quite common for defense lawyers and prosecutors to negotiate a plea bargain, which amounts to a compromise in which each side gains something and neither side loses everything. In the case of the young man on trial for drunk driving, the prosecutor and defense lawyer could agree to a lesser charge so that the young man would avoid the harsh consequences of a drunk driving conviction but would still suffer some penalty for having been driving after drinking. In such a situation both sides would argue in front of a judge in a way that would be intended to work out a compromise that is fair and appropriate. Accordingly, the defense lawyer would employ different strategies and make different claims than he did when he argued in front of a jury. The purpose of negotiating the conflict changes what and how he argues.

*Restate what you just heard*

Arguing to negotiate differences is sometimes called Rogerian argument, after the influential psychotherapist Carl Rogers, who emphasized the importance of communication as a means to resolve conflicts (see Figure 1-5). Rogers believed that most people are so ready "to judge, to evaluate, to approve or disapprove" that they fail to understand what others think. He urged people to "listen with understanding" and recommended a model for communication in which listeners are required to restate what others have said before offering their own views. This restatement should be done fairly and accurately, without either praise or blame, so that the original speaker is able to confirm, "Yes, that is what I said."

Although this model might seem simple, Rogers cautioned that it takes courage to listen carefully to views that are contrary to one's own, especially in volatile situations or on charged and difficult issues (such as abortion or capital punishment). It is extremely hard to listen when feelings are strong. The greater the conflict, the greater the chance of misinterpreting what others have said. Moreover, it's easy to think of situations in which any kind of listening seems impossible because the people involved are engaged in such deep conflict. Rogers envisioned situations in which individuals are engaged in dialogue, and his commitment to the importance of restating others' ideas (without evaluating them) rests on the assumption that language can be completely neutral — an idea that has been seriously questioned by modern linguists and philosophers. And Rogers's emphasis on the importance of listening may be more helpful to people who are used to speaking than to those who have been silenced. Feminists, for instance, have argued that because public discourse has long been dominated by men, women need to learn how to assert themselves, and men need help in learning to listen. For these reasons, many scholars questioned the extent to which Rogers's ideas can be applied to written

### FIGURE 1-6

**Nelson Mandela**

In helping to reconstruct his country after apartheid was dismantled in 1991, former president of South Africa Nelson Mandela made many speeches that can be considered Rogerian argument.

arguments. (To learn how to organize an argument according to a Rogerian model, see pages 127–128.)

Nevertheless, if you think carefully about the role of argument in resolving conflict and achieving social cooperation, Rogers's perspective on communication can be useful in helping you formulate effective arguments. And the examples we have cited here underscore the advantages of approaching argument in this way when a situation is characterized by a difficult conflict. Indeed, given the scale of the conflicts we face today within our communities, in our cultures, and in the world, a Rogerian perspective might be the most ethical way to approach an argument and might offer the only viable alternative available in certain situations. Think, for example, of the situation faced by Nelson Mandela as the new president of South Africa after the previous apartheid government was dismantled (see Figure 1-6). The long history of oppression and conflict that characterized South Africa and the terrible struggle that Mandela and his supporters endured to defeat apartheid and achieve equality would have made it easy for Mandela to argue for his new government's policies with only the goal of domination and victory in mind. Instead, Mandela recognized that even supporters of the defeated apartheid government were citizens of his country and that it was in everyone's interest to confront and negotiate their differences. As a result, he often argued with the goal of resolution in mind.

The usefulness of an approach to argument that emphasizes negotiating differences extends to much more common situations. For example, neighbors in conflict over a drainage problem on the boundary between their properties might be better served by arguing to their town supervisor for a resolution that fairly addresses the problem on both sides of the boundary rather than for one neighbor to try to force the other to fix the problem by winning the case in court. Or you might find yourself working with other classmates as part of a group project for one of your college courses; if a conflict arises between group members, it's possible that a "victory" by one group member over another could result in a project that is less effective and therefore earns a lower grade for all group members. In short, arguing to negotiate differences rather than to defeat an opponent might best serve your own interests as well as those of the other people involved, and it may be the best way to avoid further conflict.

There is no question that some differences may be irreconcilable. The news headlines about bombings in the Middle East or religious conflict in Europe remind us that no matter how genuinely we engage with one another in arguments, negotiation and resolution might not always be possible. And there are certainly times when winning an argument, rather than negotiating differences, may be ethical. Still, in all but the most extreme situations, genuine engagement in argument as a way to solve a problem, negotiate serious differences, and work toward resolution can offer the best alternative for all concerned. As a writer, you also benefit from writing arguments in this way, in the sense that your engagement in such argumentation may lead to a greater understanding of the situation, which can enrich your perspective on conflict and enhance your ability to engage in future arguments.

## 2

## STRATEGIES FOR ARGUMENT

STRATEGIES F

**W**hen you write an argument, you might feel confident about what you want to say or about the position you wish to take on an issue. In such a case your primary challenge is to examine the issue carefully so that you can develop the most effective argument. In other situations you might be faced with the prospect of arguing about an issue about which you are unsure or have mixed emotions. In that case writing your argument will involve exploring the issue more fully and perhaps even discovering your own position as you write. In both cases, however, you are engaged in what classical rhetoricians termed *invention*, that is, exploring and developing ideas about a specific topic to make an effective argument about it. Aristotle, whose treatise on rhetoric is still an important work for rhetoricians today, defined *rhetoric* as "the faculty of observing in any given case the available means of persuasion." In other words, rhetoric is finding an effective way to persuade other people to believe or do something. We can usefully think of argumentation in similar terms.

OR ARGUMENT

In his *Rhetoric* Aristotle identified three primary modes of persuasion:

- Logical, or arguments based on reason
- Emotional, or arguments that appeal to the emotions
- Ethical, or arguments based on the speaker's character

Obviously, these categories can overlap. You can, for example, make a logical argument that also appeals to your audience's emotions. In practice, most arguments use all three modes of persuasion in some way. But we can use these categories to identify arguments on the basis of the primary strategy the writer (or speaker) employs, and understanding these strategies will help you write effective arguments of your own.

## LOGICAL ARGUMENTS

Logic is often associated with objectivity. We tend to think of a logical argument as one that is made objectively on the basis of facts or reason rather than emotion. Consider the following letter written in 2002 by Gerald Gordon to the *New York Times* in response to an editorial by David Plotz. In his editorial Plotz criticized Fairfax County, Virginia, for its policies concerning growth and development. (You can read Plotz's editorial on pages 274–277.) At the time Gerald Gordon was president of the Fairfax County Economic Development Authority:

> I disagree that the county is in crisis. In 2001, my agency helped 164 companies that said they would create more than 11,500 jobs here. Compare that with tech centers like San Jose, California, and Atlanta, which have been shedding jobs by the tens of thousands.
>
> Also, Mr. Plotz says there is only enough "greenery left for a side salad." Funny line, but the county has more than 30,000 acres of dedicated parkland, including a national wildlife refuge established to protect bald eagles and one of the largest urban marshes on the east coast.

Gordon makes his main argument — that Fairfax County is not in crisis — by claiming that the county has plenty of jobs as well as substantial open green spaces. He cites specific figures (the potential creation of 11,500 jobs by 164 companies, 30,000 acres of parks) to support his claim. His position as president of the Fairfax County Economic Development Authority would suggest that Gordon does have an emotional stake in this issue, but he seems to remain objective, using facts to make his case. His argument relies on logic:

Jobs and open spaces are indicators of a healthy county.

Fairfax County has both; therefore, it is a healthy county (it is not in crisis).

His major assumption is that jobs and open spaces are good for a county. If you share that assumption, his argument will probably be persuasive to you; if you don't, then the support he offers becomes meaningless. For example, you might assume that a truly healthy county is one in which the majority of residents are homeowners and have median incomes above the national average. If so, then the existence of jobs alone would not indicate a healthy county, nor would the existence of green space. In other words, the effectiveness of a logical argument depends in large part on whether or not the main assumption — usually called the *main premise* in formal logic — is valid or acceptable.

Arguments rarely rely on logic alone, but the use of logic in an argument can be extremely effective, in part because we tend to think of reason as being superior to emotion when it comes to argumentation. As a result, objective, rational arguments are often considered more valid than openly emotional ones. Of course, the very idea of objectivity can be (and has been) questioned, and since we often engage in argument over complex and important issues that matter deeply to us, avoiding or eliminating emotion is rarely possible and not necessarily even desirable. (Some scholars argue that the distinction between logic and emotion is invalid in the first place.) Nevertheless, logic can be a powerful component of a writer's effort to engage in argumentation, and even when we make arguments that appeal to emotion or character, we will probably incorporate some elements of logic and reason.

Logical arguments can take several different forms. The two most common, which derive from classical rhetoric, are arguments based on *inductive reasoning* and those based on *deductive reasoning.*

## REASONING INDUCTIVELY

When we use induction, we are drawing a conclusion based on specific evidence. Our argument rests on a foundation of details that we have accumulated for its support. This is the type of reasoning we use most frequently in daily life. In the morning we look at the sky outside our window, check the outdoor temperature, and perhaps listen to a weather forecast before dressing for the day. If the sun is shining, the temperature is high, and the forecast is favorable, we are drawing a reasonable conclusion if we decide to dress lightly and leave the umbrella at home. We haven't *proved* that the day will be warm and pleasant; we have only *concluded* that it will be. This is all we can usually do in an inductive argument: arrive at a conclusion that seems likely to be true on the basis of our available evidence. Ultimate and positive proof is usually beyond reach. In this sense, induction can be seen as a way for a writer of an argument to deal with probability.

Listen, for example, to literary critic Sven Birkerts as he considers the technological changes he sees around him in the 1990s. Birkerts is concerned that new electronic media, especially those driven by computers, are adversely affecting our lives, in particular how we read and write, without our being very aware of it. "A change is upon us," he asserts, "away from the patterns and habits of the printed page and toward a new world distinguished by its reliance on electronic communication":

> The evidence of the change is all around us, though possibly in the manner of the forest that we cannot see for the trees. The electronic media, while conspicuous in gadgetry, are very nearly invisible in their functioning. They have slipped deeply and irrevocably into our midst, creating sluices and circulating through them. I'm not referring to any one product or function in isolation, such as television or fax machines or the networks that make them possible. I mean the interdependent totality that has arisen from the conjoining of parts — the disk drives hooked to modems, transmissions linked to technologies of reception, duplication, and storage. Numbers and codes and frequencies. Buttons and signals. And this is no longer "the future," except for the poor or the self-consciously atavistic — it is now. Next

to the new technologies, the scheme of things represented by print and the snail-paced linearity of the reading act looks stodgy and dull. Many educators say that our students are less and less able to read, or analyze, or write with clarity and purpose. Who can blame the students? Everything they meet with in the world around them gives them the signal: That was then, and electronic communications are now.

Notice that Birkerts offers a series of observations about the impact of the technological changes he sees in our lives. He cites examples to illustrate the effects that these changes seem to be having on how we communicate. He then concludes that students no longer learn to read and write as they did before the advent of these new technologies. He cannot be certain of this result; no one can. But the evidence around him suggests that such a result is not only possible but perhaps even likely.

This kind of reasoning is common in scientific research. A scientist may have a theory that explains some phenomenon, but she or he must carry out many experiments to prove the theory is valid. These experiments will enable the scientist to eliminate certain variables and gather enough data to justify a generally applicable conclusion. Ideally, a well-researched scientific conclusion will reach a point at which it seems uncontestable. One such example is the warning on cigarette packages. Over the years so much evidence has accumulated to link cigarette smoking to cancer that the warning has evolved from a probability to a veritable certainty. Most writers of arguments cannot hope to reach such certain conclusions through induction. Instead, like Sven Birkerts, they try to draw reasonable conclusions based on their observations and the evidence they present. If a writer is careful and thorough and has gathered sufficient evidence, his or her conclusion will usually seem valid to readers.

## REASONING DEDUCTIVELY

When an argument rests on a fundamental truth, right, or value, rather than on available evidence, it employs deductive reasoning. Whereas in inductive reasoning a writer begins with observations or evidence and draws conclusions from those, in deductive reasoning the writer begins with a basic truth or belief and proceeds from there. Evidence is still cited in support of the argument, but evidence is of secondary importance. The writer's first concern is to define a commonly accepted value or belief that will prepare the way for the argument she or he wants to make.

One of the most famous examples of an argument based on deductive reasoning is the Declaration of Independence, written by Thomas Jefferson. (To read the Declaration of Independence, go to page 297.) Although Jefferson cited numerous grievances against England, he rested his argument on the belief that "all men are created equal" and that they have "certain unalienable Rights," which King George III had violated. This was a revolutionary idea in the 18th century, and even today there are people who question it. But if we accept the idea that all people are created equal and have an inherent right to "Life, Liberty, and the pursuit of Happiness," as Jefferson asserted, then certain conclusions follow. The writer's task is to work logically toward those conclusions. Accordingly, Jefferson argued for a specific action — the separation of the colonies from England — based on the basic idea of equality. In other words, having established the fundamental truth of the equality of all people, he reasoned that the king's actions were unacceptable and concluded that the colonies must become independent.

The truth, right, or belief from which a writer deduces an argument is called the *premise*. Often, the main premise of a deductive argument is not immediately obvious, but even when we don't recognize it, it is the crucial element holding together the argument. Let's look at a more current example of an argument based on deductive reasoning, a *New York Times* editorial written in 2002 in response to a controversial court ruling that declared the Pledge of Allegiance unconstitutional:

> Half a century ago, at the height of anti-Communist fervor, Congress added the words "under God" to the Pledge of Allegiance. It was a petty attempt to link patriotism with religious piety, to distinguish us from the godless Soviets. But after millions of repetitions over the years, the phrase has become part of the backdrop of American life, just like the words "In God We Trust" on our coins and "God bless America" uttered by presidents at the end of important speeches.
>
> Yesterday, the United States Court of Appeals for the Ninth Circuit in California ruled 2 to 1 that those words in the pledge violate the First Amendment, which says that "Congress shall make no law respecting an establishment of religion." The majority sided with Michael Newdow, who had complained that his daughter is injured when forced to listen to public school teachers lead students daily in a pledge that includes the assertion that there is a God.
>
> This is a well-meaning ruling, but it lacks common sense. A generic two-word reference to God tucked inside a rote civic exercise is not a prayer. Mr. Newdow's daughter is not required to say either the words "under God" or even the pledge itself, as the Supreme Court made clear in a 1943 case involving Jehovah's Witnesses. In the pantheon of real First Amendment concerns, this one is off the radar screen.
>
> The practical impact of the ruling is inviting a political backlash for a matter that does not rise to a constitutional violation. We wish the words had not been added back in 1954. But just the way removing a well-lodged foreign body from an organism may sometimes be more damaging than letting it stay put, removing those words would cause more harm than leaving them in. By late afternoon yesterday, virtually every politician in Washington was rallying loudly behind the pledge in its current form.
>
> Most important, the ruling trivializes the critical constitutional issue of separation of church and state. There are important battles to be fought virtually every year over issues of prayer in school and use of government funds to support religious activities. Yesterday's decision is almost certain to be overturned on appeal. But the sort of rigid overreaction that characterized it will not make genuine defense of the First Amendment any easier.

Obviously, the editors of the *New York Times* disagree with the court's ruling. They support the idea of the separation of church and state, which is a fundamental principle contained in the U.S. Constitution. Notice that they are not arguing for or against this principle; they accept it as true and good. Their argument proceeds from that principle. But in this case they criticize the ruling not because it violates this principle, but because they see no genuine threat to this principle that would justify the court's decision. According to the editors, the ruling is intended to help maintain the constitutional separation of church and state, which they believe is admirable. But in their view, common sense indicates that the words "under God" in the Pledge of Allegiance do not represent a significant threat to that constitutional principle. So we might articulate the editors' main premise as follows:

> Serious threats to the constitutional separation of church and state should be opposed.

In this instance no serious threat exists in the editors' view; therefore, the ruling makes no sense. They develop their argument by examining what they consider to be some of the negative consequences of the ruling.

This kind of argumentation is quite common. Glance at an editorial page of any newspaper, and you're likely to see one or more examples of an argument based on deductive reasoning. But as the preceding example shows, formulating — or identifying — a good premise can be a challenge. A good premise should satisfy at least two basic requirements:

**1.** It should be general enough that an audience is likely to accept it, thus establishing a common ground between writer and audience.
**2.** It should be specific enough to prepare the way for the argument that will follow.

In this example the editors can be confident that most of their readers will understand the idea of the separation of church and state. Certainly, not all of their readers will agree that this principle is a good one that should be maintained, but most readers very likely will agree. So the editors' task is to build an argument that might convince those readers that no threat to that principle exists in this case.

What makes formulating a good premise difficult is that a premise usually refers to or invokes fundamental values or beliefs that we don't often examine consciously. In the case of the Declaration of Independence, Jefferson clearly articulated a fundamental belief in equality, which most of us today understand and accept. The *New York Times* editors invoke a constitutional principle that, while controversial, is nevertheless well known and easily identified. In some cases the premise will be harder to identify. But being able to identify the basic premise of an argument is an important skill that will help you more effectively evaluate arguments you encounter; it will also help you write effective arguments.

**The Syllogism**    If you look closely at the examples in this section, you'll notice that having a main premise is only part of the writer's task. Deductive reasoning often follows a pattern of what is called a *syllogism,* a three-part argument in which the conclusion rests on two premises, the first of which is the *major premise,* because it is the main assumption on which the argument rests. Here's a simple example of a syllogism:

| Major Premise: | All people have hearts. |
|---|---|
| Minor Premise: | John is a person. |
| Conclusion: | Therefore, John has a heart. |

If both premises are true — as they are in this case — then the conclusion should also be true. Note that the major and minor premises have a term in common (in this example, *people* or *person*). In a written argument the minor premise usually involves a specific case that relates to the more general statement with which the essay began. For instance, we might set up a syllogism based on the *New York Times* editorial on page 27 like this:

| Major Premise: | Serious threats to the constitutional separation of church and state should be opposed. |
| Minor Premise: | The phrase "under God" in the Pledge of Allegiance does not constitute a serious threat to the constitutional separation of church and state. |
| Conclusion: | Therefore, the Pledge of Allegiance should not be opposed. (That is, the appeals court ruling that the Pledge is unconstitutional is incorrect.) |

Notice that the minor premise cites a specific threat, whereas the major premise refers to a more general principle or belief. You can see from this example, however, how quickly syllogistic reasoning can become complicated. You can also see that the major and minor premises are not universally held to be true or valid; many people may disagree with either or both of them. The writers of this editorial surely knew that, and they probably calculated that most of their readers would accept their major premise as true.

**The Enthymeme**    Because it can be difficult to follow the rules of logic, faulty reasoning is common. Consider another simple example:

| Major Premise: | All women like to cook. |
| Minor Premise: | Elizabeth is a woman. |
| Conclusion: | Therefore, Elizabeth likes to cook. |

Technically, the *form* here is correct. The two premises have a term in common, and if we accept both premises as true, then we also have to accept the conclusion. But the major premise is faulty. Elizabeth, like many women (and men) might *hate* to cook, preferring to go out bowling at night or to read the latest issue of the *Journal of Organic Chemistry.* A syllogism may be valid in terms of its organization, but it can be *untrue* if it rests on a major premise that can easily be disputed. Usually, the major premise is a generalization, as in this example, but some generalizations make sense and will be widely accepted, while others will not. And it is easy to confuse generally accepted truths with privately held beliefs. In this case some people might well believe that all women like to cook, but many will not hold that belief. You can argue in favor of a private belief, but you cannot expect an audience to accept an easily debatable opinion as the foundation for an argument on behalf of yet another opinion.

It is also important to realize that in many arguments a premise might be implied but not stated. You might overhear a conversation like this one:

"I hear you and Elizabeth are getting married."
"Yes, that's true."
"Well, now that you've got a woman to cook for you, maybe you could invite me over for dinner sometime."
"Why do you think that Elizabeth will be doing the cooking?"
"Because she's a woman."

The first speaker has made a number of possible assumptions. He or she might believe that all women like to cook or perhaps that all women are required to cook whether they like it or not. But these assumptions were not stated. If they were, it would be easy for the other speaker to point out the flaw in the first speaker's reasoning.

This example suggests why many people see formal logic as too rigid for everyday arguments. Although formal logic can help us understand arguments and identify the assumptions we use in argument, rarely do writers of arguments consciously try to follow its rules. However, we do routinely use logic in our day-to-day discussions and arguments, though more informally. We regularly make and support claims, make and evaluate assumptions, and draw or oppose conclusions, and doing so according to the rules of formal logic would be cumbersome and perhaps even silly. Consider the following statement:

"I'd better close the windows, because the sky is getting darker."

If we examined this statement carefully, we could devise a syllogism to reveal the logic inherent in the statement:

| | |
|---|---|
| Major premise: | A dark sky indicates rain. |
| Minor Premise: | The sky is getting darker. |
| Conclusion: | Therefore, it will probably rain (and I should close the windows). |

You'll notice that in the original statement the major premise is implicit. Yet the statement is a form of logic nonetheless. Indeed, it would sound quite silly if we spoke in formal syllogisms in such situations. The point is that we need to make claims and provide reasons as we conduct our day-to-day affairs, but we need to do so efficiently. And we can usually assume certain beliefs or knowledge on the part of our listeners without having to state them explicitly.

In fact, for centuries theorists have been exploring the uses of such informal logic in arguments. Aristotle called this kind of informal logic a rhetorical syllogism, or an *enthymeme*. You might think of an enthymeme as a syllogism that consists of only two parts. In the example above, the major premise is missing. But it might be more helpful to think in terms of practical logic. In other words, rather than trying to follow the rigid rules of formal logic when making an argument, you are applying logic where it is most useful to you. Aristotle understood that in most situations such informal uses of logic are not only efficient and practical but effective as well.

There are two important ways in which understanding logic and employing informal logic, such as enthymemes, can be helpful to you: (1) as a reader (or listener) who is trying to make sense of and evaluate an argument and (2) as a writer who is trying to construct an effective argument. As a reader, you are often confronted with arguments — on a newspaper editorial page, in a reading assignment for a college course, in a political flyer you received in the mail. Being able to identify the premises on which an argument is based, especially when they are implicit, enables you to evaluate the argument and perhaps to uncover problems or flaws in the argument. For writers logic can be a powerful way not only to make a persuasive case for a position but also to organize an argument. (See pages 125–144 for a discussion of organizing an argument.)

**Cultural Differences in Logical Arguments**   It is also important to keep in mind that people from different cultural backgrounds might make different assumptions that they take for granted their audience shares. For example, in making an argument against sweatshops in which U.S. corporations employ young workers in Asian countries, an American writer might assume that her readers share her belief that child labor is a bad thing. Indeed, that would be a safe assumption with an American audience, since child labor has long been illegal in the United States (except under certain circumstances), and Americans generally seem to agree that it should be illegal. However, a reader from a rural community in Bangladesh, for instance, where children routinely work on local farms, might not share that assumption. In such a case the writer's argument would likely have very different effects on these different readers. You can easily think of more dramatic examples of such cultural differences and how they might affect logical argument. The suicide bombings taking place in the struggle between Israelis and Palestinians in the Middle East have been the subject of intense debate, which has revealed deep differences in how the participants view violence, suicide, national identity, and religious belief. In such a charged and difficult context a writer cannot safely assume, for instance, that his or her readers will accept the view that suicide is inherently wrong. You might not often engage in argumentation about such difficult issues, but you will almost certainly encounter the need to understand how cultural difference might influence the way readers will react to your assumptions.

## THE TOULMIN MODEL OF ARGUMENTATION

Formal logic, although it is a powerful framework for argumentation, has its limitations. Most people prefer not to be bound by a predetermined method of structuring an argument and regard the syllogism, in particular, as unnecessarily rigid. Many writers will therefore combine inductive and deductive reasoning in making an argument and often make arguments without the use of formal logic. Partly for these reasons scholars have long explored alternative ways of employing logic so that it becomes more practical and effective in arguments. One of the best-known systems for doing so was developed by a British philosopher named Stephen Toulmin in the 1950s. Emphasizing that logic is concerned with probability more often than with certainty, Toulmin provided a new way of analyzing arguments that focused on the nature of claims.

Toulmin's model includes three main components: the *claim,* the *data* or *reasons,* and the *warrant.* According to Toulmin, the basis of all arguments is the *claim,* which is the writer's (or speaker's) statement of belief — the conclusion or point he or she wishes to prove. The *data* or reasons are the evidence or information a writer or speaker offers to support the claim. The *warrant* is a general statement that establishes a trustworthy relationship between the data and the claim; it is a fundamental assumption (similar to the major premise in formal logic) on which a claim can be made and supported. In an argument the claim and data will be explicit, but the warrant is often implied, especially if the person making the argument assumes that the audience accepts the warrant. In that case the task is simply to present sufficient evidence to support the claim. However, if the audience disagrees with the warrant or finds it unacceptable, then the writer must defend it to make the claim.

To better understand these terms, let's consider an example adapted from one of Toulmin's examples:

Claim:       Raymond is an American citizen.

Data:        Raymond was born in Puerto Rico.

Warrant:     Anyone born in Puerto Rico is an American citizen.

### ELEMENTS OF THE TOULMIN SYSTEM OF ARGUMENT

| | |
|---|---|
| Claim: | The conclusion or the main point being argued. |
| Data: | The evidence supporting the claim. Also called the *reasons*. |
| Warrant: | Basic principle or assumption that connects the data and the claim. |

These three statements might remind you of the three elements in a deductive argument. If arranged as a syllogism, they might look like this:

Major Premise:    Anyone born in Puerto Rico is an American citizen.

Minor Premise:    Raymond was born in Puerto Rico.

Conclusion:       Raymond is an American citizen.

The advantage of Toulmin's model becomes apparent when we realize that the major premise here might not be true. For example, Raymond might have been born to French parents who were vacationing in Puerto Rico, or perhaps he was an American citizen but became a naturalized citizen of another country. Because the rigid logic of the syllogism is designed to lead to a conclusion that is *necessarily* true, Toulmin argued that it is ill suited for working toward a conclusion that is *probably* true. Believing that the syllogism was overemphasized in the study of logic, Toulmin saw a need for a "working logic" that would be easier to apply in the rhetorical situations in which most people find themselves — a kind of logic that would function in the kinds of arguments that people engage in every day. His model therefore easily incorporates *qualifiers* such as "probably," "presumably," and "generally." Here is a revision of the first example, employing Toulmin's model:

Claim:    Raymond is probably an American citizen.

Data:     Raymond was born in Puerto Rico.

Warrant:  Anyone born in Puerto Rico is entitled to American citizenship.

Both the claim and the warrant have been modified. Toulmin's model does not dictate any specific pattern in which these elements must be arranged, which is a great advantage for writers. The claim can be made at the beginning of an argument, or it can just as easily be placed after a discussion of the data and the warrant. Similarly, the warrant may precede the data, it may follow it, or it may be implied, as we already noted.

It is easy to see that claims and warrants can be extremely complicated and controversial, and one advantage of Toulmin's system is that it not only offers writers great flexibility in constructing effective arguments but also provides readers with a way to evaluate arguments carefully. In Chapter 5 we'll explore how Toulmin's model can help you structure your own arguments. For now it's important to examine some of the complexities of claims and warrants.

**Understanding Claims and Warrants**    There are different kinds of claims: claims supported by facts, claims supported by expert opinion, claims supported by values. For example, if you wanted to argue that the stock market should be subject to greater regulation, you could base your claim primarily on facts: You could define current regulations, report on laws governing markets, cite specific abuses and scandals involving insider trading, and include figures for the money lost to investors as a result of unethical trading practices. You would present these various facts to support your claim that greater regulation is needed. By contrast, another writer might argue in favor of regulating the stock market on the basis of the values of honesty and fair play. Of course, when we argue, we often use several different kinds of claims. For example, if you wanted to argue against capital punishment, your data might consist of facts (such as the numbers of executions performed annually, differences in these figures by state or by race, the number of death row inmates, and so on), the views of criminologists or legal experts regarding the death penalty, and an appeal to moral value (such as the sanctity of human life) that you believe your audience might share. In short, you would present different types of data depending on the nature of the claim you are making.

Warrants are also complex, and the nature of a warrant will differ from one argument to another. Some warrants may be relatively straightforward. For example, law often constitutes a warrant. A lawyer arguing on behalf of someone claiming American citizenship might invoke the Jones Act of 1917, which guarantees U.S. citizenship to citizens of Puerto Rico. That law would become the lawyer's warrant for the claim that a person born in Puerto Rico should be considered a U.S. citizen. But because warrants sometimes reflect assumptions or beliefs, they can be disputable and controversial. If you base a claim that capital punishment should be banned in the United States on a belief that taking any human life is wrong, you should be prepared to defend that warrant, since many people would not accept it. In such a case you would strengthen your argument against capital punishment if you explained and defended your view about the wrongness of taking human life. Simply stating or implying such a controversial warrant would likely result in some readers dismissing your argument altogether.

These examples reflect the challenges that writers — and readers — can often face when they engage in argumentation about difficult or charged issues, and they remind us that no model, including Toulmin's, will always lead to effective arguments. But if our goal is to understand the issues adequately in order to address a problem or negotiate differences that create conflict or discord, then Toulmin's model can be a useful framework for both writers and readers.

**Evaluating Claims and Warrants**   Being able to make strong claims and support them adequately is a crucial part of what makes an argument effective. It is also a challenge, largely because most claims deal with probability rather than certainty. If you engage in serious argumentation out of a desire to address an important issue or solve a problem, you need to understand how claims function and how to evaluate claims effectively. Toulmin's ideas about claims, data, and warrants can be useful tools in helping us make and evaluate claims.

Let's look at an example of an argument about an issue that became deeply important to Americans after the terrorist attacks on the United States on September 11, 2001: national security. In response to those attacks, the U.S. government began removing information that had previously been available on many of its Web sites. Among the kinds of information removed were environmental statistics, emergency plans, and data on health and safety risks to Americans. A year after the attacks and several months after the government began censoring its Web sites, writer Mary Graham argued in *The Atlantic Monthly* that keeping such information secret in the interest of national security is not only wrong but dangerous. She asserted that "the wholesale censorship of information on Web sites carries insidious costs." To support this central claim, Graham describes how this censorship policy can undermine, rather than increase, national security. She also asserts that this kind of censorship is unfair, and she questions whether secrecy will actually accomplish the goal of enhancing security: "National security is everyone's concern, and the idea that openness can be more effective than secrecy in reducing risks has received too little attention."

Evaluating Graham's argument requires us to examine how these assertions relate to her central claim. We might restate her claim as follows:

Claim:     The censorship of information on U.S. government Web sites should
           end because it is unfair to Americans and does not necessarily increase
           Americans' security.

Here we see that Graham offers two main reasons for her claim: (1) Censorship is unfair, and (2) secrecy might not enhance security. So far so good. But this claim rests on a basic assumption — her warrant — that isn't as obvious. We might state her warrant as follows:

> Warrant:     Americans have a right to information related to their security.

Notice that this warrant invokes a legal principle (a specific legal right that Americans have to information); it also invokes more general ethical values (openness and fairness). Because such a warrant is likely to be acceptable to most readers of the *Atlantic Monthly,* Graham need not defend it and can therefore concentrate on supporting her claim by offering reasons why the government's censorship policy won't achieve its goal of enhancing security. In short, her claim is clear, supported with various reasons, and strengthened by a warrant that is generally acceptable to her intended audience. As a reader, you can disagree with her claim, and no doubt some readers will also disagree with her warrant (believing, for example, that only government officials should have access to the kinds of information that has been censored from government Web sites). But if you accept her warrant, you can evaluate her argument against censorship on the basis of the evidence she presents.

If a claim is based on a warrant that isn't necessarily acceptable to an audience, the writer might have to defend that warrant. Otherwise, the argument for the claim might be less persuasive to the audience. Sometimes, it is the warrant and not the claim that is problematic for an audience. Let's examine an example in which the writer might have misjudged his audience and relied on a warrant that might be questionable for that audience. The following passage was taken from an essay arguing against a national boycott of gasoline — called a "gas out" — that some consumer advocates and environmental groups proposed in 2000, when gas prices were rising quickly in the United States. The writer, Gary Foreman, disagreed with this proposal. He made his claim against the boycott:

> I can pretty much tell you that "Gas Out 2000" won't work. It might draw some media attention. But it won't change the price you pay at the pump by one penny. And if you'll consider the facts you'll understand why.

Let's restate Foreman's claim:

> It's useless to participate in "Gas Outs," because they won't reduce the price of gas.

If we restate his claim in this way, his main reason supporting his claim also becomes clear: The boycott won't reduce gas prices. Most of Foreman's essay is devoted to an explanation of the economics of gasoline production and distribution, which he uses to support his claim. In other words, he relies on facts about the economics of the gasoline market to demonstrate why a boycott cannot reduce prices. But what is his warrant? Later in his essay he writes,

> So if a "Gas Out" won't help, what can you do? One very practical thing. Use less gas. Carpool, take public transportation, combine trips or get your car tuned up. Anything you can do to save gas will put more money in your pocket. And that's the one "statement" that oil producers will notice. More importantly, you'll notice it in your wallet, too.

Here he implicitly conveys his warrant, which we can restate as follows:

> Paying less money for gas is desirable.

Notice that this warrant is likely to be acceptable to many people. But this essay was published in a newsletter called *Simple Living,* which promotes an environmentally sound lifestyle. The readers of that newsletter are likely to be as concerned about the environmental effects of gasoline combustion as they are about gasoline prices. In other words, for such an audience, Foreman could safely use a much more environmentally conscious warrant; he could have made an argument that focused on environmental impact as well as price. Such an argument would likely have resonated with the readers of *Simple Living.* In fact, it is likely that many of those readers would find Foreman's argument *less* persuasive precisely because he focuses on reducing gas prices and ignores the ethical and environmental concerns that those readers probably share. In this case, readers of *Simple Living* might very well accept Foreman's claim that a boycott may not be a good idea while resisting his warrant.

This last example highlights the fact that claims and warrants, like other aspects of argument such as style or tone, must be understood in rhetorical context. No claim is universally valid; no warrant is universally acceptable. The audience, the cultural context, and the rhetorical situation all influence the impact of an argument. It's worth noting here too that because this newsletter was published on the World Wide Web, the writer might have assumed his audience to be much larger than just the subscribers to the newsletter. If so, we can see how the medium can influence an argument's warrant. (See Chapter 4 for a discussion of how media can affect argument.)

## FALLACIES

If you look closely at some of the examples in this chapter, you can find problems with the arguments. Any apparently logical argument can reveal serious flaws if you take the trouble to examine it carefully. Here is an excerpt from a letter written by a person opposed to a federal appeals court decision in 2002 ruling that the phrase "under God" in the Pledge of Allegiance is unconstitutional:

> In light of the events of this past September (9/11/01), I think it would be hypocrisy to omit an acknowledgement of a divine being under which the ideals and beliefs of this nation were created. And if you don't think so, ask everyone how many of them prayed to God that day.

flaw reasoning

This writer suggests that a large number of people praying is evidence of the existence of God. Obviously, whether or not you agree with him that there is a God, you can easily see that the number of people who pray does not necessarily prove God's existence. This flaw in the writer's reasoning is called a *logical fallacy* (specifically *attributing false causes,* which is discussed on page 38). Fallacies are often unintentional. We might think that we are making a strong argument but have actually engaged in flawed reasoning without realizing it, as is likely to have been the case with the writer in this example. Sometimes, however, writers know that their reasoning may be suspect but deliberately use it to win an argument. Some fallacies can in fact be powerful strategies for writers of arguments. But if we are concerned about truth — about addressing a problem or negotiating a conflict — then it makes sense to guard against fallacies so that we do not undermine our efforts to come to a reasonable resolution. And it is important to be able to identify fallacies in the arguments of others. In this section, we discuss some common fallacies.

## APPEALING TO PITY

Writers are often justified in appealing to the pity of their readers when the need to inspire this emotion is closely related to whatever they are arguing for and when the entire argument does not rest on this appeal alone. For example, someone who is attempting to convince you to donate one of your kidneys for a medical transplant would probably assure you that you could live with only one kidney and that there is a serious need for the kidney you are being asked to donate. In addition to making these crucial points, the arguer might move you to pity by describing what will otherwise happen to the person who needs the transplant.

When the appeal to pity stands alone, even in charitable appeals in which its use is fundamental, the result is often questionable. Imagine a large billboard advertisement for the American Red Cross. It features a close-up photograph of a distraught (but nevertheless good-looking) man, beneath which, in large letters, runs this caption: PLEASE, MY LITTLE GIRL NEEDS BLOOD. Although we might already believe in the importance of donating blood, we should question the implications of this ad. Can we donate blood and ask that it be reserved for the exclusive use of children? Are the lives of children more valuable than the lives of adults? Few people would donate blood unless they sympathized with those who need transfusions, and it might be unrealistic to expect logic in advertising. But consider how weak an argument becomes when the appeal to pity has little to do with the issue in question. Someone who has seldom attended class and has failed all his examinations but then tries to argue, "I deserve to pass this course because I've had a lot of problems at home," is making a fallacious appeal to pity. The "argument" asks the instructor to overlook relevant evidence and make a decision favorable to the arguer because the instructor has been moved to feel sorry for him. You should be skeptical of any appeal to pity that is irrelevant to the conclusion or that seems designed to distract attention from the other factors you should be considering.

## APPEALING TO PREJUDICE

Writers of argument benefit from appealing to their readers' values. Such appeals become fallacious, however, when couched in inflammatory language or when offered as a crowd-pleasing device to distract attention from whether the case at hand is reasonable and well informed. A newspaper that creates a patriotic frenzy through exaggerated reports of enemy "atrocities" is appealing to the prejudices of its readers and is making chances for reasonable discussion less likely. Racist, sexist, classist, and homophobic language can also be used to incite a crowd — something responsible writers should take pains to avoid doing. Appeals to prejudice can also take more subtle forms. Politicians might remind you that they were born and raised in "this great state" and that they love their children and admire their spouses — all of which are factors that are believed to appeal to the average voter but that nevertheless are unlikely to affect performance in office. When candidates linger on what wonderful family life they enjoy, it might be time to ask a question about the economy.

## APPEALING TO TRADITION

Although we can learn from the past and often benefit from honoring tradition, we can seldom make decisions based on tradition alone. Appealing to tradition is fallacious when tradition becomes the only reason for justifying a position. "We cannot let women join our club because we've never let women join in the past" is no less problematic that arguing, "We shouldn't buy computers for our schools, because we didn't have computers in the past." The world changes, and new opportunities emerge. What we have done in the past is not necessarily appropriate for the future. If you believe that a traditional practice can guide us in the future, you need to show why this is the case. Do not settle for claiming, "This is the way it always has been, so this is the way it always has to be."

## ARGUING BY ANALOGY

An analogy is a comparison that works on more than one level, and it is possible to use analogy effectively when reasoning inductively. You must first be sure that the things you are comparing have several characteristics in common and that these similarities are relevant to the conclusion you intend to draw. For example, you might argue that competition is good for schools, since it is considered to be good for businesses. But the strength of this argument would depend on the degree to which schools are analogous to businesses, so you would need to proceed with care and demonstrate that there are important similarities between the two. When arguing from analogy, it is important to remember that you are speculating. As is the case with any type of inductive reasoning, you can reach a conclusion that is likely to be true but not guaranteed to be true. It is always possible that you have overlooked a significant factor that will cause the analogy to break down.

Unfortunately, analogies are often misused. An argument from analogy that reaches a firm conclusion is likely to be fallacious, and it is certain to be fallacious if the analogy itself is inappropriate. If a congressional candidate asks us to vote for him because of his outstanding record as a football player, he might be able to claim that politics, like football, involves teamwork. But because a successful politician needs many skills and will probably never need to run across a field or knock someone down, it would be foolish to vote on the basis of this questionable analogy. The differences between football and politics outweigh the similarities, and it would be fallacious to pretend otherwise.

## ATTACKING THE CHARACTER OF OPPONENTS

If you make personal attacks on opponents while ignoring what they have to say or distracting attention from it, you are using what is often called an *ad hominem* argument (Latin for "to the man"). Although an audience often considers the character of a writer or speaker in deciding whether to trust what he or she has to say, most of us realize that good people can make bad arguments, and even a crook can sometimes tell the truth. It is always better to give a thoughtful response to an opponent's arguments than to ignore those arguments and indulge in personal attacks.

## ATTRIBUTING FALSE CAUSES

If you assume that an event is the result of something that merely occurred before it, you have committed the fallacy of false causation. Assumptions of this sort are sometimes called post hoc reasoning, from the Latin phrase *post hoc, ergo propter hoc,* which means "after this, therefore because of this." Superstitious people offer many examples of this type of fallacious thinking. They might tell you, "Everything was going fine until the lunar eclipse last month; *that's* why the economy is in trouble." Or personal misfortune might be traced back to spilling salt, stepping on a sidewalk crack, or walking under a ladder.

This fallacy is often found in the arguments of writers who are determined to prove the existence of various conspiracies. They often seem to amass an impressive amount of "evidence," but their evidence is frequently questionable. Or, to take a comparatively simple example, someone might be suspected of murder simply because he or she was seen near the victim's house a day or two before the crime occurred. This suspicion might lead to the discovery of evidence, but it could just as easily lead to the false arrest of the meter reader from the electric company. Being observed near the scene of a crime proves nothing by itself. A prosecuting attorney who would be foolish enough to base a case on such a flimsy piece of evidence would be guilty of *post hoc, ergo propter hoc* reasoning. Logic should always recognize the distinction between *causes* and what might simply be *coincidences.* Sequence is not a cause because every event is preceded by an infinite number of other events, not all of which can be held responsible for whatever happens today.

This fallacy can be found in more subtle forms in essays on abstract social problems. Writers who blame contemporary problems on such instant explanations as "the rise of violence on television" or "the popularity of computers" are no more convincing than is the parent who argues that all the difficulties of family life can be traced to the rise of rock and roll. It is impossible to understand the present without understanding the past, but don't isolate at random any one event in the past and then try to argue that it explains everything. And be careful not to accidentally imply a cause-and-effect relationship where you did not intend to do so.

## ATTRIBUTING GUILT BY ASSOCIATION

This fallacy is frequently apparent in politics, especially toward the end of a close campaign. A candidate who happens to be religious, for example, might be maneuvered by opponents into the false position of being held accountable for the actions of all the men and women who hold to that particular faith. Nothing specific has been argued, but a negative association has been either created or suggested through hints and innuendo.

## BEGGING THE QUESTION

In the fallacy known as begging the question, a writer begins with a premise that is acceptable only to anyone who will agree with the conclusion that is subsequently reached — a conclusion that is often very similar to the premise itself. Thus, the argument goes around in a circle (and is sometimes referred to as *circular reasoning*). For instance, someone might begin an essay by claiming, "Required courses like first-year Composition are a waste of time" and end with the conclusion that "first-year Composition should not be a required course." It might indeed be arguable that first-year Composition should not be required, but the author who begins with the premise that first-year Composition is a waste of time has assumed what the argument should be devoted to proving. Because it is much easier to *claim* that something is true than to *prove* it is true, you may be tempted to beg the question you set out to answer. This temptation should always be avoided.

## EQUIVOCATING

Someone who equivocates uses vague or ambiguous language to mislead an audience. In argumentation, equivocation often takes the form of using one word in several different senses without acknowledging the change in meaning. It is especially easy to equivocate when using abstract language. Watch out in particular for the abuse of such terms as "right," "society," "freedom," "law," "justice," and "real." When you use words like these, make sure your meaning is clear. And make doubly sure your meaning doesn't shift when you use the term again.

## IGNORING THE QUESTION

When someone says, "I'm glad you asked that question!" and then promptly begins to talk about something else, that person is guilty of ignoring the question. Politicians are famous for exploiting this technique when they don't want to be pinned down on a subject. Students (and teachers) sometimes use it too when asked a question that they want to avoid. Ignoring the question is also likely to occur when friends or partners have a fight. In the midst of a quarrel, we might hear remarks like "What about you?" or "Never mind the budget! I'm sick of worrying about money! We need to talk about what's happening to our relationship!"

## JUMPING TO CONCLUSIONS

This fallacy is so common that it has become a cliché. It means that the conclusion in question has not been supported by an adequate amount of evidence. Because one green apple is sour, it does not follow that all green apples are sour. Failing one test does not mean that you will necessarily fail the next. An instructor who seems disorganized on the first day of class might eventually prove to be the best teacher you ever had. You should always try to have more than one example to support an argument. Be skeptical of arguments that seem heavy on opinion but weak on evidence.

## OPPOSING A STRAW MAN

Because it is easier to demolish a man of straw than to address a live opponent fairly, arguers are sometimes tempted to pretend that they are responding to the views of their opponents when they are only setting up a type of artificial opposition that they can easily refute. The most common form of this fallacy is to exaggerate the views of others or to respond only to an extreme view that does not adequately represent the arguments of one's opponents. If you argue against abolishing Social Security, you should not think that you have effectively defended that program from all criticisms of it. By responding only to an extreme position, you are doing nothing to resolve specific concerns about how Social Security is financed and administered.

## PRESENTING A FALSE DILEMMA

A false dilemma is a fallacy in which a speaker or writer poses a choice between two alternatives while overlooking other possibilities and implying that no other possibilities exist. A college freshman who receives low grades at the end of the first semester and then claims, "What's wrong with low grades? Is cheating any better?" is pretending that there is no possibility other than cheating or earning a low grade — such as that of earning higher grades by studying harder, a possibility that is recognized by most students and teachers.

## REASONING THAT DOES NOT FOLLOW

Although almost any faulty argument is likely to have gaps in reasoning, this fallacy, sometimes called the *non sequitur* (Latin for "it does not follow"), describes a conclusion that does not follow logically from the explanation given for it.

Gaps of this sort can often be found within specific sentences. The most common type of non sequitur is a complex sentence in which the subordinate clause does not clearly relate to the main clause, especially where causation is involved. An example of this type of non sequitur would be "Because the teacher likes Joe, Joe passed the quiz in calculus." Here a cause-and-effect relationship has been claimed but not explained. It might be that Joe studied harder for his quiz because he believes that his teacher likes him, and that in turn resulted in Joe passing the quiz. But someone reading the sentence as written could not be expected to know this. A non sequitur can also take the form of a compound sentence: "Mr. Blandshaw is young, and so he should be a good teacher." Mr. Blandshaw might indeed be a good teacher but not just because he is young. On the contrary, young Mr. Blandshaw might be inexperienced, anxious, and humorless. He might also give unrealistically large assignments because he lacks a clear sense of how much work most students can handle.

Non sequiturs sometimes form the basis for an entire argument: "William Henderson will make a good governor because he is a friend of working people. He is a friend of working people because he has created hundreds of jobs through his contracting business." Before allowing this argument to go any further, you should realize that you've been asked to swallow two non sequiturs. Being a good governor involves more than being "a friend of working people." Furthermore, there is no reason to assume that Henderson is "a friend of working people" just because he is an employer. He might have acquired his wealth by taking advantage of the men and women who work for him.

## SLIDING DOWN A SLIPPERY SLOPE

According to this fallacy, one step will inevitably lead to an undesirable end. An example would be claiming that legalized abortion will lead to euthanasia or that censoring pornography will lead to the end of freedom of the press. Although it is important to consider the probable effects of any step that is being debated, it is fallacious to claim that people will necessarily tumble downhill as the result of any one step. There is always the possibility that we'll be able to keep our feet firmly on the ground even though we've moved them from where they used to be.

## EMOTIONAL ARGUMENTS

There is perhaps no more powerful way to construct an argument than to appeal to your readers' emotions. No argument is completely devoid of emotional appeal. But some arguments rely on emotions much more than others do. And because emotional appeals can be so powerful, they carry risk for both writer and reader.

One reason that emotional arguments don't work in all circumstances is that emotion itself is so complex and often poorly understood. Think for a moment about the range of emotions that might figure into an argument about, say, capital punishment: anger, pity, worry, fear, sadness, relief. Trying to anticipate how readers might react emotionally to a specific point about such charged issues can be daunting. You might try to inspire sympathy among your readers by, for instance, invoking a call to patriotism in an argument about measures to be taken against terrorism but find that your argument sparked anger among some readers instead. In fact, it is impossible to know with certainty what emotional responses you might elicit with a particular line of argument; you can only try to anticipate their responses on the basis of your experience, your knowledge of them, and your understanding of the rhetorical context.

Because of this uncertainty and because emotions will very likely be involved in any argument, it is a good idea to think of the use of emotion in argument as an ethical matter. You might suspect that a line of argument may evoke very strong emotions in some readers and, as a result, make those readers more susceptible to that line of argument. In other words, you might be able to "push the buttons" of your readers intentionally to elicit strong emotions. Doing so might enable you to win the argument, but will it truly solve the problem about which you are arguing? Is it the right way to address the issue at hand?

Used carefully and ethically, emotional appeals can be very effective. Let's consider how one writer employs emotion in an argument about the ongoing controversy over gun control. In this case the writer, Jeanne Shields, argues in favor of restricting the sale and ownership of handguns. But she writes from an especially wrenching position: Her own son was murdered by someone using a handgun. Here are the opening paragraphs of her essay:

> If the telephone rings late at night, I always mentally check off where each child is, and at the same time get an awful sinking feeling in the pit of my stomach.
>
> Four years ago, April 16, we had a telephone call very late. As my husband answered, I checked off Pam in Long Beach (California), Nick in San Francisco, David in New Brunswick (New Jersey) and Leslie outside Boston. The less my husband spoke, the tighter the knot got in my stomach. Instinctively, I knew it was bad news, but I wasn't prepared for what he had to tell me. Our eldest son, Nick, 23, had been shot dead on a street in San Francisco.
>
> Nick was murdered at about 9:30 p.m. He and a friend, Jon, had come from lacrosse practice and were on their way home. They stopped to pick up a rug at the

home of a friend. While Jon went in to get the rug, Nick rearranged the lacrosse gear in the back of their borrowed Vega. He was shot three times in the back of the head and died instantly, holding a lacrosse stick.

Nick was the fourteenth victim of what came to be called the "Zebra killers." Between the fall of 1973 and April 16, 1974, they had randomly killed fourteen people and wounded seven others — crippling one for life. Four men were subsequently convicted of murder in a trial that lasted thirteen months.

Shields goes on to describe how she and her husband eventually became involved in efforts to strengthen gun laws in the United States, arguing that current laws were too weak to control the proliferation of handguns like the one that killed her son. In setting up her argument, Shields describes a situation that she knows is likely to evoke strong emotions among her readers. Readers who are parents themselves will surely identify with Shields and her husband, and other readers are likely to feel empathy for them as well. Those feelings can make readers more likely to be open to Shields's support for tougher gun laws, even if those readers are not in favor of gun control in principle. Notice how the opening paragraphs of her essay describe two vivid scenes: two parents receiving a dreaded late-night phone call and an innocent young man shot in cold blood while doing an everyday task. Such a strategy is likely to give many readers pause, since the emotions surrounding these scenes can be deep and powerful.

Shields isn't just tugging at her readers' heartstrings here. Later in her piece, despite her own unequivocal support for stronger gun laws, she discusses both the pros and cons of gun control, and she refers to well-funded lobbies that oppose such laws. In this way she is making a reasoned, logical argument. But she employs emotion as well, appealing to her readers' empathy and perhaps also appealing to their emotional commitment to their own children. In short, her emotional appeal becomes an integral part of the logical argument she makes regarding gun control.

This example illustrates that emotional appeals must be used judiciously and ethically. It is easy to imagine some readers rejecting Shields' argument in favor of gun control and turning her appeal to the opposite position. The same emotions she invokes in favor of gun control can be used in an argument opposing it. For example, a parent whose child was murdered might well take the position that arming oneself with a handgun can help to prevent violent crime and might have saved his or her child. In evaluating positions like these, it is important to sort out the emotional appeals as well as the specific logical arguments each person is making.

Arguments about controversial issues such as gun control are fertile ground for emotional appeals, but emotion can be used in any argument. Here's an excerpt from an essay by Filip Bondy published the day after Brazil's soccer team won the 2002 World Cup:

> He cried, he laughed, he scored. Ronaldo put his mark on this special World Cup Sunday with a redemptive samba — two second-half goals in the 2-0 championship victory by Brazil over Germany, and eight goals in seven matches.
>
> Ronaldo's tale is now one for the ages, from the streets of Rio to the Yokohama stadium where he trotted about the field in triumph, hugging everyone, with a Brazil flag draped from his broad shoulders.
>
> The son of a drug-addicted father and a rock-steady mother, Ronaldo had blown off school as a youngster to play street soccer, to become that odd athletic combination of bull and gazelle that made him such a unique talent.

He wouldn't listen to his mother, who wanted him to study hard and to become a doctor. Instead, he aimed for something even more impossible — a career in soccer — and somehow succeeded. The trail, however, was not always as direct as his style.

In this argument celebrating Ronaldo, Bondy appeals not only to his readers' admiration for Ronaldo's achievement, but also to the joy that sports fans so often feel when they witness a victory by a great champion. In addition, in referring to the story of Ronaldo's difficult childhood, Bondy is also likely to stir up positive feelings about family, hard work, and the pursuit of individual dreams. Although he is not writing about something as complex and controversial as gun control, Bondy's appeal to these emotions may help make his argument about Ronaldo's achievement more convincing to his readers, whether they are fans of Brazil's soccer team or not.

This example illustrates that emotional appeals can work on several different levels. Notice, for example, that the idea of a world championship in sports can be used to evoke pride or admiration in readers. A writer like Bondy can try to employ that emotion throughout his or her argument. In other words, the very idea of a championship elicits certain emotions that become integral to the entire argument. By contrast, the brief descriptions in Bondy's essay of Ronaldo's childhood can elicit different emotions, which the writer uses for different purposes — in this case, to help support his point that Ronaldo's achievement is a special one and perhaps to create additional admiration for Ronaldo as an individual. Visual details and individual words or phrases can have the same effect. For example, think about your own reaction to the description of Ronaldo "hugging everyone, with a Brazil flag draped from his broad shoulders" or of Ronaldo's father as "drug-addicted." Certain words have powerful associations; in this case "drug-addicted" might create greater sympathy for Ronaldo. Terms such as *family values, environmentally friendly, freedom of choice,* and *American* are often used precisely because of the emotions they evoke. As a writer you can employ such carefully chosen words as you build your argument. But be mindful of the potential pitfalls of doing so. A single word, such as "drugs," can elicit very different responses in different readers, and it is important to try to understand the associations that a particular word or phrase might carry for readers. It is equally important to recognize how such words might influence you when you encounter them in someone else's argument.

How we use the power of emotion in an argument, of course, depends not only on our ability to assess the impact of a line of reasoning or an emotional appeal on our audience; it depends as well on what we hope to accomplish with an argument. If our purpose is to address a problem or to negotiate differences regarding a difficult or complex issue, then we must take care to employ emotional appeals appropriately and ethically.

## CHARACTER-BASED ARGUMENTS

"You can count on her."

"I wouldn't trust a word he says."

How many times have you heard — or spoken — some version of those two statements? Very likely, you have done so often, perhaps without realizing that you were engaging in one of the most basic and long-standing strategies for argument: invoking character. Aristotle identified character, or *ethos,* as one of the most powerful components of persuasion available to a speaker: "We believe good men [and women] more fully and more readily than others," he wrote, adding that a speaker's character "may almost be called the most effective means of persuasion he [or she] possesses" (*Rhetoric,* p. 25). But character is not just a strategy; it is also a quality. Like Aristotle, the famous Roman rhetorician Quintillian believed that the most effective orator is a "good" person. Above all, Quintillian wrote, the effective orator "must possess the quality which . . . is in the very nature of things the greatest and most important, that is, he [or she] must be a good man [or woman]" (*Institutio Oratoria,* Book XII, p. 355). In short, the best way to sound or appear ethical in an argument is to *be* ethical.

We often rely on our sense of someone's character when making decisions in our daily lives. For example, you might seek advice about attending graduate school from a relative or a teacher you trust and whom you know to be careful with advice about such matters. In some cases character might grow out of one's authority and expertise: Your professor's knowledge of universities and education can lead to useful advice about graduate school. You wouldn't necessarily have the same confidence about such advice from, say, a friend who is a chef. From her you might seek suggestions for a good restaurant or recipe. One's authority or expertise is not the same thing as character (a professor can be unethical and untrustworthy, for instance), but it is usually part of one's character and can be a powerful source of appeals in argument.

This kind of appeal is common in advertising. Corporations select celebrities to represent them or their products — for example, basketball star Michael Jordan for Nike shoes. The implicit argument is that if someone like Michael Jordan endorses this product, it must be good. An advertising campaign for the soft drink Sprite even parodied this strategy. In several television ads, professional basketball players, such as Grant Hill, were shown drinking Sprite. The ads seemed to suggest that drinking Sprite would enable anyone to perform the athletic feats of a player like Hill. But at the end of the ad, a person fails to perform such a feat after drinking Sprite. The ads end with the line "Obey your thirst." The suggestion was that you shouldn't trust a celebrity for advice about how to quench your thirst. These ads presented a twist on the common approach to using celebrities to sell products, suggesting how routine that approach has become in American culture.

Character is especially important in the arenas of law and politics. In court, for instance, lawyers will try to establish or undermine the credibility of witnesses as they try to convince a judge or jury about a person's guilt or innocence. Defense lawyers sometimes call "character witnesses" to establish that the defendant was a particular kind of person (usually, of course, a good person). Similarly, when it comes to politics, character often looms large. Consider how often candidates for elected office try to establish their own credibility as trustworthy and dependable. Advertisements showing a candidate's family, for example, are standard fare in U.S. elections. Such advertisements intend to convey that politicians who are married and have children are more reputable than candidates who are single — an old-fashioned idea that has been strangely enduring even though most people these days recognize that there's nothing necessarily odd about being single and that families who smile together are not necessarily happy. Just as common are advertisements attacking an opponent's credibility. Often such "attack ads" will suggest that a candidate is not concerned with issues affecting voters and therefore isn't to be trusted.

A writer can raise questions about someone's credibility to support a particular point or position on an issue. Consider, for instance, the following excerpt from an editorial by *Chicago Tribune* columnist Clarence Page. Page is arguing in favor of a controversial policy at the University of North Carolina requiring all incoming first-year students in 2002 to read a book about the Koran. The purpose was to encourage students to learn and think carefully about an important book that they might not be familiar with. Page is reacting specifically to an appearance by a University of North Carolina professor on *The O'Reilly Factor*, a popular television news talk show hosted by journalist Bill O'Reilly:

> The important thing, as Robert Kirkpatrick, the professor who chose the book, explained on "The O'Reilly Factor" TV show is this: First-year students need to know that "as a member of an academic community they have to learn to think and to read and to write and to defend their opinions."
>
> That's right. Start pushing a book on college freshmen and, who knows? They might try reading another one.
>
> That's what college is supposed to be about. It is not just a time for learning but a time to arouse curiosity in preparation for a lifetime of learning.
>
> That process begins when you learn not only to have opinions but also how to express and defend them.
>
> "And defending the right not to read the book is something that will be very interesting to read," the professor said.
>
> Indeed, it should be at least as interesting as listening to showman-journalist O'Reilly explain why he will not read the book. According to a Fox transcript, he called UNC's assignment "unbelievable," compared it to assigning "Mein Kampf" during World War II and asked why should freshmen be required to study "our enemy's religion."
>
> Yes, there is a lot more to Islam than Osama bin Laden and his violent brethren, but apparently not in O'Reilly's mind.
>
> "I mean, I wouldn't give people a book during World War II on [how] the emperor is God in Japan. Would you?"
>
> "Sure," Kirkpatrick said. "Why not? Wouldn't that have explained kamikaze pilots?"
>
> That's a sensible answer, not that sensibleness gets you anywhere on high-energy cable TV news-talk shows these days or, for that matter, in politics — especially religious politics.

Here, Page supports his own position in favor of the reading requirement by questioning O'Reilly's credibility (and even his common sense) on the issue. He suggests that O'Reilly's interest as a TV talk-show host is not in arriving at a "sensible" answer to the question raised by the University of North Carolina requirement but rather in being a "showman." Such a strategy can be effective when a person advocating a certain position is well known and likely to be considered credible by many people. Because of his television show, Bill O'Reilly was widely known in the United States in 2002, and it is likely that many of his viewers saw him as an important voice on issues such as public education.

By calling O'Reilly's credibility on the issue into question, Page could weaken O'Reilly's position and strengthen his own argument that the reading requirement is justified and sound.

A writer can take the opposite approach in making a character-based argument; that is, the writer can invoke certain positive aspects of someone's character to advance an argument. In the following passage, notice how sports columnist Harvey Araton establishes Pakistani tennis player Qureshi as a committed professional athlete who overlooks political and religious affiliations and focuses on winning at tennis (see Figure 2-1). As you read, keep in mind that Qureshi was harshly criticized by other Pakistanis for agreeing to have an Israeli player as his doubles partner. These criticisms came during the 2002 Wimbledon tennis tournament at the same time that the conflict in the Middle East between Israelis and Palestinians was intensifying and had become especially bloody.

They played together, then sat together, Pakistani and Israeli, Muslim and Jew, and wanted everyone to know it was no big deal. There was no statement made, no cause advanced, other than the bid to go as far they could in the Wimbledon draw. Pragmatism, not peacemaking, made doubles partners of Aisam ul-Haq Qureshi and Amir Hadad.

"We are not here to change anything," said Qureshi, 22, of Lahore, Pakistan. "I don't like to interfere religion or politics into sport."

Hadad, 24, of Ramala, Israel, near Tel Aviv, said: "I know Aisam is very good on grass, good serve, good volley, and also I like him as a person. When he asked me to play, we didn't even think it's going to get so big."

Then they survived the qualifying tournament and won two rounds in the main draw last week. No Pakistani had lasted past this round at Wimbledon, or in any Grand Slam event. What would have been a feel-good story in Pakistan became an inflamed issue when Qureshi, the country's No. 1 player, from a family with a rich tennis history, made a bit of his own history with Hadad — until they were dispatched by the Czechs Martin Damm and Cyril Suk yesterday, 6-1, 7-6 (5), 6-4.

It was, for them, a productive pairing, one they said they might reprise at the United States Open next month, no matter the ominous reports from Pakistan that Qureshi has read on the Internet.

His family, stationed by Court 5 yesterday in the shadow of Center Court, was only interested in what was happening here, saying they had received support from Pakistanis all over London. His mother, Nosheen, formerly No. 1 in Pakistan and still an active player at 41, kissed the Israeli, Hadad, on the cheek and called him a good boy. The father, Ihtsham, a 50-year-old businessman, videotaped the third-round match, right down to the volley his son misplayed on match point. An uncle, Khalid Rashid, dismissed the protests, calling them the work of "Al Qaeda and extremists in the north."

The reports, without subtlety, said otherwise. A former Pakistani champion, Saeed Haid, was quoted in *The Times* of London saying, "The bloodshed in the

Middle East means his pairing with an Israeli is wrong." A director of the country's official Sports Board, Brig. Saulat Abbas, told Agence France-Presse: "Although he is playing in his private capacity, we officially condemn his playing with an Israeli player and an explanation has been sought from him. Since we have no links with Israel, Qureshi may face a ban."

In the heart of aristocratic-mandated civility, the lawns neatly manicured and the sportswear lily white, this sounded like hardened geopolitical zealotry bordering on lunacy. A cautious Ihtsham Qureshi said it was his understanding that the Pakistani news media were supporting his son, and many positive e-mail messages had been received. His wife, whose father was the best player in India before partition in 1947, said, "People with the right perspective don't think like that."

Within this insular sport, which rears wandering citizens of the world, the players sounded mature and wise as they spoke of a friendship formed along the endless road of small-time events for those on the far periphery of fame. They joked about how their greatest faith must be in their ability to stay fit and focused in the pursuit of almighty computer points.

"I don't pray at all, but I practice a lot," Hadad said.

In this editorial Araton is not just establishing the two tennis players as credible and principled people; he also shows them to be committed to excellence in their sport. He implies that such a commitment allows them to be open-minded about others who might have different religious beliefs or political views from their own. Obviously, not all Araton's readers will agree that such character is a good thing in view of the ongoing conflict between Arabs and Israelis — a conflict in which Qureshi and Hadad are indirectly involved. But Araton uses the character of these two players to make his larger argument that we must get beyond our religious differences if we will ever solve this terrible conflict. Here is Araton's final paragraph:

He [Qureshi] said he had played with Israelis before, but on nothing like the world Wimbledon stage. Here, as Hadad said, the point was to "improve our ranking, make some money." A Muslim and a Jew partnered and got the job done in a game that begins with the score at love. If only doubles were that easy in settling conflicts plagued and prolonged by hate.

If Araton had not established that Qureshi and Hadad have a certain kind of integrity and commitment to their profession, his argument would not have the same impact. Araton believes that it is precisely the kind of character possessed by Qureshi and Hadad that can help us overcome prejudice and cultural conflict. In this regard, he is employing a character-based argument as a way to try to address a horrible conflict; his is an example of an argument whose ultimate purpose is to negotiate deep religious differences that seem intractable and that have led to great suffering.

**FIGURE 2-1**    Qureshi (left) and Hadad

SOURCE: AP, July 4, 2002.

The character of the writer himself or herself can also play a powerful role in an argument. In the previous example readers who don't know anything about Harvey Araton can still find his argument, based on the character of the two tennis players, effective. But sometimes it is the writer's character that becomes an important basis for an argument. As we noted above, the advice of a professor about graduate school or of a chef about a recipe carries weight because of who is giving the advice. Similarly, many arguments have force because of the authority or character of the writer. Consider the following letter to the editor of the *Cleveland Plain Dealer*, written in response to an editorial about the promise of medical technology:

The *Plain Dealer's* Aug. 13 editorial "Miracles on demand" was right that emerging medical breakthroughs hold incredible promise in overcoming serious diseases like cancer and heart failure. And it was right that, in our imperfect world, it is impossible to provide an absolute guarantee of the safety of medical technology. But it missed the fact that manufacturers and the Food and Drug Administration are doing an excellent job making sure new tests and treatments are as safe as possible.

. . .

FDA data on product recalls show that the agency's system of pre-market and post-market regulations is working well. Even as the number and complexity of medical technologies has increased, the total number of recalls has remained steady over the last 10 years. The vast majority of recalls are not considered a serious public-health issue and are due to issues like labeling errors that can be easily corrected. Are medical technologies always perfect? Unfortunately, no. But manufacturers and the FDA have maintained an impressive safety record as a result of their mutual commitment to the safest possible products.

The agency itself concludes: "The public's confidence in FDA is well justified." After examining the facts, we wholeheartedly agree.

The letter was signed as follows:

Pamela G. Bailey.

Bailey is president of the Advanced Medical Technology Association, which represents more than 1,100 innovators and manufacturers of medical devices, diagnostic products and medical information systems.

Obviously, Bailey is making a logical argument here about the safety of medical technologies. But her argument might have greater impact on readers who notice that she is president of an organization of medical technology professionals. You might consider whether you assign greater credibility to this argument on the basis of your knowledge of Bailey's position. (Of course, your reaction would depend in part on your opinion of large companies that manufacture medical technologies. For some readers, knowing who Bailey is will undermine her argument.)

The public prominence of a person can work in much the same way in an argument. In the summer of 2002, the *New York Times* published an essay in favor of school vouchers by the famed economist Milton Friedman. After the Supreme Court decision in June 2002 upholding the voucher program in the Cleveland, Ohio, city schools, many editorialists wrote arguments supporting or opposing the Court's ruling. Many of those writers had no authority as either legal experts or educators. In that regard, their character probably did not figure prominently into their arguments — or in readers' reactions to their arguments. Friedman, by contrast, is an internationally known figure who is one of the most influential economists of the 20th century. Consider how this blurb, which was included at the end of his essay, might influence your reaction to his argument:

Milton Friedman, the 1976 recipient of the Nobel Prize in economics, is a senior research fellow at the Hoover Institution.

Writers of arguments need not have such impressive reputations as Friedman's to employ character effectively. Establishing credibility is an important strategy in argumentation that all writers can use. When you refer to your own experiences, for example, as a way to indicate to your readers that you know something about a situation or an issue, you are establishing credibility that can give your argument greater weight. Here is writer Joshua Wolf Shenk addressing the issue of legalizing drugs:

> There's no breeze, only bare, stifling heat, but Kevin can scarcely support his wispy frame. He bobs forward, his eyes slowly closing until he drifts asleep, in a 45-degree hunch. "Kevin?" I say softly. He jerks awake and slowly rubs a hand over his spindly chest. "It's so hot in here I can hardly think," he says. . . .
>
> This July I spent a long, hot day talking to junkies in New York City, in a run-down hotel near Columbia University. Some, like Kevin, were reticent. others spoke freely about their lives and addictions. I sat with Melissa for 20 minutes as she patiently hunted her needle-scarred legs for a vein to take a spike. She had just fixed after a long dry spell. "I was sick," she told me. "I could hardly move. And Pap" — she gestures toward a friend sitting across from her — "he helped me out. He gave me something to make me better. . . ."
>
> Making drugs legally available, with tight regulatory controls, would end the black market, and with it much of the violence, crime, and social pathology we have come to understand as "drug-related." And yet, history shows clearly that lifting prohibition would allow for more drug use, and more abuse and addiction.
>
> I spent that day in New York to face this excruciating dilemma. It's easy to call for an end to prohibition from an office in Washington, D.C. What about when looking into Kevin's dim eyes, or confronting the images of crack babies, shriveled and wincing?

Shenk uses his own experience not only to make his point about the horrors of drug addiction, but also to establish himself as someone who knows about this problem from direct experience. Notice, too, that Shenk's gentle, sympathetic descriptions of the addicts he met help to convey a sense of him as caring and deeply concerned, which might add to his credibility for many readers. (Obviously, there is an emotional appeal here, too.)

There are other ways for a writer to establish credibility as well. Establishing an honest, straightforward voice as a writer can help to convince readers that you are credible and believable and that they can take you seriously. Indeed, the very quality of your writing can help establish your credibility by demonstrating your competence to readers. Acknowledging your own limitations can be an effective strategy for establishing credibility, too. For example, imagine that you wish to contribute to a discussion of standardized testing in your community, an important educational issue that affects all students (including you). In writing a letter to your local school board, for instance, you might concede at the outset that you are not an expert in educational testing but that your own experiences as a student give you insight into the problems associated with testing. Such a statement can gain you credibility by showing that you are not trying to claim expertise that you don't have, yet you are genuinely concerned about the issue at hand. In this sense you are being honest with your readers and thereby communicating to them that they can trust you. You are, in other words, establishing your own character as the writer of an argument.

Sometimes, claiming authority as the writer of an argument can backfire. You have no doubt heard or read statements by someone engaged in argument who claims to know more than someone else about the issue being discussed. For instance, let's return to the example in the previous paragraph. Imagine that your letter to the school board has provoked a response from a school board member who is an expert in educational testing. Imagine further that he explicitly refers to that expertise in his attempt to call your position into question. In effect, he says, "I know what I'm talking about, because I'm an expert in this area. This other person, on the other hand, doesn't know what he's talking about." Even if your purpose is to dominate, such an approach can undermine your credibility, since readers could find you arrogant. The school board member in this example might well have expertise in testing, but residents of the school district might reject his position if they believe that his arrogance gets in the way of the best interests of the students. If your purpose in this argument, by contrast, is to address a problem involving the testing of students in your school district, then perhaps the strategy is inappropriate. Like all appeals, the appeal to character can be complicated and should always be assessed in terms of the specific situation at hand.

# 3

# THE CONTEXTS OF
# ARGUMENT

THE CONTEXTS

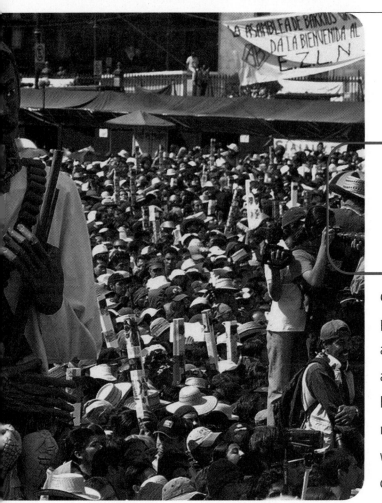

**W**henever we engage in argumentation, we must do more than examine the topic carefully and construct a sound argument in support of our position. We must also take into account our audience, the specific situation we and they are in, the cultural factors that might affect how an audience responds to a particular argument, even the historical moment we are in as we argue. In short, we always argue within a context — actually, within several contexts simultaneously — and we must address context if we expect to argue effectively.

O F   A R G U M E N T

Let's imagine for a moment that you have been given an assignment in your composition course to take a position on the issue of racial profiling and write an argument justifying your position. Let's assume further that you will be asked to read your essay to your class, which includes students of different racial groups. Obviously, racial profiling is a controversial topic, and you know that your classmates' views about the topic are likely to be varied and strong. After reading a number of articles and essays, you have decided that despite some problems with racial profiling, you believe that it can be an important tool for fighting crime if used carefully. You write an argument in which you acknowledge the serious problems that can occur as a result of racial profiling by law enforcement agencies, but you justify its use on the grounds of security and public safety. In your argument you try to address your teacher as well as your classmates, some of whom have voiced strenuous opposition to profiling. You wish to make an effective argument that your classmates, even those who are opposed to profiling, will take seriously, though you are mindful that some of them might reject what you have to say because of their own passionate engagement with the issue. You also know that your teacher will be assessing your argument and that your classmates' reactions might influence her assessment. So you have gathered some evidence that profiling can reduce some kinds of crime, and you have identified what you consider to be good arguments in support of profiling policies that can protect citizens' privacy and civil rights. But you also know that the charged nature of the topic will make some of these arguments seem less than convincing to some of your classmates. What will you write?

As a writer you might not have faced a situation quite as challenging as the one described here, but if you have engaged in argument, you have had to think about some of the same problems you would encounter in this situation. The answer to the question "What will you write?" in a given situation requires that you consider the context of your argument. No matter what kind of argument you wish to make, no matter what your purpose, there are at least three main contexts you should consider as you construct an argument:

- The rhetorical situation
- The cultural context
- The particular moment in which we are arguing, which we can call the historical context

## THE RHETORICAL SITUATION

Rhetoricians have long used the metaphor of a triangle to help define the rhetorical situation (see Figure 3-1). The classical rhetorical triangle reminds us that when we write an argument, we are engaged in an interaction with a particular audience about a particular subject. Both audience and writer have a connection to the subject matter in the form of knowledge about the subject, opinions about it, experience with it, and so on. But the writer and the audience will never have identical connections to that subject. A big part of the challenge, then, is to try to understand your audience and its connection to your subject so that you can address your audience effectively as you construct your argument.

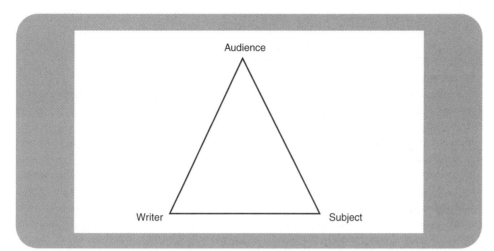

FIGURE 3-1

**The Rhetorical Situation**

## ANALYZING YOUR AUDIENCE

Obviously, the audience for a particular argument can vary dramatically from one situation to another, and as we'll explain in more detail later in this chapter, the specific characteristics of the rhetorical situation (when and where someone is making an argument, for example) can profoundly affect how a writer addresses an audience and how an audience might respond to an argument. But because an argument is very often an attempt to communicate with an audience about a conflict or a problem, and because ideally an argument will effectively address that conflict or resolve the problem, it is essential for writers to try to understand their audience to the extent that they can. And there are some general guidelines for doing so.

First, try to determine what you already know about your intended audience. In some cases, the audience for an argument will be very specific. In our hypothetical example, you would literally know your audience (your teacher and your classmates), and you would have some sense of their knowledge and opinions about your subject (racial profiling). Moreover, because you would have engaged in class discussion about racial profiling, you might even know how some of your classmates (and perhaps your teacher) might react to specific arguments in favor or against racial profiling. You can imagine other situations in which you might know your audience well. For instance, if you were writing a letter to your local school board in support of a proposal for, say, a new swimming pool at the high school, you would know something about the members of the school board and community members who might read your letter. You might even know them personally. If you wrote a letter to the editor of your local newspaper, you would have a good sense of who the readers would be, since they live in your community. A writer can draw on such knowledge to identify effective arguments. In some ways this is almost an ideal situation for a writer, because there would be very little of the uncertainty about the audience that writers usually face in writing an argument. And if the goal is to try to solve a problem, then knowing the audience can lead to a better understanding of their positions and a more genuine engagement with them about the issue.

In most cases, however, writers are likely to have much more general knowledge — or very little knowledge — about their audience. Imagine the difference between writing a letter to the editor of a local newspaper, which is read by a few thousand people, almost all of whom live in the same town, and writing a letter to the editor of a national publication such as *USA Today*, which is read by millions of people from all over the country. The assumptions that you can reasonably make about these audiences can differ dramatically. But it is not really feasible to analyze a general audience, such as the readership of *USA Today*, in depth because that audience is far too diverse for you to know anything about it in detail. At the same time, you can approach such an audience in a way that is likely to engage a majority of readers and address them effectively. In other words, even though there is a limit to what you can really know about an audience (after all, even a close friend can surprise you), you can make some general assumptions about your audience that will help you to argue effectively.

You can begin by assuming an intelligent and fair-minded audience. Assume as well that intelligent and fair-minded people tend to be skeptical about sweeping generalizations and unsupported claims. (Indeed, they might be skeptical about the generalization made in that sentence!) In some cases you might be able to expect your audience to agree with you. For example, if you are the keynote speaker at a political convention, chances are that most people in the audience will share your viewpoint. But if you are attempting to reconcile differences or solve a conflict through argument, you should probably assume that your audience will disagree with you. Some members of your audience might be neutral about the issue you're addressing. But imagining a skeptical audience will enable you to anticipate and respond to opposing views or objections to your position, thus building a stronger case.

## IMAGINING YOUR AUDIENCE

In some ways imagining an audience is a creative act. Well-known 20th century scholar Walter Ong wrote a famous article called "The Writer's Audience Is Always a Fiction," in which he argued that when writers write, they must always create a sense of an audience that doesn't necessarily correspond directly to a "real" audience. This act of "fiction," Ong maintained, is necessary because rarely do writers know in detail just whom they are writing to or for. But this imagined audience is always based on a general sense of who might read what we are writing, our experiences with people in general, our experiences as readers of other people's writing, and our knowledge of the conventions of writing. All these figure into our imagined audience. In other words, our imagined audience is based on our real experiences with writing and with other people. When it comes to argument, this act of imagining an audience influences the specific arguments you will make in support of your position on an issue.

Even when imagining a general audience, writers often make specific assumptions about their readers beyond assuming that they are intelligent but skeptical. Consider, for example, the following letter, which was written to the editors of *Newsweek* in response to an essay by columnist Allan Sloan criticizing greed and unethical behavior by large corporations:

> Right on, Allan Sloan! I have long thought that no economic system, certainly not capitalism, can function successfully without the moderating effects of virtuous, ethical behavior on the part of the key players. That said, I'm afraid that we have yet to widely acknowledge that such behavior can never be reliably coerced by endless rounds of civil regulation. In a free society there will always be loopholes to be identified and exploited by those with selfish, greedy attitudes.

Notice that this writer implicitly assumes that his readers are not necessarily those with "selfish, greedy attitudes," nor are they likely to be the "key players" in the capitalist system. In other words, he assumes that his readers are more "average" people who share his basic values regarding ethical behavior. He can further assume that his readers have read Allan Sloan's essay and that they probably have a basic understanding of the principles of capitalism that Sloan discussed. The point is that even a "general" audience can be specific in certain respects. Narrowing an audience in this way can help a writer determine how to cast an argument so that it effectively addresses that general audience.

Sometimes, a writer can define a general audience more directly by explicitly excluding specific kinds of readers. In the following letter, which was also written to the editors of *Newsweek,* the writer is responding to an article about electroshock therapy:

> I was surprised to find no mention of neurofeedback in your article "Healthy Shocks to the Head." Noninvasive, relatively inexpensive and proving to be effective with a long list of central nervous-system disorders, this procedure should be given an opportunity to demonstrate its effectiveness before more invasive procedures are tried. It's too bad the medical community is so enamored with drugs and surgery.

Notice that this writer refers to "the medical community" in a way that excludes members of that community from his audience. In effect, he is addressing everyone outside "the medical community." Of course, this writer probably knows that members of that community are likely to read his letter, too, so indirectly he is also addressing them — as well as criticizing them — and perhaps inspiring an Ong-like fiction: "You're a *good* doctor or nurse, not one of those types I am referring to here." But by referring to them as he does, he defines his intended audience as those readers who are not members of that community, thus narrowing his "general" audience and assuming that they might well share his concerns.

It is worth noting here that if the writer in the preceding example hoped to try to negotiate the apparent conflict that exists among those who advocate noninvasive techniques for treating disorders of the central nervous system, as he does, and those in the medical community who might have a different view, then he would ultimately need to address the medical community directly, too. In other words, a sense of purpose for an argument will shape the writer's sense of audience.

The audience for an argument is also influenced by the specific circumstances in which the argument is being made. In the previous example the writer is addressing a general audience made up of readers of *Newsweek,* and he is doing so in response to a specific article that appeared in that magazine. Imagine if he were making the same argument — in favor of noninvasive techniques for treating disorders of the central nervous system — in a letter written to the *Journal of Mental Health.* In that case the audience would likely include some of the same readers of *Newsweek,* but it would now be composed primarily of mental health professionals who read that journal — that is, members of the "medical community" that he criticized in his original letter. Although his argument might not change, this writer would now be able to use more technical language and would likely have to address his readers differently if he wished them to take him seriously. Imagine further that he is not responding to an article in *Newsweek* but instead is writing about the issue of electroshock therapy in general. In this case he must introduce his topic differently, since he would not be able to refer to a specific article that he could assume his readers had read. But he *could* assume that his audience knew more about these treatments than the readers of *Newsweek* are likely to know, which would affect what information he might include in his argument and how he might present it. The circumstances for his argument would therefore affect several important aspects of his argument even if his basic position is the same.

As these examples suggest, the circumstances within which an audience is being addressed can also have a big impact on how that audience will respond to a specific argument. Obviously, it is impossible for a writer to know about everything that is part of a rhetorical situation, just as it is impossible for a writer to be able to anticipate how every member of the audience will react to a specific word, phrase, tone, fact, or line of argumentation. Human beings are simply too complex. But effective arguments are usually effective only within a specific rhetorical situation. What works in one situation might not work in another. So it is crucial for writers of arguments to examine the rhetorical situation they are in and make their best judgments about how to address their audience in that situation. And although trying to understand an audience in itself takes time and effort, it offers a great reward: knowledge about human nature that can make it easier for you to live and work with others.

## CULTURAL CONTEXT

When writers engage a particular audience in argumentation, they never address generic readers, even when they are addressing the kind of general audience discussed in the previous section. Instead, they address human beings, each of whom brings a different set of experiences, knowledge, beliefs, and background to the interaction. In other words, who we are as individuals shapes how we will react to an argument. And who we are is a complex matter that encompasses our racial, ethnic, gender, and cultural identities. In this regard, *culture* will always be part of any rhetorical situation and thus shape any argument.

### UNDERSTANDING CULTURE

Culture can be understood in several ways when it comes to argumentation. As was suggested in the preceding paragraph, we can think of culture as our sense of identity as it relates to our racial and ethnic backgrounds, our religious upbringing (if any), our membership in a particular social class (working class, for example), and the region where we live (for example, rural West Virginia versus urban Los Angeles). These aspects of our identity affect how we understand ourselves as individuals in relation to others and as members of various communities. Culture in this sense will shape how we view the world, what we believe and value, and how we experience various aspects of life. We can also think of culture as a setting within which we live and interact with each other, as in the culture of New York or the culture of Japan. These ways of understanding culture overlap, of course, but they provide a sense of the powerful influence that culture will have on individual writers and readers as they engage in argumentation.

Let's return to the example at the opening of this chapter. Consider how classmates with different cultural backgrounds might react to your argument in favor of racial profiling. Obviously, an African American student might be highly sensitive to the subject — and perhaps passionate about it — because the controversy about the subject has directly involved Blacks in many communities. In addition, if that student grew up in an urban neighborhood where relations between residents and police are strained, he or she might have strong feelings related to his or her experience as well as his or her identity as a Black person. Compare that student to, say, an exchange student from Japan, where racial issues have a very different history. A Japanese student might also have a different sense of authority and of the relationship between individuals and the government than Americans students have. To invoke a somewhat different example, what if one of your White classmates was raised in a Quaker household that emphasized a lifestyle based on nonviolence? How might that person react to an argument in favor of racial profiling? All these hypothetical examples indicate the various ways in which culture can influence both the writing and reading of an argument.

These examples tell us something else: that culture is complex. The student who was raised as a Quaker, for example, is White but can legitimately claim a different cultural identity from other White students in your class, even though all of them can claim to be part of American culture. The same can be said of two different Black students: one who might have grown up in a middle-class suburb and another whose parents might be working-class immigrants from the Caribbean. In other words, even if two people have similar cultural backgrounds, they will not have *identical* cultural backgrounds and will not have identical experiences as members of that culture. As a writer of arguments you can't be expected to sort out all these subtle complexities, but you should always be sensitive to culture and assume that culture will play an important role in argumentation. Brian Fay, a philosopher of social science, describes the influence of culture in this way:

> My experience has been deeply shaped by the fact that I am male, a (former) Catholic, American, and middle class. Because of these characteristics I look at the world in a certain way, and people treat me in a particular manner. My Catholic upbringing, for example, gave me a view of myself as fallen and as needing to be redeemed by something other than myself or the natural world; it made me think that certain desires and behaviors are bad, and led me to (try to) repress them; even my body was shaped by certain typical Catholic disciplines (kneeling, for instance). Even when in later life I reacted against this upbringing, I was still reacting against my particular Catholic heritage, and in this way this heritage continues to shape me; it will do so until I die.

It seems obviously true that I am in part who and what I am in strong measure because of the groups to which I belong (to which in many cases I had no choice but to belong). If I had been born and raised in New Guinea then I would be quite other than what I am: I would not only describe the world differently, I would experience it differently.

Fay does not use the term *culture* in this passage, but he is referring to aspects of one's background — such as religious upbringing, social class, gender, and national origin — that are usually associated with culture and considered part of one's cultural identity. Think of how these aspects of Fay's cultural identity might affect his reaction to an argument about racial profiling or school voucher programs.

## CONSIDERING CULTURE IN ARGUMENT

We can return to another example to examine the role of culture in argument more closely. Earlier, we referred to an essay by Harvey Araton about a tennis doubles team comprising a Muslim player and a Jewish player (see pages 46–48). Araton's essay was published in the *New York Times,* whose readership certainly includes Arabs and Jews, both in the United States and abroad. But that readership is composed primarily of people living in the United States, the great majority of whom are American citizens. Those in that audience who are neither Jewish nor Muslim are likely to react differently to Araton's argument than Jews or Muslims will. In fact, Araton quotes former Pakistani tennis champion Saeed Haid as criticizing Qureshi, the current Pakistani tennis player, for playing with a Jewish partner in view of the bloodshed between Arabs and Jews; Araton quotes the Pakistani sports director as condemning Qureshi as well. Araton suggests that these criticisms amount to zealotry and lunacy, but his argument grows out of a cultural context (that of the United States) in which pluralism and religious diversity are deeply held values. The former Pakistani tennis champion and sports director are arguing out of a different cultural context (that is, an Arab and Muslim nation in Asia) that does not necessarily share those values. In such a context the criticisms of Qureshi would not sound like zealotry at all. As is often the case in situations in which different cultures come into conflict, this situation is not simply a matter of differing opinions or a disagreement about whether or not Qureshi was right to take Hadad as his doubles partner; rather, the different cultural contexts complicate the matter. Araton brings to his argument a different worldview, which grows out of his cultural identity, from that of the Pakistani tennis champion or the sports director. These cultural differences profoundly shape not only how these individuals view the situation with Qureshi and Hadad, but also what kinds of claims or assertions are likely to be persuasive to each.

Culture not only influences how individual readers or writers might react to an argument, but it also can affect how people engage in argumentation. Different cultures might have different values, as we saw in the previous example of the Pakistani tennis player Qureshi, and they might have different ways of engaging in argument as well. For example, in some cultures it is considered impolite or even disrespectful to question another's statements, claims, or credibility. In such cultures people follow certain implicit protocols that govern what they can say to each other. In Japan, for example, if it is raining and you are without an umbrella, it would be impolite to directly ask a person who has an umbrella if you may borrow it. Instead, you would be expected to make a statement such as "It's raining very hard" or "We are likely to get wet," which the other person would know to interpret as a request to borrow the umbrella. Such cultural protocols govern how a writer might structure an argument and how he or she might support his or her position on an issue. A Japanese writer arguing in favor of, say, having American troops leave Okinawa, which is a Japanese-controlled island, might focus his argument on the capabilities of the Japanese security forces to protect Okinawa rather than asserting that Americans have no business occupying that island.

## CONSIDERING GENDER

We can also think of culture as encompassing important aspects of our identity such as gender, sexual orientation, and age. It is risky to generalize about such things, and many arguments are directed toward audiences without regard to gender, sexual orientation, age, or other such factors. But it is important to be sensitive to how these factors can influence the way an audience might react to an argument. Moreover, there are times when it is appropriate to take those factors into account in making an argument. Sometimes an argument is intended specifically for an audience of, say, young women or retired men. Sometimes the topic might be one that has different implications for different audiences. An argument in favor of a woman's right to choose an abortion will mean something different to women than it will to men, and it will mean something different to young women than to older women — no matter whether men and women of any age agree with the argument. In such cases writers will make certain assumptions based on these important aspects of their readers' identities and will adjust their claims and appeals accordingly.

Consider the following two examples, both of which are arguments about differences in how men and women are treated. The first is a letter written to the editor of *Health* magazine, which is devoted to health-related and lifestyle issues for women. The writer was responding to an article about changing ideas of beauty:

> Dorothy Foltz-Gray's article "The Changing Face of Beauty" [*Mind,* July/August] is a stunning example of a woman co-opted by our patriarchal society's focus on skin-deep appearance.
>
> She writes that the power of beauty gets you "more than just admiration." And that "it was exhilarating to think I had a little of that power, too."
>
> After 15 years in the corporate world, I have had my fill of women getting ahead because of their looks. Foltz-Gray was careful to assert that she got the "homely" woman's job based upon her own merits, even though she does acknowledge that her looks played a part. She did "feel uncomfortable" with that but accepted the job.
>
> I would have liked to see the article point the finger at the real culprit (men in power) and advocate for change, rather than continuing to accept the status quo. I believe that the media has an obligation to expose abuses of power, especially a magazine devoted to women's total wellness.

This writer is obviously addressing the magazine's editors directly, but she makes it clear that she assumes *Health* to be a magazine for and about women. She also makes an assertion that might be acceptable to most readers of this magazine (most of whom are women) but would certainly be controversial for other audiences: that "men in power" are the reason for women's struggles to advance in the workplace. Given the audience for *Health,* she perhaps doesn't need to worry about alienating male readers. She seems to be saying to her female readers, "C'mon, let's call this problem what it is!" If she were writing for a different audience — say, a more general audience that would include as many men as women or readers of a business-oriented publication such as the *Wall Street Journal* — she would have to assume that her assertion would not be accepted by many in her audience, and she would probably have to defend it.

The second example also addresses the issue of differences in how men and women are treated, but it does so in a less strident way and for a less specific audience. Nevertheless, although the writer, Susan Brownmiller, is addressing a broader audience than the readers of *Health* magazine, she seems to address male and female readers differently. This excerpt is taken from her book *Femininity:*

> We are talking, admittedly, about an exquisite esthetic. Enormous pleasure can be extracted from feminine pursuits as a creative outlet or purely as relaxation; indeed, indulgence for the sake of fun, or art, or attention, is among femininity's great joys. But the chief attraction (and the central paradox, as well) is the competitive edge that femininity seems to promise in the unending struggle to survive, and perhaps to triumph. The world smiles favorably on the feminine woman: it extends little courtesies and minor privilege. Yet the nature of this competitive edge is ironic, at best, for one works at femininity by accepting restrictions, by limiting one's sights, by choosing an indirect route, by scattering concentration and not giving one's all as a man would to his own, certifiably masculine, interests. It does not require a great leap of imagination for a woman to understand the feminine principle as a grand collection of compromises, large and small, that she simply must make in order to render herself a successful woman. If she has difficulty in satisfying femininity's demands, if its illusions go against her grain, or if she is criticized for her shortcomings and imperfections, the more she will see femininity as a desperate strategy of appeasement, a strategy she may not have the wish or the courage to abandon, for failure looms in either direction.

Here Brownmiller is addressing the same basic issue as the previous writer: the potential effect of being a woman on one's success in life. Brownmiller knows that her readers will be both men and women. Yet there seems to be a subtle difference in the way she addresses readers who are men compared to readers who are women. For one thing, she is writing as a woman, and in doing so, she refers to experiences that only women readers will be able to relate to. For example, she describes the "enormous pleasure" of "feminine pursuits." Although she always uses the third person and never speaks of women as "we," these references to the female experience seem to create a bond between her and women readers that cannot exist with male readers because women readers will be able to share these experiences with her. But she makes these references without referring to men in a way that might alienate them (as the previous writer seems to do). No doubt Brownmiller understands that men and women might react very differently to her argument, but she takes advantage of those different reactions in presenting her argument — assuming, it seems, that women will know what she is talking about and perhaps inviting men to try to understand the experience of femininity that she is describing.

## CONSIDERING AGE

Look again at the passage written by Susan Brownmiller and imagine that she is writing for an audience composed mostly of older readers — for example, the readers of *Modern Maturity*, a magazine published by the American Association of Retired Persons. She might wish to handle the issue of femininity somewhat differently, since many of those readers would probably experience gender in different ways than younger readers would. In this sense the age of an intended audience can influence how a writer makes an argument. In some cases an argument is intended for readers of a very specific age, and the writer's language, strategies, and even topics will be shaped accordingly. An argument in favor of a particular kind of retirement fund might play well with readers of *Modern Maturity*, but it wouldn't appear in *Seventeen* magazine or in a flyer from a college career development service. Sometimes, the effect of the age of intended readers is more subtle. Consider what assumptions journalist Camille Sweeney makes about the age of her readers in the following passage, taken from the beginning of an article in which Sweeney argues that the appeal of Internet chat rooms for teens has to do with the age-old adolescent struggle to establish an identity:

> "Yo yo yo, what's up what's up?" The lines scroll up my screen. Difference fonts, different colors, the words whiz by, everyone's screen name sounding vaguely pornographic. I'm on America Online, in a chat room for young adults. There are hundreds of such chat rooms on AOL, and it has taken a lot of Net navigating simply to find one that has room enough to let me in.
>
> For all the crowds and clamoring, there's not much being said in this chat room, or rather, not much that's being paid attention to. A 16-year-old girl is talking about her baby due in two months. A grumpy 15-year-old guy reluctantly wishes her well. Another girl, 17, asks, "Are your parents cool with it?" The lines continue to scroll, a word here, a phrase there, live text that reads much like a flow of conversation you might overhear in a crowded high-school hallway or parking lot between classes in old-fashioned meat space (that is, anyplace not in the cyberworld).

Sweeney goes on to tell readers that she spent several months visiting chat rooms in an effort to "determine if there is such a thing as a cyberself," and she ultimately takes the position that what goes on in cyberspace with teens isn't really new: Teens are just trying to discover who they are. It's obvious that Sweeney isn't addressing her essay to teens themselves; she knows that teenagers will make up only a small number of her readers. But older readers might be much less familiar with the cyberworld Sweeney is describing. As a result, she not only must try to give her readers a sense of what happens in chat rooms, but she also must explain some terms (such as "meat space"). Perhaps more important, Sweeney refers to teens as "other" — that is, she discusses teens as if they are different from her readers. In this way she tries to connect with her readers on the basis of age. And that sense of connection — of older readers observing unfamiliar teen social behavior — runs throughout her essay and gives it some of its persuasive impact. To appreciate that impact, imagine how different her opening paragraphs might be if they had been written for readers of *Teen* magazine.

## CONSIDERING SEXUAL ORIENTATION

To turn to another kind of cultural context, consider the implications of the simple question "Do you have a family?" When one adult asks it of another in the United States, the question usually means "Are you married with children?" So how is a single gay man to respond? He might cut the conversation short by interpreting it to be a query about marriage and children and simply respond, "No." Or he might take the question literally (or subversively) by saying, "Yes, I have two brothers and several nieces," although this response could trigger annoyance, confusion, or a more direct question about his own household.

What might happen, then, if you use an expression such as "family values" or "our children" in an argument? Strictly speaking, no one is excluded from these words on the basis of sexual orientation. Anyone can create a family, and increasing numbers of same-gender couples are adopting children. Nevertheless, someone who is gay, lesbian, bisexual, or transgendered might associate expressions such as "family values" and "our children" with a heterosexual majority to which they do not belong. The phrase "family values" is especially problematic because it has often been used in rhetoric designed to limit the rights of minorities — as in the campaign that led to the Defense of Marriage Act, a 1996 federal law that excludes same-gender couples from the right to have a civil marriage.

If it can be problematic for writers to assume that all members of their audience are heterosexual, it can be challenging to write about sexual orientation. Words such as "gay" and "queer" are emotionally charged, and occasions for stereotyping abound. For example, a reference to the "gay community" implies that all gay individuals (regardless of religion, race, or social class) socialize together. And it might not be clear whether the "gay community" includes women, since there are women who describe themselves as "gay," while others insist on the use of "lesbian" on the grounds that "gay" was taken over by men. Unless we assume that it is reasonable to write about "the heterosexual community," which would be a very big community indeed, it is better to write about "gay and lesbian communities" instead of lumping diverse people into a single group about which a generalization is going to be made.

In the introduction to *A Queer Geography,* Frank Browning writes,

> As an American, as a white man, as a creature of the late twentieth century, as a male who grew up when the *New York Times, Time, Life, Newsweek,* and all of television and radio regarded homosexuality as either criminal or diseased, I am incapable of experiencing my desires as either a young Neapolitan in Italy or a Sambia tribesman in New Guinea — two places where homosexuality has a rich and ancient history and few make much effort to disguise. The strategies of social and psychological survival I have employed set me apart radically from middle-class Brazilians or Filipinos and even from most of the young men I write about in this book.

In other words, Browning sees his cultural context as being defined by nationality (American) race, (white), gender (male), and age (being no longer young in the late twentieth century) in addition to sexual orientation (homosexual). As you read and write arguments, recognize that sexual orientation is an element of culture but cannot exist separately from other aspects of cultural context. It would be risky to assume that anyone could be either completely defined by sexual orientation or completely understood without some consideration of it.

## HISTORICAL CONTEXT

The previous example of Harvey Araton's essay about Qureshi, the Pakistani tennis player (see pages 46–48), points to another crucial kind of context for argumentation: the moment at which an argument is being made. Araton's essay might have had a certain impact because it was published in the midst of intense, terrible fighting between Israelis and Palestinians in the Middle East in 2002. It was also published during the Wimbledon tennis championship, the world's most prestigious tennis tournament. If Araton had written his essay a year earlier (assuming that Qureshi and Hadad were playing as doubles partners at that time), when the conflict in the Middle East was not as intense and when international attention was not focused on that part of the world, his argument might have been less provocative or persuasive for many readers. It might even have had an entirely different significance. Araton's main argument, which focused on achieving a peaceful solution to a long-standing and bloody conflict, was really not about tennis at all, but he used the decision by Qureshi and his tennis partner Hadad — and the controversy surrounding their decision — to give his argument a timeliness and force it might not otherwise have had. In other words, *when* an argument is made can be as important as how it is made.

The ancient Greek rhetoricians used the term *kairos* to describe an opportune moment for making a specific argument or trying to persuade an audience to act in a specific situation. We might think of *kairos* as making the right argument at the right time. Araton's essay is a good example of an author taking advantage of a particular moment to make his argument. Historical context, then, can refer to understanding when to make a particular argument. A particular appeal might be persuasive at one time but not at another. Circumstances change, and that change can affect what a writer chooses to write in an argument as well as how readers respond to that argument. After the horrible events of September 11, 2001, for example, many people thought that certain kinds of statements and criticisms were inappropriate. Comedians refrained from skewering politicians, especially President George W. Bush; editorialists and political commentators did likewise. In such a climate arguments that relied on criticisms of the President would widely be considered not only ineffective but inappropriate and even disrespectful. Indeed, filmmaker and political essayist Michael Moore found himself in this very situation when his publisher hesitated to release Moore's book *Stupid White Men* after the events of September 11. Given the sudden change in the American political climate as a result of September 11, the publisher asked Moore to rewrite the book, which was a humorous but irreverent attack on the Bush presidency. In effect, Moore was asked to change his argument about the Bush administration because the times had changed. Although Moore refused to do so, it took many months before his book was finally made available for sale to the public. Moore's experience is a dramatic but revealing example of how events can profoundly affect what audiences will accept as appropriate in argumentation.

Historical context encompasses more than just making the right argument at the right time, however. The time in which an argument is made can profoundly affect not only how an audience reacts to it but also its very meaning and import. Consider the opening paragraph of the Declaration of Independence, one of the most famous arguments ever written:

> When in the course of human events, it becomes necessary for one people to dissolve the political bands which have connected them with another, and to assume among the powers of the earth, the separate and equal station to which the Laws of Nature and Nature's God entitle them, a decent respect to the opinions of mankind requires that they should declare the causes which impel them to the separation.

Jefferson's well-known words are general, even abstract, but we know that they refer to a specific situation and to specific events that occurred in 1776 and before. But some of the abstract ideas in this passage carry different meanings in 1776 than they do today. For example, the very idea of a colony or state separating from a monarchy such as ruled Great Britain at that time was radical and even unthinkable to many people. Today, such a notion does not seem so radical. Similarly, what Jefferson meant by "Nature" and "Nature's God" is not necessarily what we might mean if we used those terms today. Indeed, the most famous lines from the Declaration of Independence make an argument that most Americans probably accept as universal but which Jefferson knew to be extremely radical in his day:

> We hold these truths to be self-evident, that all men are created equal, that they are endowed by their Creator with certain unalienable Rights, that among these are Life, Liberty and the pursuit of Happiness.

Such "truths" were not widely considered "self-evident," as Jefferson surely knew, which gave his argument a kind of shock value it would not have today. Perhaps an even more revealing illustration of how the historical context can affect the meaning of an assertion is contained in the famous statement that "all men are created equal." Today such a statement might carry a sexist message that it would not have had for readers in 1776. Indeed, today this statement might be interpreted as a negative one because of what we now consider to be sexist language.

We need not look back 200 years for examples of how historical context can alter meanings in this way. Think of the connotations of the contested and often controversial term *patriotism* in the United States. At times — for example, at the height of the anti–Vietnam War protests in the early 1970s — that term carried largely negative connotations for some audiences and positive connotations for others. At other times — during the takeover of the U.S. embassy in Iran in the late 1970s, say — a writer could assume that the term would be interpreted positively by most American readers. Even in cases that are not quite as dramatic as these, historical context is part of any argument and affects how that argument works and what it means. Good writers attend to historical context, and careful readers are attuned to it as well.

Obviously, in composing an argument, you can never address every possible contextual factor, and very likely you will not even be aware of the potential impact of some of those factors. But you will always be making your argument about a specific issue at a specific moment in time in a specific rhetorical situation. The more carefully you consider those factors, the more effective your argument is likely to be.

# 4

## THE MEDIA FOR
## ARGUMENT

THE MEDIA

**G**eorge Will is a well-known conservative commentator who appears regularly on television shows devoted to political affairs. Will also writes a syndicated column for newspapers as well as essays for publications such as *Newsweek*. His arguments about political and social issues are conservative; his basic message regarding the limits of government in American social and economic life is constant. But do his arguments change in any way when he is making them on a political affairs television show as compared to his columns or essays? Here's the opening paragraph of a *Newsweek* essay Will wrote in 2002:

> These are the best of times for the worst of people. And for the toxic idea at the core of all the most murderous ideologies of the modern age. That idea is that human nature is, if not a fiction, at least so watery and flimsy that it poses no serious impediment to evil political entities determined to treat people as malleable clay to be molded into creatures at once submissive and violent.

OR ARGUMENT

Will goes on in his essay to pursue this philosophical point about human nature. You will probably agree that even this brief passage reflects a sophisticated writing style and a learned voice. Look at the third sentence, for example; it is complex and sounds scholarly. Do you think Will would use this same kind of language to make this point if he were speaking on a television talk show? Would he write the essay differently if he intended to publish it on the Web? In other words, what role does the medium play in his arguments — or anyone's arguments?

In this chapter we examine the role of the medium in argumentation. As you will see, many elements of argumentation, such as addressing an audience appropriately and using evidence effectively, apply to all medium. So some of what we discuss in relation to print will be important for arguments in any medium. But although print remains an important medium for making arguments, other media, including television, radio, and newer online media such as Internet discussion groups and the World Wide Web, have become increasingly significant as forums for public discourse. To argue effectively in these media requires an understanding of how media might influence or change the way you construct and present an argument.

## ANALYZING ARGUMENTS IN PRINT

We live in a culture defined by print — so much so that we take it for granted. We tend to see print as a "natural" medium for literacy and for communication. But print isn't natural. It is a technology — or rather, a set of technologies — for transforming human language into something other than oral speech. Historians tell us that the invention of the printing press in the 15th century changed the way writing and reading were done and the role they played in Western culture. Five hundred years later, print permeates our lives, and we probably engage in written argumentation without ever thinking about the way print can shape arguments. In this section we examine how arguments tend to be made in print so that you can become a more careful reader of written arguments.

### READING ARGUMENTS CRITICALLY

Reading is not a passive activity. When you read a newspaper editorial, for example, you are not simply trying to understand the writer's point. You are also engaged in a sophisticated intellectual and social activity in which you try to analyze, evaluate, and react to the argument. The more carefully you do so, the more substantive will be your engagement with the argument and the better will be your understanding of the issue under discussion. Ideally, reading an argument should be as careful and sophisticated an act as writing an argument.

The more you know about the strategies writers use in constructing their arguments, the better able you will be to analyze and evaluate those arguments without falling victim to subtle persuasive techniques that a writer might use. In addition, the more you know about yourself as a reader, the easier it will be for you to identify appeals or lines of reasoning that might be questionable or flawed. But as we have already noted, human beings react in countless ways to their experiences and to each other in various situations. One

**FIGURE 4-1**

**Wooden Screw Printing Press, circa 1450**

Gutenberg's technology still influences how written arguments are made.

of the challenges of reading arguments critically, then, is to try to manage the complexity that is inherent in human interactions, especially when it comes to the kinds of difficult issues about which we tend to engage in argument.

Print is often considered the traditional medium for formal argument (even though formal arguments have always been made orally as well, for example, in a courtroom, government hearing, or political rally). And print can influence arguments in other media. For example, arguments delivered as speeches are usually written out first; similarly, radio or television essays are also crafted in written form first. But print is not a monolithic medium for arguments. There are countless varieties of print forums within which people can argue:

- Magazines and newspapers of all kinds
- Flyers and circulars
- Memos, letters, and pamphlets
- Essays written for college classes
- Books

Reading an argument carefully requires you to take into account the specific print forum in which that argument appears, for different forums lend themselves to different kinds of arguments. For example, an editorial in the conservative business newspaper the *Wall Street Journal* will usually differ in tone, style, and content from an essay in the left-leaning magazine *Mother Jones.* Each of these publications has a different purpose and addresses a somewhat different audience. To understand an argument published in each of these print forums requires you to have some sense of those differences.

Let's look at arguments in two very different publications to see how the nature of the publication affects the way each writer approaches his argument. The first example is taken from an essay in *USA Today* by its founder and publisher, Al Neuharth. In the opening paragraphs of his essay, Neuharth introduces the issue of the early starting dates for the school year:

> "Back to School." The three most wonderful words for the ears of most parents.
>
> This year, more classrooms in grades K-12 are opening sooner than ever. August has become back-to-school month. Some will open as early as next week. Many on August 12. Most by August 19.

The audience for *USA Today* is a very general one, and Neuharth knows that. The style of writing on the opinion page of *USA Today,* where this essay appeared, tends to be informal, and the topics tend to be current events or controversies. Notice that although Neuharth implicitly addresses the broad audience of all readers of his newspaper, he also narrows the audience somewhat by referring to parents of school-age children. By attempting to establish this connection with a specific audience, Neuharth might strengthen his argument, appeal to those many readers who share his experience of preparing children for school in August. As a reader, you might want to evaluate the extent to which sharing that experience affects your response to his argument, which rests on the assumption, as he writes, that "most kids get a little bored with fun and games by August." While that might be true — and it might resonate with parents who must deal with their own bored children — it might not address more complex implications associated with starting school earlier in August. For example, businesspeople who rely on summer tourism for their livelihood might point to income that is lost as a result of families not vacationing in August. For such readers, Neuharth's appeal might ring hollow. However, given the nature of *USA Today's* opinion page and its broad audience, Neuharth probably doesn't need to address such specific aspects of the issue. In short, his general argument and his strategy of trying to establish a connection with his readers as parents are appropriate for this publication.

Compare Neuharth's approach to the following excerpt from an essay in *Climbing* magazine, in which editor Duane Raleigh addresses a very specialized topic for a much narrower audience:

> You've seen the ads in this magazine and you've visited the websites. Euro dot.coms selling top-brand merchandise for as much as half what you'd pay for the same gear at your local shop. High-end shoes for $60, ropes for $70, ice tools for less than retailers pay at wholesale. Crazy! These are the prices I used to pay for much, much lower-tech gear back in the 1970s. Something screwy must be going on — what's the catch?
>
> The catch is not simple, and takes a tangled, often convoluted and contradictory path. Mostly, foreign dot.coms, because they typically buy directly from the

manufacturer (usually also European) and sell directly to you, bypass the usual distribution (the importers here in the U.S.) and sales channels (your retail climbing shops). Cutting out these two channels eliminates two U.S.-based markups, which largely explains why their prices are so low.

In this instance Raleigh's audience is obviously composed of people who climb and would therefore be interested in the prices of climbing gear. His magazine has a very specific focus on climbing-related issues, which would perhaps seem esoteric to a more general audience. If you are not a climber, Raleigh's appeal might not have much impact on you; indeed, if you are not a climber, he might not care, since it is unlikely that you buy climbing gear or are concerned about the effect of Internet sales on U.S. climbing retailers. Moreover, nonclimbers would probably not understand the importance of the prices Raleigh quotes in his first paragraph. (In 2002, climbing shoes typically sold in the U.S. for between $100 and $160, ropes for $120 to $180; you need to know this to understand his argument.)

If you look a bit more closely, you can see other ways in which Raleigh's argument is shaped by the nature of the magazine he writes for. For one thing his conversational writing style is typical of *Climbing* magazine. An assertion like "Crazy!" fits here, whereas it might be inappropriate for other publications. In addition, Raleigh refers to the 1970s in a way that establishes his authority as someone who understands the markets for climbing gear as a result of his many years of experience as a climber. That strategy is likely to be persuasive to his readers, since climbers often identify credibility with climbing experience. In these ways, Raleigh's argument is very specifically tuned to his magazine.

In these examples the writers tailor their strategies to the audiences that read their publications. In a sense they write in a way that assumes a kind of community of readers, defined by the publication as a medium. But writers can also intentionally provoke an audience in making their argument. For example, a person who is opposed to teaching evolution in schools and is responding to an editorial in favor of teaching evolution might intentionally criticize advocates of evolution on moral grounds, knowing that such readers would very likely not be persuaded by an antievolution argument in any case, and the writer's criticisms would play well with supporters of his or her stance. Such a strategy is common in some kinds of publications, such as letters to newspaper editors, but it might be inappropriate for others.

In reading an argument critically, you should try to account for these strategies and be aware of how an argument can be shaped by the specific print publication for which it is written. Some teachers might advise you always to read skeptically, and that can be good advice because it can help you guard against subtle but powerful appeals that can shape your reaction to an argument. In sum, reading critically means looking carefully at the way a writer tries to address a specific audience for a specific publication; it means being aware of how your own perspective, beliefs, and values might influence your reaction to particular arguments.

## EVALUATING ETHOS

If writers of arguments try to establish a connection with readers in a print medium, readers also gain a sense of connection to a writer through that same medium. But as a reader you have the option of resisting that connection. In other words, you might not identify with the writer — or with the audience he or she directly addresses — or you might not *wish* to identify with the writer. There can be many reasons to resist such a connection, but one important reason has to do with your sense of the writer's credibility. You are not likely to be persuaded by a writer whose credibility you question, no matter how inclined you might be to agree with his or her argument. In Chapter 2 we examined how ethos — a writer's persona and credibility — can be a powerful strategy for writers of arguments. Here we'd like to explore the control *you* exercise as a reader in analyzing and evaluating a writer's *ethos.*

Writers can establish their ethos in a variety of ways. For example, the following excerpt is the opening paragraph of an essay entitled "The Laments of Commuting" by Daisy Hernandez, which was published in the *New York Times:*

> It's hard to make commuters happy. So much is working against us. Virtually no subway platforms have air conditioning. Express lines suddenly go local. And it's a long-distance hike through the underground pedestrian connection between ACE and the NRQWS1237 trains.

Notice that Hernandez immediately identifies herself as a commuter in her essay. Readers will be more likely to consider her credible because of her knowledge and her experience as a commuter. In addition, her conversational tone suggests that she is reasonable and personable — someone you might find yourself sitting next to on the train as you commute to work. Even though commuting is a serious matter for millions of people, Hernandez adopts a tone that isn't overly serious, and her lighter tone might invite readers — especially those who do not commute — to engage her argument. So in this case Hernandez's experience as a commuter as well as her tone may help establish her credibility with readers. As a reader, you will want to take note of your own reaction to Hernandez's experience and tone and decide whether they do make her a more credible writer in this instance.

Compare Hernandez's approach with that of the following writer, whose letter to the editor of *USA Today* was written in response to an article about actor Mike Myers:

> The sheer stupidity of what many Americans find entertaining never ceases to amaze me. Another tired, hackneyed sequel to the foolish *Austin Powers* series is dragged out for the people who wouldn't get a joke if it didn't include obvious "you're-supposed-to-laugh-now" cuts.
>
> The debate still rages as to who is less funny: Jim Carrey or *Austin Powers'* Mike Myers. Both couldn't act their way out of a wet paper bag, so instead they pump out inane movies with a grade-school humor level. It's as if IQ is unwelcome in movie production these days.
>
> Honestly, who couldn't star in *Austin Powers?* The only difference between Myers' embarrassing himself and any number of fools we've all had to tolerate is that Myers has cultivated an entire career by being gratingly unfunny.
>
> I gave in this past weekend and managed to suffer through about 15 minutes of *the Spy Who Shagged Me,* playing on cable. I want my 15 minutes back, Mr. Myers.

This writer's opening sentence immediately creates a distinction between him and the "many Americans" who find Myers' movies entertaining. That distinction might serve the writer's purpose, since he obviously excludes himself from that category of readers. So he might not be concerned if such readers dismiss his argument. However, consider how the writer's tone might affect his ethos among other readers, who might even agree with his assessment of Myers. This writer criticizes Myers's comedy, but he offers no evidence to support his main contention that Myers's acting ability is poor; instead, he offers simple assertions to that effect. Although readers who share the writer's opinion might nod in agreement, it is worth considering how other readers, who might have no strong opinion one way or the other about Myers, might react to this argument. For such readers this writer might sound arrogant or unreasonable, and his credibility therefore suffers. In this case, then, the writer's ethos might undermine his argument for some readers while enhancing it for others.

Usually, writers of arguments convey their ethos in much more subtle ways. We've already discussed several strategies:

- The writer's tone
- The writer's knowledge and/or experience
- The specific evidence a writer offers to support his or her points

Writers can also invoke values that they assume their readers will share as a way to establish themselves as credible. Here is well-known television news anchor Dan Rather writing about the AIDS epidemic:

> Eighty-five million. It's a big number, more than one percent of the total world population. Eight-five million is what the world health experts say will be the total number of cases of HIV/AIDS in eight years, if the epidemic continues its terrible advance.
>
> Twenty-five million — also a big number. By the end of the decade, that's the number of children worldwide that the United Nations believes will be growing up having lost one or more parents to AIDS.
>
> These figures are terrifying, in purely human terms and in view of their larger social implications.

Rather's column appeared in hundreds of newspapers and was therefore read by a large audience, most of whom probably already knew him as a television news anchor. So he already had credibility among many of his readers. But notice that Rather does not rely exclusively on his fame as a news anchor; he does not simply assert that the AIDS epidemic is terrifying, assuming that readers will believe him. Instead, he offers statistics to establish the scale of the epidemic, and then he appeals to his readers' sense of humanity, to their concern for the human suffering that this epidemic will cause. This appeal helps to establish a connection with his readers as caring human beings, but it also helps to reinforce his credibility as someone who shares their concerns and not someone who simply reports the news. Such an ethos might make his argument more persuasive to his readers. Does it do so for you?

Ethos plays a role in all arguments, but in print it is primarily how a writer chooses his or her words that establishes ethos. As a reader you can gain a better sense of the way a writer tries to present himself or herself to an audience by attending carefully to how words are used in an argument. In arguments that are intended to address problems or negotiate differences, ethos becomes even more important, for the credibility of participants in the argument can deeply affect our sense of purpose and motivation in an argument: We are more apt to believe those we trust.

## APPRAISING EVIDENCE

One of the most important — and difficult — aspects of making effective arguments is identifying and using appropriate evidence. Being able to appraise evidence is a crucial part of evaluating arguments, but appraising evidence can be challenging. Consider the following examples. The first is a letter to the editors of *Consumer Reports* magazine; in this letter the writer challenges a recommendation the magazine made in a report on how to save money:

> I disagree with your money-saving recommendation to stick with regular gasoline. I own a 2001 *Chrysler Sebring* and a 1996 *Ford Taurus GL,* both of which are supposed to use regular. But I've found that using midgrade 89-octane fuel increases highway mileage by 2 to 5 mpg.

Here's the editors' response:

> It's good to hear that something yields better fuel economy, but we wouldn't credit the fuel. We have found that temperature and climate conditions affect mileage more than octane.

Who is right? Or we might rephrase the question: Whose evidence is more convincing? The writer of the letter provides evidence of good fuel economy using a higher-octane fuel; the magazine editors refer to their own tests as evidence suggesting otherwise. How do we judge the evidence in such a case?

As these examples suggest, almost anything can be used as evidence: statistics, opinions, observations, theories, anecdotes. It is not always easy to decide whether a particular kind of evidence might be appropriate for a specific claim. Moreover, what counts as appropriate and persuasive evidence always depends upon context. Personal experience might be acceptable to readers of a popular consumer magazine but not necessarily for a technical report on fuel economy for a government agency. The rhetorical situation in which an argument is made will help determine not only what kinds of evidence are most appropriate for that argument but also whether that evidence is likely to be persuasive.

With that in mind, let's look at four commonly used kinds of evidence:

**1.** Facts or statistics
**2.** Personal experience
**3.** Authority
**4.** Values

**Facts as Evidence**    In the following excerpt from an essay published in the online public interest journal *TomPaine.com,* writer Joan Wile argues against a tax refund that President George W. Bush sponsored in 2001. Wile contends that opposition to the Bush tax policies is important, even a year after the policy was adopted. Writing in 2002, she asserts,

> However, the tax abatement issue is still, if not more, critical today than a year ago. Our needs are even greater but with less revenue to address them — our receding economy; our health care crisis; our worsening environment; our failing education system; the reestablished deficit; our increasing numbers of poor with the

concomitant smaller numbers of rich controlling greater amounts of wealth, as well as the necessity for greater defense (but sane and non-threatening to our civil liberties) measures against terrorism.

Wile tries to establish the importance of the tax abatement issue by presenting evidence that the nation's ongoing "needs" continue to be great. Her evidence consists of references to the problems facing the United States: "our receding economy; our health care crisis; our worsening environment; our failing education system; the reestablished deficit; our increasing numbers of poor." Notice that Wile refers to these problems as facts without necessarily establishing them as such. For example, she refers to the "receding economy" without providing, say, statistics on economic activity or stock market performance to demonstrate that the economy is indeed in recession. She can do so because in September 2002, when her essay was published, the U.S. economy was in recession. So simply referring to the economic situation suffices as evidence in this instance. Similarly, she cites "our worsening environment" and "failing education system" without specific information about them. Given the audience for *TomPaine.com,* Wile can assume that most of her readers will accept these references as adequate evidence, because she knows that those readers are likely to view both the environment and the education system as being in crisis; they will not demand further information to support those "facts." But what if she were writing for a politically conservative journal? In that case she would most likely have to supply additional evidence — perhaps in the form of figures indicating increased air and water pollution or declining scores on standardized educational tests — to persuade readers that such crises do exist. In short, what counts as a fact and what is considered ample evidence depend on context and audience.

Whatever the writer's intended audience, a reader must ultimately decide whether the evidence presented in support of a claim is adequate. In this example Wile's argument that the tax refund was a bad idea rests on her claim that the nation has pressing problems that require tax dollars. She supports that claim by listing those problems. If you agree that the problems she lists are real and pressing, then you will likely accept her claim and find her argument persuasive. If you don't agree that such problems exist, her evidence will not be adequate to persuade you that the tax refund should be opposed. Sometimes, simply referring to something won't suffice. More specific evidence is required. Here is part of an essay by a college president who believes that the problems in U.S. schools will not be solved unless teachers are adequately supported in their work:

> We often marginalize our teachers rather than celebrate and reward their contributions. Recent national data reveal that the average annual earnings of young teachers between the ages of 22 and 28 was 30 percent less than similarly aged professionals in other fields. By the time these teachers reach 50, the salary gap almost doubles — a little more than $45,000 for veteran teachers versus almost $80,000 for non-teachers. Of course, many of these new teachers don't stay in the profession to age 50. We lose 30 percent of our new teachers in their first five years of teaching and more than 40 percent in large metropolitan areas like New York City.

This writer, R. Mark Sullivan, provides statistical data to support his claim that teachers are not celebrated and rewarded for their contributions. His audience is a general one: the readers of a regional newspaper. He can assume that they will be familiar with some of the problems facing schools, but he probably cannot assume that all his readers will accept his claim that teachers are not supported adequately. To establish that point, he cites evidence showing income disparities between teachers and other professionals. For many readers such figures can be very compelling, since income is such an important factor in most people's lives. As a result, many readers will likely see figures demonstrating lower incomes for teachers as very good evidence that teachers are not in fact well supported.

But look carefully at the second set of statistics Sullivan offers: the percentage of new teachers who quit teaching within five years. Does this evidence really support his claim that teachers are not well supported? On the surface it might seem so. One explanation for the seemingly high number of teachers leaving the profession might be their low salaries (which is what Sullivan suggests). Another explanation (which Sullivan does not suggest) might be that teachers' working conditions are difficult. These figures might also suggest that not everyone can be a good teacher, and you might believe that those who quit shouldn't be teaching anyway. If it is true that these young teachers quit because they simply have not been effective teachers, then the figures Sullivan cites might actually work against his claim: They could suggest that the best teachers remain in the classroom, while ineffective ones leave. Moreover, we are never told what the attrition rates are for other professions. How many accountants or engineers quit their jobs within five years, for example? That information could change the significance of the figures that Sullivan cites. If 25 percent of accountants or engineers quit in their first five years, then 30 percent of teachers might not seem so high a number — in which case it would not be very persuasive evidence for Sullivan's claim.

This example suggests the importance of examining evidence carefully to determine whether it actually supports a claim. As a reader, you should pay close attention to *how* a writer is using evidence as well as to *what* evidence is presented. In this example Sullivan uses statistical evidence, which is usually considered valid and can be persuasive for many audiences. But as we noted, it is important to examine just what the statistics might indicate. Even if statistical evidence is accepted as true, it may still be open to interpretation. Think about the ongoing debates about global warming. In these debates participants often point to statistics showing the rising average temperature of the earth. Most scientists seem to agree that the average global temperature has increased in the past century, but they do not agree about what that means. Do rising global temperatures *prove* that humans have caused global warming? Or do they reflect natural cycles of warming and cooling? A statistical fact by itself has no inherent significance. How it is used and in what context it is used make all the difference.

**Personal Experience as Evidence**   In the previous example writer R. Mark Sullivan's use of statistics can be seen as a savvy strategy because many readers are likely to accept statistical evidence as valid. But Sullivan might have used other kinds of evidence to support his claim that teachers are not adequately rewarded for their work. For example, he might have included statements from people who have left teaching because they didn't feel supported. Or he might have referred to his own experience as a teacher (assuming that he had such experience) or perhaps to the experience of someone he knows well — say, a brother or neighbor — who left teaching for that reason. The readers of a regional newspaper might well find that kind of evidence as compelling as statistical evidence. Consider how the writer of the following passage uses his own experience as evidence; the passage is taken from an essay that argues against the designation of New York's Adirondack Mountains as "wilderness":

The irony is that one actually has a truer "wilderness experience" in Adirondack lands designated "wild forest" than in those designated "wilderness." How can this be? The answer is in the numbers — of people, that is. Without the "status" of wilderness, the lowly wild forest just grows on, with little to no human molestation. While there may be a road or two, it is the road less traveled. There may not be a High Peak to bag, but chances are you'll see real wildlife . . . and some lower elevation vistas that fewer eyes have seen. And amazingly enough, you will probably not see another human. I can say this because I have experienced it.

This writer supports his claim about the wilderness experience in "wild forest" areas by stating that he has had that experience himself. It can be hard to deny the validity of such experience. Think of the weight often given to eye-witness testimony in legal cases: if a person saw something, it must be true. But the extent to which readers will find such first-hand evidence compelling will vary. And we can question this kind of evidence, just as we can question statistical data. For one thing, where exactly did this writer go in the Adirondacks? It's possible that he visited a few very unusual locations that are not representative of most "wild forest" areas. Also, *when* did he go? He would almost certainly encounter fewer (or no) other hikers in February than he would in July. And how often did he visit these places? If he visited them only once or twice, then his experience might not be typical for those areas. If so, that experience becomes much less forceful as evidence for his claim than it would be if he regularly visited these areas throughout the year. As a reader, raising questions like these will help you evaluate personal experience that is used as evidence. It can also keep you alert to questionable evidence and help you spot evidence that simply does not support the claim being made.

**Authority as Evidence**   Citing experts or authorities as evidence is common in all kinds of arguments, but it is especially important in many academic disciplines. Here is an excerpt from *Ecological Literacy*, in which environmental studies scholar David Orr argues that perpetual economic growth cannot be sustained without irreparable damage to the earth's ecosystems:

> In a notable book in 1977, economist Fred Hirsch described other limits to growth that were inherently social. As the economy grows, the goods and services available to everyone theoretically increase. . . . After basic biological and physical needs are met, an increasing portion of consumption is valued because it raises one's status in society. But, "If everyone in a crowd stands on tiptoe," as Hirsch puts it, "no one sees better." Rising levels of consumption do not necessarily increase one's status.

In this passage Orr draws on the work of a respected economist to support his claim about the dangers of constant economic growth. Notice that Orr underscores the authority of Hirsch's work by describing his book as "notable." Then he presents Hirsch's views about economic growth. Following this passage, Orr summarizes what Hirsch describes as the effects of the desire for more consumption, including such unhappy consequences as "a decline in friendliness, the loss of altruism and mutual obligation, increased time pressures," and so on. Then Orr concludes, "In short, after basic biological needs are met, further growth both 'fails to deliver its full promise' and 'undermines its social foundations.' "

In this case Orr does not offer factual evidence; rather, he cites Hirsch's theories to make the claim that unchecked economic growth is undesirable. In effect, Orr is deferring to Hirsch's expertise as an economist to support this claim. Although what Hirsch offers is essentially an interpretation of economic data and social and economic developments, rather than the data themselves, his status as an expert gives his interpretation weight. Orr relies on that status in using Hirsch's ideas as evidence.

In evaluating an argument like Orr's, you must decide how credible the authority or expert really is. If you know nothing about the work of Fred Hirsch, you have to take Orr's word for it or find Hirsch's book and examine it for yourself. Notice that Orr summarizes Hirsch's key ideas in this passage. He probably assumed that many of his readers would not be familiar with Hirsch's theories. So telling us that Hirsch is an economist who authored a "notable" book helps to establish Hirsch's authority on the subject. Orr's claim depends in large measure on whether his readers accept that authority as credible.

In many cases writers cite a well-known authority or expert in supporting a claim. Using such an authority to support a claim has obvious advantages. Not only will readers be familiar with the authority, but a widely accepted authority can have an established credibility that a writer can rely on. Consider how Martin Luther King, Jr., in this passage from his famous "Letter From a Birmingham Jail," draws on biblical and historical figures to support his claim that being an extremist for freedom is just and right:

> But though I was initially disappointed at being categorized as an extremist, as I continued to think about the matter I gradually gained a measure of satisfaction from the label. Was not Jesus an extremist for love: "Love your enemies, bless them that curse you, do good to them that hate you, and pray for them which despitefully use you, and persecute you." Was not Amos an extremist for justice: "Let justice roll down like waters and righteousness like an overflowing stream." Was not Paul an extremist for the Christian gospel: "I bear in my body the marks of the Lord Jesus." Was not Martin Luther an extremist: "Here I stand; I cannot do otherwise, so help me God." And John Bunyan: "I will stay in jail to the end of my days before I make a butchery of my conscience." And Abraham Lincoln: "This nation cannot survive half slave and half free." And Thomas Jefferson: "We hold these truths to be self-evident, that all men are created equal."

Clearly, King expects these names to have credibility with his readers. The moral weight of the names he cites will give force to the quotations he uses as evidence in this passage.

**Values as Evidence**   The passage from Martin Luther King's "Letter From a Birmingham Jail" points to a final kind of evidence: values or beliefs. (You can read King's Letter From a Birmingham Jail on pages 298–310.) Although King uses the authority of the names he cites in this passage, he is also invoking deeply held moral values. Elsewhere in his "Letter" he uses these values directly as evidence to support specific claims. For example, in arguing that he and his followers were justified in breaking laws prohibiting Blacks from visiting public places, King cites a moral principle:

> One has not only a legal but a moral responsibility to obey just laws. Conversely, one has a moral responsibility to disobey unjust laws. I would agree with St. Augustine that "an unjust law is no law at all."

In effect, King uses the value of justice as evidence that his disobedience was justified and even necessary. Of course, using values or beliefs as evidence can be tricky. If you invoke a principle or value that your readers do not share, your evidence will not be very per-

FIGURE 4-2    **Presenting Information Visually**

Charts such as these, which include data related to driving and fuel economy, present information efficiently and effectively.

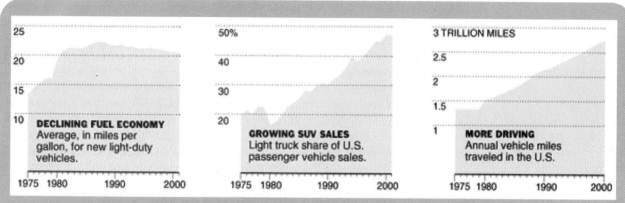

SOURCES: World Resources Institute, Dr. James J. MacKenzie, American Council for an Energy-Efficient Economy, Federal Highway Administration, Environmental Protection Agency

suasive to them, and your argument may be weakened. In addition, values and beliefs can be open to interpretation, just like factual evidence or personal experience. Consider, for example, the ongoing controversies about capital punishment. Both opponents and supporters of capital punishment cite moral values to support their arguments — sometimes, the very same value or principle (for example, "Thou shalt not kill"). In assessing such evidence, be aware of how it might be received by readers.

**Presenting Evidence in Visual Form**    Evidence, especially factual or statistical evidence, is sometimes presented in visual formats within a written argument. In some cases presenting evidence graphically can be more effective than simply incorporating it into the text.

Imagine that you are writing an essay in which you argue that American driving habits are a prime contributor to environmental destruction and possibly to global warming. The charts in Figure 4-2 present three sets of statistical data:

- Changes in average fuel economy for light-duty vehicles in the United States
- Increasing sales of sport utility vehicles (SUVs)
- Changes in the number of miles driven annually by American drivers

All three charts show data over a twenty-five-year time period, and all three include data that you could use as evidence to support a claim that U.S. driving habits have changed over time in ways that potentially damage the environment.

But notice that each of these charts actually represents a *set* of data, not just a single fact. For example, the first chart reveals that average fuel economy rose dramatically from 1975 to about 1989, from less that 15 miles per gallon to approximately 22 miles per gallon. The same chart shows that fuel economy declined steadily from about 1989 to 2000; the decline was about 2 or 3 miles per gallon, or about 10 percent. The chart also indicates that the steepest rise in fuel efficiency occurred around 1980. All of this information might be relevant as evidence for your claim. You might include several sentences with selected statistical information, much as we have done in this paragraph. Or you can present the chart, which includes all the information we have just described efficiently and in a format that makes it easily accessible to your readers. Indeed, the chart might make your evidence more effective because of the visual impact of the line indicating the decline in fuel efficiency since 1989. Placed next to the other two charts, which present different but related data, the chart becomes a means to convey important evidence efficiently and with a potentially powerful impact on readers. In effect, the format of the chart lets your readers "see" the evidence.

Word processing and desktop publishing computer software, along with the rise of the World Wide Web as a medium with multimedia capabilities, make it easy for writers to incorporate visual elements into their arguments. At the same time these technologies make it even more important for readers to develop the ability to evaluate evidence carefully. Evidence presented visually, as in the charts above, can be appealing and persuasive, but it should be subjected to the same careful scrutiny that you would use to assess any evidence.

## ANALYZING ARGUMENTS IN VISUAL MEDIA

Images have power. It is no coincidence that in the months following the terrible events of September 11, 2001, the American flag and the colors red, white, and blue began to appear everywhere: in television and print advertisements, on flyers and posters, on book and magazine covers, on the windows of cars and trucks. At that time the well-known clothing company, Ralph Lauren, was running a series of ads featuring images of attractive models in Ralph Lauren clothing to show "the world of Ralph Lauren." Shortly after September 11, those same ads began to include images of the American flag, including one displayed discreetly but clearly on the final screen of the television commercial.

We take for granted that images are used in this way. We live in an age of multimedia communications, and we are surrounded by images on television, in print, and on the World Wide Web; on signs and billboards; on flyers and pamphlets; from the logos on race cars to the Nike swoosh on golfer Tiger Woods's ever-present baseball cap. Not only advertisers, but politicians, advocates for all kinds of causes, institutions like schools and hospitals, even individuals — all use and manipulate visual elements to communicate an idea or position and to influence a particular audience. They all use *visual rhetoric* to make an argument.

To appreciate the power of images to convey ideas, look at the photograph of President George W. Bush in Figure 4-3, which appeared in August 2002 when the President was trying to generate support for his proposed new Department of Homeland Security. This photo was taken by an Associated Press photographer, but it was certainly set up by the President's staff. For example, the staff would have determined where photographers could stand during the news conference; in that way they set the angle from which photographs of the President could be taken. Those photographs would thus produce the desired effect: to show the President along with the famous faces of past American presidents carved into Mount Rushmore.

FIGURE 4-3    **President George W. Bush at a News Conference at Mount Rushmore**

What does this photograph communicate about President Bush? What argument does it seem to make?

What does such a photograph communicate about President Bush? How might it influence readers' opinions about him and about his proposal for a Department of Homeland Security? Consider the cultural significance of the Mount Rushmore national monument and what it means to Americans. It not only invokes the idea of patriotism for many Americans, but it also suggests greatness with its gigantic figures of four revered American presidents. The photograph associates President Bush — and, by extension, his proposal — with those ideas of patriotism and greatness. Now consider how different the impact of a photograph of the President might be if the background at his press conference had been a wall at an airport or a dark blue curtain in a hotel conference room rather than the striking and deeply symbolic stone visages of Mount Rushmore.

The effects of visual elements can of course be much more subtle and complex than the photograph in Figure 4-3. Consider the use of the American flag in the Ralph Lauren

**FIGURE 4-4**    **Patriotic Advertisements**

The use of an American flag in commercials after September 11, 2001, associated companies like Ralph Lauren with patriotism.

television ads (see Figure 4-4). Like many ads, those employed appealing images to convey a positive sense of Ralph Lauren's clothing and of the company in general. The attractive models not only are well dressed, but also appear in appealing poses, doing things we associate with affluence and leisure, such as boating or horseback riding. Those images invite us to imagine ourselves enjoying such a life and suggest that Ralph Lauren's clothing is part of that life. But the addition of the American flag communicates something different, though equally powerful: that this company is an American company, even a patriotic one. It suggests that aspiring to the kind of life portrayed in the ads is patriotic. It may also convey the more serious suggestion that this company is a good citizen, united with the rest of us as Americans. Sometimes companies avoid associations with patriotism for fear of alienating U.S. consumers who might be cynical about politics and about their government. After September 11, 2001, however, when the Ralph Lauren ads appeared, an association with patriotism was likely to evoke positive feelings among Americans.

It would be difficult to communicate all those ideas succinctly in words during a thirty- or sixty-second television advertisement. The image of the American flag does so in ways that words alone might not do. Part of the power of visual elements, then, is their capacity to communicate complex messages efficiently (see Figures 4-5 and 4-6). Recognizing this capacity can enable you to employ visual elements to enhance your own arguments and to understand their impact on you as a reader or viewer.

To an extent, arguments in visual media can be categorized in the same way as arguments in print media: Visual elements used in argumentation can appeal to our emotions, they can make logical appeals, and they can address character. However, it is important to distinguish between argument and persuasion. While we can describe an advertisement like the Ralph Lauren commercial as an argument (for example, in favor of buying American-made clothing, in support of an affluent lifestyle, or even to assert that clothing is an important part of who you are), the primary purpose of such ads is to persuade you to purchase a product. Genuine argumentation, by contrast, seeks to clarify thought in an effort to address an issue or solve a problem; ideally, it aspires to truth. Persuasion of the kind generally used in advertising has no such goal. The appeal to patriotism in advertising like the Ralph Lauren commercials is intended to persuade you to buy that company's products; if that appeal is successful, it is not likely to have been the result of careful, critical evaluation on your part, but rather the result of the strength of your emotional response to that patriotic appeal.

Despite these differences between advertising and genuine argument, examining advertising can help us understand the subtlety and complexity of visual elements in argument. Consider, for example, the advertisement for Evian Natural Spring Water in Figure 4-5. At first glance, the advertisement seems directed exclusively at pregnant women. The use of the second person, as in "If you plan to breast feed, experts say you should drink up to *30% more water* every day," seems to exclude anyone who is *not* planning to breast feed. But although the written text seems to target only a small percentage of potential buyers of imported spring water, the ad as a whole is designed to persuade a much larger group. By associating their product with motherhood, the advertisers have made an appeal to emotion. According to an old adage, mothers are as American as apple pie, so by associating a European product with motherhood, the advertisers are appealing to a widely held American value. Mother figures are revered in many different cultures, however, so the ad has the potential to reach a very large market. The opening line, "Mommy, can I have a drink of water?" perhaps invites readers to assume the role of

## ARGUING WITH IMAGES

Consider the ideas conveyed by this graphic, which appeared on the Web site of a political activist group called NoLogo.org. How would you explain in words the argument being made by these images? Do they make a point about strength in numbers? About organizing for power? About individuals versus large and powerful organizations? About all these ideas?

SOURCE: http://nologo.org/ (10/13/02).

**FIGURE 4-5**

### Complexity in Visual Rhetoric

This ad for bottled water suggests how subtle and complex visual elements can be in communicating ideas. What impressions do you take away from this ad? Why?

children. To put this ad's message simply: "Mothers are good. Evian water is good for mothers. If you are a good mother, you should buy some. If you are a good child, you should also buy some."

On closer examination we can see that the persuasive appeal of this ad relies on visual elements that are more subtle than just the image of an expectant mother. For one thing, the woman is wearing a white dress, emphasizing the purity that apparently comes with drinking the product in question. She is thoroughly at ease, reclining, a book in hand. What could be more peaceful? The image suggests the comfort that comes with wealth. After all, for every pregnant woman who can lounge in the French Alps, there are many hundreds who are working for a living. Thus, in addition to being the drink of mothers, Evian water becomes the drink of wealth and privilege; it is presented as the right water for those who are healthy, wealthy, and sophisticated. Obviously, the careful manipulation of visual elements can be very powerful in conveying a message.

## DESIGN AND COLOR

Our discussion of the Evian advertisement highlights two important aspects of visual rhetoric: design and color. Notice how your eye is initially drawn to the large photograph placed prominently near the center of this ad. The image of the relaxed and slightly smiling (and attractive) woman is the first thing you focus on, and it sets the tone for the ad. If you look closely, you'll notice that the photo is placed slightly above the exact center of the advertisement. That makes it more prominent. (This is why photographers usually display their photographs slightly above center in the frame, leaving more space below it than above it. Such placement attracts your eye and focuses attention on the image.) Notice, too, the symmetry of the advertisement: It is arranged in a rectangular format that is familiar to the eye, and the text at the bottom is placed in equal proportions around the Evian logo, which appears at the bottom center of the ad. Because such a layout is familiar and proportional, it can evoke feelings of comfort, which reinforce the relaxed image of the woman. Finally, the wavy appearance of the Evian logo not only suggests the flow of water but also contributes to the feeling of relaxation.

The size, style, color, and placement of text also contribute to the effect of the page. In this case the one line of text above the photograph is larger and darker than the text below it. Its size and placement draw your eye before you move to the smaller-sized text below the photograph. The first thing you are likely to read, then, after noticing the larger and stylized word *Evian* at the bottom of the page, is the question "Mommy, can I have a drink of water?" That question, which carries positive associations with childhood, highlights the connection between Evian water and family — another positive association. It also invites us to read the smaller text at the bottom of the ad. Notice as well that the larger, stylized font of the Evian logo draws your eye to it and emphasizes it, connecting the word *Evian* with the appealing photo.

The use of color in this ad also contributes to its persuasive power. We have already noted the white dress of the woman. White has powerful associations with purity and goodness. The colors of the sky and the mountains evoke feelings of relaxation, and the darker color of the text helps to emphasize it for viewers. Even the color of the word *Evian* conveys a positive sense of relaxation.

These design principles can function in much simpler illustrations than the Evian ad. For example, the following passage and illustration are taken from an essay entitled "The Seductive Call of School Supplies," by Michelle Slatalla, in which the author makes an argument about the appeal of increasingly high-tech school supplies to younger students:

> If I had to pinpoint the moment when I went wrong during the back-to-school season last year, I wouldn't necessarily say it was when I took my daughters to a local store so that they could pick out their own school supplies.
>
> I still believe the goal — to make them feel excited instead of nervous about the impending school year — was sound. The shopping trip allowed them to exercise control over their own destiny, or at least over their own three-ring-binder selections. And it's true that my plan seemed at first a success, as they headed off to the first day of class confident in their careful choices of glue (medium-size squeeze bottle) and scissors (purple molded hand grips).
>
>
>
> No, the error I made was more fundamental. Blinded by relief that they had headed back to school (for six blessed hours a day!), I let my guard down. That very night, Ella, who was 10 then but no less wily, announced calmly at supper, "I can't go back to the fifth grade, ever."
>
> The problem revolved around a product she described as the stretchable book cover, an apparently essential item that until that moment I did not know existed. As Ella explained it, the march of progress had trampled those good old-fashioned book covers that we had been cutting from brown paper bags. Instead, she said, everyone in her class had to have elasticized fabric covers.

The small, sepia-toned illustration is the only visual element in this essay, but it contributes to the author's argument in a variety of ways. In this case the rather whimsical character of the illustration reinforces the light tone of the essay. The image of the woman with a laptop helps to underscore a contradiction the author highlights in her essay: the traditional activity of buying school supplies is now focused on modern high-tech items. The sepia tones of the image contribute to this point by suggesting a bit of nostalgia for a bygone era when high-tech school supplies were not the norm. A full-color version of this illustration would not have worked as well for this purpose. Even the simple placement of this illustration at the beginning of the essay — rather than in the middle or near the end — contributes to its persuasive effect by helping to establish the tone of the piece.

Authors who understand these design principles can employ them to enhance the effectiveness of their arguments. Readers who understand these principles will be better able to evaluate those arguments.

## TWISTING AN IMAGE TO MAKE A POINT

This ad by a group called Adbusters (http://adbusters.org) makes a statement by altering an image from an advertisement for a popular vodka. The ad uses the same layout and color scheme as the original ad, the same image of the vodka bottle, and even the name of the vodka itself. But here the image of a sagging bottle and the advertising tag line ("Absolut impotence"), which parodies the original tag line, create an association between the vodka and sexual dysfunction. Consider how effectively this ad employs visual elements to make its argument. Would a print advertisement explaining the connection between alcohol and impotence work in the same way?

## ART AS VISUAL ARGUMENT

You might not associate art with argument, but the design principles discussed in the previous section apply to paintings and other kinds of art as well. You can think of any painting as an argument for the artist's vision. The painting shown in Figure 4-6 was completed in 1816, eight years after Spanish troops had suppressed a revolt in Mexico, which was still part of the Spanish Empire at the time. It is the work of Francisco José de Goya, one of the great European painters of the 19th century. Because he was such a good painter, Goya was frequently commissioned to paint portraits of Spanish royalty and aristocrats, but his sympathies were with people who struggled for freedom. This sympathy is evident in his painting of an execution in Mexico. Most of the painting is dark, symbolizing the darkness of the event. Bright color is reserved for the man who is about to be shot. He is wearing a white shirt, which implies purity, and gold trousers, a warm color that contributes to the sense that he is someone worthy of sympathy. The coloring of the lantern that is illuminating the execution echoes the color of his clothing. Light has positive connotations, especially when surrounded by darkness. So the man in white and gold is in the light created by the white and yellow lantern.

Other aspects of the design direct attention to this man, whose complexion suggests that he is a person of color. His arms are raised in

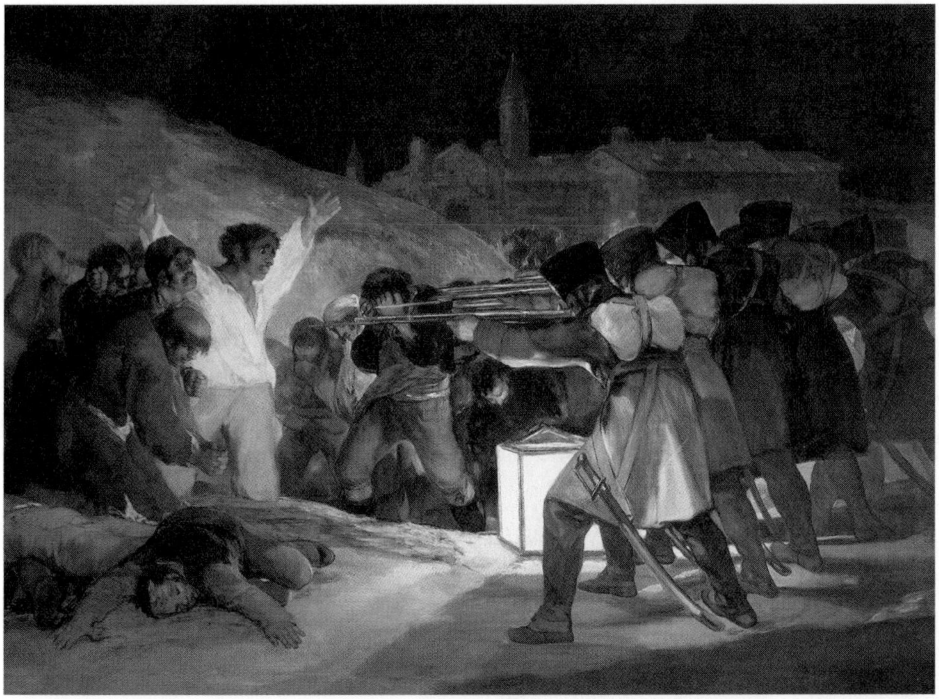

FIGURE 4-6

**Painting a Subversive Argument.**

Francisco José de Goya's famous 1816 painting of an execution in Mexico might be seen as an argument against government oppression.

## PHOTOGRAPHY AS ARGUMENT

**This photograph was taken several months after U.S. armed forces defeated the Taliban, a group that had previously imposed a strict Islamic government on Afghanistan. What argument does this photograph make? In answering that question, consider the contrast between the traditional dress of the girls in the photograph, which is intended to hide a woman's physical appearance, and the Western beauty items on the shelf, which are intended to enhance physical beauty. Consider, too, the uncovered face of the girl, placed at the center of the photo, just in front of her companion, whose face remains obscured by the traditional dress. How do these elements help to make a statement?**

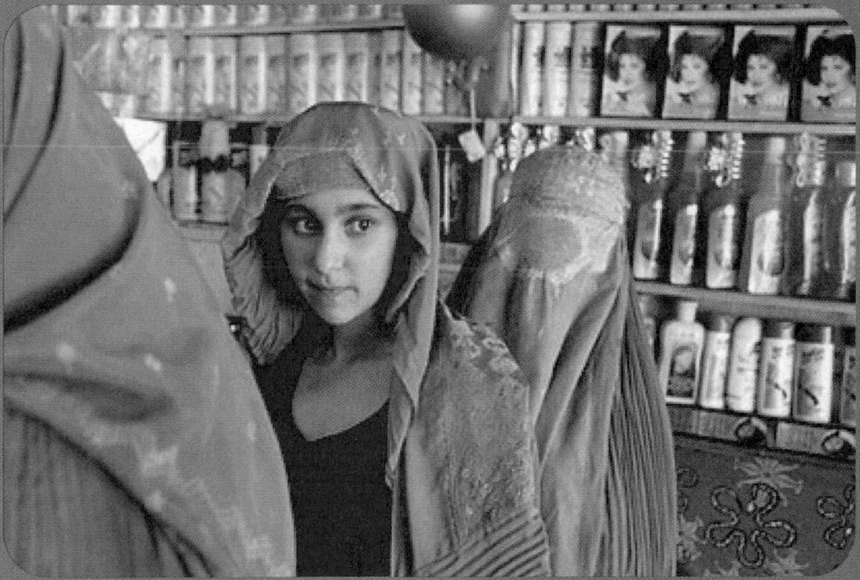

**Kabul, Afghanistan. September 13, 2002. Manizha, 13 (center), and Mina, 16, take in an array of beauty products that were not openly available under Taliban rule.**

## PAINTING AS ENVIRONMENTAL AWARENESS

The landscape paintings of the famous Hudson Valley School in the 19th century are sometimes described as making a case for environmental conservation. They presented an idealized version of nature as beautiful and sublime, worthy of our admiration and protection, at a time when many people were concerned about the destructive effects of industrialization. Consider what claim Thomas Cole might be making in this painting of a well-known mountain along the Hudson River. How does his depiction of Storm King Mountain make a case for a particular view of nature?

Thomas Cole, *Storm King of the Hudson,* c. 1825–1827.

what could be seen as either a gesture of surrender or an embrace that encompasses the soldiers and anyone viewing the picture. The guns are not only aimed at him; they also visually direct the viewers' eyes to him. Furthermore, the man in the white shirt is one of the few figures with eyes the viewers can see. (The other two are also victims.) The expression in his eyes seems tender rather than fierce, contributing to the sympathy Goya creates for him. Significantly, we cannot see the eyes of any of the soldiers; they are presented as part of a faceless mass.

So what claim does this painting make? Interpretations vary. But the painting clearly conveys sympathy for the victim. It is arguing that the repression of the revolt was brutal, that governments do wicked things under the cover of night, or that the repression of native peoples cannot last forever. It is worth noting, in this respect, that although the soldiers have all the guns, there are more victims than soldiers — a fact that suggests that the imperial authority is outnumbered. (The drama of this painting is reinforced by its size, approximately 6 feet by 8 feet. If you ever have the chance to view the original in Madrid, you will feel as if you are witnessing a life-size event.)

Sometimes art is enlisted directly in an effort to persuade or to put forth a particular position on an issue or situation. A poster designed to advertise the French State Railways (see Figure 4-7) makes more than one visually compelling argument. Train service is associated with *Exactitude,* which is French for "getting things exactly right" or, more precisely, *precision.* The streamlined appearance of the train and the uncluttered look of the platform convey the sense that the technology in question is efficient as well as reliable. The clock positioned above the engineer's head suggests that this train will leave the station at exactly the right time. Addressed to travelers, the poster makes the claim: "You can count on us."

Another argument conveyed by the poster's design emerges when we consider its historical context. The poster was published in 1932, when the economies of Western nations were in deep depression and democratic governments were at risk. In Italy, one of

France's neighbors, Benito Mussolini had won respect for his fascist government by fulfilling his promise "to make the trains run on time." One year after this poster appeared, Hitler would seize power in Germany, bringing fascism to another of France's neighbors. The fascists came to power in part because they offered a message that appealed to people during troubled times. The heart of that message was that strong government, represented by a strong leader, could preserve both capitalism and nationalism by repressing communists and any social group considered a threat to economic growth. It would do so through the imposition of a new order suitable for a new age. So in the early 1930s fascism, like the train, could claim to be modern and efficient.

With this in mind, take another look at the poster. Most of the colors are muted; the boldest color, red, highlights the word *Etat,* which means "State." The train becomes a metaphor for the power of the state. It is long,

PIERRE-FÉLIX FIX-MASSEAU (1905–1994) French
*Exactitude,* 1932. Poster / color lithograph. Printer: Edita, Paris. Designed as an advertisement for the French State (État) Railways. H: 39¼ in (99.7 cm) x W: 24¼ in (61.6 cm) // 44 in (111.8 cm) x 29½ in (74.9 cm)

## FIGURE 4-7

### A Poster as Argument

This poster for the French State Railways in the 1930s may be making several arguments. What are they?

massive, and potentially dangerous. We view the train from a position on the platform that is precariously close to the edge. One false step, and we might fall beneath the power of the state. We are, moreover, alone on the platform. Everyone else seems to have already boarded the train. Do we want to be left behind? Do we want to get hurt? So in addition to urging people to travel by train, which continues to be a widely used means of transportation in Europe, this poster argues, "Get on board for the future, or get out of my way. The government is powerful; you are not. It will be dangerous for you to resist." The future is either technology or the power of a strong central government — or both, as is the case when a central government uses technology to increase its power.

The U.S. government also used paintings and sketches during World War II to encourage enlistment in the armed forces, sell war bonds, publicize efforts to conserve items such as gasoline and butter, and generally exhort citizens to support the war effort. We might think of these images in the same way that we think of contemporary print or television advertisements: as propaganda whose purpose was to persuade rather than to engage viewers in serious argumentation. However, if you understand World War II as a moral endeavor to combat the evils of totalitarianism and ethnic extermination, then you might view these posters as part of a larger attempt to engage U.S. citizens in a collective effort to oppose evil. From such a perspective, individual posters can be seen as making an argument for a particular kind of activity associated with the war effort. Each poster might be posing a version of the question "Won't this particular activity help in the war effort?"

For example, the message in the poster in Figure 4-8 seems clear: Buy war bonds to help the U.S. airmen. In a sense the claim made in this poster is that war bonds will help the war effort by keeping U.S. airmen flying; the warrant is that sustaining the war effort is desirable. The image of the airman in the poster, with his eyes looking skyward, his hands holding his combat equipment, a determined expression on his face, is noble and inspiring. The phrase at the top of the poster seems to be a statement this airman would make, and the large, bright words at the bottom of the poster drive the argument home. But notice that this airman is African American. At a point in history (the 1940s) before the Civil Rights Movement and before the landmark U.S. Supreme Court rulings that helped to guarantee those rights to African Americans, this image would have struck many citizens as unusual and even disturbing, since this airman was fighting for a country that did not extend full rights to people of his racial background. Indeed, at that time the U.S. armed forces were still segregated. Yet the poster seems to suggest that *all* Americans are part of the war effort. And it might have spoken especially powerfully to Black Americans, whose experience of racism might have made them hesitant to support the U.S. government's efforts. The airman in this poster might suggest to those citizens that their support is needed and appropriate.

The poster in Figure 4-9 can also be seen as presenting an argument rather than simply trying to persuade. This poster was used in General Motors automobile factories in 1942, when that company was producing vehicles for the war effort. However, even during the war, companies and workers faced many of the same challenges that they face in peacetime, and labor relations were always a potentially difficult matter. In fact, strikes by auto workers in the 1930s had a serious economic and social impact on the country. But a labor conflict — especially a strike — during war time could have been disastrous. In such a context we might see this poster as making an argument about the need for good relations between workers and their employers. The claim might be stated as follows: Avoiding labor conflict will aid the U.S. war effort because it will enable the company to continue production of military vehicles. Again, the warrant is that aiding the war effort is desirable for all Americans. The design of the poster is intended to present that claim effectively. The most noticeable item is the word *together*, which appears in large red letters at the very top of the page. The images of the two fists — both clenched, both exuding strength, both exposed by rolled-up sleeves as if to suggest getting down to work — reinforce the idea of working together. Both are also identical in every respect except for the color of their shirt sleeves, which are used to reinforce their respective positions: blue for the blue-collar workers, white for management. The light yellow background not only highlights the arms by bringing them into relief, but it also conveys a sense of possibility: yellow is associated with the sun, with the idea of a new day. Notice, too, that aside from that background color and the green tank and fighter aircraft, everything else on the

### Art in Support of a War Effort

These posters were distributed by the U.S. government during World War II. Their message of support for the U.S. war effort is obvious, but what specific arguments do these posters make?

FIGURE 4-8

FIGURE 4-9

poster is red, white, or blue, colors that are obviously associated with patriotism. Every element of the design thus supports the poster's claim.

## INTEGRATING VISUAL ELEMENTS AND TEXT

The examples we have included so far in this chapter reveal that combining text and visual elements can be an extremely effective technique for argumentation. You probably have noticed a trend in television advertising in recent years toward structuring commercials around text. One widely broadcast ad for Nike shoes, for example, included a series of images of world-class athletes in many different sports preparing for their respective

## CARTOONS AS ARGUMENT

One of the most common and effective kinds of visual argument is the political cartoon. Consider this cartoon by Jim Morin. What argument does it make about weapons of mass destruction and pollution — two serious concerns in the early 21st century? How effectively does it make its argument? Compare this approach with a conventional editorial. What are the advantages and disadvantages of each?

SOURCE: Jim Morin, *Miami Herald*, September 6, 2002.

events: a sprinter getting ready at the starting blocks, a swimmer stretching at the edge of the pool before the start of the race, an archer drawing her bow. As these images appear in quick succession on the screen, the sound of an orchestra warming up gets louder. As the sound reaches a crescendo and then suddenly stops, the images also disappear, leaving a black screen on which only the words "Just do it," the famous Nike slogan, appear, with the equally famous Nike swoosh logo above them. The words on the screen seem to have greater impact without sound and color.

When you encounter textual arguments that incorporate visual elements, it is important to be aware of the impact that the combination of text and image can have on you as a reader or viewer. Engaging these arguments critically includes assessing visual elements and what they might contribute to the author's claims. Consider, for example, the open letter in Figure 4-10, which was distributed as a newspaper advertisement by St. Lawrence Cement, a company that found itself in an environmental controversy in 2002 when it sought to build a cement plant in upstate New York. In this example the letter includes an extended written argument in which the company presents its claim that its proposed plant will not harm the environment. We might see this argument as an example of an argument to negotiate differences (see pages 18–21): It addresses its audience in a way that is respectful and direct, acknowledging the validity of its opponents' concerns; it presents evidence that supports its central claim that its plant will not cause environmental damage; and it rests this claim on a warrant that seems acceptable to its intended audience (that all residents want and will benefit from a healthy environment).

But the text of the letter in this advertisement is only part of the argument. The ad also includes a photograph along with several graphs that reinforce the claim. Those graphs ostensibly present factual evidence that the company's new plan will significantly reduce its impact on the environment. Note that the visual form of the graphs highlights facts that might otherwise be harder for readers to pick out of the lengthy text. The photograph doesn't present evidence in the way the graphs do, but it reinforces the company's message that it is staffed by concerned and competent professionals. Notice that the four people in the photograph represent racial and gender diversity as well, sending a further positive message about the company to readers. The layout of the ad also contributes to the argument. Because the photo is placed before the first paragraph, readers are likely to view it before reading the text. If they have a positive reaction to that image, they might be agreeable to the company's argument. In addition, the letter discusses environmental

# An Open Letter to the Community:

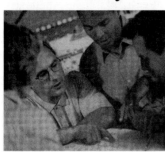

The community plays an important role in shaping the quality of life for the individuals and families who live there. Communities, and all the people who make them up, are concerned with whether a new facility, such as the St. Lawrence Cement Greenport replacement plant, will be good for the environment. They want to know if the project will stimulate the local economy and create new jobs, and whether the company will operate as a responsible community member. Overall, the community wants to be assured that any proposed facility is safe and that it upholds the high environmental standards that many have worked hard to establish.

At St. Lawrence Cement, we believe that this is all as it should be. We regard ourselves as part of this community, both Hudson and Greenport locally as well as New York State. We believe that we should be open with the community and share our plans for the new Greenport facility and its benefits. We also feel compelled to correct misinformation, misleading statements and untruths about the plant. This is especially important when issues begin to drive a wedge between community members. Finally, we are convinced that our proposed project to replace the existing Catskill plant with the new Greenport facility will provide an overall net benefit to the communities and regions in which we operate.

St. Lawrence Cement has been a community member for nearly two decades, operating a cement facility at Catskill since 1984. We are proud of our track record in Catskill, and we hold it up to the community as an indicator of the commitment we have to meet and exceed the most rigorous environmental standards in the country.

### Environmental Benefits

While the current Catskill plant is safe and emissions are well under the allowable standards, the Catskill plant is also older and unable to accommodate new environmental control technologies that are now available. Economically, it is not feasible to try to retro-fit the existing plant. This is why St. Lawrence Cement has proposed to build a replacement facility at Greenport—a new plant for a new age.

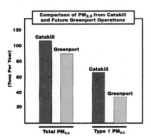

Our proposed Greenport replacement facility will incorporate a unique combination of environmental control technologies, making it one of the most environmentally friendly cement plants in the world. The replacement of Catskill with the new state-of-the-art Greenport plant will allow us to substantially lower those emissions that the public tends to be most concerned about.

Emissions of fine particulates (most commonly referred to as PM 2.5) will be cut by 14%, with the most troublesome combustion-related particulate matter dropping by 40%. Emissions of mercury will be reduced by 95% and lead emissions by 94%. Similarly, the emissions that cause acid rain—

sulfur dioxide and nitrogen oxides emissions—will be reduced by 45%. Studies by the EPA and NYSDEC corroborate these figures, providing credible and expert third-party validation that the environmental benefits we promise are real.

St. Lawrence also recognizes the community's concerns about the impact of plant emissions on historic structures and facades. Emissions from our Catskill plant are already well below allowable limits, and do not accelerate the deterioration of historic buildings and facades. The even lower emissions at Greenport should re-assure the community that St. Lawrence Cement is committed to the community and the preservation of our historic buildings—valuable community assets that enrich our area and attract tourists.

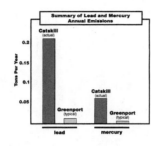

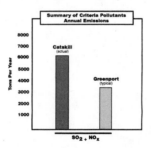

### Economic Benefits

The history of this region is grounded in the cement industry. The community recognizes the importance of industry to create a diverse economy, one that takes advantage of tourism while also providing meaningful jobs for the families who live here. The Greenport replacement plant respects this need for balance, and promises to bring economic improvements to the area while preserving and enhancing the community's overall appeal.

The replacement plant, for example, will use a different process for cement production than the Catskill facility. Instead of the current 'wet' process utilized at Catskill, the Greenport plant will employ a dry process. The net benefit here is that the replacement facility will use 99% less Hudson River water and discharge absolutely nothing back into the River. Add to this St. Lawrence's restoration of 3.0 acres of former inter-tidal wetland in South Bay, an area filled over a half-century ago (long before St. Lawrence bought the property) that has been deemed extremely well-suited, if restored, for fish and wildlife habitation.

Of course, the Greenport replacement plant also holds enormous economic promise for the community, Columbia County and upstate New York. In addition to the costs of constructing the new facility (much of which will be spent right here in Greenport), jobs will be both preserved and created, a host of products and services will be required, and local, county and state taxes will be paid. St. Lawrence Cement is committed to the local community, its economy and its future, and we've proposed a project that promises multiple benefits for all of us.

St. Lawrence Cement welcomes this opportunity to provide our community with important facts and information that will help the community better understand the environmental and economic impact of our proposed replacement plant in Greenport. For certain, we want to see a successful conclusion to the process, but we also want our fellow members of the local and regional community to know the facts, recognize the benefits and support the plant.

---

## USING PHOTOGRAPHY TO ENHANCE AN ARGUMENT

This photograph appears on the title page of *Tigers in the Snow*, a book by Peter Matthiessen about a shrinking population of tigers in a remote part of Siberia, Russia. In his book Matthiessen describes the efforts of U.S. and Russian biologists to study these tigers in order to help prevent them from becoming extinct. Matthiessen clearly supports these efforts. What do you think this photograph suggests? What might it say about the tiger? About the efforts to save it? Why do you think it was placed on the title page with nothing else aside from the title and author's name? How might this use of the photograph figure into the argument Matthiessen makes in his book?

**Photograph by Maurice Hornocker**

issues before economic ones, which seems to reinforce the company's claim that it is concerned about the environment. The subheadings ("Environmental Benefits," "Economic Benefits") highlight these concerns and make them easier for readers to access. In short, the combination of these visual elements with the text of the letter contributes subtly to the effectiveness of this argument.

This example illustrates both the importance and potential risks of using visual elements in genuine argumentation about controversial issues. If we engage in argument with an honest intent to address difficult problems, then it makes sense to employ whatever strategies and resources we have available to us, including visual elements, to make our argument as effectively as possible. In the case of the St. Lawrence Cement Company it is easy to suspect the company's motives and accuse them of trying to manipulate public opinion. (Of course, the same can be true of the company's opponents.) From such a perspective you might see the use of visual elements as part of an effort to win at any cost, and you might be right. One element in analyzing the argument in a case like this is the company's track record in such disputes. Has the company been unforthcoming about the environmental impact of its plants in the past? Has it engaged in underhanded tactics to manipulate public opinion? If so, you would have reason to be skeptical of the company's motives and you should assess its argument accordingly. You might, for example, view the photograph negatively because you may suspect that the company is trying to soften its image and divert attention from its environmental record.

But it might also be true that many long-time residents of the town work for the company and therefore have a sincere interest in ensuring that the new plant will not harm the local environment. Because those workers live in the community where the plant will be built, their interests will be similar to those of opponents of the plant who also hope to preserve the health of the local environment. From this perspective the argument made by the company — and arguments made by other parties in the conflict — can be seen as negotiating differences among the participants. Visual elements become tools that all participants employ as they seek to resolve the problems created by the company's plans to build the new plant. If it turned out that the company or other parties in the controversy did not have honorable motives, you could still engage their arguments thoughtfully and decide on their merits accordingly. Your attention to the visual elements is an important part of the process by which you make that decision.

## ANALYZING ARGUMENTS IN ELECTRONIC MEDIA

Because they offer capabilities that are not available in print forms, electronic media provide a rich context for argumentation that can differ significantly from print media. For example, radio allows speech, music, and other sound effects to be used in arguments in ways that cannot be reproduced in print. Television enables the use of sound in addition to moving images and text. And the computer-based media on the Internet and World Wide Web offer previously unseen configurations of text, image, and sound that can be more interactive than other media. Moreover, the specific characteristics of communication in these new electronic media, especially their speed and availability, might be changing the nature of communication itself.

Because of the rapid development of new technologies (such as multimedia online capabilities, digital video and audio technologies, and high-definition TV), the characteristics of electronic media are changing constantly. No one can anticipate how these media will influence the ways we engage in argumentation about important issues in our lives. (Who could have predicted ten years ago that email and cell phones would become as commonplace as the traditional telephone?) But what we can do is examine some of the important features of these media and begin to explore how they can be used to make effective arguments.

### THE INTERNET

It is probably no exaggeration to say that the Internet will eventually have as big an impact on our society as television. And because the Internet has become so important in how we interact and communicate with each other, it is inevitably influencing how arguments are made.

The emergence of the Internet and the World Wide Web as a means of communication and as a forum for public discussion has been touted by some observers as a watershed development for democratic societies, which — in theory at least — are built around the idea that citizens make collective decisions about how they should be governed. Some believe that Internet technologies like email and the multimedia capabilities for transmitting ideas and information on the World Wide Web will eventually enable many more people to participate directly in in the political process than they could have without these technologies. Today, newsgroups, email discussion lists, (such as *listserv*), Web-based bulletin boards, and online chat rooms enable millions of people to join in discussions about current issues that affect their lives. With access to these online forums, you can debate a recent Congressional decision or political election with someone from across the country almost as easily as — indeed, perhaps *more* easily than — you can debate your neighbors or roommate. Moreover, the Internet and World Wide Web enable people with similar interests or concerns to form "virtual communities," in which they can share ideas quickly and easily without having to be in the same place at the same time. Online forums now exist for every imaginable kind of group, from academics to zoologists, from sales to sailing. These forums allow participants to engage in conversations about issues that are important to them, and many professional organizations use online forums for conducting meetings, circulating petitions, voting, and similar activities. In these ways Internet technologies help people to form and maintain communities by providing a ready medium for communication, discussion, and debate.

Chances are that you have participated in one or more of the online forums now available on the Internet or World Wide Web. If so, you might share the enthusiasm expressed by many commentators for these technologies. At the same time you might also have experienced the "flame wars" that frequently occur in newsgroups, mailing lists, and chat rooms. Visit a chat room or skim the messages posted to a mailing list or newsgroup, and you quickly see that much of the discussion that occurs in some of these forums is not argumentation but more like the quarreling you see on television talk shows. This is true even in online forums devoted to serious issues and maintained by professionals such as lawyers or academics. Many critics have expressed skepticism about the possibilities of these forums to enhance public debate about serious issues. They worry about the overwhelming volume of online discussion and of information on the Internet and World Wide Web, and they raise questions about the usefulness of online discussion. Here, for example, is Mark Slouka, a well-known writer specializing in issues related to these new technologies:

> Will virtual communities help us "reclaim democracy, vent our opinions about the OJ trial, and circumvent Op-Ed newspaper editors" etc.? Clearly, there's something very powerful (and potentially very positive) about a technology that allows millions of people to share ideas and allows them to side-step the occasionally ignorant or biased "filters" like magazine Op-Ed editors. My concern (a viable one, to judge from the mass of stuff online) is that the Net will privilege "venting" over debate and knee jerk speed over reflection. There's a very real chance that what the Net will produce is not "tons of useful information," but virtual mountains of babble among which the occasionally useful tidbit of information (the kind not available in the local library) will be as easy to find as a nickel in a landfill.

Slouka expresses two of the main concerns skeptics often cite in their criticism of online forums for public discourse: the questionable nature of much of the discussion that occurs online and the sheer volume of online discussions. A single newsgroup or mailing list can generate hundreds of messages in one day, far too many for any person to sort through carefully. In addition, as Slouka notes, many online discussions are characterized by superficial exchanging of opinions instead of careful, considered debate. Genuine argumentation is often as hard to find online as it is on popular talk radio.

What does all this mean for those who are interested in argument? No one can be sure, despite the enormous amount of discussion among scholars, critics, and policy makers about the role of electronic technologies in public discourse. But the Internet and World Wide Web are not likely to disappear. They will continue to evolve, and they will very likely become more important for communication and argumentation in our society. The capabilities of these technologies seem to promise new ways of engaging in argument for the purpose of solving problems and negotiating differences. But it is also true that these technologies will complicate argumentation in ways that we cannot anticipate. In the meantime you will almost certainly encounter arguments in online forums, and you might well present your own arguments in such forums. In many respects engaging in genuine argumentation online is similar to engaging in argumentation in other forums, and the advice we have offered in this chapter and elsewhere will generally apply to on-line forums as well. But there are some characteristics of online technologies that can shape argumentation, and you should be aware of how these characteristics might affect arguments online.

Not all online forums are alike, and for the purposes of our discussion of them, we will distinguish between online forums that are used primarily for discussion — including email mailing lists, newsgroups or Web-based bulletin boards, and chat rooms — and Web sites, which can advance arguments but do not necessarily involve discussion and which have multimedia capabilities that most discussion forums lack.

## WEB SITES

The World Wide Web represents a potentially unprecedented medium for argument. Because of the Web's complexity and because of the rapid pace at which Web technologies are evolving, no one can predict how its role as a medium for argument might grow or change. What we can say is that the Web offers intriguing possibilities for structuring and presenting arguments. In this section we review some of the characteristics of the Web and their implications for argument.

**Online Versions of Print Arguments**    To begin, it is important to point out that there are different kinds of Web sites. Some Web sites essentially offer online versions of print documents. For example, many newspapers and magazines are available on the Web in more or less the same format as their print versions. If you visit a site such as the *Los Angeles Times* online (**www.latimes.com**), you will find the same articles that appear in the printed newspaper. Although the online versions of these articles might have links to other Web sites and might include graphics that do not appear in the print versions, their content and format are essentially the same as the printed versions. In terms of structure, content, and related matters, therefore, arguments on such Web sites are not very different from arguments in a print medium. An editorial essay in the *Los Angeles Times* is the same essay online and in print. Currently, most arguments on the Web are of this kind. (See Figure 4-11.)

**Hypertextual Web Sites**    True hypertext is another matter altogether. *Hypertext* refers to the capacity to link documents through *hyperlinks* that a user clicks to move from one document to another. Web sites that are truly hypertextual can differ dramatically from a print document (or an online version of a print document) in the way they are structured. Hypertextual documents need not be organized in a linear fashion, as most print essays are; rather, links can be embedded on Web pages so that users can move from one page to another in the Web site in a variety of ways: hierarchically, in a radial fashion, or randomly. The possibilities for arranging textual and graphical information in a hypertext are

endless. Moreover, hypertexts can be more interactive than print text in the sense that readers select which links they will follow as they move through a document. In a print essay, readers generally move from the opening paragraph to the final paragraph. By contrast, true hypertexts offer countless ways for readers to move through them, so it is possible that no two readers will read a hypertext in exactly the same way.

These features of hypertext offer new possibilities for authors to present their arguments. In addition to enabling authors to incorporate graphics and sound easily into an argument, hypertext allows authors to structure an argument in a variety of ways that affect the impact of the argument. Keeping in mind that arguments in print form tend to be organized in a linear fashion, consider the following example of a hypertextual Web site entitled "Argumentation on the Web," by Tom Formaro. In this hypertext Formaro examines the implications of using hypertext for argumentation, actually demonstrating his argument by presenting it in hypertext. Obviously, Formaro might have made the same argument in a conventional print format. But hypertext offers options for presenting his argument that would not be possible in print.

Figure 4-12 shows the first screen of his hypertext. Notice that this Web page doesn't really introduce Formaro's topic; rather, it gives the reader advice on how to move through, or navigate, his hypertext. Notice, too, the links on the left side of the screen. As you'll see, those links will remain visible no matter which Web page you visit in this hypertext; they help you find your way to specific pages in the document. However, Formaro has also embedded links within each page. Those links function very differently within his argument than the links on the left side of the screen. For example, a few links from this first screen will bring you to the screen in Figure 4-13. Here, Formaro raises questions that are central to his main argument — questions about the meaning of a "beginning" in a text and how the idea of a beginning or introduction can be complicated by hypertext. You can read this paragraph and then click one of the links at the bottom of the screen, which will take you to another screen related to this one — almost like

ARGUMENTATION ON THE World Wide Web

## Links

Sections

General Index

Authors Index

Topics Index

Bibliography

Navigation Tips

### How to Use This Hypertext

**A Caveat**

I've chosen to use frames because of the effect frames have on the boundaries of a work. What you'll notice throughout this piece is that when you jump to other sites from links I've provided, you haven't really left this work at all. The Links sidebar and the title remain visible. The boundary between my work and the work of others becomes difficult to discern.

Blurring the boundaries between works is the reason for the frames and illustrates an important point about hypertext on the World Wide Web. I'll discuss this idea formally throughout the work, especially when considering the World Wide Web and texts. If you are not using a frames compatible browser, you will still be able to view the work, but the boundary between this piece and others to which it is linked will be more distinct.

**Navigation Tips**

Receiving image (0 bytes of 321 bytes, 0 bytes/sec): button.home.gif

**FIGURE 4-12**

**Opening Screen of "Argumentation on the World Wide Web"**

ARGUMENTATION ON THE World Wide Web

## Links

Sections

General Index

Authors Index

Topics Index

Bibliography

Navigation Tips

### What *Is* the Beginning?

Linear designations such as beginning, middle, and end are problemitized by postmodern and hypertext theory. They are also difficult to discern on the Web. Where exactly is the beginning of the Web? Such a question is like asking "where is the beginning of the Interstate highway system in the U.S." Certainly there are many places where you can get on, drive for a while, and get off, but would that constitute the beginning, middle and end of the Interstate system? It does constitute a beginning, middle, and end of a trip, but that's not the same as the system on which the trip took place. So, like a trip, it is possible to have a beginning, middle, and end in a Web *session*; the Web itself, however, does not have such designations.

  What's in a Name? ▶ Lineraity and Print

An Introduction?

| Sections | General Index | Authors Index | Topics Index |
| Bibliography | Navigation Tips |

**FIGURE 4-13**

**A "Beginning" Web Page in "Argumentation on the World Wide Web"**

FIGURE 4-14

One Link from the
"Beginning"

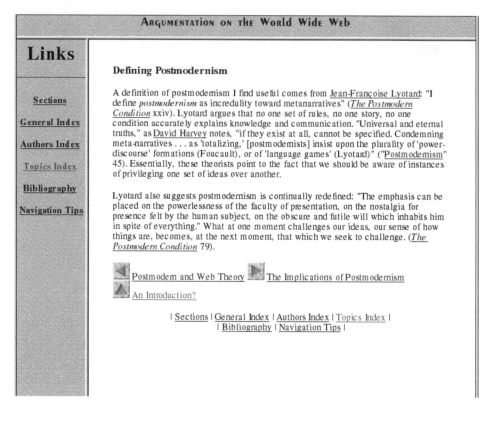

ARGUMENTATION ON THE World Wide Web

## Links

Sections

General Index

Authors Index

Topics Index

Bibliography

Navigation Tips

**Defining Postmodernism**

A definition of postmodernism I find useful comes from Jean-Françoise Lyotard: "I define *postmodernism* as incredulity toward metanarratives" (*The Postmodern Condition* xxiv). Lyotard argues that no one set of rules, no one story, no one condition accurately explains knowledge and communication. "Universal and eternal truths," as David Harvey notes, "if they exist at all, cannot be specified. Condemning meta-narratives . . . as 'totalizing,' [postmodernists] insist upon the plurality of 'power-discourse' formations (Foucault), or of 'language games' (Lyotard)" ("Postmodernism" 45). Essentially, these theorists point to the fact that we should be aware of instances of privileging one set of ideas over another.

Lyotard also suggests postmodernism is continually redefined: "The emphasis can be placed on the powerlessness of the faculty of presentation, on the nostalgia for presence felt by the human subject, on the obscure and futile will which inhabits him in spite of everything." What at one moment challenges our ideas, our sense of how things are, becomes, at the next moment, that which we seek to challenge. (*The Postmodern Condition* 79).

◄ Postmodern and Web Theory ► The Implications of Postmodernism
▲ An Introduction?

| Sections | General Index | Authors Index | Topics Index |
| Bibliography | Navigation Tips |

turning a page in a book. But you can also click one of the underlined words in the first sentence to move to a different screen. If you click the word *postmodern*, for instance, you'll see the screen in Figure 4-14.

On this Web page, Formaro defines the term *postmodernism* in a way that serves his purposes in his argument. However, if you clicked the word *hypertext* instead of *postmodern* in the previous screen, you would see the screen in Figure 4-15.

Here Formaro discusses what he sees as the key feature of hypertext for argumentation. Notice the many underlined words on this screen. Each of them is a link that leads to a different screen. As a reader you make choices about which links to follow, and these choices affect how you engage Formaro's argument. Different readers will follow different links, thus reading Formaro's text in different ways, in effect deciding how to organize Formaro's argument. As a writer, Formaro creates these links as transitions to various parts of his argument. In this sense his links are not only a means of moving through his document, but also a way to connect ideas. He can thus use them to help make his claims or provide evidence.

Because we are so used to the conventions of print and its usual linear structure, reading through a complicated argument in a hypertext such as Formaro's can be disconcerting. Hypertext forces us to read differently. It also forces the writer to think differently about how to present an argument. Because the author does not determine the precise order in which each reader will read the various pages in a hypertext, the author cannot think of his or her argument in a linear way, in which every reader moves from point to point in the same way. Instead, the author may think of an argument as a collection of large pieces, each representing a distinct topic, point, or claim. The author must then de-

| ARGUMENTATION ON THE World Wide Web |
|---|

**Links**

Sections

General Index

Authors Index

Topics Index

Bibliography

Navigation Tips

**Hypertext Theory**

The core of hypertext and the Web can be summed up in one word: freedom. Freedom for authors, for readers, for texts, freedom for the argument, and even freedom for the technology (the relationship among each of these elements relates to Burke's concept of container and the thing contained). There are some exceptions to the freedom of hypertext on the World Wide Web. However, together with my conception of privileging as the core of postmodern theory, freedom in hypertext--and particularly on the Web--are the theoretical legs on which my discussion stands.

▶ Freedom and the Author

▲ An Introduction?

| Sections | General Index | Authors Index | Topics Index |
| Bibliography | Navigation Tips |

**FIGURE 4-15**

**A Different Link from the "Beginning"**

cide how those pieces relate to each other so that the overall argument makes sense to readers, each of whom might experience the argument differently. Should a particular claim or bit of evidence appear on a main page or on a page linked to that main page? Why? What pieces of an argument should *every* reader see? Which pieces can be skipped without weakening the argument? Such questions can encourage a writer — and readers — to reexamine how an argument fits together. And the links themselves represent transitions that can support or enhance an argument. For example, an author can make a claim based on an implied warrant, then create a link to a page that defends that warrant. In a print article such a defense would have to be incorporated into the text (or perhaps included in a footnote or sidebar), which perhaps would interrupt the flow of the author's argument. Hypertext enables authors to decide on alternative ways of presenting claims, evidence, and warrants.

Notice, too, that hypertext enables an author to embed multimedia in a Web site to help support an argument. The Web enables Formaro to use color and design very easily to present and enhance his argument in ways that we discussed earlier in this chapter. If he desired, he could also link video or audio clips to specific points in his argument. These features can become powerful tools in an author's efforts to present his or her argument.

It remains to be seen whether the potential of hypertext to enhance arguments will be realized in a widespread way in the years ahead. Formaro's Web site represents a use of hypertext for argumentation that is still quite rare, despite the rapid growth of the Web. But as his hypertext suggests, the Web offers intriguing new possibilities for people to address complex issues and try to solve problems through argumentation.

**Web Sites as Arguments**    We have been discussing Web sites in which authors make arguments in hypertextual form. But Web sites themselves can also be seen as making arguments in the way that a brochure or a flyer does. Today, advocacy groups, political organizations, government and nongovernmental agencies, institutions, and community groups of all kinds maintain Web sites on which they present themselves to the public. On the surface such Web sites do not seem very different from a flyer or brochure that a group might distribute to publicize itself. But individuals or groups can take advantage of the Web's capabilities to make implicit arguments. Consider the home page of the Web site for the Minnesota Public Radio program *Marketplace*® (Figure 4-16). At first glance, this Web page seems straightforward enough, presenting information about *Marketplace* along with links to additional information and to related sites. But a closer look reveals that this site makes good use of the multimedia capabilities of the Web. For one thing it contains links to audio clips of its programs as well as links to archives of text versions of some segments of its broadcasts. It also employs a sophisticated design with careful use of layout and color, suggesting a professional operation. Notice too, the logos for several large businesses. Not only do these logos convey the information that Fannie Mae, BankOne, and Deloitte & Touche are corporate sponsors of Marketplace, but their inclusion on the front page of the Web site might also be seen as an implicit argument that the program has legitimacy as a source of business information. All three major sponsors are large corporations that are easily recognizable and associated with business success in a way that might well appeal to the Marketplace audience.

The Web site for the Digital Freedom Network, an advocacy group, takes similar advantage of the capabilities of the Web (Figure 4-17). This site presents the Digital Freedom Network overtly as an activist group with a particular view of freedom in the digital age.

Like the *Marketplace* home page, Digital Freedom Network's home page employs principles of design to present itself effectively to its audience. Graphics and color highlight ideas and links to related information. However, as an advocacy group, the Digital Freedom Network uses its Web site to present an overt stance on the issues it is concerned about. The photograph, whose prominent placement in the center of the page draws the eye, makes a powerful statement about the incarceration of activists in China. That photo is also a link to the group's report on that topic. The caption placed above the photo is colored red, which connotes danger and contrasts noticeably with the surrounding colors. In these ways this site combines some of the hypertextual capabilities of the Web with solid design to make a strong statement about its activism. In addition, notice how this site invites a visitor's participation in the group's activities. The caption above the photo

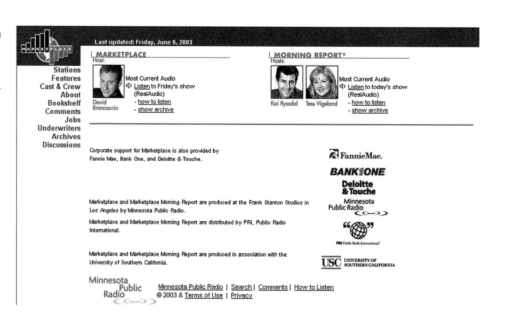

## FIGURE 4-16

**Presenting an Image on the Web**

Organizations of all kinds can use the Web to present an image of who they are to the public. The Web site for Minnesota Public Radio's *Marketplace*® is both a source of information about the show and a means of projecting its image to its audience.

FIGURE 4-17

**Advocacy on the Web**

The Digital Freedom Network, an advocacy group, uses its Web site to make a political statement.

exhorts readers to "take a stand," and the link with the same words to the right of the photograph provides readers with a way to do so: They can become members of the group, volunteer, or become involved in one of the group's activities. In this regard the site uses the interactive character of the Web to encourage participation in the group's activist work. It also implicitly makes an argument in favor of such activism.

## ONLINE DISCUSSION FORUMS

Online discussion forums have proliferated dramatically in the past few years. Today you can find a newsgroup, mailing list, or Web board on any imaginable topic. In addition, college instructors now commonly set up online forums as a component of their courses. (In courses that are offered exclusively online, online forums often replace traditional face-to-face classroom discussion.) A common use of such forums is to foster discussion among students about important course topics. In effect, students often go online to engage in argumentation about course-related issues.

One obvious advantage that an online forum has over a more traditional print medium (such as a newspaper editorial page) is that it is more immediate and opens up the possibility for more voices to enter the conversation. You can post a message to a newsgroup in which you defend a position on an issue, and within a few hours or even minutes several people might have responded to your post. Many more people can join in the conversation in this way than could possibly do so on a newspaper editorial page or in the letters-to-the-editor section of a magazine. In *asynchronous* forums such as mailing lists, newsgroups (in which messages remain available to participants at any time that they log on — the electronic equivalent of a bulletin board containing many messages pinned to it), or Web boards, readers can sort through messages and analyze them before posting a response. In this respect asynchronous forums have an advantage over face-to-face discussion (such as in a classroom or at a public meeting) in that they allow participants time to consider their responses before posting them. Usually, in a face-to-face discussion a response must be made soon after someone has spoken, providing little time for discussants to formulate their responses carefully. If the conversation moves quickly, you might not even get the chance to make your comment before the conversation moves to another point. On a mailing list, newsgroup, or Web board, by contrast, you can write and even revise your response offline before posting it. Of course, it's possible to respond prematurely in an asynchronous forum, just as it is possible to respond rashly in a face-to-face discussion or to damage a relationship by responding to an email in anger.

Here's part of a discussion about plagiarism that occurred on the Usenet newsgroup soc.college.admissions. The discussion began when one participant posted part of a news report about plagiarism in American colleges and universities. Several other people joined in. (The lines preceded by >'s are quoted passages from previous messages.)

> Plagiarism is running rampant on American college campuses, and everyone
> knows that technology is partly to blame. After all, any student with a few
> dollars can go to one of the many Web sites that sell research papers and
> buy the perfect paper for the assignment.

I fail to understand why plagiarism is so hard to define and understand. If every teacher in every class started out on the first day of class to define plagiarism as:

1. submitting ideas or words that are not one's own without properly and accurately attributing them to their true author
2. papers that are copies of papers someone else wrote or which have been previously submitted to another class
3. whatever else the teacher does not want in original works (specifically "cut and paste" items from the Internet) along with examples of what is permitted and what is not permitted, the students would know upfront specifically what is allowed and not allowed.

Each student should then be required to write a brief summary of the rules in his/her own handwriting, sign it., and turn it into the teacher. This can be done even by very young children. Nothing affects understanding so much as having to put it in one's own words (how ironic for a definition of plagiarism). Then if someone is found to have violated the rules, he or she fails the class. And schools must back up the teachers, not be weakened by litigious parents.

Kate

------------------------

"Kate" wrote in #1
> I fail to understand why plagiarism is so hard to define and understand.
> If every teacher in every class started out on the first day of class to
> define plagiarism as:
> 1. submitting ideas or words that are not one's own without properly and
> accurately attributing them to their true author

This is precisely why it's so hard to define. Most students (or people for that matter) go through entire days without thinking a single original thought. How is a student expected to write an entire paper of almost entirely unoriginal ideas and credit every single 'true author'. I obviously know what your point is, I'm just saying the line isn't that clear. I know that one of the greatest feelings for a teacher is discovering new ideas coming from his students, but can you really expect this from everyone (the C student as well as the B and A students?)

How strict would you propose enforcing your Rule No. 1? Would you like to end up with papers with citations noted after every single sentence? I think plagiarism is awful, I just think its not as clear-cut as you say.

matt

------------------------

> I think plagiarism is awful, I just think its not as clear-cut as you say.

Hmmm. I find that I agree with a lot of this. How about: 1) I read Joe Expert's book and he lays out a few facts. I think to myself, "(Insert some conclusion from those facts here)" Then, I turn the page and Joe Expert reaches the same conclusion. Do I need to cite that? (I would, to be on the safe side, but I'm not sure I should have to)

Also, how about the line between "common knowledge" and what needs to be cited? Interestingly, Vanderbilt University defines this specifically in their honor code documentation: common knowledge is an idea that appears in 3 or more distinct sources. This is the first time in my life I have seen such a clear cut definition.

Joe

------------------------

"Joe" wrote in message #3

> How about: 1)I read Joe Expert's book and he lays out a few facts. I think
> to myself, "(Insert some conclusion from those facts here)" Then, I turn
> the page and Joe Expert reaches the same conclusion. Do I need to cite
> that? (I would, to be on the safe side, but I'm not sure I should have to)

It's not plagiarism to use the same idea another person had if you put it into your own words and expand upon it or criticize it positively or negatively. Such as: "Joe Expert says George Bush is the Anti-Christ [cite]. Many people may believe this to be true but I disagree for several reasons." . . .

The problem with plagiarism today is that it is far easier to heist information from the Internet in one's bedroom than it is to crawl through dusty library stacks before computers were everywhere. Perhaps, teachers can require that a certain percentage of citations in a paper must be from real books -- which requires real page numbers; maybe require a few xeroxed book pages in support. Maybe that's all too much.

Kate

------------------------

"Kate" wrote:

> The problem with plagiarism today is that it is far easier to heist
> information from the Internet in one's bedroom than it is to crawl through
> dusty library stacks before computers were everywhere.

Wait, is this a bad thing . . . ?

> Perhaps, teachers
> can require that a certain percentage of citations in a paper must be from
> real books -- which requires real page numbers; maybe require a few xeroxed
> book pages in support. Maybe that's all too much.

If the information is appropriate for the paper, accurate, and from a credible source, does it matter where it came from? I think it would be unhealthy to search for reasons to cling to real books (especially when the whole world is opting for change.) After all, 'real' (or perhaps not so real) books are now being published over the Net.

This excerpt is a good example of the way argumentation can occur in asynchronous online forums. The participants seem genuinely concerned about plagiarism, and the discussion seems to move toward a loose consensus about how schools might solve the problem. Notice that the participants follow some of the conventions of traditional argument. For example, they present claims (e.g., plagiarism is hard to define), support their claims (e.g., students do not generally work with original ideas, so identifying what is original and what is not can become a problem), and imply warrants (plagiarism is bad). In addition, participants address their audience — indeed, they do so directly by responding to points made by other participants. And they seem to make certain assumptions about that audience and about the larger context of the discussion. For example, the participants all seem familiar with American higher education, and they are responding to recent events involving plagiarism at American universities. In these ways this newsgroup discussion resembles traditional argumentation.

It is easy to see some of the advantages of arguing in such a forum. The medium allows for a great deal of back-and-forth discussion in a way that simply is not possible in traditional print forums. And many people can participate without the discussion becoming overwhelming. The immediacy of the forum allows participants to focus narrowly on specific claims or evidence, as you might in a face-to-face debate but without the pressure of having to respond immediately to someone else's challenge or rebuttal. But notice that argument in this forum tends to be more informal and less rigorous than it can be in print media. Because messages tend to be relatively short, and because active discussions can generate many messages very quickly, claims and evidence need to be presented concisely, without the lengthy explanations and extensive support that might be expected in the formal essays you write for your college courses. For the most part participants understand and accept this fact. But if you engage in discussions in online forums, it is worth remembering that the principles of genuine argumentation don't always apply.

The matter of ethos can also be complicated in online forums. Generally, there is no way of knowing who participants really are, whether they have any legitimate knowledge or experience related to the topic at hand, and whether they are being honest about what they say. As we noted in Chapter 2, determining the credibility of the author of an argument is an important part of analyzing that argument. Participants in online forums can establish their own ethos over time through the messages they post, but you usually have no way to verify what others say in their messages. To an extent one's ethos is always constructed, even in a respected print medium. But writers whose essays appear in a magazine such as the *Atlantic Monthly* or a newspaper such as the *Wall Street Journal* must work with editors and generally have well-established credentials. Just being published in a respected magazine gives them a measure of credibility. By contrast, anyone can log into a newsgroup such as soc.college.admissions and post a message. And a participant can claim to be a college instructor or an admissions officer without having to provide proof. If you know that the person is who he or she claims to be, you are more likely to take that person's arguments seriously. But without a way to verify their claims, you should always view their messages with at least a small measure of skepticism.

It goes without saying that your own ethos can be questioned too. So as a participant in an online discussion you are likely to be more effective in making your arguments if you can establish credibility, just as you would in a print medium. Keep in mind that other participants might take your claims about who you are with a grain of salt. Keep in mind, too, that following the protocols of arguing in online forums is one of the best ways to establish your credibility in such a forum. Posting relatively brief messages that respond to previous messages, keeping your responses to the point, and avoiding criticism or ridicule of other participants (that is, avoiding flame wars) will likely encourage others to take your arguments more seriously.

*Synchronous* forums, such as chat rooms, instant messaging, or MUDs (multi-user domains), differ from asynchronous forums in that participants post and read messages in "real time." In other words, when you are logged onto a chat room or other kind of synchronous forum, your message appears on the screens of all the other logged-on participants as soon as you write it on your computer; any messages posted by other participants appear on your screen immediately as well. And those messages do not remain available once the conversation has ended; that is, you cannot always retrieve them later, as you can on a newsgroup or mailing list.

The experience of engaging in a synchronous discussion is very much like having a face-to-face conversation, except that you are reading and writing comments rather than speaking or hearing them. As a result, discussions in synchronous forums tend to be somewhat slower than face-to-face discussions. And usually several different topics — or "threads" — occur simultaneously. These characteristics of synchronous forums result in messages that tend to be very short and, ideally, concise as well. Longer messages, even messages of a few sentences, can slow down the discussion and make it harder for participants to keep up with the conversation. Consequently, synchronous forums do not lend themselves to considered debate about complex issues that require participants to present lengthy arguments or cite extensive evidence to support their arguments. If you engage in synchronous discussions, you will be most effective if you can keep your statements short but clear and if you can focus on one claim at a time. Similarly, offer clearly identifiable support for a claim that can be easily digested by other participants.

Although the advice we have offered here applies generally to any kind of online discussion forum, all online forums are not the same. Public newsgroups such as soc. college.admissions tend to be much more freewheeling and informal than specialized newsgroups for professionals, which are often moderated (that is, a moderator reviews messages and decides whether they are appropriate for the forum; the moderator is the equivalent of a newspaper or magazine editor). The protocols governing online behavior can vary widely from one forum to another. Sarcasm and ad hominem attacks that are common on many public newsgroups might result in your removal from a moderated academic mailing list. The audiences for online forums can differ dramatically as well. Participants in a newsgroup such as soc.law may include lawyers and other legal professionals, but participants are just as likely to be people with little or no knowledge of the law. By contrast, a mailing list maintained by the American Bar Association will probably be made up mostly of lawyers. The nature of the audience will affect the kinds of topics discussed in a forum and the ways in which participants engage with each other. Flame wars, for example, are much less common in specialized professional forums than in public newsgroups and chat rooms. The expectations for claims and evidence are likely to be more rigorous in a professional forum as well. Even the length of messages and the conventions for how people identify themselves can be different in these different forums. Because of these differences, to engage effectively in argumentation in any online forum, you need to become familiar with the forum and its protocols. It makes sense to read a newsgroup or mailing list for several days or even weeks before jumping into the discussion. If you do so, you will probably find that online discussions can be fruitful and interesting and can be part of your effort to solve problems and negotiate difference through argument.

## RADIO AND TELEVISION

The differences between these two media are obvious; most important, radio is not a visual medium. When television began to come into widespread use in the 1950s, many critics feared that it would mean the end of radio. However, radio has thrived since that time, a fact that suggests that it has characteristics as a medium for communication that television lacks. At the same time radio and television share many characteristics that can escape our notice.

Perhaps the most important feature of radio and television is their reach: They are available to hundreds of millions of people worldwide — many more people than currently have access to the Internet. This reach gives them enormous power for making an argument available to a large audience. Moreover, radio and television are local, national, and international at the same time. Your local talk-radio station might have a host who addresses issues of importance to residents of your region. At the same time the station might be part of a national network, enabling it to broadcast national (and possibly international) shows as well. So someone can direct an argument to a very specific audience or to a much wider national audience on the same station. The same can be said of most television stations. Although it is true that local newspapers and other print forums also print local as well as national and international news, more people listen to radio shows and watch television news programs than read newspapers and newsmagazines. The easy availability of radio and TV seems to matter. And that ease becomes a factor in making an argument in these media.

The immediacy of radio and television is also important. If you are listening to an editorial on radio or on a television news program, you are hearing an electronic version of a speech. In most cases you will not have access to a printed version of the editorial, so you will not be able to rehear it or reread sections of it (unless of course you record it). This characteristic of radio or television arguments requires the speaker to adjust diction, style, and arrangement so that listeners can follow the argument easily. Long, complex sentences can be difficult for an audience to follow in oral arguments, and very complicated reasoning or detailed evidence can be lost on listeners. For these reasons constructing an argument in these media usually means choosing accessible words, crafting relatively simple sentences, perhaps repeating key phrases, and generally being more succinct than you might be in, say, a research paper for a college course or a newspaper editorial.

Sound is a very powerful tool in both television and radio. Listen to any commercial, an announcement for an upcoming program, or a political advertisement, and you will almost certainly hear music or some other sound effect that was specifically chosen for that spot. Political advertisements, for example, are often accompanied by patriotic music or other kinds of music intended to influence listeners positively. Television commercials for sporty cars use contemporary rock music that appeals to younger people who are likely to buy such cars. Similarly, ads for many products now include popular songs from the 1970s that would have positive connotations for viewers who grew up during that decade. As a listener or viewer you might find yourself reacting to such sound effects in ways that might influence how you think about the claim being made on behalf of a political candidate or for a particular car. Would you react to the pitch in the same way if it did not incorporate that favorite song of yours? Would your feelings about the political candidate be different if no music were played during his radio ad? Being aware of the impact of such uses of sound is part of being able to engage public arguments critically.

Earlier in this chapter, we discussed the role of visual elements in argumentation, and we referred to television advertisements and other kinds of television arguments, in which images are so central to their impact. It is worth reemphasizing here that the video and sound capabilities of television make it an enormously powerful medium, and it is important to keep in mind that much of what appears on television is persuasion rather than genuine argumentation. In fact, aside from editorials on news programs, discussions on some public affairs programs (such as *Face the Nation*), and some special documentary programs, very little of what appears on television can be described as genuine argumentation of the kind we have been exploring in this book. At the same time the power of this medium, its ubiquitous nature, and even its seductiveness are compelling reasons for you to be aware of its persuasive qualities and to be able to distinguish between the many kinds of persuasion on television and the few genuine arguments appearing in that medium.

Perhaps the most obvious instance of argumentation on television occurs during political conventions, especially during presidential elections. When the major political parties convene, they take great pains to present themselves in a certain light on the extensive television coverage of those events. The stage and backdrop for speeches, the music, the colors of banners and signs, the camera angles are all carefully arranged to communicate certain messages to voters. When a candidate addresses the convention, his or her appearance on the television screen is as important as the speech itself. Think of your own reaction to a televised political speech. How much was it influenced by your feelings about the appearance of the candidate? By his or her delivery? How much attention did you pay to the words themselves? How closely did you follow the argument, identifying and evaluating claims and evidence? Chances are that for many viewers the messages communicated by the candidate's appearance and presentation overshadow the specific claims made in the speech itself. A candidate's confident and trustworthy appearance might impress the viewer more than his or her specific arguments about, say, tax reform. The power and subtlety of visual messages thus present a challenge to those who wish to engage in genuine argumentation in this important medium.

You might never have an opportunity to make an argument on radio or television, but you will certainly encounter arguments in those media. And many of those arguments will be about important matters in your life, including political elections. Being aware of the way these media are used to communicate and persuade — as well as to argue — will make you a more savvy citizen.

■ ■ ■

The well-known critic Marshall McLuhan once famously asserted that the medium *is* the message. In this chapter we have examined some ways in which McLuhan may have been right. But we have also pointed out that in many ways argument is argument is argument. In other words, the principles of sound argumentation apply in any medium. Moreover, our motives for argument will determine much of what we say and how we make use of a particular medium. If we are genuinely committed to engaging in argumentation to solve problems, then our uses of media can enhance our arguments and contribute powerfully to our efforts to negotiate differences as we address the many complex issues that affect us as we live and work together.

**5**

# CONSTRUCTING
# ARGUMENTS

CONSTRUCTIN

**A**n assignment for your cultural anthropology course requires you to write an essay examining the ethical issues faced by Western anthropologists who study nonindustrialized societies in places such as the Amazon basin. In your essay you are to take a position on the ethical guidelines for such research that have been proposed by a professional organization for anthropologists.

■ You have been asked by other residents of your college dormitory to write a letter to the campus director of residential life to urge him not to implement new security measures that the college is considering. These measures include a new policy that would prohibit students from having visitors in their dorms except during specified hours in the early evening. You and your dorm-mates oppose these measures. Your letter to the director of residential life will try to convince him that the proposed measures would significantly restrict students' social activities without enhancing campus security.

■ A local organization that you belong to advocates sustainable community development. A national retail business has requested a permit to build a large store on farmland near a residential neighborhood in your community. Many residents are pleased because they believe that the new store will improve the community's economic status. Others worry about the impact of the new store on surrounding land, especially regarding water runoff into a nearby marsh that is part of a community park and natural area. Your organization has decided to oppose the building of the new store on the proposed site unless certain measures to protect the marsh are required. You are part of a team that will create a new Web site devoted to presenting your organization's perspective on the new store.

G A R G U M E N T S

How do you proceed?

The answer to that question is the same for each of these situations. It is also different for each of them.

In each of these cases you would try to present and support your claims to your intended audience in a way that is persuasive. To make an effective argument, you must examine the issue carefully so that you understand it well, which might require some research. You must also gather and present evidence to support the claims you will make in your argument. You will want to consider how your intended audience is likely to respond to your claims and warrants in each case. And you must adopt a style — and, in the case of the Web site, a design — that most effectively presents your case.

But each of these situations is different, and arguing effectively means understanding the specific factors involved in each case.

1.  *The rhetorical situation.* The audience and circumstances for each of these writing tasks are very different. Your anthropology teacher, for instance, will have different expectations for your paper than the director of residential life will have for your letter. And the audience for the Web site would be an entire community, with complex and perhaps divergent expectations for a persuasive argument.

2.  *The goals for argument.* Although we can see each of these arguments as part of an effort to solve a problem, the problems in each instance represent different challenges to you as writer. In your anthropology course you hope to understand the ethical issues of anthropology research sufficiently to make an effective argument to earn you a good grade. Your letter to the residential life director is intended to convince him not to implement new security rules that would have a direct impact on your living situation. And your organization hopes that its Web site will generate support among community residents for environmental restrictions on a very large construction project.

3.  *The medium.* The anthropology paper will have to adhere to the conventions of academic writing in the field of anthropology. The letter to the residential life director is also a print document, but one that follows different conventions for writing. And the Web site is an entirely different medium that requires you to consider such matters as layout, color, and hyperlinks.

Adapting to different situations like these is part of making effective arguments. Everything included in the first four chapters of this book is intended to help you understand argumentation in order to construct effective arguments in any situation. The principles we have examined apply to all kinds of arguments. But in this chapter we offer a more focused discussion of how to construct arguments, whatever the situation.

## MANAGING THE COMPOSING PROCESS

### UNDERSTANDING COMPOSING AS INQUIRY

In some ways composing an argument, whatever the medium, is like any other kind of writing: You must define your topic, develop your ideas, gather sufficient information, organize your material, revise accordingly, and edit so that your writing is accurate, effective, and correct. In other words, you must move through the composing process. Composing arguments can make that process both easier and harder. It can make the process easier in the sense that some of the conventions of argumentation will help you determine what you will say and how you will say it. For example, in an argument you will generally be expected to make your claims clearly and support them with adequate evidence. Knowing that can help you generate ideas and organize the information more easily. But as we have seen throughout this book, argumentation involves confronting the complexities of human beliefs and opinions. Part of your challenge in composing your argument is managing that complexity and showing that you are knowledgeable and fair-minded. For example, the essay for your anthropology course will probably address issues of racial diversity, and you will have to consider how the controversial nature of race relations might figure into your argument. In addition, if your goal is to address a serious issue and try to solve a problem through argumentation, you will always be concerned about arguing ethically and honestly. In other words, your goal isn't to win but to engage with others in order to work through a difficult problem. That goal requires you to consider the implications of your argument and the potential effects of your claims on your audience.

Of course, you can't hope to do everything at once. Think of the process of composing an argument as an ongoing process of inquiry. By composing an argument, you are carefully exploring an issue, learning about that issue and about yourself and others as well. That learning might require you to rethink your claims or your position on the issue at hand. For instance, you might begin your essay for your anthropology course believing that strict ethical guidelines for anthropology research are not necessary, but you might find as you compose your essay that the issue is more complicated than you initially thought. That process of inquiry might therefore lead you to revise your original position.

If you approach the writing of an argument in this way — as a process of inquiry — you are more likely to construct effective arguments. Moreover, you might gain a deeper understanding of the issue at hand and perhaps address the problem more effectively as well.

## DEFINING YOUR TOPIC

In the scenarios at the beginning of this chapter the topic for argument in each case may seem clear. But it is important to distinguish between a *subject* and a *topic*. That distinction is even more important if you are faced with a situation in which you are asked to write an argument about anything you want (which is not uncommon in a college writing class). In the case of the anthropology essay, for example, the subject is anthropology, or more specifically, *anthropology research;* we might define the topic as *the ethical problems facing anthropologists who study other cultures.* We can narrow that topic even further: *the specific ethical problem of the relationship between the anthropologist and the people he or she is studying.* Because issues like this are so complex, narrowing the topic will enable you to address it adequately in your essay. It would be impossible to write anything but a very superficial five-page essay about an issue as big as the ethics of anthropological research. Entire books have been written about that issue. But you can feasibly write a five-page essay arguing for specific ethical guidelines relating to the personal relationship between an anthropologist and the people being studied.

If you are given the flexibility to write an argument on any topic, part of your challenge is to select a suitable topic worth arguing about. The best topics are those that are complex: They are about issues that matter to people; they generate controversy; and usually there is a variety of views about them. The topics in the scenarios at the beginning of this chapter are good topics for those reasons. But it is important that the topic you choose matter to *you*. Composing an effective argument is an intellectually rigorous process. There is no point in carefully examining an issue that you're not interested in or concerned about.

Almost all intelligent arguments involve *opinions,* but not all opinions lead to good arguments. Simply having an opinion about something is not the same thing as being able to make a considered argument about it. And some opinions are just not worth arguing. What would be the point of making an argument that golden retrievers are more handsome dogs than poodles? You might love golden retrievers, but will such a topic generate much interest among your classmates? Probably not. It would be better to choose a topic that will matter to others.

Be careful to distinguish between opinions that are a matter of taste and those that are a question of judgment. Some things — broccoli, for example — are a matter of personal preference. You might be able to write an amusing essay about broccoli, but no matter how hard you try, you will not convince someone who hates green vegetables to rush to the produce department of the nearest supermarket. And why would you want to? Questions of judgment, on the other hand, are more substantial. Our judgments are determined by our beliefs, which in turn grow out of basic principles to which we try to remain consistent. These principles ultimately lead us to decide that some judgments are correct and others are not. Should a university require first-year students to live in dormitories? Should it restrict their social activities? Does the state have a right to execute criminals? Should couples live together before getting married? All these are to a great extent questions of judgment.

Questions like these provide rich topics for argumentation because they are complex and offer many avenues to explore. But the very richness of these topics can also be challenging when you are composing an argument. Arguments written about these topics can take many directions. Trying to explore too many directions at once can lead to confusing and ineffective arguments. For this reason defining your topic is only one step in the process of composing an argument. As we noted earlier, composing an argument amounts to engaging in inquiry — that is, exploring your topic fully, and perhaps changing it along the way. In some cases you might have a clearly defined topic even before you begin to write. The letter to the director of residential life in our example at the beginning of this chapter is one such instance. But often you will find that your specific topic will change as you explore the issue you are writing about.

Whatever your topic, the following questions can help you define it carefully and begin to explore it:

- Do I know what my specific topic is?
- Is the topic suitable for the assignment or situation for which I am writing?
- Do I have an opinion about this topic? What is that opinion based on?
- On what grounds might anyone disagree with my opinion?
- Can I hope to persuade others to agree with my opinion?
- Can I support my opinion with evidence?

## CONSIDERING AUDIENCE

The questions above remind us that an argument is always made with an audience in mind. That audience will shape an argument from the very beginning of the composing process. So carefully considering your audience is an important part of the process of exploring your topic and developing your argument. In Chapter 3 we examined the rhetorical context of argument and discussed the role of audience in argumentation. As you prepare to compose your argument, it is a good idea to review that chapter. Here we will focus on how audience considerations will affect the *composing* of your argument.

**Identifying Your Audience**  In some situations your audience is already well-defined. That letter in which you argue against new dormitory restrictions has a very specific audience: the director of residential life. Your essay about the ethical problems facing anthropologists also has a specific audience — your teacher, though your teacher will probably expect you to assume a larger audience (for example, people interested in anthropology). The Web site about the new store proposed for your town has a more general audience, though even this audience is relatively specific (residents of your community). As you work through the process of composing your argument, try to identify what you know about your audience's interests, views, and knowledge of the topic you are addressing. Your sense of what your audience knows or believes can help you define your topic in a way that will connect with that audience; it can also help you explore that topic so that you can develop ideas for making your argument. For example, in writing the letter to the director of residential life at your college, you can assume that your audience (the director) has detailed knowledge of the problems associated with security in campus housing. He most likely feels a great sense of responsibility for the security of students living on campus. And he probably wants students not only to feel secure on campus, but to enjoy their living arrangements as well. As you develop your argument against new restrictions on dormitory visitors, you can use these assumptions to identify claims and warrants that are likely to be acceptable to the director, and you can more easily identify common ground. For example, you might point out that you and the other students in your dorm share his concerns about safety in the dorms. You can research problems with security on your campus and use that information to support your contention that the new visitor restrictions will not likely enhance security. In short, your understanding of your audience can help to generate specific ideas for your argument and

### A METHOD FOR EXPLORING YOUR IDEAS AND YOUR AUDIENCE IN ARGUMENT

Whenever you are making any argument, it can be useful to make a list of the reasons why you believe as you do about the issue. You will probably not be able to discuss, in a short essay, all the points you have listed about the issue, and it is likely that as you compose and revise your argument, you will generate even more ideas — ideas that might prove to be even more important than those on your list. But you can benefit from identifying the reasons for your position, ranking them in order of their importance, and considering the impact they might have on your intended audience. In the case of an essay opposing capital punishment, you might list as one of your reasons "Killing is always morally wrong." If you think about how readers who support the death penalty might react to such a statement, you can begin to anticipate their objections (for example, that killing can be justified in certain cases) or even discover common ground (the idea that human life is sacred).

You can also benefit from making another list: reasons why people might disagree with your position. Then, having explored opposing points of view, you can ask yourself why you have not been persuaded by those reasons. Are there flaws in those reasons? Do you hold beliefs that make it impossible for you to accept those reasons? Adding a brief response to each of these reasons can help you anticipate objections to your position and generate ideas for presenting and supporting your claims. And you are likely to discover that those who hold views opposed to yours have at least one good argument that you cannot answer.

formulate those ideas in ways that might resonate with that audience. Moreover, if you approach argumentation as problem solving, you will tend to see your audience not as an opponent but as a partner in your effort to address the issue at hand. You and your dorm-mates might have different priorities than the residential life director, and obviously your responsibilities are different. But all of you care about safety, and all of you hope for a pleasant and enjoyable campus lifestyle. Understanding that shared ground can lead you to formulate an argument that works toward a solution rather than a victory. The same can be true even when your audience is more general.

At times, you and your audience might hold very different views on an issue, and your respective positions can seem irreconcilable. In fact, because arguments are so often made about controversial matters, it is quite likely that you will find yourself construct-ing an argument for an audience that might be passionately opposed to your point of view. Just skim the newspaper on any morning, and you'll quickly find such issues: capital punishment, sustainable development, tax increases, school funding, religious free-dom. Because such issues are so important to people, they can make the process of con-sidering your audience more complicated, and they require that you take greater care in understanding your audience.

Imagine, for instance, that you are making an argument to a general audience — say, in an article for your local newspaper — about an issue as emotional and complicated as capital punishment. You can be certain that some members of that audience will hold views that are opposed to your own. As you develop your argument, assume that such readers will be skeptical. But don't dismiss their views; rather, consider their reasons for opposing your viewpoint, and try to address their concerns as you build your own case. Doing so not only will help you make a more convincing argument, but might also en-able you to find common ground with those readers.

**Making Concessions**    Often, especially when we are addressing complex and contro-versial issues such as capital punishment, we can find ourselves believing that our position is right and those who believe otherwise are simply ignorant or harbor dubious motives. But serious controversies almost always continue because each side of the issue has valid concerns that cannot be dismissed. Identifying these concerns enables you to understand the issue better and to construct an argument that might be not only more convincing but also more useful. This might mean conceding a point or two to those who oppose your position. If you have no rebuttal to a particular point and recognize that your op-ponents' case has some merit, be honest and generous enough to say so. Making such a concession should not be considered simply a strategic move on your part. Rather, it also signals your willingness to take your audience seriously, even when they disagree with you, and it reflects your genuine interest in addressing the problem at hand effectively and eth-ically. In this way you might bridge the gap between you and members of your audience who oppose your position, making it easier to reach a more substantial agreement. Insisting in a belligerent way that your opponents are completely wrong will hardly con-vince them to take you seriously. Life is seldom so simple that one side is unequivocally right and the other wrong.

Having a good sense of your audience will help you decide what concessions to make. Different audiences will have different expectations. Some might want to hear concessions before listening to opposing views. Some might expect lengthy discussions of conceded points; others might not. When making concessions, address what you think are your audience's most pressing concerns. Doing so can help you develop important points in your argument and organize them more effectively.

**Understanding Audience Expectations**    Having a good sense of audience can also help you decide on the examples and evidence that will best illustrate and support your claims. You will want to use examples that your audience will understand, and you will want evidence that will be convincing to them. Examples of actual cases in an argument opposing capital punishment can be persuasive for a general audience, such as readers of your local newspaper. For a college course in legal theory, however, you will probably need to use a court's formal opinion or statistical data if you wish to be persuasive.

There is a great difference, however, between responding to the interests of your audience by discussing what it wants to know and twisting what you say to please an audience with what it wants to hear. A writer should try to tell the truth as he or she sees it. What we mean by "truth" can have many dimensions. When limited space forces us to be selective, it is wise to focus on the facets of a topic that will be most effective with the audience we are hoping to convince. But it is one thing to focus and quite another to mislead. Never present anything to one audience that you would be compelled to deny to another. Doing so not only damages your credibility, but also undermines any legitimate effort to solve problems through argumentation.

You should bear in mind, too, that all of our advice about considering audience can be profoundly influenced by culture. The very idea of truth, for example, can vary from one culture to another or between two people who follow different religious practices. Even the idea of "factual evidence" can be shaped by cultural background. Western societies such as the United States place a high value on scientific evidence, but some cultures do not share that faith in science. Indeed, even in the United States there are communities that, because of religious beliefs or ideological leanings, harbor a deep mistrust of science. You might never have to address such audiences in an argument, but it is always important to remember that whenever you make an argument to an audience, you do so in a cultural context.

**How One Student Addresses Her Audience**    The following essay, which was originally published as an editorial in a college newspaper, illustrates the importance of taking audience into account in argumentation.

---

To Skip or Not to Skip: A Student Dilemma

This is college, right? The four-year deal offering growth, maturity, experience, and knowledge? A place to be truly independent?

Because sometimes I can't tell. Sometimes this place downright reeks of paternal instincts. Just ask the freshmen and sophomores, who are by class rank alone guaranteed two full years of twenty-four-hour supervision, orchestrated activities, and group showers.

But the forced dorm migration of underclassmen has been bitched about before, to no avail. University policy is, it seems, set in stone. It ranks right up there with ingrown toe nails for sheer evasion and longevity.

But there's another university policy that has no merit as a policy and no place in a university. Mandatory Attendance Policy: wherein faculty members attempt the high school hall monitor–college instructor maneuver. It's a difficult trick to justify as professors place the attendance percentage of their choice above a student's proven abilities on graded material.

Profs rationalize out a lot of arguments to support the policy. Participation is a popular one. I had a professor whose methods for lowering grades so irritated me I used to skip on purpose. He said, "Classroom participation is a very important part of this introductory course. Obviously, if you are not present, you cannot be participating."

Equally obvious, though not stated by the prof, is the fact that one can be perpetually present but participate as little as one who is absent. So who's the better student — the one who makes a meaningless appearance or the one who is busy with something else? And who gets the points docked?

The rest of his policy was characteristically vague, mentioning that absences "could" result in a lower grade. Constant ambiguity is the second big problem with formal policies. It's tough for teachers to figure out just how much to let attendance affect grade point. So they doubletalk.

According to the UWSP catalog, faculty are to provide "clear explanation" of attendance policy. Right. Based on the language actually used, ninety-five percent of UWSP faculty are functionally incapable of uttering a single binding statement. In an effort to offend no one while retaining all power of action, profs write things like (these are actual policies): "I trust students to make their own judgments and choices about coming, or not coming, to class." But then continues: "Habitual and excessive absence is grounds for failure." What happened to trust? What good are the choices?

Or this: "More than three absences may negatively affect your grade." Then again, they may not. Who knows? And this one: "I consider every one of you in here to be mature adults. However, I reserve the right to alter grades based on attendance."

You reserve the right? By virtue of your saying so? Is that like calling the front seat? Another argument that profs cling to goes something like, "Future employers, by God, aren't going to put up with absenteeism." Well, let's take a reality pill. I think most students can grasp the difference between cutting an occasional class, which they paid for, and cutting at work, when they're the ones on salary. See, college students are capable of bi-level thought control, nowadays. (It's all those computers.)

In summary, mandatory attendance should be abolished because:

1. It is irrelevant. Roughly the same number of students will either skip or attend, regardless of what a piece of paper says. If the course is worth anything.

2. It is ineffective. It automatically measures neither participation, ability, or gained knowledge. That's what tests are for. Grades are what you end up knowing, not how many times you sat there to figure it out.

3. It is insulting. A college student is capable of determining a personal schedule, one that may or may not always meet with faculty wishes. An institution committed to the fostering of personal growth cannot operate under rules that patronize or minimize the role an adult should claim for himself.

4. It is arbitrary. A prof has no right and no ability to factor in an unrealistic measure of performance. A student should be penalized no more than what the natural consequence of an absence is — the missing of one day's direct delivery of material.

5. It abolishes free choice. By the addition of a factor that cannot be fought. We are not at a university to learn conformity. As adults, we reserve the right to choose as we see fit, even if we choose badly.

Finally, I would ask the faculty to consider this: We have for some time upheld in this nation the sacred principle of separation of church and state; i.e., You are not God.

Karen Rivedal

*Editor*

In this essay Karen chose a topic that would certainly interest many college students, the audience for whom she saw herself writing. Her thesis is clear: Mandatory class attendance should not be required of college students. And her writing is lively enough to hold the attention of many readers. All this is good.

But Karen's argument also has some weaknesses. In her sixth paragraph she offers what logicians call a *false dilemma:* offering a choice between only two alternatives when others exist (see page 40). By asking, "So who's the better student — the one who makes a meaningless appearance or the one who is busy with something else?," she has ignored at least two other possibilities. Appearance in class is likely to be meaningful to at least some students, and cutting class may be meaningless if the "something else" occupying a student's attention is a waste of time. The comparison in the tenth paragraph between reserving the right to lower grades because of poor attendance and "calling the front seat" is confusing. In the twelfth paragraph Karen claims, "Roughly the same number of students will either skip or attend, regardless of what a piece of paper says," but she offers no evidence to support this claim, which is really no more than guesswork. And because Karen herself admits that many students skip class despite mandatory attendance policies, her claim in the sixteenth paragraph that required attendance "abolishes free choice" does not hold up.

These lapses in logic aside, the major problem with Karen's argument is that she misjudged her audience. She forgot that professors, as well as students, read the school newspaper. Students cannot change the policies of their professors, but the professors themselves usually can, so she has overlooked the very audience that she most needs to reach. Moreover, not only has she failed to include professors within her audience, but she has actually insulted them. Although her criticisms of professors will strike some students as funny, a professor who is told that she or he is "functionally incapable of uttering a single binding statement" (paragraph 8) is unlikely to feel motivated to change. Only in the very last paragraph does Karen specifically address the faculty, and this proves to be simply the occasion for a final insult. There may be professors who take themselves too seriously, but are there really that many who believe that they are divine?

Although it might be easy to poke holes in this argument, Karen deserves credit for boldly calling attention to policies that might indeed be wrong. Recognizing that her original argument could be stronger but still firmly believing that mandatory class attendance is inappropriate for college students, Karen decided to rewrite her editorial as an essay. Here is her revision:

Absent at What Price?

Karen Rivedal

This is college, right? A place to break old ties, solve problems, and make decisions? Higher education is, I always thought, the pursuit of knowledge in a way that's a step beyond the paternal hand-holding of high school. It's the act of learning performed in a more dynamic atmosphere, rich with individual freedom, discourse, and debate.

But sometimes I can't tell. Some university traditions cloud the full intent of higher education. Take mandatory attendance policies, wherein faculty members attempt the high school hall monitor–college instructor maneuver. It's a difficult trick to justify as professors place the attendance percentage of their choice above a student's proven abilities on graded material.

This isn't to say that the idea of attendance itself is unsound. Clearly, personal interaction between teacher and students is preferable to textbook teaching alone. It's the *mandatory* attendance policy, within an academic community committed to the higher education of adults, that worries me.

Professors offer several arguments to support the practice. Participation is a popular one. I had a professor whose methods for lowering grades so irritated me that I used to skip class out of spite. He said, "Classroom participation is a very important part of this introductory course. Obviously, if you are not present, you cannot be participating."

Equally obvious, though, is the fact that one can be perpetually present, but participate as little as one who is absent. Participation lacks an adequate definition. There's no way of knowing, on the face of it, if a silent student is necessarily a learning student. Similarly, an instructor has no way of knowing for what purpose or advantage a student may miss a class and therefore no ability to determine its relative validity.

As a learning indicator, then, mandatory attendance policy is flawed. It automatically measures neither participation nor ability. That's what tests are for. A final grade should reflect what a student ends up knowing rather than the artificial consequences of demerit points.

Some faculty recognize the shortcomings of a no-exceptions mandatory attendance policy and respond with partial policies. Constant ambiguity is characteristic of this approach and troublesome for the student who wants to know just where he or she stands. It's tough for teachers to figure out just how much to let attendance affect grade point. So they double-talk.

This, for example, is taken from an actual policy: "I trust students to make their own judgments and choices about coming, or not coming, to class." It then continues: "Habitual and excessive absence is grounds for failure." What happened to trust? What good are the choices?

Or this: "More than three absences may negatively affect your grade." Then again, they may not. Who knows? And this one: "I consider every one of you in here to be mature adults. However, I reserve the right to alter grades based on attendance."

This seems to say, what you can prove you have learned from this class takes a back seat to how much I think you should know based on your attendance. What the teacher says goes — just like in high school.

Professors who set up attendance policies like these believe, with good reason, that they are helping students to learn by ensuring their attendance. But the securing of this end by requirement eliminates an important element of learning. Removing the freedom to make the decision is removing the need to think. An institution committed to fostering personal growth cannot operate under rules that patronize or minimize the role an adult should claim for himself or herself.

A grading policy that relies on the student's proven abilities certainly takes the guess work out of grade assigning for teachers. This take-no-prisoners method, however, also demands a high, some say unfairly high, level of personal student maturity. Younger students especially may need, they say, the extra structuring that a policy provides.

But forfeiting an attendance policy doesn't mean that a teacher has to resign his humanity, too. Teachers who care to can still take five minutes to warn an often-absent student about the possible consequences, or let the first test score tell the story. As much as dedicated teachers want students to learn, learning is still a personal choice. Students must want to.

A "real-world" argument that professors often use goes something like "Future employers aren't going to put up with absenteeism, so get used to it now." Well, let's take a reality pill. I think most students can differentiate between cutting an occasional class, which they paid for, and missing at work, when they're the ones on salary.

Students who intelligently protest an institution's policies, such as mandatory attendance requirements, are proof-in-action that college is working. These students are thinking; and learning to think and question is the underlying goal of all education. College is more than its rules, more than memorized facts. Rightly, college is knowledge, the testing of limits. To be valid, learning must include choice and the freedom to make mistakes. To rely on mandatory attendance for learning is to subvert the fullest aims of that education.

In revising her essay, Karen has retained both her thesis and her own distinctive voice. Such phrases as "the high school hall monitor–college instructor maneuver," the "take-no-prisoners method," and "let's take a reality pill" are still recognizably her own. But her argument is now more compelling. In addition to eliminating the fallacies that marred her original version, Karen included new material that strengthens her case. The third paragraph offers a much needed clarification, reassuring readers that an argument against a mandatory attendance policy is not the same as an argument against attending class. The seventh paragraph begins with a fairly sympathetic reference to professors, and the eleventh paragraph opens with a clear attempt to anticipate opposition. The twelfth paragraph includes another attempt to anticipate opposition, and the thirteenth paragraph, with its reference to "dedicated teachers," is much more likely to appeal to the professors in Karen's audience than any statements in the original version did. She still makes a hard-nosed argument, but she doesn't lapse into insults. Finally, the conclusion of this essay is much improved. It successfully links the question of mandatory attendance policies with the purpose of higher education as defined in the opening paragraph.

You might think that Karen's revision has suppressed the strong, critical voice of her original version. As a result, you might feel that her revised essay will not resonate as well with students. However, consider this: If we think of Karen's essay as an effort to address a legitimate concern for both students *and* faculty, is her revised version a more effective attempt to solve the problem of cutting classes?

## DEFINING YOUR TERMS

To make sure that your ideas are understandable in an argument, it is important to clarify any terms that are essential to your argument. Unfortunately, many writers of argument fail to define the words they use. It is not unusual, for example, to find writers advocating (or opposing) gun control without defining exactly what they mean by *gun control.* Many arguments use words such as *censorship, society, legitimate,* and *moral* so loosely that it is impossible to decide exactly what the writer means. When this happens, the entire argument can break down.

Don't feel that you need to define every word you use, but you should define any important term that your audience might misunderstand. Avoid defining a word by using the same term or another term that is equally complex. For example, if you are opposed to the sale of pornography, you should be prepared to define what you mean by *pornography.* It would not be helpful to tell your audience that pornography is "printed or visual material that is obscene" because this only raises the question: What is *obscene?* In an important ruling, the U.S. Supreme Court defined *obscene* as material that "the average person, applying community standards, would find . . . as a whole, appeals to the prurient interest," but even if you happened to have this definition at hand, you should ask yourself whether "the average person" understands what *prurient* means — not to mention what the Court might have meant by *community standards.* Unless you define your terms carefully, avoiding unnecessarily abstract language, you can end up writing an endless chain of definitions that require further explanation.

### USING A DICTIONARY

If you consult a dictionary to help you define a term, remember that dictionaries are not all the same. For daily use, most writers usually refer to a good desk dictionary such as *The American Heritage Dictionary, The Random House Dictionary,* or *Merriam Webster's Collegiate Dictionary.* A good general dictionary of this sort will usually provide you with an adequate working definition. You might also want to consider consulting the multivolume *Oxford English Dictionary,* which is available in most college libraries and is especially useful in showing how the usage of a word has changed over the years. Your audience might also appreciate the detailed information that specialized dictionaries in various subject areas can provide. Many such dictionaries are likely to be available in your college library. For example, if you are working on an English literature paper, you might consult *A Concise Dictionary of Literary Terms* or *The Princeton Handbook of Poetic Terms.* For a paper in psychology, you might turn to *The Encyclopedic Dictionary of Psychology,* or for a paper on a musical topic, you could consult *The New Grove's Dictionary of Music and Musicians.* There are also dictionaries for medical, legal, philosophical, and theoretical terms as well as for each of the natural sciences. When using specialized dictionaries, you will often find valuable information, but remember that the definition that appears in your paper should not be more difficult than the word or phrase you originally set out to define.

Dictionaries can be helpful when you're defining your terms. But often the important terms in an argument cannot be satisfactorily defined with a dictionary. Consider the term *sustainability*, which is sometimes used in arguments about environmental issues. Such a term has specific and specialized meanings in environmental debates, and it would not suffice to supply only a dictionary definition. So instead of relying exclusively on dictionaries, try to define such key terms in your words. You can choose from among several strategies:

- Give synonyms.
- Compare the term with other words with which it is likely to be confused, and show how your term differs.
- Define a word by showing what it is *not*.
- Provide examples.

Writers frequently use several of these strategies to create a single definition. Sometimes an entire essay is devoted to defining one term; in doing so, the writer makes an argument in which that term is central. For example, a writer can focus an essay on defining *free speech*, in the process making an argument for a particular conception of that term.

When writing an argument, you will usually need to define your terms within a paragraph or two. In addition to achieving clarity, definition helps to control an argument by eliminating misunderstandings that can cause an audience to be inappropriately hostile or to jump to a conclusion that is different from your own. By carefully defining your terms, you limit a discussion to what you want to discuss. This increases the likelihood of your gaining a fair hearing for your views.

## STRUCTURING AN ARGUMENT

One of the biggest challenges in composing an argument is structuring it. Once you have explored your topic and developed your ideas, you will need to consider the following questions:

- How should I begin my argument?
- In what order should I arrange the points I want to make?
- How can I most efficiently respond to opposing arguments?
- How should I conclude?

The answers to these questions will vary from one essay to another and from one kind of argument (such as a newspaper editorial) to another (a Web page). Even if no single plan will work for all arguments, you can benefit from being familiar with some basic principles of argumentation that may help you organize your argument effectively. Here we will discuss three traditional ways of structuring an argument:

- Classical arrangement
- Rogerian argument
- Logical arrangements

## CLASSICAL ARRANGEMENT

Because classical theories of rhetoric developed at a time when most arguments were oral, the great works of classical rhetoric recommended strategies that could be easily understood by listeners. If speakers adhered to essentially the same plan, listeners were able to follow long, complex arguments because the main components were easily recognizable and the order in which they appeared signaled what was likely to follow.

The common plan for organizing an argument along classical lines included six main components: introduction, statement of background, proposition, proof, refutation, and conclusion, as follows.

| | |
|---|---|
| **Introduction** *(Exordium)* | In the introduction you urge your audience to consider the case that you are about to present. This is the time to capture your readers' attention and introduce your issue. |
| **Statement of Background** *(Narratio)* | In the statement of background you narrate, or tell, the key events in the story behind your case. This is the time to provide information so that your audience will understand the nature of the facts in the case at hand. |
| **Proposition** *(Partitio)* | This component divides (or partitions) the part of the argument focused on information from the part focused on reasoning, and it outlines the major points that will follow. You must state the position you are taking, based on the information you have presented, and then indicate the lines the rest of your argument will follow. |
| **Proof** *(Confirmatio)* | Adhering carefully to your outline, you now present the heart of your argument: You make (or confirm) your case. You must discuss the reasons why you have taken your position and cite evidence to support each of those reasons. |
| **Refutation** *(Refutatio)* | In this key section you anticipate and refute opposing views. By showing what is wrong with the reasoning of your opponents, you demonstrate that you have studied the issue thoroughly and have reached the only conclusion that is acceptable in this case. |
| **Conclusion** *(Peroratio)* | The concluding paragraph(s) should summarize your most important points. In addition, you can make a final appeal to values and feelings that are likely to leave your audience favorably disposed toward your case. |

Classical rhetoricians allowed variations on this plan, depending on, as the great Roman orator and scholar Cicero wrote, "the weight of the matter and the judgment of the speaker" (*De Oratore* I, 31). For example, a speaker was encouraged to begin with refutation when an audience was already strongly committed to an opposing point of view. But because this basic plan remains strong and clear, it can still help writers organize their thoughts.

One advantage of this method of arrangement is that it helps writers generate ideas for their arguments. If you follow the common classical plan for organizing your argument, you will have to generate ideas for each of the main parts. For example, you will have to provide background information about the issue at hand and include arguments to refute opposing points. As a result, your argument will tend to be thorough.

Much of classical rhetoric focused on political discourse, in which speakers publicly debated issues that required action by elected officials or legislatures. Because of this, classical arrangement can be especially useful when you feel strongly about an issue and you are trying to convince an audience to undertake a proposed course of action. Since classical rhetoric tends to assume that an audience can be persuaded when it is presented with solid evidence and a clear explanation of the flaws in opponents' reasoning, this plan for arranging an argument might be most effective when you are writing for people who share your basic values.

## ROGERIAN ARGUMENT

In Chapter 1 we briefly discussed how the ideas of psychotherapist Carl Rogers have influenced scholars interested in argumentation. Rogers focused on listening with understanding in order to avoid miscommunication that can too often accompany serious conflicts. For Rogers the key to resolving conflict is to try honestly to understand what others mean.

Despite questions raised by some scholars about the extent to which Rogers's ideas can be applied to written arguments, you can benefit from viewing persuasion as a means to resolve conflict and achieve social cooperation instead of thinking that the point of an argument is to defeat your opponents. Accordingly, planning a Rogerian argument means emphasizing concessions rather than refutations and placing concessions early in your essay. Like classically arranged arguments, Rogerian arguments have six identifiable parts, as follows.

| | |
|---|---|
| **Introduction** | State the problem that you hope to resolve. By presenting your issue as a problem in need of a solution, you raise the possibility of positive change. This strategy can interest readers who would not be drawn to an argument that seems devoted to tearing something down. |
| **Summary of Opposing Views** | As accurately and neutrally as possible, state the views of people with whom you disagree. By doing so, you show that you are capable of listening without judging and that you have given a fair hearing to people who think differently from you — the people you most need to reach. |
| **Statement of Understanding** | Having summarized views different from your own, you now show that you understand that there are situations in which these views are valid. In other words, you are offering a kind of concession. You are not conceding that these views are always right, but you are recognizing that there are conditions under which you would share the views of your opponents. |
| **Statement of Your Position** | Having won the attention of both your opponents and those readers who do not have a position on your issue, you have secured a hearing from an audience that is in |

need of or is open to persuasion. Now that these readers know that you've given fair consideration to views other than your own, they should be prepared to listen fairly to your views.

**Statement of Contexts**

Similar to the statement of understanding, in which you have described situations where you would be inclined to share the views of your opponents, the statement of contexts describes situations in which you hope your own views would be honored. By showing that your position has merit in a specific context or contexts, you establish that you don't expect everyone to agree with you all the time. The limitations you recognize increase the likelihood that your opponents will agree with you at least in part.

**Statement of Benefits**

You conclude your argument by appealing to the self-interest of people who do not already share your views but are beginning to respect them because of your presentation. When you conclude by showing how such readers would benefit from accepting your position, your essay's ending is positive and hopeful.

(Adapted from Richard Coe, *Form and Substance.* New York: Wiley, 1981.)

Depending on the complexity of the issue, the extent to which people are divided about it, and the points you want to argue, any part of a Rogerian argument can be expanded. It is not necessary to devote precisely the same amount of space to each part. You should try to make your case as balanced as possible, however. If you seem to give only superficial consideration to the views of others and then linger at length on your own, you are defeating the purpose of a Rogerian argument.

Throughout this book we have advocated an approach to argumentation that draws on some of the principles of Rogerian argument, especially the importance of working toward solutions to conflicts. Any style of arrangement — classical, Rogerian, or otherwise — can strive toward the goal of solving problems through argumentation. But a Rogerian argument might be most effective in situations in which people are deeply divided as a result of different values or perceptions. It is especially useful when you are trying to reconcile conflicting parties and achieve a compromise. However, there will be situations in which such an approach might not be the most effective one. If you hold very strong views about a particular issue, for instance, you might find that it is better to consider other ways of organizing your argument. In some situations presenting a strong argument for a specific course of action or viewpoint might be the most ethical way to proceed, even if the ultimate goal is to resolve a conflict. The point is that planning and organizing your argument should be thought of in the larger context of your purposes for engaging in argument.

Here is a student essay about a very complicated and controversial issue: gay adoption. As you'll see, Rachel uses the principles of Rogerian argument to make her case in favor of a national policy for adoption by same-sex couples:

A Reasonable Approach to Gay Adoption

by Rachel Guetter

Adoption by gay parents recently became an open topic with the help of talk show host Rosie O'Donnell. O'Donnell, who went public with her sexuality in 2001, has adopted several children and is a foster mother (Huff and Gest 2). She is currently taking on a Florida law that bans homosexuals from adopting. In doing so, she is prompting everyone to address a situation that is likely to become more common: gay couples seeking to adopt children.

Currently, there is no national policy regarding gay adoptions, and state laws offer a mixed bag of approaches and restriction. For example, Florida is the only state that has enacted a law explicitly banning gay adoptions. In the states that do not have prohibitory laws, gays and lesbians can file for adoption in court (Maxwell, et al.). It is then up to each court to decide whether a petition for adoption meets the state's adoption policies. Many homosexuals have children from previous marriages, or they become parents by donating their own sperm or egg. Only California, Connecticut, and Vermont have legislation that would allow gays and lesbians to adopt their partner's child (Berman). The forty-six other states must rely on their individual judges to consider the petition. One would hope that a judge would not let personal preference get in the way of a fair ruling, but unfortunately this does not always happen.

The many different state laws may reflect the resistance of many Americans to the idea of gay adoption. Those who feel that children should not be brought up in homosexual households state that their concerns are not the product of homophobia, but are the product of what they find to be in the best interest of the children. These people believe that the best way for a child to be raised is in a family with married mother and father. Also, some opponents of gay adoption argue that children who grow up with same-sex parents are not provided with the same legal benefits and securities as those who are raised in heterosexual, married households.

One reason for this resistance is that America is still dealing with the lack of acceptance for and recognition of homosexuals. Until homosexuality is more widely received, children with gay and lesbian parents will have to deal with the fact that their family is viewed as pejoratively different. Glenn Stanton, senior research analyst for Focus on the Family, says, "While there may be very nice people who are raising kids in homosexual situations, the best model for kids is to grow up with mom and dad" (Stanton). It seems reasonable to believe that having both a mother and father benefits children. Women and men have different parenting traits that give a strong balance for the development of a child. Stanton also states, "Fathers encourage children to take chances ... mothers protect and are more cautious." There exist in parents different disciplining, communication, and playing styles that can be advantages in raising a child. Sandy Rios, president of Concerned Women for America, agrees, "As the single mother of a son, I can see quite clearly that having a mother and father together would be far better for my son" ("Pediatrics").

Another problem is that children who have gay and lesbian parents are not necessarily given the same benefits as children from two-parent, heterosexual families. Often, one person in a same-sex relationship is the biological parent and the other will help raise the child as his or her own. According to the American Academy of Pediatrics (AAP), children in this situation lose "survivor benefits if a parent dies and legal rights if the parents break up" (Berman 1). Both situations leave a dramatic impact on the child, who then is caught in the middle of legal battles. Another benefit that the child would not be given is health insurance from both parents. In all of these cases, the child is not given the same economic stability as one who has a married mother and father.

Many gays and lesbians are like any other people who dream of one day having a family. But they face great obstacles. Often, one parent in a same-sex family is not given the same rights as the other when one partner has a biological child. Sometimes neither partner in a same-sex family is able to obtain a child through adoption. Despite such obstacles, it cannot be denied that homosexual families exist. Depending on which study you consult, there are anywhere from 1.5 to 5 million children being raised in gay and lesbian families (Maxwell, et al.). The children, however, are the ones who are being hurt by the lack of legality of the situation that they are in. We owe it to these children — and to the same-sex couples who are committed to raising them — to address this problem in a way that is satisfactory for all concerned.

This issue needs to be examined from a national point of view for two reasons. First of all, people who wish to adopt a child are not restricted to adopting within their own states. Often, the demand for certain children requires couples to look in another state. Secondly, people tend to move from state to state. A couple may adopt a child in one state and later decide to move to another with different laws governing parenthood. The adoption needs to be legally recognized in all states, so if a couple adopts in one state, they can move to another and still be protected by law as legal parents. Instead of allowing each state to make its own decision concerning this matter, federal legislation needs to be enacted that would not only permit homosexuals to adopt their partner's child, but also allow gay couples to adopt children together. Obviously, such legislation would make it easier for same-sex families to raise their children in safe and happy homes. But it might also address the problem of children who need to be adopted. If homosexuals are legally permitted to adopt, more children waiting to be adopted can be given homes and the homosexual families that currently exist will become legally recognized.

There are children who are constantly being shifted from one foster home to another and deservingly need to be placed in a permanent and stable environment. There are currently not enough homes that children can be adopted into. In 1999, about 581,000 children were a part of the U.S. foster care system. Of those, 22 percent were available for adoption ("Foster Care Facts"). A report by the Vera Institute of Justice states that children raised without a permanent home are more likely to exhibit emotional and behavioral problems and be involved with the juvenile justice system ("Safe and Smart"). This is not to say that the foster care system is bad, but it suggests how important a permanent home and family are for children. Same-sex couples could provide such a home for many of these children.

Florida, the state that bans homosexuals from adopting, nevertheless allows homosexuals to become foster parents (Pertman). It is interesting to think that someone could be allowed to clothe, feed, discipline, and love a child yet not be allowed to call that child their own. By allowing a couple to be foster parents, the state has made a statement about what kind of people those foster parents are: responsible and caring and able to provide a good home and family environment. Why should they not be allowed to become legal parents of their own adopted children?

Both sides agree that children need to be raised in loving and caring families. It is wrong to think that a gay couple cannot provide that. A study in Minnesota shows that "in general, gay/lesbian families tended to score the most consistently as the healthiest and strongest of the family structures" (Maxwell, et al.). Married couples placed a strong second, and unmarried heterosexual couples were found to be the least healthy and least strong, especially when children were a part of the family (Maxwell, et al.). The study done by the courts discloses that homosexual couples deliberately plan to have children and arrange their lives so that both parents are significantly involved with raising the child (Maxwell, et al.). Opponents say that it takes more than just a loving environment; it takes both a mom and dad. As the Minnesota study proved, though, perhaps mother-father households are not as stable as once thought. Gays and lesbians have to make extensive plans in order to obtain or even conceive a child, so the likelihood that a child was an "accident" or unwanted is rare.

In February 2002, AAP issued a new statement titled, "Coparent or Second-Parent Adoption by Same-Sex Parents." It explains the AAP's stance on what is in the best interest of children being raised in same-sex families. Dr. Steven Berman offers a summary: "The AAP concluded that legalizing second-parent adoptions is in the best interest of the children" (Berman). Also in this statement is the reassurance that children are not more inclined to become homosexual or to possess homosexual tendencies from being raised by homosexual parents. Although the AAP does not endorse or condemn homosexuality, they, like the rest of the U.S., cannot ignore the growing number of same-sex families and must deal with what truly would be in the best interest of the children who are caught in the middle.

Whether the stance is for or against gay and lesbian adoption, both sides base their reasoning on what is in the best interest for the children. It would be safe to say that most would agree that having a child brought up in a loving, same-sex family is better than having a child moved from foster home to foster home or raised in an abusive home. Being homosexual does not mean that one loses the right to raise a child. Being an unwanted child does not mean that one loses the right to find a loving home, whether that home is single parent, married, heterosexual or even homosexual.

## Works Cited

Berman, Steven. "Homosexuals and Adoption." *Rocky Mountain News* 23 Feb. 2002:1, final ed.: 1 W.

"Foster Care Facts." The Evan B. Donaldson Adoption Institute. 10 Apr. 2002

   <http://www.adoptioninstitute.org/FactOverview/foster.html>.

Huff, Richard, and Emily Gest. "Rosie Takes on Prez About Gay Adoption." *New York Daily News* 14 Mar. 2002, final

   ed.: 2.

Maxwell, Nancy G., Astrid A.M. Mattijssen, and Charlene Smith. "Legal Protection for All the Children: Dutch-

   American Comparison of Lesbian and Gay Parent Adoptions." *Electronic Journal of Comparative Law* 3.1

   (August 1999) 20 Sept. 2002 <http://www.ejcl.org/ejcl/31/art31-2.html>.

"Pediatrics Academy's Endorsement of Homosexual Adoption." *US Newswire* 04 Feb. 2002.

Pertman, Adam. "Break Down Barriers to Homosexual Adoption." *The Baltimore Sun* 20 Mar. 2002, final ed., sec.

   A: 23.

"Safe and Smart." Vera Institute of Justice. 10 Apr. 2002

<http://www.vera.org/project/project1_1.asp?section_id=6&project_id=5>.

Stanton, Glenn T. "Why Children Need a Male and Female Parent." Focus on the Family. 13 May 2002

<http://www.family.org/cforum/tempforum/A0020006.html>.

Notice that Rachel follows the general Rogerian structure described on pages 127–128. After her introduction she presents the views of those who oppose gay adoptions, and she does so without criticism. She offers a statement of understanding, conceding that the concerns of opponents are valid. But she also offers her own concerns, which are based on the same basic goal of protecting children that opponents of gay adoptions hold. This is the common ground that enables her to present her proposal for national legislation regarding gay adoptions — legislation that she believes will protect children in such situation as well as foster children waiting to be adopted. She clearly lays out the benefits of such legislation.

Although you do not need to follow the Rogerian structure, you can see that it might help you organize your argument in a way that is likely to connect with your opponents — which is one of the goals of Rogerian argument. As in the case of Rachel's essay, an argument structured according to a Rogerian approach structure places your opponents' concerns first. Notice, too, that Rachel's tone is measured, respectful, and concerned throughout her essay, another indication of her desire to seek common ground and find a solution to the problem she is writing about.

## LOGICAL ARRANGEMENTS

Arguments can also be shaped by the kind of reasoning a writer employs. In Chapter 2 we discussed the two basic kinds of logic: *inductive reasoning* and *deductive reasoning*. We also discussed informal logic, in particular the Toulmin model. These kinds of logic represent strategies that writers can use to make their arguments, and like the classical and Rogerian approaches, they can be helpful in deciding how to structure an argument.

**Inductive Reasoning**  When you base an argument on inductive reasoning, you are drawing a conclusion based on evidence that you present. For example, let's say you are making an argument for more stringent enforcement of driving laws in your state. In doing so, you might present a variety of relevant information:

- Experiences you've had with speeding drivers
- Anecdotes about friends or family members who have been in accidents that resulted from reckless driving
- Statistics from the U.S. Department of Transportation about automobile accidents and their relationship to speed limits
- Quotations from law enforcement officials or experts who advocate lower speed limits but admit that posted speed limits are often not vigorously enforced.

From all this evidence you draw the conclusion that higher speed limits are dangerous and that drivers would be safer if laws were enforced more rigorously. Such an argument would be based on inductive reasoning.

In making an argument based on inductive reasoning, keep the following considerations in mind:

■ *Try to arrange your evidence so that it leads your readers to the same conclusion you have reached.* Obviously, you need to introduce the issue and demonstrate to your readers that it is a problem worthy of attention. But the primary challenge will be to decide which evidence to present first and in what order the remaining evidence will be presented. Consider, too, how best to begin. You might, for example, cite a particular observation that strikes you as especially important. Or you might begin with an anecdote. Whatever approach you use, your introduction should address your particular audience so that they will want to continue reading. A well-structured inductive essay would then gradually expand as the evidence accumulates so that the conclusion is supported by numerous details.

■ *Consider how specific kinds of evidence you have gathered will affect your readers.* Will some kinds of evidence likely be more compelling to them than others? If so, will it be more effective to present such evidence earlier or later in the argument? Answering those questions not only can help you decide how best to organize your essay, but also can generate additional ideas for evidence that will make your conclusion as persuasive to your audience as possible.

■ *Decide how much evidence is enough.* Eventually, you will reach a point at which you decide that you have offered enough evidence to support your thesis. You might reach this point sooner in some contexts than others. For example, in an essay for your college writing class, you are not likely to cite as much evidence as you might be expected to include in a research report for a course in freshwater ecology; an essay in a respected political journal such as *Foreign Affairs* will include more extensive evidence than an editorial in your local newspaper. But whatever the context, the process is essentially the same.

■ *Interpret and analyze your evidence for your audience.* When you stop citing evidence and move to your conclusion, you have made what is known as an *inductive leap.* In an inductive essay you must always offer interpretation or analysis of the evidence you present. For example, if you use an anecdote about an accident involving a speeding driver in an essay on the enforcement of driving laws, you will have to explain the significance of that anecdote — what it means for your argument. There will always be a gap between your evidence and your conclusion. It is over this gap that the writer must leap; the trick is to do it agilely. Good writers know that their evidence must be in proportion to their conclusion: The bolder the conclusion, the more evidence is needed to back it up. Remember the old adage about "jumping to conclusions," and realize that you'll need the momentum of a running start to make more than a moderate leap at any one time.

The advice we offer here suggests that organizing an argument inductively offers you a great deal of flexibility. As always, the decisions you make will reflect your purpose and your sense of how best to address your audience.

**Deductive Reasoning**   Deductive reasoning begins with a generalization and works to a conclusion that follows from that generalization. In that respect it can be thought of as the opposite of inductive reasoning, which begins with specific observations and ends with a conclusion that goes beyond those observations. The generalization you start with in a deductively arranged argument is called a *premise* and is the foundation for your argument. As we saw in Chapter 2, it takes much careful thought to formulate a good premise. Nevertheless, because so many arguments employ this kind of logic, deductive reasoning can be a powerful way to construct an effective argument.

The process of reasoning deductively might be difficult to grasp in the abstract, but you can follow some general steps that will help you explore your topic and generate an outline for your argument. In effect, you work backward from the conclusion you wish to reach.

---

## A METHOD FOR REASONING DEDUCTIVELY

Because it can be difficult to formulate a good premise, it is often useful to work backward when you are planning a deductive argument. If you know the conclusion you want to reach, write it down, and number it as statement 3. Now ask yourself why you believe statement 3. That question should prompt a number of reasons; group them together as statement 2. Now that you can see your conclusion as well as some reasons that seem to justify it, ask yourself whether you've left anything out — something basic that you skipped over, assuming that everyone would already agree with it. When you can think back successfully to what this assumption is, knowing that it will vary from argument to argument, you have your premise, at least in rough form.

---

1.  *Identifying Your Conclusion.* Suppose that you have become concerned about the consequences of eating meat. Because of worries about your own health, you have reconsidered eating meat, and you have begun to adopt a plant-based, or vegetarian, diet. But in exploring a vegetarian diet, you have also learned that meat production has potentially harmful environmental consequences. In particular, you are concerned about the destruction of forests that are cut down to allow cattle to graze. You believe that if eating meat leads to such environmental damage, it should be stopped.

    Obviously, given how prevalent meat consumption is and its prominent place in the American diet, you can't reasonably argue for eating meat to be made illegal or restricted by law in some way. But you can argue that it be discouraged — perhaps in the same way that smoking is discouraged. Most important, you believe that people should at least eat much less meat than they currently do.

    So your conclusion is clear: People should eat less meat. Now you begin to write down your outline in reverse:

    3. Americans should not consume so much meat.

    2. Consuming meat can be unhealthy, and meat production damages the environment.

2.  *Examining Your Reasons Carefully.* Before going any further, you realize that not all of your reasons for opposing meat consumption can be taken with equal degrees of seriousness. For one thing, diet can be a personal choice, and your concerns about your own health are not sufficient grounds to argue against other people eating meat. So you need to make sure that your point about the health risks of eating meat does not sound self-serving but has validity for others as well. Your own research has shown that eating meat involves a number of health risks.

You also know that a vegetarian diet has health benefits. You will want to discuss these risks and benefits in a way that makes them relevant to people in general so that you are not simply discussing your own health choices.

Your greater concern is the possible environmental damage associated with meat production. Here, too, it might be difficult to convince people who enjoy eating meat that the loss of forests thousands of miles away from their backyard grill should concern them. So it will be important for you to establish not just that meat production leads to the loss of forest, but also that there might also be other environmental consequences closer to home. For example, most livestock in the United States is fed grain, and the production of feed grain not only uses up vast amounts of farmland, but also contributes to pollution through agricultural runoff. Furthermore, the raising of livestock generates pollution in the form of animal waste. There is, as well, the problem of the chemicals and drugs that are used on livestock, which you have heard can be risky for humans who eat meat. All these reasons can be compelling to others who might enjoy eating meat but might be unaware of the problems that can be caused by meat production.

3. *Formulate Your Premise.* You should now be ready to formulate your premise. Your conclusion is that eating meat should be curtailed, and you will urge others to stop or reduce their meat consumption and adopt an alternative diet. So near the beginning of your argument, you need to establish the principle that supports this conclusion. In this case you believe that it is wrong for people to engage in a practice that is ultimately destructive of the environment, especially when there is an alternative to that practice. In effect, you are suggesting that if what we do has damaging consequences (in this case eating meat has negative consequences for the environment and our health), then it is unethical to continue doing it when we have other options. This is your main premise.

A premise can be a single sentence, a full paragraph, or more, depending on the length and complexity of the argument. The function of a premise is to establish a widely accepted value that even your opponents should be able to share. You would probably be wise, therefore, to make a fairly general statement early in your argument — something like this:

> It is unethical to continue engaging in an activity that is harmful and environmentally destructive.

Obviously, such a statement needs to be developed, and you will do so not only by showing how destructive meat production and consumption can be, but also by offering alternatives to eating meat. You will want to suggest that our individual choices about things like diet can affect others. That makes those choices ethical ones. Now you have the foundation for a logical argument:

> If engaging in a practice or activity is harmful to people and their environment, then it should be stopped. Eating meat is such an activity; therefore, we should avoid eating meat and instead adopt an alternative diet.

This example can help you see the utility of structuring an argument deductively. You can see, too, that generating an argument in this way can deepen your engagement with your topic and eventually lead to a more substantive and persuasive essay. The following student essay by Kristen Montgomery, in which she argues against eating meat, is one example of an argument structured in this way. Notice that Kristen presents her main premise — that doing something harmful and environmentally destructive is unethical — implicitly in her second paragraph, after introducing her topic. In this case Kristen's question, "Do we have the right to support eating habits that have such negative consequences, especially when these habits are unnecessary?," implies her main premise. Often in a deductive argument, the main premise is explicitly stated at the beginning. Kristen chose a slightly different strategy. But it is clear that she will argue from this basic principle that we have no right to engage in harmful practices when alternatives to those practices exist. Kristen could have stated her premise explicitly in her opening paragraph and then proceeded to her specific evidence. Either approach is acceptable for an argument that is structured deductively. The important point is to establish the main premise early in the essay and then argue on the basis of that premise, which Kristen does.

*Carnivorous Concerns*

by Kristen M. Montgomery

Baseball? Apple pie? Shopping? Most Americans love these things, but there is perhaps nothing more American than eating meat. Birthdays, ballgames, and the most American of holidays, the Fourth of July, are all celebrated with barbeques and cookouts featuring burgers, dogs, and steaks. A burger and fries may be the most American meal of all. Each day, Americans eat 46 million pounds. And each year, the average American eats two times his or her weight in meat.

But what if this all-American meal is actually damaging health and home? Is it right to engage in a practice that is not only harmful to our physical health but also destructive to our environment? Do we have the right to support eating habits that have such negative consequences, especially when these habits are unnecessary? Many people oppose eating meat on the grounds that meat production is cruel to animals. And it is. But the consequences for the human population are arguably as bad. And it simply unethical to engage in a practice that is so damaging to the earth and its inhabitants.

A careful look at meat production shows why eating meat contributes to human illness. The animals we eat are pumped full of chemicals that are often unhealthy to them and to humans; they are also neglected and tortured. Meanwhile, their living conditions are feces-ridden and disease-infested. The animals live in their own excrement next to others that are themselves full of disease. It is only reasonable to expect that these conditions contribute to human illness. In fact, the USDA estimates that salmonella, a dangerous pathogen that can cause serious illness and even death in humans, is present in 35 percent of turkeys, 11 percent of chickens and 6 percent of ground beef. Each year, food-borne pathogens cause 76 million illnesses and 5,000 deaths, according to the Centers for Disease Control. And it is alarming to note that certain bacteria in meat have shown evolutionary changes into more dangerous substances. For example, O157:H7 is a mutant strand of E. coli, which is very hard to treat because of its evasiveness in medical tests. Ultimately, for those who eat meat contaminated with O157:H7, organ failure is the cause of death. It is reasonable to assume that this strand of E. coli is not the only bacterium which may have developed strengths against human antibodies. There are likely more out there and more to come.

Exposing ourselves to such illnesses is unnecessary. We have healthier alternatives to meat as a food source. Although many people view a plant-based diet as unthinkable because of their love of meat, a plant-based diet, with a little bit of research and practice, can have more variety and is much healthier than a meat-based diet. Meat is deficient in carbohydrates and vitamins. Not only is meat lacking important nutrients for proper health, but it is also abundant in harmful substances, such as calories and saturated fat. When cooked, most meats produce a variety of benzenes, among other carcinogenic compounds. Benzene is commonly found in paints, cleaners, and cigarettes, and it is poisonous to humans. In addition, the average American gets five times the amount of needed protein in his or her diet, which strains the kidneys with luric acid and can actually cause nephritis.

By contrast, a plant-based diet enables us to avoid such potentially serious problems. And contrary to popular opinion, there is no nutrient necessary for good health that cannot be obtained from a plant-based diet. That is why mom always made us eat our vegetables. High fruit and vegetable consumption has been associated with a lowered risk for heart disease, several types of cancers, and other chronic illnesses. Also, there is a growing body of medical evidence that eating such things as beans, peanuts, lentils, and peas, which contain a variety of beneficial ingredients, may protect against disease. For example, according to the Journal of American Dietetic Association, soybean consumption is linked with a decreased risk of prostate cancer and increased bone density in post-menopausal women. These facts are just the beginning. If we look at the overall benefits of eating a plant-based diet, it doesn't make sense to risk our health by eating meat.

But if eating meat is unhealthy for our bodies, it may be even worse for our planet. And this alone should make us reconsider our reliance on meat as a food source. Some people worry about big business eating away at rural and suburban land, but urban sprawl is not the leading cause of deforestation. Meat production is to blame: "For every acre of forest land consumed by urban development, seven acres are devoured by the meat industry, for grazing and growing feed. If water used by the meat industry were not subsidized by U.S. taxpayers, a hamburger would cost $35." And 125,000 square miles of rain forests are destroyed each year for the purpose of producing meat. For each quarter-pounder fast-food burger made of beef that is raised on land that was once rain forest, fifty-five square feet of land is used. Every second, 2.4 acres of forest is turned into grazing land. Moreover, this use of the land is incredibly inefficient. For example, an acre of land can produce approximately 20,000 pounds of potatoes but only 165 pounds of beef. Large amounts of grain are grown to feed the animals that we butcher for food. In fact, eighty-seven percent of all agricultural land in America is used to raise the animals we eat. Instead of feeding the grain to humans, we feed it to cows and chickens. It takes twice the amount of grain to produce beef and four times the amount of grain for poultry production than to feed this grain to humans.

Not only does raising animals for food require a large amount of land, but it also requires a large amount of energy. Consider for a moment that it takes the water from 17 showers to produce a single hamburger. Or instead of driving a small car for 20 miles, consider using the same amount of energy to make that one hamburger patty. That's how much energy is needed to produce the beef for that burger. In the 1980s, one-half of the world's grain harvest was fed not to people, but to livestock. With world starvation rates as they are, this approach to food production doesn't make sense. What's more, it's unethical.

All of this resource depletion also leads to pollution. On the large portion of land on which we raise animals and the grain to feed them, raw waste is produced. Excrement is produced at a rate of 130 times more than what is produced by the entire human population. It must go somewhere, and where it goes is everywhere, sometimes in nearby waterways. According to *Scientific American,* this waste has increased the pathogenic organisms in the water, which has poisoned humans as well as millions of fish, which serve to maintain the delicate balance of the oceanic ecosystem. Not only are the feces poisoning the soil and waterways, but some people living near these areas must actually wear face masks because of the overwhelming stench. In addition to water and land pollution, the EPA estimates that the world's animal population is responsible for 25 percent of anthropogenic emissions of methane gas, which contribute to the greenhouse effect. Therefore, meat production also contributes to air pollution. These facts are compounded by the fact that since the 1950s, the livestock population has increased more rapidly than the human population. So as our consumption of meat increases, so does the damage we are doing to our earth.

Eating meat is enjoyable for many people, but it is an impractical approach to food production that cannot be sustained. We may neglect to see the consequences of depleting our resources and letting our planet become overburdened with animal waste, because the consequences are not immediate and we are a society where immediate is considered best. Few of us see the dramatic effects described above. But we all must seriously consider what our heavy meat consumption means for our future. The slaughtering of animals to satisfy our hunger contributes to the depletion of our world's valuable resources, results in pollution, and causes human disease. The consequences of our murderous appetite may eventually be as deadly for us as for the animals we kill to satisfy this appetite. Perhaps knowing this may curb our appetite for meat. It's time we adopted more sustainable and ethical eating habits, before we eat ourselves — and our world — to death.

**Using the Toulmin Model**   Even when you are using logical arrangement to organize your argument, you will rarely follow the rules of logic rigidly. Because most people use logic informally in arguments, the Toulmin model (see pages 31–35) can be extremely useful in helping you construct your argument. The Toulmin model focuses on the *claim* you want to make — that is, the conclusion you are trying to reach or the assertion you hope to prove. Your task, simply put, is to state your claim clearly and offer persuasive reasons (what Toulmin calls *data*) for that claim. The third element in the Toulmin system is the *warrant,* which is the assumption that connects the claim and the data. As we noted in Chapter 2, the warrant is usually a fundamental value or belief that, ideally, is shared by writer and audience (like the premise we discussed in the section above on deductive reasoning).

This model dictates no specified pattern for organizing an argument, so the challenge is to determine how best to present your claim to your intended audience and then to of-

fer adequate reasons for your claim. But the value of this model for constructing an argument lies in the way it requires you to articulate your claim precisely and to pay close
attention to the adequacy of your reasons and your evidence, without having to follow the
rigid rules of formal logic. In this way the Toulmin model can help you refine your claim
and develop convincing support for it. This model also encourages you to think through
the often unstated assumptions that lie behind your claim: the warrants. Identifying your
warrant can lead to a much more effective argument because it can help you see points of
possible contention between you and your audience.

Let's imagine that you live in a small town where a businessperson wishes to build a
large meat-processing facility. This person has recently applied to the town board for a
permit to begin construction of the plant. As a resident who values the quiet lifestyle of
your town as well as its clean and safe environment, you worry about the social and environmental damage the plant might cause. So you decide to write to the town supervisor to express your concerns and urge him to reject the permit for the plant.

Using the Toulmin model for your letter, your first step would be to try to articulate
your central claim clearly. You might state your claim as follows:

> We should not allow a meat-processing facility to be built in our town.

Before moving to your reasons for your claim, you should consider carefully whether that
statement accurately represents the position you want to take. Can you be more specific?
Can you focus the claim even more narrowly? In thinking about these questions, you
might amend your claim as follows:

> Building a meat-packing facility would damage the quality of life and the environ-
> ment of our town.

Notice that although this version of your this claim is related to the first version, it is a
bit narrower and more precise. It also points directly to the kinds of data or the reasons
you can offer to support the claim. Being clear about your claim is crucial because your
reasons must fit that claim closely in order to be persuasive. Now you can begin exploring your reasons.

At this point it is a good idea to brainstorm, listing the main reasons for your belief
that the plant should not be built in your town. You have many reasons: the possible damage to local streams from the waste and runoff from the plant, the increased traffic to and
from the plant, the odor, the negative impact of a large plant on the quality of life in a
small town. You should examine these reasons and try to identify those that are most compelling. So now you have your claim and main reasons for it:

Claim:         Building a meat-packing facility would damage the quality of life and
               the environment of our town.

Reasons:       Meat-packing facilities can cause pollution, endanger the health of lo-
               cal residents, and increase truck traffic on local roads.

Before you begin to develop evidence to support these reasons for your claim, you
should think about your warrant — the assumptions that lie behind the claim and connect your reason and claim. This is a crucial step in using the Toulmin model because it
helps you identify the assumptions behind your claim or the principles on which you base
your claim. In Toulmin's model, the warrant is what provides the basis for a claim.

Without an acceptable warrant the claim becomes weak or even invalid. In this case you might state your warrant as follows:

Warrant: We all have a right to live in clean, safe environments.

You can probably be confident that your audience — the town supervisor — would accept this warrant, so you probably don't need to defend it. However, you might decide to state it in your letter, and you might even defend it in order to drive it home. The point is that you have identified a basic value or belief that you assume others share and without which your claim has no foundation.

Now you can begin developing specific evidence to support your claim and your reasons. The reasons stated above suggest the kinds of evidence you might gather. For example, to support the assertion that meat-processing facilities damage the environment, you might find reports of increased pollution in streams near existing meat-packing plants. You can perhaps find similar reports about the impact of truck traffic around such plants. Evidence to support the assertion that your town's lifestyle would be adversely affected might be trickier. First, you will want to establish the character of the town as it is. That might mean providing facts about the number of residences as compared to businesses, the size and use of roads, and so on. The point is to identify specific and persuasive evidence that fits your reasons for your claim — and to gather evidence that will be acceptable and convincing to your audience.

Here's a letter by a student that takes up this issue. In this letter Kristen Brubaker is writing to the supervisor of her small town in rural Pennsylvania. She expresses concern about a resident's request to build a factory hog farm in the town.

---

Dear Mr. Smithson:

As township supervisor of Wayne Township, you have had a great impact on our community for the past several years. In the coming months, your service will be needed more than ever. Jack Connolly, a resident of our township, has put forth a plan to build a factory hog farm, called a CAFO. His proposed facility will house 5,600 breeding sows, 100,000 piglets, and will cover nearly five acres of buildings (Weist). I am aware that you support this project, but I think there are some points you may be overlooking. We need to work together to ensure that our basic rights as property owners and citizens are not infringed upon and to protect the quality of life in our community.

I know we share similar values when it comes to the protection of our environment. In fact, you are one of the people who helped to shape my view of the environment. When I was younger, I attended the Dauphin County Conservation Camp that you helped to sponsor. I remember several of our activities, including the stream improvement project we completed and the stocking of trout in Powells Creek. Because of these experiences, I was surprised to find out you did not strongly oppose this project. Were you aware that CAFOs have caused extensive damage to trout streams in many states? I hope we don't have to face the destruction of our creek and surrounding valley before we realize that we made a mistake.

Although the risks to our environment are numerous, the first problem most people associate with CAFOs is the smell. In Powells Valley, we have traditionally been an agricultural community, so we're not afraid of the natural, inevitable odor of farms. Although factory farmers argue that the odor of animal waste is simply part of living in a rural, agricultural area, the air pollution caused by CAFOs is often more than a minor inconvenience. Imagine being unable to hang your clothes out to dry because of a thick, permeating smell that saturates everything it touches. The smell is not harmless either. CAFOs produce dangerous levels of ammonia and methane, gases suspected of causing nausea, flu-like symptoms, and respiratory illness, especially in children or the elderly. These chemicals also return to the ground as rain, polluting our water (Satchell). Another potentially harmful gas produced is hydrogen sulfide. In as small a concentration as 10 parts per million, it causes eye irritation. At 50 parts per million, it causes vomiting, nausea, and diarrhea. At 500 parts per million, hydrogen sulfide causes rapid death (Weist).

Another problem with the proposed location of this facility is its close proximity to houses and the small size of the valley. More than 35 houses are located within a half-mile radius of the proposed operation. Our valley is only a mile wide, so there will be nowhere for the odor to go. It will sit in our valley on hot summer days, saturating the air and everything in it. If this facility must be built, why can't it go somewhere less densely populated or somewhere that would handle odors more effectively?

But the most frightening aspect of having a CAFO in our valley is the strong possibility that we would face severe water pollution. Because of the immense scale of CAFOs, they often produce much more manure than the surrounding land can handle effectively. In cases where overspreading occurs, excess nutrients can run into the streams, disrupting the ecological balance and killing fish. Powells Creek, like most small creeks, sits in a very delicate balance and a small increase of nutrients can seriously alter the habitat of the stream. Nutrients contribute to increased plant and algae life, which can clog waterways and rob them of oxygen. Excess nutrients can also seep into the ground water, creating a problem with illness-causing pathogens such as salmonella (Satchell).

Another cause of water pollution among CAFOs is the waste lagoons used to store manure. Because fields may be spread only certain times of the year, there is a need for immense storage facilities. Most farms use lagoons that can be several acres long, sometimes holding up to 25 million gallons of waste. In North Carolina, waste lagoons are being blamed for the catastrophic fish kills and pollution of the coastal waters that took place in 1996 (Satchell). In the recent flooding in North Carolina due to Hurricane Floyd, over 50 lagoons overflowed, and one burst. Although it is not yet known how these recent spills will affect the environment, more fish kills and contaminated drinking water supplies are virtually guaranteed (Wright).

There are many other problems Powells Valley could face as a result of this facility. The operation that Mr. Connolly is proposing would produce 12 million gallons of waste per year. This waste is going to be spread throughout three townships in our valley. This is a lot of waste for one small stream, yet this is the best-case scenario. Can you imagine what would happen in the case of a leak or spill. Powells Creek is located about 350 feet downhill from these proposed facilities. In the case of an overflow, flood, or leak, the waste would go directly into the creek. To make matters worse, this operation is going to be located in an area that has frequent problems with flooding. In 1996, a small flood destroyed the bridge that crosses Powells Creek just below the proposed operation. If a spill or leak were to occur, the creek's aquatic life would be destroyed. If this facility is approved, we may not have to worry about stocking Powells Creek anymore.

The local increase in traffic is another issue that must be addressed. If this facility goes into operation, there would be approximately 1,750 truck trips per year delivering feed and supplies and transporting the 100,000 piglets to finishing operations. In addition to this, there will be an estimated 3,500 trailer truck trips needed to transport the 12 million gallons of waste (Weist). The roads in our area are not equipped for this kind of traffic. It would put a much greater burden on Wayne Township for the upkeep of its roads. The Carsonville Fire Company, which would be charged with the responsibility of handling any accidents, is dangerously underequipped to handle a large spill. Additionally, the roads entering the area of the proposed operation are small, curvy, and unsafe for large trucks. There are school busses from two school districts traveling these roads. The risk of having a serious accident is simply too high to justify this operation.

One of the key factors that allows these problems to exist largely unchallenged is the lack of regulation for these factory farms. If someone were to build a factory producing the same amount of contaminating waste, they would face numerous regulations. Human waste treatment plants also follow strict environmental controls that ensure that they do not pollute. Because CAFOs are technically agriculture, and not industry, they face virtually no regulations. They are also protected by the "Right to Farm Act," which was originally passed to protect family farms from harassment and lawsuits by developers. This law is making us defenseless because it will back any lawsuit we could make against the owner of the CAFO. Although nutrient management plans are required for a large operation, such a requirement is not enough protection.

As expected, Jack Connolly's plans have not been stifled by the protests of over 100 citizens. His nutrient management plan was recently rejected by the Dauphin County Conservation District, but he continues to build. He realizes that although many people in the community are afraid of his plans, just as many are unwilling to interfere with his right to do what he wants with his property. We don't like being told what we can and cannot do with our land, and when we give up those rights, we feel it starts a dangerous trend. At the same time, we must think of the property rights of those who have inhabited this valley their whole lives. Operations like this can seriously lower property values. People who can't stand the smell would have two choices. They could sell their homes, their sole investments, for a fraction of their worth or live with the smell.

There are some possible benefits to having this operation in our valley. For one, the factory is expected to create between 20 and 30 local jobs. We don't have a problem with unemployment in our valley, though, so it's likely that these jobs will be filled with outsiders. Also, they aren't going to be the high-quality jobs that most of us would want. Another possible benefit, one I'm sure you're aware of, is the possibility of cheap fertilizer. I noticed on the nutrient plan that you were listed among the recipients. Are you aware that if there is an accident with the waste on your land, you are responsible, not Mr. Connolly? If you still decide that this plan is in the best interests of everyone it will affect, do some research of your own to ensure you're not part of the problem by accepting more manure than your land can safely handle. Also, make sure Mr. Connolly hasn't increased your projected amount without your knowledge in order to satisfy his nutrient management plan.

If you agree that his CAFO is not good for our community, there are steps you should take to postpone, or even reject, this proposal. First, you, as township supervisor, can reject his building permits until he gets the necessary approval from the county and state. These agencies will be more likely to approve his plan if he already has a multi-million dollar complex built to house it. You could also pass ordinances to prevent the growth of this "farm." A common scenario is that after the nearby property values are sufficiently lowered due to the offensive smell, a factory farm owner will buy the surrounding land and build more operations. It only makes sense when you consider that the operation Mr. Connolly has proposed is a breeding facility. This means that the piglets will need to be transported to a finishing facility. Wouldn't it be cheaper and more cost effective to build a near-by facility that could house the hogs as they were prepared for slaughter? After that, why not just build a slaughtering facility as well. It's happened before, and it could happen in our valley. Although people tend to be against zoning in rural communities such as ours, sometimes it is imperative to prevent negative changes.

Please think about the possible effects this will have on our valley. As a life-long resident, you must value its beauty. I also assume that you value the right of every person in this community to live in a safe and clean environment. Imagine a day when you couldn't sit on your porch to eat breakfast because of the overwhelming odor that permeates everything it touches. Imagine your grandchildren getting ill because of water-borne bacteria caused by this CAFO. Imagine the day when you can no longer fish in the creek you helped improve. This day could be upon us if we don't take action now. You're a vital part of this equation, and I trust that we can count on you to help us maintain the land that raised us.

Sincerely,

Kristen Brubaker

References

Cauchon, Dennis. "N.C. Farmers, Scientists Begin Taking The Toll." *USA Today* 27 Sept. 1999: 6A.

"Hog Factories vs. Family Farms and Rural Communities." Powells Balley Conservation Association. 8 Oct. 1999.
   Pennsylvania Department of Environmental Protection. 15 Oct. 1999 <www.dep.state.pa.us>.

Satchell, Michael. "Hog Heaven — and Hell." *U. S. News and World Report* 22 Jan. 1996: 57.

Weist, Kurt, "Petition to Intervene of the Powell's Valley Conservation Association, Inc." Powell's Valley Conservation
   Association, Inc. 1999.

Wright, Andrew G. "A Foul Mess." *Engineering News Record* 4 Oct. 1999: 26.

Notice that Kristen's claim is implicit in her first paragraph, in which she indicates concern about the hog farm, but she doesn't explicitly state that the permit should be denied until the second-to-last paragraph. Notice, too, that she states her warrant in her second paragraph and then reinforces it in her final paragraph. The Toulmin model does not require that the essay be structured in this way. Kristen might just as easily have begun by stating her claim explicitly and proceeded from there; similarly, she might have left her warrant unstated or waited until the final paragraph to state it. Those choices are up to the writer. But using the Toulmin model can help to identify these elements so that you can work with them in constructing an argument.

We should also point out that Kristen has chosen to document her evidence with a list of references, an unusual step in a letter. However, that decision can make her letter more persuasive, since it indicates to the town supervisor not only that Kristen has taken the time to research this issue thoroughly, but also that her facts and figures have been taken from reputable sources.

In considering these different models for arranging an argument, you should understand that they are not mutually exclusive. In a classically arranged argument, for example, the statement of background can be done in the kind of nonjudgmental language emphasized in Rogerian argument. Similarly, the summary of opposing views in a Rogerian argument requires the kind of understanding that a writer following a classical arrangement would need to have before engaging in refutation. In both cases, the writers need to be well informed and fair-minded. And both classical arrangement and Rogerian argument encourage the use of concessions. The difference between the two is best understood in terms of purpose. Although any argument is designed to be persuasive, the purpose of that persuasion varies from one situation to another (see Chapter 1). You might be writing to assert a position or to inquire into a complex issue. Your plan should fit your purpose.

It is also worth remembering that contemporary arguments rarely follow rigid guidelines, except in certain academic courses or in specialized documents, such as legal briefs, or situations like formal debates. For that reason many teachers today advocate the Toulmin model, emphasizing its flexibility in adapting an argument to a specific situation. Moreover, different media represent different opportunities and challenges for how to present an argument (see Chapter 4). All of this means that you have many options for structuring your argument. The more familiar you are with the principles of organization in argumentation, the more likely it is that you will be able to structure your argument effectively.

## SUPPORTING CLAIMS AND PRESENTING EVIDENCE

The letter by Kristen Brubaker (page 140) highlights the importance of presenting good evidence to support your argument. Without compelling evidence even the most carefully articulated claim won't be persuasive. But as we noted in Chapter 4 (pp. 76–82), what counts as good evidence will vary from one context to another. So an important part of generating evidence for your argument is considering your audience and its expectations for evidence as well as the rhetorical situation in which you are making your argument. In Kristen's case the audience is very specific: her town supervisor. And she offers evidence that directly addresses a number of issues regarding quality of life that would concern a person in his position. Indeed, one of the strengths of Kristen's argument is that her evidence fits her audience. Another strength is the amount of evidence she provides. She includes statistics and other facts to support her assertions about pollution, road use, odor, and health problems. She also uses values as evidence, appealing to the supervisor's sense of the importance of private property and community well-being (see page 140). Moreover, the amount of evidence suggests that Kristen has done her homework. By presenting so much appropriate evidence so carefully, she helps to establish her credibility. And although she is writing specifically to one person, Kristen's evidence would probably resonate with a broader audience — say, readers of the local newspaper — if Kristen were addressing such an audience. Implicitly addressing a broader audience might strengthen her argument as well, since the supervisor will probably be sensitive to the views of other people in the community.

Your audience can affect not just the kind of evidence you use, but also whether you need evidence for a particular point. For example, if you are confident that your readers will accept your warrant, then you might decide that you don't need to support it. If it is likely that your audience will disagree with your warrant, then you will need evidence to back it up. Imagine, for instance, if Kristen were writing for a much broader audience — let's say she was making an argument against CAFOs for a newspaper like *USA Today.* Some of her readers might be willing to give up some of the characteristics of a small town for greater economic development. For such readers Kristen might want to defend her warrant about a clean environment, perhaps showing that economic development doesn't have to mean damaging the environment. The point is that your sense of audience and its expectations will affect what you decide to present as evidence and even *whether* some kinds of evidence should be included in your essay.

As you construct your argument and develop your supporting evidence, then, consider the following questions:

- What specific claims and/or warrants am I making that will need supporting evidence?
- What kinds of evidence are available for those claims or warrants?
- Where can I find such evidence?
- What expectations will my audience have for the evidence I present?
- Have I included sufficient evidence for my audience?
- Does the kind of evidence I have included (factual, firsthand experience, philosophical reasoning, expert testimony) make sense for the claims I am making?

## USING LANGUAGE EFFECTIVELY

In his famous *Rhetoric,* Aristotle wrote that "the way in which a thing is said affects its intelligibility" (*Rhetoric* 165). We might add that the way in which something is stated also affects its impact and, potentially, its persuasive force. Style matters. It matters because it is sometimes a reflection of the fact that you have followed the appropriate conventions for a particular argument — for example, you have used the right legal terminology in a letter to your insurance company about a pending lawsuit. And it matters because the way an idea or opinion is presented can profoundly affect how an audience reacts to it. In constructing an effective argument, you should attend to how you employ the power of language — how you use diction, sentence structure, tone, rhythm, and figures of speech. Usually, these are matters you can focus on once you have defined your topic, developed your claims and supporting evidence, and arranged your argument appropriately. But how you use language can be an important consideration in constructing an argument, even from the very beginning.

As always, audience is a primary consideration as you decide upon an appropriate style for your argument. Different audiences will have different expectations for what is acceptable — and persuasive — when it comes to your use of language in an argument. You will want to use much more formal language in a cover letter to a potential employer (which is a very common kind of argument) than you might in a letter to the editor of your school's newspaper. Similarly, an essay advocating a specific research method in a biology class will require a different kind of language than an argument in favor of decriminalizing marijuana laws for the campus newsletter of a student advocacy organization. The specific medium in which you are presenting your argument will also influence your decisions about language. *Wired* magazine publishes writing that is noticeably different in style and tone from those of the essays that appear in public affairs magazines such as *Commentary.* The audiences for each magazine are different, but so is each magazine's sense of purpose. *Wired* sees itself as techy, edgy, and hip, and the language its writers use reflects that sense of itself. By contrast, *Commentary* is a more erudite, staid publication, and the writing style reflects its seriousness. As you work through your argument, think carefully about what kind of language will be most effective for the specific audience, rhetorical situation, and medium you are encountering.

Even within a specific rhetorical situation you have a great deal of latitude in deciding on the style and tone you will adopt for your argument. Consider the following excerpts from an essay that appeared on *Commondreams.org,* a Web site that publishes essays and news with alternative views about important social and political issues. In the essay from which the following excerpts were taken, the writer, John Borowski, a science teacher from Oregon, harshly criticizes efforts by interest groups to ban school science books that present an environmentalist perspective, and he argues for parents and others to oppose such efforts:

> Remember this phrase: "Texas is clearly one of the most dominant states in setting textbook adoption standards," according to Stephen Driesler, executive director of the American Association of Publisher's school division. And this November the Texas school board inflamed by the anti-environmental science rhetoric by the likes of Texas Citizens for a Sound Economy and Texas Public Policy Foundation (TPPF) may bring Ray Bradbury's "Fahrenheit 451" to life. Recall that "Fahrenheit 451" (the temperature at which paper bursts into flames) depicts a society where independent thought is discouraged, wall-to-wall television and drugs sedate a numb population and "firemen" burn books.
>
> This past fall "book nazis" at the TPPF, led by Republican Senator Phil Gramm's wife (Wendy) and Peggy Venable, director of the 48,000 member Texas Citizens for a Sound Economy, put several environmental textbooks in their "crosshairs." *Environmental Science: Toward a Sustainable Future* published by Massachusetts-based publisher Jones and Bartlett was canned due to political "incorrectness."

We as parents, defenders of the constitution and the vigilant flame-keepers of the light of democracy must rise to meet the challenge.

There is no doubt about how Borowski feels about groups like TPPF. Nor is there any doubt about his goal: to exhort people who share his concerns to action against such efforts to ban books from schools. You might find Borowski's language inflammatory. There is a good chance that he intended it to be so. He certainly knew that the audience for *Commondreams.org* would not likely include many people from organizations such as TPPF. Rather, it would be composed mostly of people who share his political perspective and are likely to be as appalled as he is about these efforts to ban textbooks. Nevertheless, we can ask how those sympathetic readers might react to the strong and very critical language Borowski employs. Will such language be more likely to convince those readers that Borowski is right than a more measured style and a less derogatory tone might be? How does it affect his credibility with his readers? Sometimes, provocative language may be warranted. Is this one of those times?

Posing such questions about your own use of language in constructing your argument can lead to a more effective argument. The rhetorical situation and the issue being addressed will help to determine your approach to using language from the outset. In this case Borowski might well have been angry and concerned enough to have decided, even before he began writing his essay, to adopt a harsh and sarcastic tone. Sometimes, however, you might not have a clear sense of the most appropriate tone or style until after you have completed a draft. And often you will have much less flexibility in adopting a tone or style. (A science report or legal brief, for example, has very strict conventions for such matters.) And bear in mind that at times the choice of a single word can make a great difference in the impact a statement will have on an audience. For example, consider how different this sentence of Borowski's might be if the verb *canned* were replaced by *removed*: *Environmental Science: Toward a Sustainable Future* published by Massachusetts-based publisher Jones and Bartlett was canned due to political "incorrectness."

The passage from Borowski's essay illustrates another set of concerns about language in argument: the use of figurative language. At one point Borowski writes that "the vigilant flame-keepers of the light of democracy must rise to meet the challenge." Here he invokes the common metaphors of light and dark to suggest good opposed to evil, right against wrong. Those who share his concerns are "flame-keepers of the light of democracy," a figurative phrase that is clearly intended not only to address his audience in a positive way, but also to stir them to action. Borowski's is a rather extreme example of the use of figurative language, and it suggests the power such uses of language can have in efforts to move an audience. But figurative language can also have a more subtle but no less important impact in helping to clarify an important point or emphasizing an idea. Here, for example, is *USA Today* sports columnist Mike Lopresti in an essay about the significance of a loss by an American basketball team to Yugoslavia in the 2002 World Championships:

But the big issue is the big picture. The years, the Olympiads, and the World Championships ahead. Because American basketball is like an empty soda cup on the field house floor.

Lopresti's use of a simile — in which he compares the international status of American basketball to an empty soda cup — vividly drives home his point with an appropriate

## FIGURARE LANGUAGE

For an example of the use of metaphor in an argument, see Gregory Cizek's essay, "Unintended Consequences of High Stakes Testing," on page 250. Cizek uses religion as a metaphor for the debates about standardized tests.

image that readers who follow sports will quickly recognize. (Notice, too, the informal style of his writing, which is typical of many sports columnists.)

Writers can also make references to myths, literature, or legends that will have significance for readers. Henry David Thoreau, for example, in criticizing what he believed was the wasteful and wasting lifestyle of his fellow citizens, wrote,

> The twelve labors of Hercules were trifling in comparison to those which my neighbors have undertaken.

The reference to the well-known Greek myth would have driven home his point to his readers. And his use of farm labor as metaphor for life in the following sentence not only emphasized his primary claim but did so elegantly:

> The better part of the man is soon ploughed into soil for compost.

As these examples show, a few carefully chosen words can do a great deal of work as you build your argument.

When you are constructing your own argument, pay close to attention to your tone and style. Asking yourself the following questions can help you determine whether your style and tone are appropriate for your purpose, your audience, and the situation about which you are arguing:

- Is my overall tone likely to offend my intended audience? If so, what specifically about my tone might be offensive to my audience? How can I revise to avoid that problem?
- Have I used appropriate words and phrases? Will my audience understand the key terms I have used? Will my audience expect me to use any special language that I have not used?
- Can I use figurative language in any way to enhance my argument?

# PART II

# WORKING WITH SOURCES

6 | Doing Research

7 | Documenting Your Sources

**6**

# DOING RESEARCH

DOING R

**W**riting effective arguments requires being able to locate and
draw on information that will help
you develop and support your ideas. Often,
writers discover that they must look beyond
themselves to gather the necessary information — They must engage in research.

ESEARCH

You might think of research as what you do when you are assigned long papers that are due at the end of a semester, but there are many other occasions when you engage in research. Any time you look for information before making a decision, you are doing research. If you are trying to decide whether to buy a particular car, for example, you might talk to people who already own the same model, read magazine articles about the car, search the Internet for other drivers' opinions about the car, and take a dealer's vehicle out for a test drive. In other words, you interview people with expertise on your topic, you conduct a periodical search, you search electronic resources, and you undertake trial testing. Academic research requires all of these activities and more, although the degree to which you need to pursue a specific research activity is likely to vary as you move from one project to another. Academic research also requires that you follow specific conventions by using sources responsibly and documenting where your information comes from. But the prospect of doing research shouldn't be intimidating. The key to successful research is simple: Be curious enough about your topic to look in different places until you find what you need.

Traditionally, academic researchers distinguish between primary and secondary research:

1. *Primary research* requires firsthand experimentation or analysis. This is the sort of research that is done in laboratories, in field locations, or in libraries or archives that house original manuscripts. If you interview someone, design and distribute a survey, conduct an experiment, or analyze data that have not been previously published, you are conducting primary research.

2. *Secondary research* involves investigating what other people have already published on a given subject — in other words, finding information about your topic in books, magazine or journal articles, Web sites, and similar sources. College students are usually expected to be proficient at secondary research.

Writing arguments often requires secondary research, and to do such research efficiently, you must know how to develop a search strategy. Different projects will require different strategies. The strategy outlined in this part of the book assumes that you will be writing arguments using material from Part III of *The Informed Argument* and that you will supplement this material with additional information you find elsewhere. As your research needs change from one assignment to another, you will probably use different sources. But the illustrations in this chapter will provide you with sufficient information to help you proceed efficiently when you decide to move beyond the articles gathered in Part III of this book.

## READING CRITICALLY

Secondary research obviously involves reading, but it requires a kind of reading that might differ from the way you read the morning paper or an article about your favorite musician on a Web site. The kind of critical reading that is required for good research is active and engaged; it involves careful thinking about what you are reading. Critical reading is going beyond the obvious meaning of a text to gain a more sophisticated understanding of it. Gaining this understanding involves being able to identify key points, such as an author's thesis, and any points that you find difficult to understand. But beyond understanding the material itself, you should also be prepared to *evaluate* it. As a student, you will sometimes be confronted with more information than you can digest with ease. You will also find that different writers might make contradictory statements. Being able to recognize what material deserves the closest reading and what sources are the most reliable is essential to coping successfully with the many academic demands made on your time. By learning to read critically, you will acquire a skill that will help you in any college course. And you will be developing an ability that will enable you to write more effective arguments.

You can learn to read critically by engaging in four related activities:

- Previewing
- Annotating
- Summarizing
- Synthesizing

## PREVIEWING

Even before you begin to read, you can take steps to help you better understand the reading you are about to undertake and to place it in rhetorical context (see pages 54–58). A quick preview or survey of a written text should give you an idea of how long it will take to read, what the reading will probably reveal, and how useful the reading is likely to be. When you glance through a newspaper to identify which stories you want to read and which you want to skip over, you are practicing a simple type of preview, one that is often guided primarily by your level of interest in various issues. But when previewing reading material in college, it is usually wise to ask yourself some questions that go beyond whether you happen to find a topic appealing:

- *How long is this work?* By checking the length of a work before you begin to read, you can estimate how much reading time the material will demand, based on the speed and ease with which you normally read. The length might also be a clue in determining how useful a text may be. Although quantity is no sure guide to quality, a long work might contain more information that is useful for your topic than a short work. And when doing research, you can usually learn the length of a work before you even hold it in your hand. This information is included in periodical indexes, book catalogs, and many Web sites. (See the illustrations on pages 170–172 and 174.)

- *What can I learn from the title?* Although some titles are too general to convey adequately the content of an article or book, a title often reveals an author's focus. Obviously, an article called "Drugs and the Modern Athlete" will differ in focus from one called "Drug Testing and Corporate Responsibility." Moreover, a title can often indicate the author's point of view. For example, an essay entitled "Keep the Borders Open" tells you quite clearly what the author's position on immigration will be. Be aware, however, that titles can sometimes be misleading.

- *Do I know anything about the author?* Recognizing the names of established authorities in a field becomes easier as you do more reading, but many written sources offer information that can help you estimate an author's credibility even when that author is unfamiliar to you. A magazine article might identify the author at the beginning or the end of the piece or on a separate page (often called "Notes on Contributors" and listed in the table of contents). A biographical sketch of the author can usually be found on a book jacket, and a list of his or her other published works sometimes appears at the front or the back of the book. Anthologies often include introductory headnotes describing the various writers whose work has been selected.

■ *What do I know about the publisher?* An important work can be published by an obscure publisher, and a small magazine might be the first to publish an author who is destined to win a Pulitzer Prize. The publisher's reputation is not an automatic guide to the reliability of a source, but there are a few factors that can help you determine whether a source is likely to be worthwhile. University presses tend to expect a high degree of scholarship, and academic journals usually publish articles only after they have been examined by two or three other experts in that field. If you read widely in periodicals, you will eventually find that some magazines and newspapers consistently reflect political positions that might be characterized as either liberal or conservative. Once you get a sense of the general orientation of such publications, you can usually anticipate what kind of stand will be taken by authors whose articles appear in one of these periodicals. This will help you to be sensitive to any bias that the author might hold on the topic at hand. Once again, remember that you are only making a preliminary estimate when previewing. The best way to judge a work is to read it carefully.

■ *Is there anything else I can discover by skimming through the material?* A quick examination of the text can identify a number of other features that can help you orient yourself to what you are about to read:

1. *Average paragraph length.* Long paragraphs might indicate a densely written text that you will need to read slowly.
2. *Special features.* Tables, figures, or illustrations can provide visual aids for the content.
3. *Subtitles.* Subtitles can provide you with a rough outline of the work and the main topics it addresses.
4. *Abstracts.* In some cases, a writer will provide you with a summary. Articles from scholarly journals are often preceded by an *abstract* (or summary) that can help you understand the article and determine whether it will be useful to you. Many magazines include brief summaries with each article, usually at the beginning of the text. Often, checking the first few and last few paragraphs can give you a good sense of what the article is about and the stance the writer has taken on the topic.
5. *Bibliography.* Finally, check to see whether the work includes a reference list. Scanning a bibliography, noting both how current the research seems and how extensive it is, can help you appraise a writer's scholarship and alert you to other sources that you may want to read on your own.

## ANNOTATING

Marking a text with notes, or *annotating* it, can be a great help when you are trying to understand your reading. Annotation can also help you to discover points that you might want to question when you evaluate this work. One of the advantages of owning a book

or having your own photocopy of an excerpt from a book or magazine is that you
can mark it as much as you wish. When
you are annotating a text that is important
to you, you will usually benefit from reading that text more than once and adding
new annotations with each reading.

When you are able to spend more time
with a text and want to be sure that you understand not only its content but also its
strengths and weaknesses, then additional
annotations are in order:

- Use the margins to define new words
  and identify unfamiliar allusions.
- Write comments that will remind
  you of what is discussed in various
  paragraphs.
- Jot down questions that you might subsequently raise in class or explore in a paper.
- Make cross-references to remind yourself of how various components of the work
  fit together and also identify apparent contradictions within the work.
- Write down your own response to an important point in the text before you lose
  the thought. An annotation of this sort can be useful when you are reviewing material before an exam, and it might very well be the seed from which a paper will
  later grow.

> ## HIGHLIGHTING VERSUS SIMPLE ANNOTATING
>
> Many students use colored highlighter pens to mark passages that seem im-
> portant to their research. Highlighting makes these passages easy to find if
> you need to return to them for specific information or quotations. But high-
> lighters can be hard to write with. So consider reading with a pen or pencil,
> too. As you read, you can make notes or marks in the margins:
>
> - a **check** when a line seems important
> - an **exclamation point** when you find surprising information or an un-
>   usually bold claim
> - a **question mark** when you have trouble understanding a particular
>   passage or find yourself disagreeing with what it says
>
> This simple form of annotation can be done very easily, and if you use a pen-
> cil, you will be able to erase any marks that you later find distracting.

Figure 6-1 shows an annotated excerpt from the Declaration of Independence. As you
examine it, remember that different readers annotate a text in different ways. Some annotations are more thorough and reflective than others, but there are no "correct" responses against which your own annotations must be measured. You might notice
different aspects of a text each time you reread it, so your annotations are likely to accu-
mulate in layers.

## SUMMARIZING

On many occasions, you will be required to summarize what others have said or written — or even what you yourself have said or written. This skill is especially important in
argumentation. You will have to be able to summarize the main arguments of your opponents if you want to write a convincing argument of your own. And researched papers will
become long, obscure, and unwieldy if you lack the ability to summarize your reading.

There is no clear rule to determine which passages are more significant than others.
The first sentence of a paragraph might be important if it introduces a new idea, but
sometimes it is simply a transitional sentence, linking the new paragraph with whatever
has preceded it. Often, a paragraph will have a *topic sentence,* which may appear anywhere
in the paragraph, that states the key idea or point of the paragraph.

When writing a summary, be prepared to *paraphrase* — to restate in your own words
something you've read or heard. There are many different reasons for paraphrasing, and

**FIGURE 6-1**

**An Annotated Text**

1776 | When in the Course of human events, it becomes nec-
essary for one people to dissolve the political bands
which have connected them with another, and to assume among the powers of the earth, the separate and
equal station to which the Laws of Nature and of Nature's God entitle them, a decent respect to the opinions of mankind requires that they should declare the
causes which impel them to the separation.

We hold these truths to be self-evident, that all
men are created equal, that they are endowed by their
Creator with certain unalienable Rights, that among
these are Life, Liberty and the pursuit of Happiness.
That to secure these rights, Governments are instituted among Men, deriving their just powers from the
consent of the governed. That whenever any Form of
Government becomes destructive of these ends it is
the Right of the People to alter or to abolish it, and to
institute new Government, laying its foundation on
such principles and organizing its powers in such
form, as to them shall seem most likely to effect their
Safety and Happiness. Prudence, indeed, will dictate
that Governments long established should not be
changed for light and transient causes; and accordingly
all experience has shewn, that mankind are more disposed to suffer, while evils are sufferable, than to right
themselves by abolishing the forms to which they are
accustomed. But when a long train of abuses and
usurpations, pursuing invariably the same Object
evinces a design to reduce them under absolute
Despotism, it is their right, it is their duty, to throw
off such Government, and to provide new Guards for
their future security. Such has been the patient sufferance of these Colonies; and such is now the necessity
which constrains them to alter their former Systems of
Government. The history of the present King of Great
Britain is a history of repeated injuries and usurpations, all having in direct object the establishment of
an absolute Tyranny over these States. To prove this,
let Facts be submitted to a candid world.

*Handwritten annotations:*

Why should nations have "equal station" when some are more powerful than others?

such as Americans

such as English

Is "Nature's God" different from "God"?

Does this include women ???

Why "self-evident"?

Couldn't he prove them?

Permanent, "not to be separated"

If the rights to life & liberty are "unalienable" how come we have capital punishment and prisons?

So the Civil War was ok?

wrongful seizure

What's the difference between a "right" and a "duty"?

George III (ruled from 1760 to 1820)

impartial

Why is the capitalization so weird?

you've probably been practicing this skill for a long time —
for example, paraphrasing the words of others to soften
an unpleasant fact. But in writing a summary, you
should paraphrase only to make complex ideas more easily
understandable.

Summarizing requires good editorial judgment. A writer
has to be able to distinguish what is essential from what is
not. If the material being summarized has a particular bias,
a good summary should indicate that the bias is part of the
work in question. *But writers should not interject their own
opinions into a summary of someone else's work.* The tone of
a summary should be neutral. You might choose to summarize someone's work so that you can criticize it later, but
do not confuse summary with criticism. When summarizing, you are taking the role of helping other writers to
speak for themselves. Don't let your own ideas get in the
way.

Summaries vary in length, depending on the length and
complexity of the original material and on how much time or
space is available for summarizing it. When summary is being
used as a preliminary to some other type of work, such as argument or analysis, it is especially important to be concise.
For example, if you are summarizing an argument before offering a counterargument of your own, you may be limited to
a single paragraph. The general rule to follow is this: Try to do
justice to whatever you are summarizing in as few words as possible, and make sure that
you have a legitimate reason for writing any summary that goes on for more than a page
or two.

Experienced writers know that summary is a skill worth practicing. If you find summary difficult, try the method described in the sidebar on page 158.

## SUMMARY VERSUS PARAPHRASE

The distinction between summary and paraphrase can be
subtle and sometimes confusing, but it is important to
understand. A *summary* is a brief statement, usually no
more than a paragraph or two, summing up the main
points or ideas of a text. A summary may include direct
quotations from the original text, and it will often include
paraphrase.

A *paraphrase*, by contrast, is a restatement — a re-
phrasing — in your own words of something you've read.
A paraphrase can be as long as the original material; under some circumstances it can even be longer.

A paraphrase of a text is *not* a summary of it. In a paraphrase you restate a specific quotation or passage from
a book or article in your own words; you don't necessarily
sum up the entire book or article, as you would in a
summary.

Summary is important in research in part because it
enables you to make the ideas in a long work manageable and accessible in your own essay. Paraphrase is important because it helps you understand what you have
read and avoid plagiarizing (see page 161).

## SYNTHESIZING

Synthesizing ideas from two or more different sources is an essential skill in constructing effective arguments. Synthesis requires identifying related material in two or more
works and tying them together smoothly. Synthesis is often an extension of summary
because writers may need to summarize various sources before they can relate these
sources to one another. However, synthesis does not necessarily require you to cover *all*
the major points of the individual sources. You might go through an entire article or
book and identify only one point that relates to another work you have read. And the
relationships involved in your synthesis may be of various kinds. For example, two different authors might have made the same claim, or one might provide specific information that supports a generalization made by the other. On the other hand, one
author might provide information that makes another author's generalization seem inadequate or even wrong.

When reading material that you need to synthesize, ask yourself, "How does this material relate to whatever else I have already read on this topic?" If you are unable to answer this question, consider a few more specific questions:

- Does the second of two works offer support for the first, or does it reflect an entirely different thesis?
- If the two sources share a similar position, do they arrive at a similar conclusion by entirely different means or do they overlap at any points?
- Would it be easier to compare the two works or to contrast them?

This process of identifying similarities and differences is essentially what synthesis is all about.

When you have determined the points that link your various sources to one another, you are ready to write a synthesis. One challenge in writing a synthesis is organizing it. For example, suppose you have read four articles on the subject of AIDS written, respectively, by a scientist, a clergyman, a gay activist, and a government official. You were struck by how differently these four writers responded to the AIDS epidemic. Although they all agreed that AIDS is a serious problem, each writer advanced a different proposal for fighting the disease. Your synthesis might begin with an introductory paragraph that includes a thesis statement such as "Although there is widespread agreement that AIDS is a serious problem, there is no consensus about how this problem can be solved." Each of the next four paragraphs could then be devoted to a brief summary of one of the different points of view. A final paragraph might emphasize the relationship that exists among the several

## A METHOD FOR SUMMARIZING

A summary should be clear, concise, and easy to read. There is no right way to summarize a text, but here is a general method for summarizing that is straightforward and useful:

1. Identify the topic sentences of the paragraphs you are summarizing, and mark any important supporting details. Limit yourself to marking no more than one or two sentences per paragraph.

2. Copy the material you have noted onto a separate sheet of paper. What you now have are the notes for a summary: a collection of short quotations that are unlikely to flow smoothly together.

3. Read over the quotations you have compiled, and look for lines that seem too long and ideas that seem unnecessarily complicated. Paraphrase these lines. As you do, you might also be able to include important details that appeared elsewhere in the paragraph. Keep in mind that you should not have to restate everything that someone else has written. A summary can include direct quotations, as long as the quotations are relatively short and have a clarity that you yourself cannot surpass.

4. Reread your paraphrasing and any quotations that you have included. Look for gaps between sentences, where the writing seems awkward or choppy. Eliminate all repetition, and subordinate any ideas that do not need to stand alone as separate sentences.

5. Check to be sure that any direct quotations are placed within quotation marks.

6. Rearrange any sentences that would flow better in a different sequence, and add transitional phrases wherever they can help smooth the way from one idea to the next.

7. Make sure that your sentences follow in a clear and readable sequence, and correct any errors in grammar, spelling, or syntax.

8. Read over your summary one more time, making sure that the content accurately reflects the nature of the text you are summarizing.

sources, either by reviewing the major points of disagreement among them or by emphasizing one or two points about which everyone agreed. Your outline for this type of synthesis would be as follows:

PARAGRAPH ONE:          Introduction
PARAGRAPH TWO:          Summary of first writer (scientist)
PARAGRAPH THREE:        Summary of second writer (clergyman)
PARAGRAPH FOUR:         Summary of third writer (gay activist)
PARAGRAPH FIVE:         Summary of fourth writer (government official)
PARAGRAPH SIX:          Conclusion

Any good outline allows for some flexibility. Depending on the material and what you want to say, your synthesis might have fewer than or more than six paragraphs. For example, if two of your sources were especially long and complex, there is no reason why you couldn't devote two paragraphs to each of them, even though you were able to summarize your other two sources within single paragraphs.

An alternative method for organizing a synthesis involves linking two or more writers within paragraphs that focus on specific issues or points. This type of organization is especially useful when you have detected a number of similarities that you want to emphasize. Suppose that you have read six essays about increasing the minimum age for obtaining a driver's license. Three writers favored increasing the minimum age, at least to 20, for much the same reasons; three writers opposing such an increase offered arguments that they shared in common. Your assignment is to identify the arguments most used by people who favor increasing the minimum driving age and those most used by people who oppose it. Your outline for synthesizing this material might be organized like this:

PARAGRAPH ONE:          Introduction
PARAGRAPH TWO:          One argument in favor of increasing the minimum
                        driving age that was made by different writers
PARAGRAPH THREE:        A second argument in favor of increasing the mini-
                        mum driving age that was made by different writers
PARAGRAPH FOUR:         One argument against increasing the minimum driv-
                        ing age that was made by different writers
PARAGRAPH FIVE:         A second argument against increasing the minimum
                        driving age that was made by different writers
PARAGRAPH SIX:          Conclusion

There are other ways of organizing a passage of synthesis in your argument, but however you do so, the key is to present the ideas of the other writers clearly and draw connections among them in a way that will support your argument.

## TAKING NOTES

Note taking is essential to research. Unfortunately, few researchers can tell in advance exactly what material they will want to include in their final paper. Especially during the early stages of your research, you might record information that will seem unnecessary when you have become more expert on your topic and have a clear thesis. So you will probably have to discard some of your notes when you are ready to write your paper.

It is important to distinguish between *note taking* and *annotating*, which we discussed on page 154. Annotating involves making notes about a specific text; note taking involves keeping notes on all your sources, ideas, and information for a single essay or project.

Some writers simply make notes in notebooks, on looseleaf, or on legal pads. Many writers now make their notes using a word processing program such as Microsoft Word. Such programs make it easy to keep separate files for different kinds of notes. (There are also specialized computer programs that are designed to help researchers organize their notes.) Unless you have a laptop computer, however, using a word processing program might not be practical if you must take notes in a library or somewhere else outside your home. Newer technologies called *personal digital assistants* are small but powerful alternatives to computers; many of them allow users to make notes.

A more traditional note card system can also be an effective means of taking notes. Such a system allows for flexibility when you are ready to move from research to composition. By spreading out your note cards on a desk or table, you can study how they best fit together. You can arrange and rearrange the cards until you have them in a meaningful sequence. This system works, however, only when you have the self-restraint to limit yourself to recording one fact, one idea, or one quotation on each card, as shown in Figure 6-2. Whether you use a note card system, a word processing program, or some other system of note taking, sorting your notes is one of the easiest ways to determine whether you have enough material to write a good paper.

**FIGURE 6-2**

**A Sample Note Card**

This note card includes a quotation from the writer's source. Notice that the topic and source information are included at the top of the card.

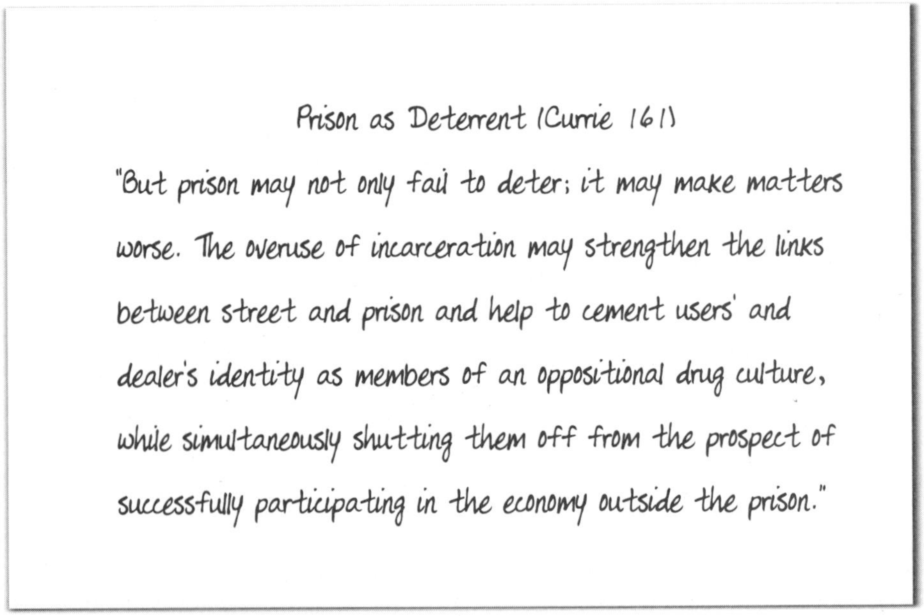

Prison as Deterrent (Currie 161)

"But prison may not only fail to deter; it may make matters worse. The overuse of incarceration may strengthen the links between street and prison and help to cement users' and dealer's identity as members of an oppositional drug culture, while simultaneously shutting them off from the prospect of successfully participating in the economy outside the prison."

## AVOIDING PLAGIARISM

Plagiarism is a legitimate concern for anyone engaged in research. To plagiarize (from *plagiarius,* the Latin word for "kidnapper") is to steal — to be guilty of what the Modern Language Association calls "intellectual theft." Plagiarism is also a form of cheating; someone who plagiarizes a paper is losing out on an opportunity for learning in addition to running a serious risk. In the workplace intellectual theft (of an essay, a song, or a proposal) can lead to lawsuits and heavy financial penalties. In a college or university students who commit intellectual theft face penalties ranging from a failing grade on a paper to expulsion from the school. They are not the only ones who are hurt, however. In addition to hurting themselves, plagiarists injure the people they steal from; the professors who take the time to read and respond to the work of writers who are not their own students; classmates, whose grades might suffer from comparison if a clever plagiarism goes undetected; and the social fabric of the academic community, which becomes torn when values such as honesty and mutual respect are no longer cherished.

The grossest form of plagiarism involves submitting someone else's paper as your own. Services that sell papers advertise on many college campuses, and obliging friends or roommates can sometimes be persuaded to hand over one of their own papers for resubmission. In cyberspace the World Wide Web provides ample opportunities for downloading a paper written by someone else. Those who are electronically sophisticated can also piece a paper together by lifting paragraphs from a number of sources on the Internet. No one engages in such overt plagiarism accidentally.

On the other hand, it is also possible to plagiarize without meaning to do so. Students sometimes plagiarize by drawing too heavily on their sources. They might forget to put quotation marks around lines that they have taken word for word from another source, or they might think they don't need to quote if they have changed a few words. The important point to keep in mind is that you must give credit for the *ideas* of others, as well as for their *words,* when you are using sources in your writing. If you take most of the information another writer has provided and repeat it in essentially the same pattern, you are only a half-step away from copying the material, even if you have changed the exact wording.

Here is an example:

Original Source

Hawthorne's political ordeal, the death of his mother — and whatever guilt he may have harbored on either score — afforded him an understanding of the secret psychological springs of guilt. *The Scarlet Letter* is the book of a changed man. Its deeper insights have nothing to do with orthodox morality or religion — or the universal or allegorical applications of a moral. The greatness of the book is related to its sometimes fitful characterizations of human nature and the author's almost uncanny intuitions: his realization of the bond between psychological malaise and physical illness, the nearly perfect, if sinister, outlining of the psychological techniques Chillingworth deployed against his victim.

Plagiarism

Nathaniel Hawthorne understood the psychological sources of guilt. His experience in politics and the death of his mother brought him deep insights that don't have anything to do with formal religion or morality. The greatness of *The Scarlet Letter* comes from its characters and the author's brilliant intuitions: Hawthorne's perception of the link between psychological and physical illness and his almost perfect description of the way Roger Chillingworth persecuted his victim.

This student has simplified the original material, changing some of its wording. But he is still guilty of plagiarism. Pretending to offer his own analysis of *The Scarlet Letter,* he in fact owes all of his ideas to another writer, who is unacknowledged. Even the organization of the passage has been followed. This "paraphrase" would still be considered plagiarism even if it ended with a reference to the original source (page 307 of *Nathaniel Hawthorne in His Times,* by James R. Mellow). A reference or footnote would not reveal the full extent to which this student is indebted to his source.

Here is an acceptable version:

Paraphrase

As James R. Mellow has argued, *The Scarlet Letter* reveals a profound understanding of guilt. It is a great novel because of its insight into human nature — not because of some moral about adultery. The most interesting character is probably Roger Chillingworth because of the way he was able to make Rev. Dimmesdale suffer (307).

This student has not only made a better effort to paraphrase the original material, but has also introduced it with a reference to the original writer. The introductory reference to Mellow, coupled with the subsequent page reference, clearly shows us that Mellow deserves the credit for the ideas in this passage. Additional bibliographical information about this source is provided by the list of works cited at the end of the paper:

Mellow, James. *Nathaniel Hawthorne in His Times.* Boston: Houghton, 1980.

One final caution: It is possible to subconsciously remember a piece of someone else's phrasing and inadvertently repeat it. You would be guilty of plagiarism if the words in question embodied a critically important idea or reflect a distinctive style or turn of phrase. When you revise your draft, look for such unintended quotations. If you use them, show who deserves the credit for them, and *remember to put quoted material within quotation marks.*

## FINDING RELEVANT MATERIAL

Up to this point in the chapter we have been discussing how to read and use sources. Obviously, you must have relevant sources before you can read them critically and use them effectively in your argument. Finding those relevant sources encompasses an important set of research skills.

### GETTING STARTED

One of the first goals of any researcher is to decide where to focus. The more specific your search, the greater is your chance for efficiently locating the material you need and then writing a well-supported paper. When you know what you are looking for, you can gauge what you should read and what you can probably afford to pass over — a great advantage when you are confronted by the staggering amount of information that a good college library, or the Internet, makes available.

In many cases you will begin your research with your topic already identified. For instance, you might be assigned to write about a specific issue. Or your class might have discussed an issue that interests you enough to want to write an argument about it. Or you might be addressing a problem for which you are seeking a solution, such as a controversy on campus involving a dorm policy or an inflammatory editorial in the student newspaper. In such cases you have a good starting point for your research.

But sometimes you might find yourself in a situation in which you have no clear topic. In such a situation you can take steps to identify a workable topic for your argument. Sometimes, for example, a specific topic will emerge as you scan information on your subject area periodical indexes, online databases, and search engines for navigating the Internet. By beginning with a general idea of what you plan to write about and then using key words to check different sources, you can refine your topic or even discover topics that have generated recent interest — topics that will interest you as well. You can judge, at this point, which topics would be the most manageable ones to research. As you proceed, keep two general rules in mind:

1. If you are overwhelmed by the number of citations you find in your research area, you probably need to *narrow your topic.*
2. If you have difficulty finding material, you might need to *broaden your search.*

If you're unsure about your topic, consider discussing it with other people — in particular, your instructor. (For additional information on choosing a topic, see pages 115–116.)

## AVOIDING SELECTIVE RESEARCH

Although you might have a tentative thesis in mind when you begin your search, it's often a good idea to delay formulating your final thesis until your research is complete. Think of your search strategy as an attempt to answer a question. For instance, suppose you are writing an argument about drug-related crime. You can proceed as if you are addressing the following question: "What can be done to reduce drug-related crime?" This is very different from starting your research with your thesis predetermined. If you begin already convinced that the way to reduce drug-related crime is to legalize drugs, you might be tempted to take notes only from sources that advocate this position, rejecting as irrelevant any source that discusses problems with this approach. In this case research is not leading to greater knowledge or understanding. On the contrary, it is being used to reinforce personal beliefs that might border on prejudice. Even if you feel strongly about the issue at hand, keeping an open mind during your research can often lead to a better understanding of that issue — and a more effective argument.

We have seen that anticipating the opposition (see sidebar on page 117) is important even in short arguments. It is no less important in a researched paper. Almost any topic worth investigating will yield facts and ideas that could support different conclusions. It is possible to take significantly different positions on issues such as immigration law, environmental protection, and education. These are extremely complex issues, and it is important to remember that fact as you conduct your research. Your own research might ultimately support a belief that you already hold, but if you proceed as if you are genuinely trying to solve a problem or answer a question, your research might deepen your understanding of the issue and lead you to realize that you were previously misinformed. For this reason, try not to overlook relevant material just because you don't agree with it. Ultimately, your argument will be stronger if you recognize that disagreement about your topic exists and then demonstrate why you favor one position over another or show how different positions can be reconciled.

With this advice in mind you can more effectively make use of the many resources now available to you as you research your topic. In addition to more traditional sources such as books and articles in magazines, journals, and newspapers, you have access to an astonishing amount of information on the Internet. In the remainder of this chapter we will discuss how best to use these resources.

## USING THE INTERNET

The kind of information that can be found on the Internet is incredibly diverse; it includes library catalogs, government documents and data, newspaper and magazine articles, excerpts from books and even entire books, and all kinds of information and material published by commercial organizations, special interest groups, and even individuals who wish to make contact with others who share their concerns.

Today, most of us access all this information through the World Wide Web, which is a graphical interface for navigating the Internet. Current software, such as Internet Explorer or Netscape Navigator, makes it very easy to browse the Web. But the enormous scale of the Web can also make it difficult to find relevant information easily. The very richness of the Web can be its drawback, and searching for the right information can be time consuming and sometimes frustrating. You might find yourself scrolling through an endless series of documents and losing sight of your main objective while pursuing an elusive loose end. For this reason it's important to understand some basic principles for searching the Web.

You should also be aware of a key difference between much of the material published on the Internet and material published in print. Writers who publish in print receive professional editorial support. Editors decide what material is worth printing and then assist writers in preparing work for publication. Most of the Internet operates without editors, however. Anyone with a little knowledge of computers can publish whatever comes to mind. In a sense the Internet is wonderfully democratic, and many people have enjoyed activities such as creating a Web site for their cat and connecting with other cat fanciers. On the other hand, the Internet also carries a great deal of misinformation, hate speech, and crank editorials. When searching the Internet, you must carefully evaluate the material you locate and recognize that this material can range from first-rate scholarship to utter trash.

Despite these potential problems, the Internet is an increasingly important resource for research. The challenge is finding your way through the huge amount of material that is floating around in cyberspace. Computer experts have developed systems called *search engines* that work as indexing services for the World Wide Web. Among the most commonly used today are Google, Yahoo!, Alta Vista, Infoseek, and Lycos. Once you learn how to use one of these systems, you can easily learn how to adapt to the others. No search engine provides a complete, error-free index to electronic documents, so you might have to use more than one system, just as you would use more than one periodical index when looking for information in your library.

Search engines require you to identify your research topic by typing key words or phrases into an entry box. After you have entered your search terms, you will be given a list of Web sites that match your request. Each of these sites can, in turn, lead you to others. Many search engines also enable you to refine your search by entering more specific information, such as dates or kinds of publications (see Figure 6-3). And Internet directories allow you to browse through broad subject categories to find subtopics that you might be looking for (see Figure 6-4). Like other electronic resources, search engines provide help screens with

## LEARNING TO SEARCH THE WEB

To learn more about efficiently searching the World Wide Web, check to see whether your library or academic computing office provides workshops or similar services. These workshops can help you learn about various search engines available on the Web as well as sophisticated strategies for searching the Web.

## EVALUATING INTERNET RESOURCES

The advice we provided earlier about reading critically (see page 152) applies to Internet resources as well. But because of the dizzying variety of material on the Internet and the fact that anyone can publish anything on a Web site, you might have to take special care in evaluating the reliability of information you find on the Web. Most libraries have information on their own Web sites about evaluating Internet resources. Here are a few very good ones:

- *Evaluating Web Resources*, Wolfgram Memorial Library, Widener University: http://www2.widener.edu/Wolfgram-Memorial-Library/webevaluation/webeval.htm
- *Evaluating Web Resources*, Cornell University Library: http://campusgw.library.cornell.edu/t/help/res_strategy/evaluating/evaluate.html
- *Thinking Critically About World Wide Web Resources*, UCLA College Library: http://www.library.ucla.edu/libraries/college/help/critical/index.htm

FIGURE 6-3

**FIGURE 6-3**

**Google's Advanced Search Screen**

The advanced search screen enables you to refine your search, making it more efficient.

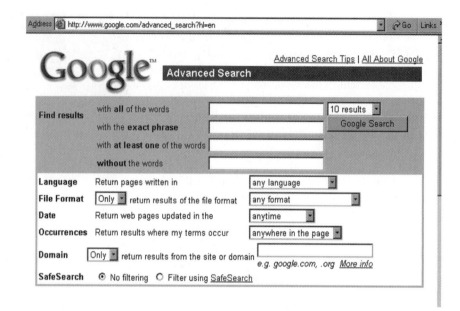

**FIGURE 6-4**

**The Introductory Screen for the Google Web Directory**

One of the most popular search engines, Google is easy to use and can be a powerful tool for research on the Web.

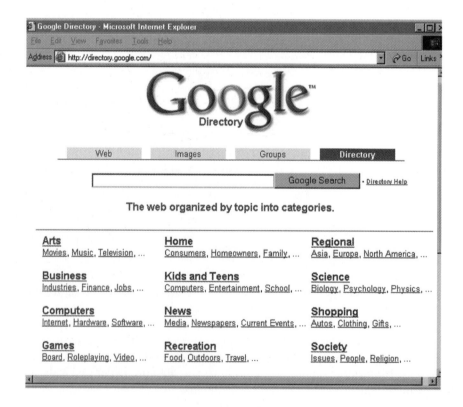

instructions on the best ways to search. These in-structions change as the technology changes, and it is wise to review them whenever you are in doubt about how to proceed.

Remember that the Internet is constantly chang-ing. New sites are launched on the Web constantly — literally every minute. And new search systems are always being developed; hundreds now exist. Because the Internet contains so much information, some researchers make the mistake of thinking that anything they need to find must be available elec-tronically. Not every scholar chooses to make com-pleted work available electronically, so you can miss important material if you try to do all your research on the Internet.

At the same time many resources that have tra-ditionally been available only in print form are be-coming available on the Internet. Many journals, newspapers, and magazines now offer full-text ar-ticles online, which means that you don't always have to go to your library to get a copy of an arti-cle you might need for your research. In addition, some publications appear only online. For exam-ple, *Slate* magazine and *Salon.com* are two re-spected publications that do not appear in print form; you can access their articles only through the Internet. And organizations of all types sponsor online archives and other sources related to their areas of interest. For example, you can visit the Web site of the U.S. Department of Health and Human Services to find a great deal of information on a range of topics related to health issues (see Figure 6-5). Thousands of such sites exist on the Web. Once you learn to navigate the Web efficiently and to evaluate Internet sources carefully, the wealth of informa-tion that is available online can enrich your research.

## TIPS FOR EFFICIENT WEB SEARCHING

Doing research on the Web is more than visiting a popular search engine such as Google and typing in your topic. Here are a few suggestions for making your Web searching more efficient and successful:

■ Visit your library's Web site to see whether it has information about searching the Web. Many libraries offer excellent ad-vice for using the Web effectively.

■ Read the search tips that are usually available on the Web sites of search engines. These tips can help you learn to use specific search engines more efficiently.

■ Learn how to use *Boolean operators* in your searches. Most search tools support Boolean, or logical, operators, such as *and, or,* and *not.* These terms help you narrow your search so that the search tools will return the most relevant docu-ments. Most search engines include basic instructions for us-ing Boolean terms.

■ Learn to recognize Internet *domains* in Web addresses, such as .com, .edu., .gov, and .org. Understanding what these do-mains mean can help you decide whether to visit specific Web sites that you find with a search engine.

## SEARCHING FOR MAGAZINE AND JOURNAL ARTICLES

Magazines, bulletins, and scholarly journals are all called *periodicals* because they are pub-lished on a regular schedule — once a week, once a month, and so on. Although re-searchers can seldom afford to rely exclusively on periodicals for information, the indexes and abstracting services that enable them to locate relevant periodical articles are essential in most searches. Periodicals often include the most current information about a research area, and they can alert you to other important sources through book reviews as well as through the citations that support individual articles. In addition, as we noted in the pre-vious section, many periodicals are now available on the Internet, which makes them eas-ily accessible to researchers.

The best-known periodical index is the *Readers' Guide to Periodical Literature,* which is now available online through OLLC FirstSearch (a service that provides access to over

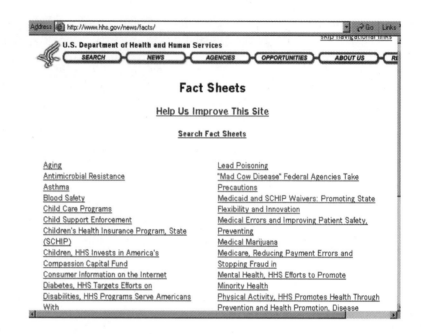

**FIGURE 6-5**

**Web Site of the U.S. Department of Health and Human Services**

Fact sheets available at this Web site contain easily accessible health-related information.

forty electronic indexes), in addition to being published in the familiar book form available in your library. The *Readers' Guide* covers hundreds of magazines; material is indexed by subject and by author. Because it indexes popular mass-circulation periodicals, it can lead you to articles that are relatively short and accessible. InfoTrac, another computerized index for periodicals in general circulation, offers a similar advantage.

Most college libraries have a variety of other indexes that will point you toward more specialized material, and you should be prepared to move beyond the *Readers' Guide* in any serious search. Almost every academic field has its own index available in regularly printed volumes, and most electronic versions of these indexes are now including *abstracts* (short summaries of the articles indexed).

If you have difficulty finding material or if you are in difficulty because you have found too much, you can broaden or narrow an online search by using *Boolean operators* — words that instruct a database to narrow a search or to broaden it. For example, searching for *drugs* in a database would yield an unwieldy amount of material, much of which might be irrelevant to your topic. If you were interested in, say, the relationship between drug use and violent crime, you might enter *drugs and crime* as your search terms. In that case your search would yield only articles that mention both drugs and crime. To narrow your search further, you could enter

**SPECIALIZED INDEXES**

The following indexes can be useful if you're searching for information specific to an academic discipline or a profession. Your college library will probably have several or all of these.

| | |
|---|---|
| *Applied Science and Technology Index* | *Business Periodicals Index* |
| *Index to Legal Periodicals* | *Philosopher's Index* |
| *Art Index* | *Education Index* |
| *Index Medicus* (for medicine) | *Science Citation Index* |
| *Biological and Agricultural Index* | *Humanities Index* |
| *Music Index* | *Social Sciences Index* |
| *MLA International Bibliography* | *Essay and General Literature Index* |

additional search terms, such as *gender,* which would limit the search to articles about gender in drug use and crime. Adding *women,* or *youth,* on the other hand, would identify articles mentioning both drugs and crime and either women or youth. By playing with terms in this way and discovering how much material is available on any given combination, you can find a specific topic for a researched paper within a larger subject area.

The advantage of consulting the *Readers' Guide* online is readily apparent from the accompanying illustrations. After instructing the computer to search for the subject *globalization,* the person conducting this online search in 2002 discovered 1,621 articles, many of them published just a few weeks or months earlier, citations that would not be available in the print version of

## USING BOOLEAN OPERATORS

*Boolean,* or logical, operators are words that command a search engine to define a search in a specific way. The most common Boolean operators are *AND, OR,* and *NOT.* Understanding how they work can help you search the Internet and databases more efficiently:

- *AND* tells the search engine to find only sources that contain both words in your search. For example, if you entered *sports AND steroids,* your search would yield sources that deal with steroids in sports and would not necessarily return sources that deal with steroids or sports in general.
- *OR* broadens a search by telling the search engine to return sources for either term in your search. Entering *sports OR steroids,* for instance, would yield sources on either of those topics.
- *NOT* can narrow a search by telling the search engine to exclude sources containing a specific keyword. For example, entering *steroids NOT sports* would yield sources on steroids but not sources that deal with steroids in sports.

In addition, keep these tips in mind:

- You can use parentheses for complex searches: *(sports AND steroids) NOT (medicine OR law);* this entry would narrow the search to specific kinds of sources about sports and steroids that did not include medical or legal matters.
- With most search engines you can use quotation marks to find a specific phrase. For example, *"steroid use in sports"* would return sources that included that exact phrase.
- Generally, you should capitalize Boolean operators.

the *Readers' Guide* (see Figure 6-6). To discover additional articles through printed volumes would require consulting other volumes and following up on a range of cross-references. A computer can do that task within seconds.

Be aware, however, that the *Readers' Guide* will usually locate sources that many college professors are likely to consider inappropriate for academic assignments, such as *People* or *Time.* If you have access to the *Readers' Guide* through FirstSearch, you should also have access to other databases that can help you locate the kind of material you would locate through the *Readers' Guide* as well as much more scholarly work.

Although there is some overlapping from one index to another, each index covers different periodicals. The records that you find in one will usually vary from the records that you find in another. This is worth remembering, for two reasons:

1. If you cannot locate any material in the past few years of one index, you can try another index that seems as if it might include records on your subject.
2. Many subjects of general interest will be found in more than one index. If you consult more than one index, you are increasing the likelihood of being exposed to different points of view.

Let's say you're searching for material on drugs and crime. Of the various specialized indexes that can lead you exclusively to material in professional journals, the *Social Sciences Index* is especially useful for locating information on such topics, since it indexes

**FIGURE 6-6**

*Reader's Guide Abstracts*

The online version of the *Reader's Guide* provides citations and sometimes direct access to articles you locate when using this service.

literature in sociology, psychology, and political science. Like the *Readers' Guide,* it can be consulted in bound volumes or online, with the online service providing abstracts as well as citations.

Figure 6-7 shows the results of a search of *Social Science Abstracts* on FirstSearch. The screen displays the first four of 515 citations located in a search for articles on the relationship between drug use and crime. The first article listed is from the *Journal of the American Academy of Child and Adolescent Psychiatry,* a scholarly publication that would not be indexed by the *Readers' Guide.* A journal like this is likely to provide more credible data on this topic than an issue of a magazine like *People* for an academic assignment. Figure 6-8 shows the abstract from this article, which can easily be accessed from the main list of articles shown in Figure 6-7.

Very often, if you are using a database such as FirstSearch through your library's Web site, the search results will indicate whether your library has the articles you are interested in — a great convenience when you're doing research.

## SEARCHING FOR NEWSPAPER ARTICLES

You can also access many newspaper articles by using a database such as FirstSearch, or you can use an Internet search engine to find archives of articles that are now maintained online by many newspapers. The *Readers' Guide* will also lead you to some newspaper articles. For a serious electronic search of newspaper articles on a research topic involving a public policy issue, use Lexis-Nexis, a powerful database that searches for news articles and legal documents worldwide, often locating material only a day or two after its

FIGURE 6-7

**Results of a Search of *Social Sciences Abstracts* on FirstSearch**

This screen shows the first four of 515 articles on drug-related crime located with FirstSearch.

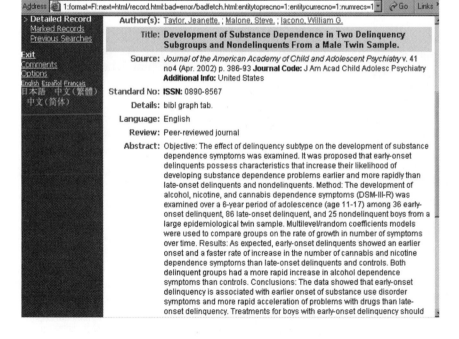

FIGURE 6-8

**Sample Abstract from *Social Sciences Abstracts***

This screen shows the abstract from one of the articles listed in Figure 6-7.

FIGURE 6-9

Search Screen in the
Lexis-Nexis Academic
Database

The Lexis-Nexis database indexes many newspapers and
magazines that are not listed in
other databases.

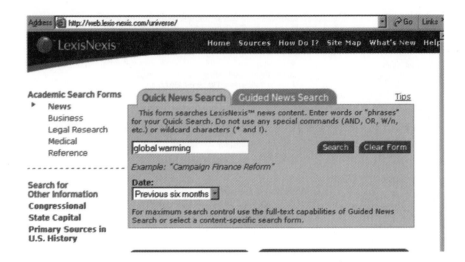

publication. Lexis-Nexis now organizes its vast databases into several subdatabases, such
as Lexis-Nexis Congressional and Lexis-Nexis Academic. Figure 6-9 shows an introductory screen for the Lexis-Nexis academic database, which, as you can see, is broken down
into additional categories (news, business, etc. — visible on the left side of the screen).
From this screen you can narrow or expand your search by limiting yourself to articles
from today, a week ago, or two years ago. If you were writing an argument on global
warming, for example, you could enter those terms. Figure 6-10 shows the results of that

FIGURE 6-10

The Results of a
Search on Lexis-Nexis

This search of Lexis-Nexis found
700 articles on global warming.

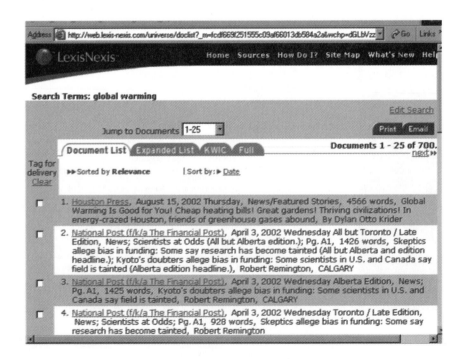

search, limited to the previous six months. By clicking on the tabs above the list, you can choose whether to view citations only, citations with summaries, and — when you find something that seems especially promising — the full text of the article, which you might then be able to print out, depending on the nature of the service your library provides. (Note: Not all libraries have access to Lexis-Nexis, and some that do have it charge for this service.)

Your college or community library might also provide you with the equipment to search online for articles in a local paper. If you are unable to search for newspapers online, look for printed volumes of the *New York Times Index,* which has been published annually since 1913 and is updated frequently throughout the current year.

## USING ABSTRACTING SERVICES

Although many electronic indexing services such as *Readers' Guide Abstracts* and *Social Science Abstracts* are now offering summaries of current articles along with the citations a search identifies, they do not consistently provide abstracts for all of the material they index. There are other services that specialize in abstracts. Important abstracting services in printed volumes include the following:

| | |
|---|---|
| *Abstracts in Anthropology* | *Biological Abstracts* |
| *Historical Abstracts* | *Psychological Abstracts* |
| *Academic Abstracts* | *Chemical Abstracts* |
| *Physics Abstracts* | *Sociological Abstracts* |

These abstracts are organized in different ways, and you might need to consult one volume for the index and another volume for the matching abstracts. When using bound volumes, consult the instructions that can be found within them. However, there is no reason to consult printed volumes of abstracts unless you do not have access to electronic databases. Almost all college libraries provide access to at least a few electronic databases. Ask your reference librarian whether there are electronic resources in your library that are appropriate to your research.

Because it can be hard to tell from a title whether an article will be useful, abstracts offer an advantage over simple bibliographical citations. The summary provided by an abstracting service can help you to decide whether you want to read the entire article. Keep in mind that an abstract written in English does not mean that the article itself is also in English; be alert for notations such as *(Chin), (Germ),* or *(Span),* which indicate when an article is published in another language. Also, remember that good researchers never pretend to have read an entire article when they have read only an abstract of it. Use abstracts as a tool for locating material to read, not as a substitute for a full-length reading.

## LOOKING FOR BOOKS

The convenience of the Internet and online databases can tempt you to avoid looking for books on a subject. Yet books remain essential to research. Although the books you locate in your library might vary in quality, they often represent the final and most prestigious result of someone else's research. It is common, for example, for a scholar to publish several journal articles in the process of writing a book. Much of the best information you can find appears somewhere in a book, and you should not assume that your research subject is so new or so specialized that your library will not have books on it. A topic that seems new to you is not necessarily new to others.

Because books take time to read, some researchers look for books at the beginning of their search. Others turn to books after they have investigated the periodical literature to focus their interests and identify the most influential works in their field. Whenever you choose to look for books on your topic, be sure that you do so well before your paper is due. A book full of important information will be of little help if you haven't left yourself time to read it.

Although some libraries still use catalogs consisting of alphabetically arranged cards in multiple drawers, most college libraries now have electronic card catalogs, which are usually accessible both within the library and via the Internet. This accessibility makes it convenient to search the library catalog without having to go to the library itself. Computerized catalogs enable users to search for books by author, title, or subject. Most of these catalogs also permit a search for material via a call number or a *key word* — a word that is likely to appear somewhere in the title or description. In addition to providing all of the information about a book that could be obtained from a card catalog, computerized catalogs are usually designed to report whether the book is currently available.

Figure 6-11 shows the catalog entry for a book entitled *Urban Sprawl.* It contains information about the author, when and where the book was published, and whether it is available in the library. Every library has its own system for displaying information about the books it holds. As you do research, you should expect to find variations on this example. The precise format of a computerized entry depends on the program employed by

**FIGURE 6-11**

**Online Library Catalog**

This screen shows an entry for a book that was found by searching this library's online catalog.

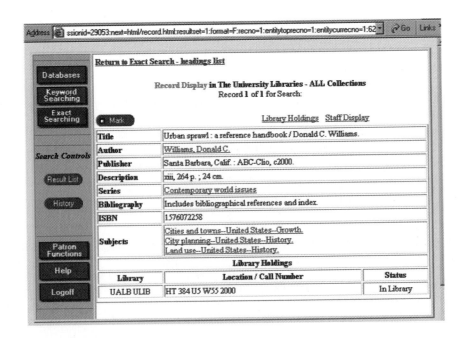

the library you are using. (If your library still uses index cards in a card catalog, you will find the same basic information displayed on those cards.)

There is no foolproof method for determining the quality or usefulness of a book from a catalog entry. The best way to judge a book's usefulness is to read it. But a catalog listing can reveal some useful clues if you know how to find them:

- *The date of publication.* There is no reason to assume that new books are always better than old books, but unless you are researching a historical or literary topic, you should be careful not to rely heavily on material that may be out of date.
- *The length of the book.* A book with 300 pages is likely to provide more information than a book half that size. A book with a bibliography might help you to find more material.
- *The reputation of the publisher.* Academic publishers generally publish books that have gone through rigorous review, which is not always the case with some commercial publishers.

## USING OTHER LIBRARY RESOURCES

Because of the great amount of material being published, libraries save space in several ways, most commonly by using microform, digital technology, and interlibrary loan. In doing research, you might need to use one or more of these resources.

*Microform* is printed material that has been reduced in size through microphotography. Libraries that use microform provide users with special devices to read the material, whether it is available on microfilm or microfiche (which is a flat sheet of microfilm).

*Digital technology,* in the form of CD-ROMs or online media, makes articles and other resources available to users electronically rather than in print form. Sometimes, you must read these resources at a computer terminal.

*Interlibrary loan* enables libraries to give their users access to books held at other libraries. You can usually request articles as well as books through this service, and today many libraries enable you to make your requests online. Keep in mind, however, that in can take several days or weeks for requested materials to arrive.

## CONDUCTING INTERVIEWS AND SURVEYS

In some cases you might want to conduct original research on your topic. For example, if you are writing an argument about a campus controversy over new parking fees, you can gather useful information by talking to people on campus (such as the person in charge of parking) or soliciting opinions by those affected by the new fees. There are many kinds of original research, but two of the most common are interviews and surveys.

*Interviews* might be inappropriate for some kinds of papers (for example, science reports), but they can often be useful sources of information. If you are writing a paper on identity theft, for example, you might interview someone working in law enforcement, such as a police officer or a public defender. You might also interview someone who might have had their identity stolen or talk to professionals at a bank or credit card company who deal with identity theft. Whom you interview will depend in large measure on your topic, but you should always evaluate the credibility of anyone you interview. Here are some other tips for interviewing:

- *Plan ahead for your interviews.* It's a good idea to prepare a list of questions before you go. It also helps to learn something about the person or persons you will interview so that you can ask appropriate questions and avoid inappropriate ones.

- *Ask good questions.* Try to compose questions that will take several sentences to answer rather than questions that might be answered with a single word. Good questions usually elicit more useful responses for your research.

- *Be flexible.* Don't necessarily adhere rigidly to the questions you prepare in advance. A good interviewer knows how to ask a follow-up question that is inspired by a provocative response to an earlier question. However, try not to get so caught up in the interview that you forget to take careful notes.

- *Consider using a tape recorder.* A tape recorder will usually preserve more of the interview than you can preserve in your notes, and it will enable you to take notes on important points without having to write everything down. If you want to use a tape recorder, ask permission to do so when you arrange for the interview. Also, make sure that the recorder is working properly before you begin the interview, and check your batteries.

- *Record the date of the interview and the full name and credentials or position of the person you interviewed.* You will need to include this information in your bibliography.

When you ask the same questions of a number of different people, you are conducting a *survey.* When a survey is long, complex, and administered to a large sample group, researchers seeking to analyze the data they have gathered will benefit from having a working knowledge of statistics. But for many undergraduate research projects, a relatively simple survey can produce interesting and useful data. The earlier hypothetical example of a campus controversy about new parking fees illustrates the usefulness of a survey. If you were writing an argument about that controversy, you could gather information about students' attitudes toward the new fees. Such information can be important and potentially persuasive support for your position on the controversy.

Here are some things to consider if you want to use a survey:

- *Carefully compose a list of relevant questions.* Each question should be designed to elicit a clear answer that is directly related to the purpose of the survey. This is more complicated than it might seem, since the kind of questions you ask will determine what results you get. For example, if you ask students whether they agree with the parking fees, you will get a basic yes-or-no response. However, if you ask students whether they would pay higher fees if they were guaranteed a parking space, you might get different results.

- *Decide whether you want to administer the survey orally or distribute it in a written form.* One advantage of an oral survey is that you get your results immediately; with a written survey, weeks can pass before you discover how many people responded to your request for information. On the other hand, written surveys give you clear records to work from. A good rule to follow when conducting a written survey is to distribute at least twice as many copies as you really need to have returned to you.

- *Decide how many people you will need to survey to have a credible sample of the population that concerns you.* For example, in the case of the campus parking fees, let's say there are 4,000 students at your school but only 1,000 drive to campus. You might want to survey both drivers and nondrivers to see whether you get different results. In that case, if you surveyed 100 students, you might want to make sure that twenty-five of them are drivers (which would match the 25 percent of student drivers on your campus).

■ *Consider whether it would be useful to analyze your results in terms of such differences as gender, race, age, income, or religion.* If so, you must design a questionnaire that will provide this information. In the campus parking controversy it might be that older students are most affected, so you would want to account for the age of your respondents.

■ *Take steps to protect the privacy of your respondents.* Ask for no more information than you need, and ask respectfully for that information. Give respondents the option of refusing to answer any question that makes them uncomfortable, and honor any promises you make about how you will use the data you gather.

As this chapter reveals, there are many aspects to doing research and many kinds of resources for the information you need. Which resources you consult and how you search for them will depend on your topic and the specifics of your assignment, such as your deadline and the length of the argument you are writing. But whether you will engage in extensive research or simply look for a few essays about your topic, the general principles guiding research are the same. And the more effective you are as a researcher, the more likely you will be to find the information you need to write an effective argument.

**7**

# DOCUMENTING
## YOUR SOURCES

DOCUMENTING

I n Chapter 6 we discussed many of the strategies that you can use to conduct research for an argument. Doing such research, in our view, is part of the process of inquiry that you engage in when you make an argument. By researching an issue or controversy carefully, you can gain a better understanding of that issue or controversy and construct a more effective argument that may lead to a satisfactory resolution. That's the goal. But the process entails some practical challenges, including organizing your paper effectively and properly documenting your sources. We take up those topics in this chapter.

YOUR SOURCES

## COMPILING A PRELIMINARY BIBLIOGRAPHY

As you use the strategies that we discussed in Chapter 6 to begin locating sources of possible value for your paper, it is important to record certain essential information about the books and articles you have discovered. You will need this information to compile a preliminary bibliography. Here are some things to keep in mind as you work with your sources:

- For books, record the full title, the full name of the author or authors, the city of publication, the publisher, and the date of publication.
- If you are using a particular part of a book, be sure to record the pages in question.
- When you have located articles in periodicals, record the author(s) of the article, the title of the article, the title of the journal in which it was published, the volume number, the issue number (if there is one), the date of the issue, and the pages between which the article can be found.
- If you are using an article or a story from an anthology that is edited by someone other than the author of the material you are using, make the distinction between the author and title of the selection and the editor and title of the volume.
- For electronic resources, such as Web sites, be sure to record the Internet address, or URL, accurately and make a note of the date you accessed the site.

Today, researchers often use a computer program to keep track of sources. You can easily use certain features of a word processing program such as Microsoft Word to maintain your preliminary bibliography, and you can also use specialized software such as EndNote that is designed specifically for constructing bibliographies. Whatever method you use, be sure to keep accurate records. It can be frustrating to discover that you neglected to record an important reference, especially if this discovery comes after the paper is written and shortly before it is handed in.

## ORGANIZING A RESEARCH PAPER

Many students think of outlines as extra work. But in fact using an outline can save you time and help you write a more effective source-based argument. It can help you keep track of your main ideas and make sure that the important parts of your argument fit together effectively. It can also help you identify areas in which you may need to do more research.

Depending on your writing process, you can outline before attempting to write or after you have completed a first draft. If you create an outline before you begin writing, the patterns discussed in Chapter 5 for classical arrangement and Rogerian argument (pages 126–128), which can be adopted for researched papers of almost any length, may be useful to you. You can also use a standard formal outline:

I. Major idea
   A. Supporting idea
      1. Minor idea
         a. Supporting detail
         b. Supporting detail
      2. Minor idea
         a. Supporting detail
         b. Supporting detail
   B. Supporting idea
II. Major idea

And so forth. Subdivisions make sense only when there are at least two categories; otherwise, there would be no need to subdivide. Roman numeral I usually implies the existence of Roman numeral II, and supporting idea A implies the existence of supporting idea B. Formal outlines are usually parallel, each part being in balance with the others.

Many writers prefer to work with less formal outlines. Two widely used alternatives to a formal outline are *listing* and *mapping*. When organizing a paper by listing, writers simply make a list of the various points they want to make without worrying about Roman numerals or indention. They then number the points on the list in the order in which they plan to discuss them. When mapping, you can create circles or blocks on a page, starting with a main idea. Each different idea is noted in a separate circle or block, and then lines are drawn to connect ideas that are related.

There is no single method that works equally well for all writers. Unless you are specifically instructed to complete a certain type of outline, practice whatever kind of outlining works best for you. And keep in mind that an outline is not an end in itself; it is only a tool to help you write a good paper. You can rewrite an outline much more easily than you can rewrite a paper, so be prepared to rework any outline that does not help you to write better.

> **PLANNING AHEAD**
>
> When planning a researched paper, allow ample time for drafting and revising. As we noted in Chapter 5, ideas often evolve during the writing process. Even if you have extensive notes, you might discover that you lack information to support a claim that occurred to you when you sat down to write. You would then need to do more research or modify your claim. The first draft might also include material that on rereading, you decide does not relate to the focus of your paper and should therefore be removed. Cutting and adding are a normal part of the writing process, so expect to make changes.

## INTEGRATING SOURCE MATERIAL INTO YOUR PAPER

One of the challenges of writing an argument involving research is integrating source material effectively into a work that remains distinctively your own. The most effective source-based arguments include source material that is woven smoothly into the paper with well-chosen quotations that are clearly introduced and properly documented. Papers with too many long quotations or quotations that seem arbitrarily placed are weaker; they lack the student's voice and might lead an instructor to be suspicious about how much of the paper is the student's own. You can avoid such problems if you work with your source material to support your own position in an argument and if you follow some basic advice for quoting and citing source material.

First, make sure that any quotations you use fit smoothly into your essay as a whole. Provide transitions that link quotations to whatever has come before them. As a general rule, anything worth quoting at length requires some discussion. After you have quoted someone, you should usually include some analysis or commentary that will make the significance of the quotation clear. Notice how Rachel Guetter, whose essay appears on pages 129–132, follows this advice to weave a quote from one of her sources effectively into her discussion of problems facing gay parents:

> Often, one person in a same-sex relationship is the biological parent and the other will help raise the child as his or her own. According to the American Academy of Pediatrics (AAP), children in this situation lose "survivor benefits if a parent dies and legal rights if the parents break up" (Berman 1). Both situations leave a dramatic impact on the child, who then is caught in the middle of legal battles.

To help keep your paper your own, try to avoid using long quotations. Quote only what you need most, and edit long quotations whenever possible. Use the ellipsis (. . .) to indicate that you have omitted a word or phrase within a sentence, leaving a space before and after each period. (When the ellipsis follows a completed sentence, include the sentence's period before the ellipsis.) When editing quotations in this way, make sure that they remain clear and grammatically correct. If the addition of an extra word or two would help to make the quotation more easily understandable, you should enclose the inserted material within square brackets [ ] to let your readers know what had been added to the quotation. Here is another passage from Rachel Guetter's essay illustrating these points:

> Until homosexuality is more widely received, children with gay and lesbian parents will have to deal with the fact that their family is viewed as pejoratively different. Glenn Stanton, senior research analyst for Focus on the Family, says, "While there may be very nice people who are raising kids in homosexual situations, the best model for kids is to grow up with mom and dad" (Stanton). It seems reasonable to believe that having both a mother and father benefits children. Women and men have different parenting traits that give a strong balance for the development of a child. Stanton also states, "Fathers encourage children to take chances . . . mothers protect and are more cautious." There exist in parents different disciplining, communication, and playing styles that can be advantages in raising a child.

Remember also that sources do not need to be quoted to be cited. As we noted in Chapter 6 (pages 155–157), paraphrasing and summarizing are important writing skills. They can help you avoid writing a paper that sounds like nothing more than one quotation after another or using quotations that are so heavily edited that readers start wondering about what you have cut out. When you put another writer's ideas into your own words (being careful, of course, to provide proper documentation), you are demonstrating that you have control over your material, and by doing so, you can often make your paper more readable.

Above all, remember that you are the writer of your argument. You are using the sources you have found to support your position or to enhance your own ideas.

## CITING SOURCES

Any time you use material from another source, you must cite it properly. Citing your sources simply means revealing the source of any information you report. When you cite your sources, you are providing your readers with information to help them evaluate the credibility of your sources, to credit the authors whose work you are citing, and to make it possible for readers to find your sources for themselves. In general, you must provide documentation for the following:

- Any direct quotation
- Any idea that has come from someone else's work
- Any fact or statistic that is not widely known

There are several different styles for documenting your sources; these styles are usually associated with different disciplines or professions. Writers in the humanities usually follow the form of the Modern Language Association (MLA). In the social sciences writers are often expected to follow the format of the American Psychological Association (APA). MLA and APA are the two most widely used systems for documenting sources, and chances are that you will be asked to use one of them for papers you write for your college courses. *The Chicago Manual of Style* (CMS) is another widely used system, though college instructors are less likely to use that system than MLA or APA. When you are writing a source-based paper, check with your instructor to see which system you should use. (If you are writing a source-based argument for publication, check with the editor about that publication's preferred system for documenting sources.)

Whichever system you use to document your sources, remember that the purpose of all these systems is the same: to provide appropriate information about your sources. And be sure to understand the relationship between the parenthetical, or in-text, citations and the bibliography, Works Cited, or References page, of your essay. When you cite a source in the body of your essay, you are telling your readers where you obtained the quotation or information you are using; your readers can then go to your bibliography for more information about that source. For example, in this passage from her essay (see pages 129–132) Rachel uses MLA style to cite the source of the quotation she is using:

According to the American Academy of Pediatrics (AAP), children in this situation lose "survivor benefits if a parent dies and legal rights if the parents break up" (Berman A1).

The information in the parentheses includes the author's last name and the page (or pages) on which the quotation appears in that author's work. Readers can then use the author's last name to find the full citation in the bibliography at the end of Rachel's essay, which looks like this:

Berman, Steven. "Homosexuals and Adoption." Rocky Mountain News 23 Feb.

2002: A1.

Here's how the same quotation would be documented in Rachel's essay if she were using APA format:

According to the American Academy of Pediatrics (AAP), children in this situation lose "survivor benefits if a parent dies and legal rights if the parents break up" (Berman, 2002, p. A1).

The citation would appear in her bibliography as follows:

Berman, S. (2002, February 23). Homosexuals and adoption. *Rocky Mountain News,*

p. A1.

## MLA AND APA SOURCES

You can find more extensive information about the MLA and APA documentation systems by consulting the official publications for each system. Notice that the following citations are the appropriate format for each system:

Gibaldi, Joseph. <u>MLA Style Manual and Guide to Scholarly Publishing</u>. 2nd ed. New York: MLA, 1998.

Gibaldi, Joseph. <u>MLA Handbook for Writers of Research Papers</u>. 6th ed. New York: MLA, 2003.

American Psychological Association. (2001). *Publication manual of the American Psychological Association* (5th ed.). Washington, DC: Author.

You can also visit their Web sites: <u>www.mla.org</u> or <u>www.apastyle.org</u>.

Notice that the same basic information is provided, no matter which documentation system is used. But the format for providing that information is different in each system. For example, MLA style requires the use of quotation marks around the title of the article, and the title is capitalized; APA style requires no quotation marks and uses lowercase letters for the title.

In the remainder of this chapter we explain the basic features of the MLA and APA systems of documentation and provide model entries for the most frequently used sources. However, a detailed discussion of these systems is beyond the range of this chapter. If you need more information about either MLA or APA format, consult the official sources for each (see sidebar on this page).

## FOOTNOTES AND CONTENT NOTES

Traditionally, footnotes were used to document sources. Strictly speaking, a "footnote" appears at the foot of the page, and an "endnote" appears at the end of the paper. However, both MLA and APA now recommend that writers use parenthetical, or in-text, citations of the kind we have been describing here; traditional footnotes are not used for documenting sources. Instead, numbered notes are reserved for additional explanation or discussion that is important but cannot be included within the actual text without a loss of focus. Such notes are called *content notes* (though APA discourages the use of such notes unless they are essential to the discussion).

If you are using MLA style, use footnotes or endnotes to provide additional information about sources or topics discussed in your essay. For example, let's return again to the passage from Rachel Guetter's essay. Let's imagine that Rachel has information about gender roles that relates to her point but is not important enough to include in her argument. In such a case by using a note, Rachel could di-

## COMMONLY USED STYLE MANUALS

MLA and APA are the two most popular style guides, but there are other manuals that you may need to consult. Here is a list of other commonly used manuals:

*The Chicago Manual of Style,* 14th ed. (Chicago: University of Chicago Press, 1993).

Huth, Edward J. *Scientific Style and Format: The CBE Manual for Authors, Editors, and Publishers.* 6th ed. New York: Cambridge University Press, 1994.

Dodd, Janet S., ed. *The ACS Style Guide: A Manual for Authors and Editors,* 2nd edition. New York: Oxford UP, 1997.

American Institute of Physics. *AIP Style Manual.* 4th ed. New York: Amer. Inst. of Physics, 1990.

Iverson, Cheryl, ed. *American Medical Association Manual of Style: A Guide for Authors and Editors.* 9th ed. Baltimore: Williams, 1998.

Harvard Law Review Association. *The Bluebook: A Uniform System of Citation.* 17th ed. Cambridge: Harvard Law Review Assn., 2000.

rect her readers' attention to another useful source that she does not cite directly in this passage. First, using MLA format, she would use a superscript number at the end of the relevant passage as follows:

> It seems reasonable to believe that having both a mother and father benefits children. Women and men have different parenting traits that give a strong balance for the development of a child.[1]

Her note (either a footnote at the bottom of the page or an endnote at the end of her essay) would look like this:

> [1] Many researchers and scholars have examined differences between men and women. For example, see Pease and Pease.

Rachel would then include the full citation for Pease and Pease in her bibliography:

> Pease, Barbara, and Allan Pease. <u>Why Men Don't Listen and Women Can't Read Maps: How We're Different and What to Do about It</u>. New York: Broadway Books, 2001.

If she were using APA format, Rachel would follow the same procedure, but she would use APA style for the citation in her bibliography:

> Pease, B., & Pease, A. (2001). *Why men don't listen and women can't read maps: How we're different and what to do about it.* New York: Broadway Books.

Also, APA format requires that content notes be placed on a separate page at the end of the essay (rather than at the bottom of the page as footnotes).

## PARENTHETICAL (IN-TEXT) DOCUMENTATION

As we noted earlier in this chapter, the two most common systems for documenting sources, MLA and APA, both recommend the use of parenthetical, or in-text, citations to cite sources. The basic principle for using these parenthetical citations is the same for both MLA and APA styles: You are providing readers with information about a source that is included in your bibliography. However, there are differences between the two systems. These differences reflect conventions within academic fields regarding which information about a source is most important:

- *MLA style,* which tends to reflect the conventions of the humanities (including the arts, literature, history, and philosophy), emphasizes the author and the author's work and places less emphasis on the date of publication.
- *APA style* emphasizes the author and the date of publication, which is more important in the social science disciplines (for example, psychology, sociology, education, and anthropology).

If you understand these basic differences, you might find it easier to become familiar with the specific differences in the formats used by each documentation system.

In the following sections we describe how to use parenthetical citations in the MLA and APA systems.

**The MLA Author/Work Style**   In a parenthetical (or in-text) citation in MLA form, the author's last name is followed by a page reference; in some cases a brief title should be included after the author's name. It is not necessary to repeat within the parentheses information that is already provided in the text.

### A.   WORK BY A SINGLE AUTHOR

If you were citing page 133 of a book called *Ecological Literacy* by David W. Orr, the parenthetical citation would look like this:

> The idea of environmental sustainability can become the centerpiece of a college curriculum (Orr 133).

Alternatively, you could use Orr's name in your sentence, in which case the citation would include only the page reference:

> David Orr has argued persuasively that that the idea of environmental sustainability should be the centerpiece of a college curriculum (133).

There is no punctuation between the author's name and the page reference when both are cited parenthetically. Note also that the abbreviation "p." or "pp." is not used before the page reference.

### B.   WORK WITH MORE THAN ONE AUTHOR

If the work you are citing has two or three authors, use the complete names of all of them in your sentence or include their last names in the parentheses:

> Cleanth Brooks and Robert Penn Warren have argued that "indirection is an essential part of the method of poetry" (573).

or

> Although this sonnet may seem obscure, its meaning becomes clearer when we realize "indirection is an essential part of the method of poetry" (Brooks and Warren 573).

Note that when a sentence ends with a quotation, the parenthetical reference comes before the final punctuation mark. Note also that the ampersand (&) is not used in MLA style.

If you are referring to a work by more than three authors, you can list only the first author's name followed by "et al." (Latin for "and others"):

> These works "derive from a profound disillusionment with modern life" (Baym et al. 910).

### C.   WORK WITH A CORPORATE AUTHOR

When a corporate author has a long name, you should include it within the text rather than within parentheses. For example, if you were citing a study by the Council on Environmental Quality called "Ground Water Contamination in the United States," you would do so as follows:

> The Council on Environmental Quality has reported that there is growing evidence of ground water contamination throughout the United States (81).

You could also include the corporate author in the parentheses; omit any initial article:

> There is growing evidence of ground water contamination throughout the United States (Council on Environmental Quality 81).

Although both of these forms are technically correct, the first is preferred because it is easier to read.

### D.   WORK WITH MORE THAN ONE VOLUME

When you wish to cite a specific part of a multivolume work, include the volume number between the author and the page reference. In this example we are quoting a passage from the second volume of a two-volume book by Jacques Barzun:

> As Jacques Barzun has argued, "The only hope of true culture is to make classifications broad and criticism particular" (2: 340).

Note that the volume number is given an arabic numeral, and a space separates the colon and the page reference. The abbreviation "vol." is not used unless you wish to cite the entire volume: (Barzun, vol. 2).

### E.   MORE THAN ONE WORK BY THE SAME AUTHOR

If you cite more than one work by the same author, you need to make your references distinct so that readers will know exactly which work you are citing. You can do so by putting a comma after the author's name and then adding a shortened form of the title. For example, if you are discussing two novels by Toni Morrison, *Song of Solomon* and *The Bluest Eye,* your citations might look like this.

> Toni Morrison's work is always concerned with the complexities of racial identity. This theme is perhaps explored most painfully in the character of Pecola Breedlove (Morrison, Bluest). But even a crowd of unnamed characters gathered near a hospital, listening to a woman break spontaneously into song and wondering "if one of those things that racial-uplift groups were always organizing was taking place," can become a reminder that race is always part of the picture (Morrison, Song 6).

If it is clear from the context that the quotation is from a work by Morrison, there is no need to include her name in the parentheses. If you're not sure, however, include it. In this example we could have left Morrison's name out of the parentheses because it is clear that we are citing her works.

### F.   A QUOTATION WITHIN A CITED WORK

If you want to use a quotation that you have discovered in another book, your reference must show that you acquired this material secondhand and that you have not consulted the original source. Use the abbreviation "qtd. in" (for "quoted in") to make the distinction between the author of the passage being quoted and the author of the work in which you found this passage.

For example, let's say you were reading a book called *The Abstract Wild* by Jack Turner and you came across a quotation by the naturalist William Kittredge that you wanted to use in your argument. You would cite the Kittredge quotation as follows:

> Many people misquote Henry David Thoreau's famous line about wilderness and the preservation of the world. William Kittredge has admitted to making this very

mistake: "For years I misread Thoreau. I assumed he was saying wilderness. . . . Maybe I didn't want Thoreau to have said wildness, I couldn't figure out what he meant" (qtd. in Turner 81).

### G.   WORK WITHOUT AN AUTHOR LISTED

Sometimes a newspaper or magazine article does not include the name of an author. In such a case, include a brief version of the title in parentheses. For example, let's say you wanted to cite an article from *Consumer Reports* entitled "Dry-Cleaning Alternatives" that listed no author:

Conventional dry-cleaning, which requires the use of dangerous solvents, can result in both air and water pollution. However, if you are concerned about potential environmental damage caused by dry-cleaning your garments, you have several environmentally-friendly options, including methods using carbon dioxide and silicone-based methods ("Dry-Cleaning" 10).

### H.   ELECTRONIC SOURCES

When citing electronic sources, you should follow the same principles you would use when citing other sources. If you are citing an article from an online journal or newspaper, cite it as you would any print article, using the author's last name or, if you don't know the author, a brief version of the title of the article. However, there are many different kinds of electronic sources, and you might not have access to the same kinds of information as are available for a published book or journal article. For example, Web sites don't usually have page numbers, and you might not be able to determine the author of an online source. In such cases incorporate sufficient information about the source into your sentence so that readers can easily find the citation in your bibliography:

On its Web site, the Sustainability Institute maintains information about global climate change ("Research").

In this case the author of the Web page being cited is unknown, so a brief version of the title of the Web page, "Research at the Sustainability Institute," is included in parentheses. Notice that the title of a Web site is enclosed in quotation marks, just like titles of articles in periodicals.

**The APA Author/Year Style**   The American Psychological Association (APA) requires that in-text documentation identify the author of the work and the year in which the work was published; where appropriate, page numbers are also included, preceded by the abbreviation "p." or "pp." This information should be provided parenthetically; it is not necessary to repeat any information that has already been provided directly in the sentence.

### A.   ONE WORK BY A SINGLE AUTHOR

If you wished to cite a book by Alan Peshkin titled *Places of Memory*, published in 1997, you might do so as follows:

Native American students face the challenge of trying to maintain their cultural heritage while assimilating into mainstream American culture (Peshkin, 1997).

or

> Peshkin (1997) has argued that the pressures on Native American students to assimilate into mainstream American culture can contribute to poor academic performance.

If the reference is to a specific chapter or page, that information should also be included. For example:

> Peshkin's (1997) study focuses on what he calls the "dual-world character of the students' lives" (p. 5).

Note that the date of publication (in parentheses) follows the author's name; the page reference (also in parentheses) is placed at the end of the sentence. If the author's name is not included in the sentence, it should be included in the parentheses:

> The "dual-world character" of the lives of many Native American students can create obstacles to their academic success (Peshkin, 1997, p. 5).

## B.  WORK WITH TWO OR MORE AUTHORS

If a work has two authors, you should mention the names of both authors every time a reference is made to their work:

> A recent study of industry (Cole & Walker, 1997) argued that . . .

or

> More recently, Cole and Walker (1997) have argued that . . .

Note that the ampersand (&) is used only within parentheses.

Scientific papers often have multiple authors because of the amount of research involved. In the first reference to a work with three to five authors, you should identify each of the authors:

> Hodges, McKnew, Cytryn, Stern, and Kline (1982) have shown . . .

Subsequent references to the same work should use an abbreviated form:

> This method was also used in an earlier study (Hodges et al., 1982).

If a work has six authors (or more), this abbreviated form should be used even for the first reference. If confusion is possible because you must refer to more than one work by the first author, list as many coauthors as necessary to distinguish between the two works.

## C.  WORK WITH A CORPORATE AUTHOR

When a work has a corporate author, your first reference should include the full name of the corporation, committee, agency, or institution involved. For example, if you were citing the *Buying Guide 2002,* published by Consumer Reports, you might do so like this:

> There are several strategies you can use to protect yourself when ordering merchandise online (Consumer Reports, 2002, pp. 11–12).

If the corporate name is long, you can abbreviate subsequent references to the same source. If you were citing a report from the Fund for the Improvement of Postsecondary Education (FIPSE), for example, you would use the full name when you first cited it, then use FIPSE for any subsequent references.

## D.  REFERENCE TO MORE THAN ONE WORK

When the same citation refers to two or more sources, the works should be listed alphabetically according to the first author's surname and separated with semicolons:

> Several studies have examined the social nature of literacy (Finders, 1997; Heath, 1983; Street, 1984; Young, 1994).

If you are referring to more than one work by the same author(s), list the works in the order in which they were published.

> The validity of this type of testing is now well established (Collins, 1988, 1994).

If you refer to more than one work by the same author published in the same year, distinguish individual works by identifying them as "a," "b," "c," and so on:

> These findings have been questioned by Scheiber (1997a, 1997b).

## ORGANIZING A BIBLIOGRAPHY

A bibliography is an essential component of any essay or report that includes references to sources. The bibliography, also called a Works Cited or References page, lists all the sources that you have cited in your essay or report. The purpose of a bibliography is to provide information about your sources for your readers.

MLA and APA styles for formatting the entries in your bibliography are described in this chapter. As you'll see, there are some differences between MLA and APA styles. However, no matter which style you use, your bibliography provides the same basic information about your sources:

### ITALICS OR UNDERLINES

Traditionally, both APA and MLA recommended underlining titles of books, journals, magazines, and newspapers. However, with the widespread use of word processing, it is now as easy to use italics as it is to underline, and either is generally acceptable. Nevertheless, MLA still recommends the use of underlining to avoid ambiguity; it suggests that students who wish to use italics check with their instructors first.

- The author's name
- The title of the work
- The date of publication

In addition, entries in your bibliography will provide the name of the magazine, newspaper, or journal for any articles you cite as well as page numbers (unless you are citing an electronic source without page numbers, such as a Web page).

**Works Cited in MLA Style**    In an MLA-style bibliography the works cited are arranged in alphabetical order by the author's last name. Here are the main things to remember when you are creating a bibliography in MLA style:

- Provide the author's first and last name for each entry.
- Capitalize every important word in the titles of books, articles, and journals.
- Underline (or italicize) the titles of books, journals, and newspapers.
- Place the titles of articles, stories, and poems in quotation marks.
- Indent the second and any subsequent lines one-half inch (or five spaces).

Here's how a typical entry for a single-authored book appears in an MLA-style bibliography:

Abram, David. The Spell of the Sensuous. New York: Random, 1996.

Here are the important parts of the entry:

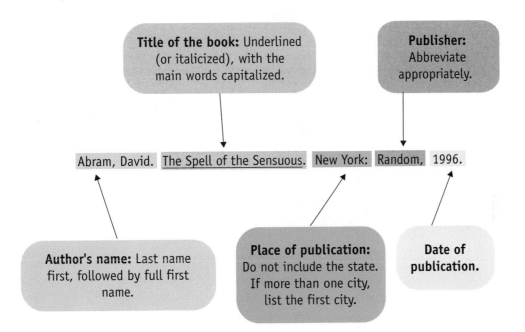

**Title of the book:** Underlined (or italicized), with the main words capitalized.

**Publisher:** Abbreviate appropriately.

Abram, David.  The Spell of the Sensuous.  New York:  Random,  1996.

**Author's name:** Last name first, followed by full first name.

**Place of publication:** Do not include the state. If more than one city, list the first city.

**Date of publication.**

Notice that there are no page numbers for this entry.

If the work you are citing is a journal article, the entry would look like this:

George, Diana. "From Analysis to Design: Visual Communication in the Teaching of

Writing." College Composition and Communication 54.1 (2002): 11–39.

Here are the parts of this entry:

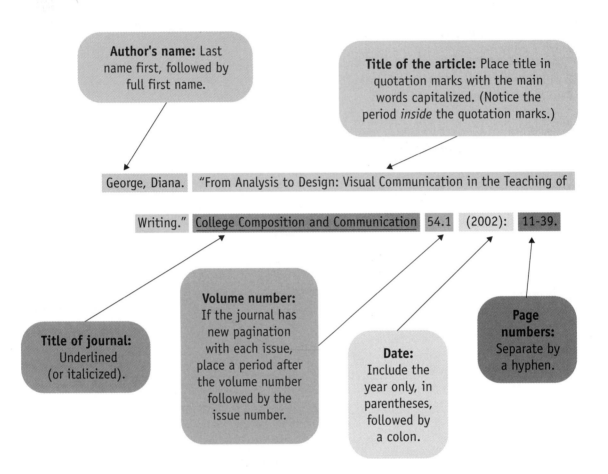

**Author's name:** Last name first, followed by full first name.

**Title of the article:** Place title in quotation marks with the main words capitalized. (Notice the period *inside* the quotation marks.)

George, Diana. "From Analysis to Design: Visual Communication in the Teaching of Writing." College Composition and Communication 54.1 (2002): 11-39.

**Title of journal:** Underlined (or italicized).

**Volume number:** If the journal has new pagination with each issue, place a period after the volume number followed by the issue number.

**Date:** Include the year only, in parentheses, followed by a colon.

**Page numbers:** Separate by a hyphen.

For online sources, you must include the Internet address, or URL, along with two dates: the publication date (if available) and the date you accessed the site. Here's an entry for an online journal article:

Luebke, Steven R. "Using Linked Courses in the General Education Curriculum."

Academic Writing 3 (2002). 16 Dec. 2002 <http://aw.colostate.edu/articles/

luebke_2002.htm>.

Notice where the dates and URL are placed in this entry:

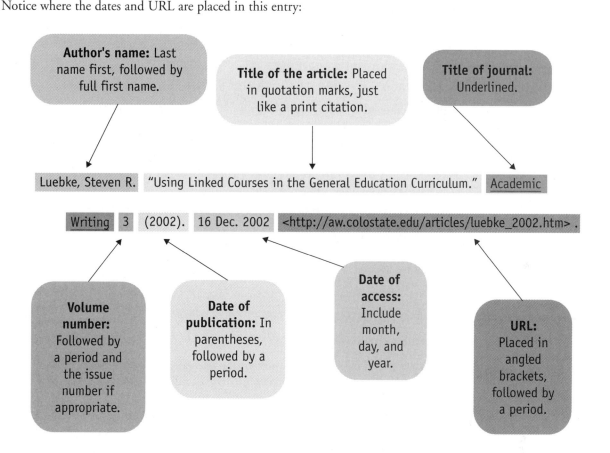

All entries in MLA format follow these basic principles, but each entry will contain slightly different information, depending on the kind of source that was cited. Keep that in mind as you look for the correct format for the sources you are citing in your bibliography.

### A.   BOOK WITH ONE AUTHOR

Abram, David. The Spell of the Sensuous. New York: Random, 1996.

### B.   BOOK WITH TWO OR THREE AUTHORS

Gilbert, Sandra M., and Susan Gubar. The Madwoman in the Attic: The Woman Writer

and the Nineteenth-Century Literary Imagination. New Haven: Yale UP, 1979.

Note that the subtitle is included, set off from the main title by a colon. The second author's name is not inverted, and abbreviations are used for "University Press" to provide a shortened form of the publisher's name. For books with three authors, put commas after the names of the first two authors (invert the name of the first author); separate the second two authors with a comma followed by "and."

### C.   EDITED BOOK

Glazer, Steven, ed. <u>The Heart of Learning: Spirituality in Education</u>. New York:

Tarcher-Putnam, 1999.

### D.   BOOK WITH MORE THAN THREE AUTHORS OR EDITORS

Black, Laurel, et al., eds. <u>New Directions in Portfolio Assessment: Practice, Critical</u>

<u>Theory, and Large-Scale Scoring</u>. Portsmouth: Boynton, 1994.

Give the name of the first author or editor only, and add the abbreviation "et al."

### E.   EDITION AFTER THE FIRST

Tate, Gary, Edward P. J. Corbett, and Nancy Myers, eds. <u>The Writing Teacher's</u>

<u>Sourcebook</u>. 3rd ed. New York: Oxford UP, 1994.

### F.   WORK IN AN ANTHOLOGY

Owens, Derek. "Sustainable Composition." <u>Ecocomposition: Theoretical and</u>

<u>Pedagogical Approaches</u>. Eds. Christian R. Weisser and Sidney I. Dobrin. Albany:

State U of New York P, 2001. 27–38.

Note that a period comes after the title of the selection but before the second quotation marks. A period is also used to separate the date of publication from the page reference, which is followed by a period.

### G.   TRANSLATED BOOK

Eco, Umberto. <u>The Aesthetics of Thomas Aquinas</u>. Trans. Hugh Bredin. Cambridge:

Harvard UP, 1988.

### H.   WORK IN MORE THAN ONE VOLUME

Leckie, Robert. <u>The Wars of America</u>. 2 vols. New York: Harper, 1992.

### I.   INTRODUCTION, PREFACE, FOREWORD, OR AFTERWORD

Dove, Rita. Foreword. <u>Jonah's Gourd Vine</u>. By Zora Neale Hurston. New York: Harper,

1990. vii–xv.

### J.   ARTICLE IN AN ENCYCLOPEDIA

Hunt, Roberta M. "Child Welfare." <u>The Encyclopedia Americana</u>. 1993 ed.

In citing material from well-known encyclopedias, give the author's name first, then the article title. If material is arranged alphabetically within the source, which is usually the case, there is no need to include volume and page numbers. You should give the full title of the encyclopedia, the edition (if it is stated), and the year of publication (e.g., 11th ed. 1996). When no edition number is stated, identify the edition by the year of publication (e.g., 1996 ed.). If the author of the article is identified only by initials, look elsewhere within the encyclopedia for a list identifying the names these initials stand for. If the article is unsigned, give the title first. (Note: This same form can be used for other reference books, such as dictionaries and the various editions of *Who's Who.*) For an example of how to cite an electronic encyclopedia, see **T.**

## K. GOVERNMENT PUBLICATION

United States. Federal Bureau of Investigation. <u>Handbook of Forensic Science</u>.

Washington: GPO, 1994.

For many government publications the author is unknown. When this is the case, the agency that issued the publication should be listed as the author. State the name of the government (e.g., "United States," "Florida," "United Nations") followed by a period. Then give the name of the agency that issued the work, using abbreviations only if you can do so clearly (e.g., "Bureau of the Census," "National Institute on Drug Abuse," "Dept. of Labor") followed by a period. The underlined title of the work comes next, followed by another period. Then give the place of publication, publisher, and date. Most federal publications are printed in Washington by the Government Printing Office (GPO), but you should be alert for exceptions. (Note: Treat a government pamphlet just as you would a book.)

## L. JOURNAL ARTICLE WITH ONE AUTHOR

Hesse, Douglas. "The Place of Creative Nonfiction." <u>College English</u> 65 (2003):

237–241.

The volume number comes after the journal title without any intervening punctuation. The year of publication is included within parentheses after the volume number. A colon separates the year of publication and the page reference. Leave one space after the volume number and one space after the colon.

## M. JOURNAL ARTICLE PAGINATED ANEW IN EACH ISSUE

Williams, Jeffrey. "The Life of the Mind and the Academic Situation." <u>College Literature</u>

23.3 (1996): 128–146.

In this case the issue number is included immediately after the volume number, and the two are separated by a period without any intervening space.

## N. ARTICLE FROM A MAGAZINE PUBLISHED MONTHLY

Brownlee, Shannon. "The Overtreated American." <u>Atlantic Monthly</u> Jan. 2003:

89–91.

Instead of citing the volume number, give the month and year of the issue. Abbreviate the month when it has more than four letters. (May, June, and July are spelled out.) For an example of how to list an article from a magazine published monthly that was obtained through a computer database, see **R.**

### O. ARTICLE FROM A MAGAZINE ISSUED WEEKLY

Kalb, Claudia. "Get Up and Get Moving." <u>Newsweek</u> 20 Jan. 2003: 59–64.

The form is the same as for an article in a magazine that is issued monthly, but you add the day immediately before the month. Note that a hyphen between page numbers indicates consecutive pages. When an article is printed on nonconsecutive pages — beginning on page 34, for example, and continuing on page 78 — give only the first page number and a plus sign: 34+.

### P. ARTICLE FROM A DAILY NEWSPAPER

Reich, Howard. "Limited Ambition." <u>Chicago Tribune</u> 9 Feb. 1997, final ed., sec. 7: 13.

If more than one edition is available on the date in question, specify the edition immediately after the date. If the city of publication is not part of a locally published newspaper's name, identify the city in brackets after the newspaper title. Because newspapers often consist of separate sections, you should cite the section number if each section has separate pagination. If a newspaper consists of only one section or if the pagination is continuous from one section to the next, then you do not need to include the section number. If separately paginated sections are identified by letters, omit the section reference (sec.) but include the letter of the section with the page number (e.g., B7 or D19). If the article is unsigned, begin the entry with the title of the article; alphabetize the article under its title, passing over small words such as "a" and "the." For an example of how to cite a newspaper article accessed through a subscription service such as FirstSearch or Lexis-Nexis, see **U**.

### Q. EDITORIAL

Terzian, Philip. "Armed Forces Work Just Fine without Draft." Editorial. <u>Albany Times</u>

<u>Union</u> 14 Jan. 2003: A14.

Editorials are identified as such between the title of the article and the title of the newspaper or magazine.

### R. PRINTED MATERIAL ACCESSED FROM A PERIODICALLY PUBLISHED DATABASE ON CD-ROM

Many periodicals and reference works such as bibliographies are now available on CD-ROMs, which are sometimes updated. Here's an example of a print article from a journal called *Managing Office Technology* that was found on a CD-ROM issued by UMI-ProQuest:

Holtzman, Henry. "Team Management: Its Time Has Come . . . Again." <u>Managing</u>

<u>Office Technology</u> Feb. 1994: 8. <u>ABI/Inform</u>. CD-ROM. UMI-ProQuest. Oct.

1994.

Notice that this entry includes the same information that would be provided for a magazine or journal article: author (if known), article title, journal title, date of print publication, and page reference. In addition, cite the database you used (in this case, ABI/Inform), the medium through which you accessed it (CD-ROM), and, if available, the vendor that made this medium available (here, UMI-ProQuest). Conclude with the date of electronic publication.

## S. EXCLUSIVELY ELECTRONIC MATERIAL ACCESSED FROM A PERIODICALLY PUBLISHED DATABASE

Many reference works today are published exclusively in electronic form on media such as CD-ROM and computer diskettes.

> African Development Bank. "1995 AFDB Indicative Learning Program." National Trade
>
> Data Bank. CD-ROM. U.S. Commercial Service. Mar. 1996.

Give the author's name (a corporate author in this case), the title of the material in quotation marks, the title of the database (here, *National Trade Data Bank*), the publication medium (in this case, CD-ROM), the vendor (here, U.S. Commercial Service), and the date it was published electronically. Note that the title of the database is underlined.

## T. NONPERIODICAL PUBLICATION ON CD-ROM

Encyclopedias and similar nonperiodical reference works are now regularly available on CD-ROM. Here is an entry for an article from *The Academic American Encyclopedia* on CD-ROM:

> Hogan, Robert. "Abbey Theater." The Academic American Encyclopedia. CD-ROM.
>
> Danbury: Grolier, 1995.

If no author is identified, begin with the work's title; if no author or title is available, begin with the title of the product consulted.

If you are citing an article from an encyclopedia that is available online, use the format for an article accessed through an online database (see **U**).

## U. PRINTED PUBLICATION ACCESSED THROUGH A DATABASE SUBSCRIPTION SERVICE

> Jeffers, Thomas L. "Plagiarism High and Low." Commentary 114.3 (2002): 54–61.
>
> Lexis-Nexis. State U of New York-Albany Lib. 28 Dec. 2002.

Follow the same pattern you would for the print equivalent (in this case, a magazine article), then add the underlined title of the database (if known), the name of the service (in this case, Lexis-Nexis), and how you accessed it (in this example, through the SUNY-Albany Libraries). Then include the date you accessed the article, followed by the URL of the service's home page (if known) in angled brackets $<>$.

## V. ARTICLE FROM AN ONLINE PERIODICAL

> Sands, Peter. "Pushing and Pulling Toward the Middle." Kairos 7.3 (2002).
>
> 15 Oct. 2002 <http://english.ttu.edu/kairos/7.3/
>
> binder2.html?coverweb.html#de>.

Cite the article as you would for a print article, but add the date you accessed the article just after the publication date (which is in parentheses followed by a period). Then add the URL in angled brackets. Remember to place a period at the end of the entry.

Follow this same pattern for articles from any online periodicals, whether they are from newspapers, popular magazines, or scholarly journals: Cite the article as you would a print article, then add the date you accessed it and the URL. The same patterns holds for on-line books.

### W.   THESIS PUBLISHED ONLINE

Increasingly, authors make their work available on Web sites. Citing these Web sites can be tricky because you do not always have access to all the publication information. Here's an entry for a thesis that the author published on a Web site:

> Formaro, Tom. "Argumentation on the World Wide Web." MA thesis. Some Random
>
> Stuff (and a Thesis). 9 May 2001. 17 Nov. 2002 <http://users.rcn.com/mackey/
>
> thesis/thesis.html>.

Notice that this entry follows the same pattern as an online periodical (see **V**): the author's name first, followed by the title of the work and of the Web site and date of publication; then add the date you accessed the text and the URL (in angled brackets). If there is no date of publication, use "n.d." for "no date."

### X.   ARTICLE ON A WEB SITE

There are many different kinds of Web sites where you can find useful information about a topic. Many sites are maintained by advocacy groups, government or nongovernment organizations, and educational institutions. If you are using information from such a Web site, follow the same basic principles for citing the source that you would follow for more conventional print sources. Here's an entry for an article found on the Web site for an advocacy group called the Center for a New American Dream:

> "In the Market? Think Green: The Center for a New American Dream's Guide to
>
> Environmentally Preferable Purchasing." Center for a New American Dream. 8
>
> Aug. 2001 <http://www.newdream.org/buygreen/index.html>.

Notice that since there is no author listed on the site, the title of the article is listed first, in quotation marks. The organization hosting the Web site is listed next, followed by the date of access and the URL of the article being referenced.

### Y.   PERSONAL HOME PAGE

> White, Crystal. Home page. 13 Jan. 2003. 22 June 2003
>
> <http://www.geocities.com/lfnxphile/>.

### Z.   INTERVIEW

> Nelson, Veronica. Personal interview. 16 Aug. 1997.

If you interview someone, alphabetize the interview under the surname of the person interviewed. Indicate whether it was a personal interview, telephone interview, or e-mail interview.

## AA. NEWSGROUP, MAILING LIST OR DISCUSSION BOARD POSTING

There are several different kinds of online discussion forums, including mailing lists and newsgroups. This example is from a Web-based discussion board:

Mountainman72. "Re: Avalanche Question." Online posting. 10 Jan. 2003. NEice Talk.

12 Jan. 2003 <http://www.neice.com/cgi-bin/ultimatebb.cgi?ubb=forum&f=1>.

Notice that the author's name (or pseudonym) is first, followed by the title of the posting, the description *Online posting,* the date of the posting, the name of the forum (if known), the date of access, and the URL.

For a mailing list or newsgroup posting, include the name of the mailing list or newsgroup after the date of the posting, as follows:

Fleischer, Cathy. "Colearn Logins." Online posting. 9 Dec. 2002. CoLEARN Research

Team Discussion List. 5 Jan. 2003 <researchteam@serv1.ncte.org>.

**References in APA Style**   In APA style, the bibliography is arranged alphabetically by the author's last name. The date of publication is emphasized by placing it within parentheses immediately after the author's name. In APA style, the bibliography is arranged alphabetically by the author's last name. The date of publication is emphasized by placing it within parentheses immediately after the author's name. The APA *Publication Manual* (5th ed.) recommends a hanging indent style of a half-inch, or five spaces, which is what is shown in the following illustrations.

Here are the main things to keep in mind when preparing a bibliography in APA style:

- Provide the author's surname, followed by an initial for the first name.
- Place the date in parentheses and follow it with a period; the date should always be the second element in an entry.
- Capitalize only the first word and any proper nouns of any title and subtitle (if there is one) in the entry.
- Italicize titles of books, journals, magazines, and newspapers.
- Do *not* place quotation marks around the titles of articles or chapters and do *not* italicize or underline them.

In APA style, a typical entry for a single-authored book looks like this:

Geertz, C. (2000). *Available light: Anthropological reflections on philosophical topics.*

Princeton, NJ: Princeton University Press.

Here are the important parts of the entry:

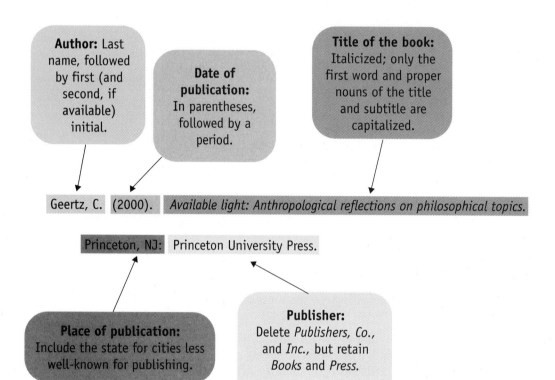

**Author:** Last name, followed by first (and second, if available) initial.

**Date of publication:** In parentheses, followed by a period.

**Title of the book:** Italicized; only the first word and proper nouns of the title and subtitle are capitalized.

Geertz, C.  (2000).  *Available light: Anthropological reflections on philosophical topics.*

Princeton, NJ:  Princeton University Press.

**Place of publication:** Include the state for cities less well-known for publishing.

**Publisher:** Delete *Publishers, Co.,* and *Inc.,* but retain *Books* and *Press.*

Here is an entry for a journal article:

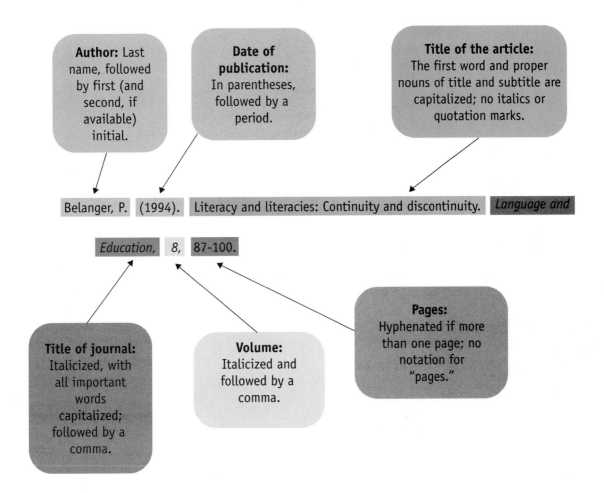

Notice the differences between the entry for a journal article and the following example of an entry for a newspaper article:

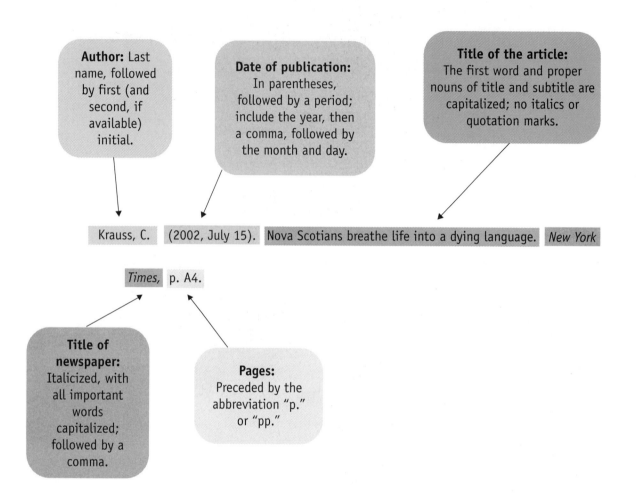

**Author:** Last name, followed by first (and second, if available) initial.

**Date of publication:** In parentheses, followed by a period; include the year, then a comma, followed by the month and day.

**Title of the article:** The first word and proper nouns of title and subtitle are capitalized; no italics or quotation marks.

Krauss, C.  (2002, July 15).  Nova Scotians breathe life into a dying language.  *New York Times,* p. A4.

**Title of newspaper:** Italicized, with all important words capitalized; followed by a comma.

**Pages:** Preceded by the abbreviation "p." or "pp."

Notice that for newspaper articles the date includes the month and day, along with the year, in parentheses; for monthly magazines, include only the year and month. Notice, too, that the page numbers are preceded by an abbreviation, unlike the entry for a journal article.

If you were citing a newspaper article that you retrieved from a database subscription service, your entry would look like this:

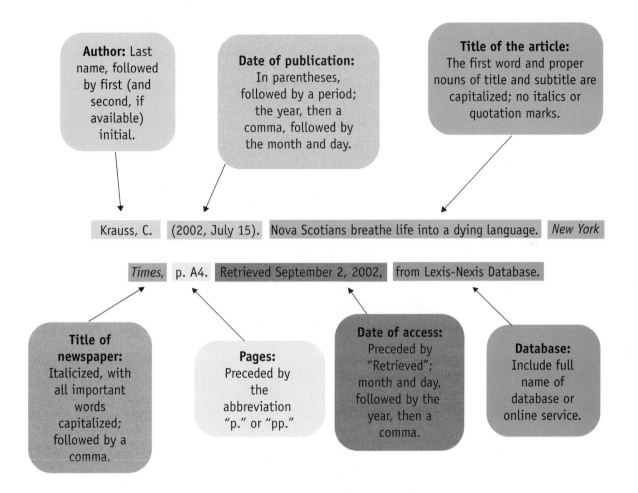

**A.  BOOK WITH ONE AUTHOR**

Loy, D. (1998). *Nonduality: A study in comparative philosophy.* Amherst, NY: Humanity

Books.

Note that the author's first name is indicated only by an initial. Capital letters are used only for the first word of the title and the first word of the subtitle if there is one. (But when a proper name appears within a title, it retains the capitalization it would normally receive; for example: *A history of ideas in Brazil.*) The name of the publisher, Humanity Books, is given in its entirety. A period comes after the parentheses surrounding the date of publication and also after the title and the publisher.

### B.  BOOK WITH TWO OR MORE AUTHORS

Blitz, M., & Hurlbert, C. M. (1998). *Letters for the living: Teaching writing in a violent*

*age.* Urbana, IL: National Council for Teachers of English.

An ampersand (&) is used to separate the names of two authors. When there are three or more authors, separate their names with commas, keeping each name reversed, and put an ampersand immediately before the last author's name.

### C.  EDITED BOOK

Street, B. V. (Ed.). (2001). *Literacy and development: Ethnographic perspectives.*

New York: Routledge.

The abbreviation for editor is "Ed."; it should be capitalized and included within parentheses between the name of the editor and the date of publication. The abbreviation for editors is "Eds." Give the names of all editors, no matter how many there are.

### D.  ARTICLE OR CHAPTER IN AN EDITED BOOK

Faigley, L. (1999). Beyond imagination: The internet and global digital literacy. In G. E.

Hawisher & C. L. Selfe (Eds.), *Passions, pedagogies, and 21st-century technolo-*

*gies* (pp. 129–139). Logan, UT: Utah State University Press.

Notice that the editor's name is not inverted when it is not in the author's position. Notice, too, that the title of the article or chapter is *not* placed in quotation marks. Use a comma to separate the editor from the title of the edited book. The pages between which the material can be found appear within parentheses immediately after the book title. Use "p." for page and "pp." for pages.

### E.  TRANSLATED BOOK

Calasso, R. (1993). *The marriage of Cadmus and Harmony* (T. Parks, Trans.). New

York: Random. (Original work published 1988).

Within parentheses immediately after the book title, give the translator's name followed by a comma and the abbreviation "Trans." If the original work was published earlier, include this information at the end.

### F.  SUBSEQUENT EDITIONS OF A BOOK

Hopkins, B. R. (1993). *A legal guide to starting and managing a nonprofit organization*

(2nd ed.). New York: Wiley.

The edition is identified immediately after the title. Note that edition is abbreviated "ed." — with a lowercase "e" — and should not be confused with "Ed." for editor; it is also placed in parentheses.

### G.  BOOK WITH A CORPORATE AUTHOR

American Red Cross. (1993). *Standard first aid.* St. Louis, MO: Mosby.

## H.   MULTIVOLUME WORK

Eisenstein, E. (1979). *The printing press as an agent of change: Communications and cultural transformations in early-modern Europe* (Vol. 2). Cambridge, England: Cambridge University Press.

The volume number is included within parentheses immediately after the title.

## I.   JOURNAL ARTICLE WITH ONE AUTHOR

Butler, A. C. (1996). The effect of welfare benefit levels on poverty among single-parent families. *Social Problems, 43,* 94–115.

Do not use quotation marks around the article title. Capitalize all important words in the journal title and italicize. Put a comma after the journal title and then give the volume and page numbers. Abbreviations are not used for "volume" and "page." To distinguish between the numbers, italicize the volume number and put a comma between it and the page numbers.

## J.   JOURNAL ARTICLE WITH MORE THAN ONE AUTHOR

Nugent, J. K., Lester, B. M., Greene, S. M., Wieczorek-Deering, D., & O'Mahoney, P. (1996). The effects of maternal alcohol consumption and cigarette smoking during pregnancy on acoustic cry analysis. *Child Development, 67,* 1806–1815.

Note that all authors' names are listed in the same format: last name followed by a comma and then the first (and second, if available) initial; commas separate all the names.

## K.   JOURNAL ARTICLE PAGINATED ANEW IN EACH ISSUE

Major, B. (1993). Gender, entitlement, and the distribution of family labor. *Journal of Social Issues, 49*(3), 141–159.

When each issue of a journal begins with page 1, include the issue number in parentheses immediately after the italicized volume number. Do not italicize the issue number.

## L.   ARTICLE FROM A MAGAZINE ISSUED MONTHLY

Baker, K. (1997, February). Searching the window into nature's soul. *Smithsonian, 745,* 94–104.

Include the month of issue after the year of publication in parentheses immediately after the author's name. Include the volume number. Follow the same form for an article in a weekly magazine issued on a specific day, but add the day after the month:

Hazen, R. M. (1991, February 25). Why my kids hate science. *Newsweek, 331,* 7.

## M.   ARTICLE FROM A DAILY NEWSPAPER

Bishop, J. E. (1996, November 13). Heart disease may actually be rising. *The Wall Street Journal,* p. B6.

Place the exact date of issue within parentheses immediately after the author. After the newspaper title, specify the page number(s). Include *The* if it is part of the newspaper title.

### N. GOVERNMENT DOCUMENT

U.S. Department of Labor. (1993). *Teaching the SCANS competencies.* Washington,

DC: U.S. Government Printing Office.

List the agency that produced the document as the author if no author is identified. Within parentheses immediately after the document title, give the publication number (which is assigned to the document by the government), if available.

### O. ANONYMOUS WORK

A breath of fresh air. (1991, April 29). *Time, 187,* 49.

Alphabetize the work under the first important word in the title, and follow the form for the type of publication in question (in this case a magazine published weekly).

### P. JOURNAL ARTICLE RETRIEVED ONLINE

If the article you are citing is from a print journal that also appears online, then cite the article as you normally would but indicate that you viewed the electronic version as follows:

Smith, K. (2001). Critical conversations in difficult times [Electronic version].

*English Education, 33*(2), 153–165.

However, if the article you are citing might be different online (for instance, it includes additional text or charts) or if it has no page numbers, then indicate when you accessed it and include the URL:

Smith, K. (2001). Critical conversations in difficult times. *English Education, 33*(2),

153–165. Retrieved December 12, 2002, from http://www.ncte.org/pdfs/

subscribers-only/ee/0332-jan01/EE0332Critical.pdf

### Q. ONLINE JOURNAL ARTICLE

For an article from a journal that appears only online (and not in print form), include the date of access and the URL of the site where the article was located:

Lassonde, C. A. (2002). Learning from others: Literacy perspectives of

middle-school English teachers. *Networks, 5*(3). Retrieved January 15, 2003,

from http://www.oise.utoronto.ca/~ctd/networks/journal/Vol%205(3).2002dec/

Lassonde.html

Notice that there is no period after the URL.

### R. INTERVIEW

Interviews are not considered recoverable data and should not be included in the References.

<table>
<tr><td>

**A Checklist for Documentation**

</td><td>

**1.** Remember to document any direct quotation, any idea that has come from someone else's work, and any fact or statistic that is not widely known. **2.** Be sure to enclose all quotations in quotation marks. **3.** Make sure that paraphrases are in your own words but still accurately reflect the content of the original material. **4.** Remember that every source cited in your text should have a corresponding entry in the bibliography. **5.** Try to vary the introductions you use for quotations and paraphrases. **6.** When you mention authorities by name, try to identify who they are so that your audience can evaluate the source. (For example, "According to Ira Glasser, Executive Director of the American Civil Liberties Union, recent congressional legislation violates . . . .") However, you need not identify well-known figures. **7.** If in doubt about whether to document a source, you would probably be wise to document it. But be careful not to overdocument your paper.

</td></tr>
</table>

## PREPARING YOUR FINAL DRAFT

After investing considerable time in researching, drafting, and revising your paper, be sure to allow sufficient time for editing your final draft. If you rush this stage of the process, the work that you submit for evaluation might not adequately reflect the investment of time you gave to the project as a whole. Unless instructed otherwise, you should be guided by the rules in the following checklist.

<table>
<tr><td>

**A Checklist for Manuscript Form**

</td><td>

**1.** Papers should be typed or word processed. Use nonerasable 8 1/2-by-11-inch white paper. Type on one side of each page. Double-space all lines, leaving a margin of one inch on all sides. **2.** In the upper left corner of page 1 or on a separate title page, include the following information: your name, your instructor's name, the course and section number, and the date the essay is submitted. **3.** Number each page in the upper right corner, 1.2 inches from the top. If using MLA-style documentation, type your last name immediately before the page number. If using APA-style documentation, type a shortened version of the title (one or two words) before the number. **4.** Make sure that you consistently follow a documentation style that is acceptable to your instructor. **5.** Any quotation of more than four lines in an MLA-style paper or more than forty words in an APA-style paper should be set off from the rest of the text. Begin a new line, indenting one inch (or ten spaces) to form the left margin of the quotation. The indention means that you are quoting, so additional quotation marks are unnecessary in this case (except for quotations within the quotation). **6.** Proofread your paper carefully. If your instructor allows ink corrections, make them as neatly as you can. Redo any page that has numerous or lengthy corrections. **7.** If you have used a word processor for your paper, be sure to separate pages that have been printed on a continuous sheet. Use a paper clip or staple to bind the pages together.

</td></tr>
</table>

# PART III

# NEGOTIATING DIFFERENCES

8 | Ownership

9 | Education

10 | Environments

11 | American National Identity

12 | Free Enterprise

13 | Globalization

# 8

## OWNERSHIP

O W N E

## Cluster
### WHO OWNS MUSIC?

① Janis Ian, "Free Downloads Play Sweet Music"

② Richard Taruskin, "Music Dangers and the Case for Control"

③ Jeffrey O.G. Ogbar and Vijay Prashad, "Black Is Back"

④ Jenny Toomey, "Empire of the Air"

CON-TEXT
**The Importance of Music**

RSHIP

# WHO OWNS

# MUSIC?

In January 2003, in a case known as *Eldred* v. *Ashcroft,* the U.S. Supreme Court upheld a law that extended the term for copyrights for books, movies, music, and other intellectual property for twenty years beyond the fifty years that previous laws already provided for. The case was considered to be one of the most important decisions involving intellectual property in recent decades, and the intense debate surrounding it reflects the importance of copyright law in the United States and the deep concerns many citizens have about it. Those concerns seem especially deep when it comes to copyrights involving music. ■ Although creative works of all kinds are protected under copyright law, music seems to generate particularly intense controversy. Perhaps that's because music is so much a part of the lives of most people; for many people, music is not so much a product as a cultural treasure to which everyone has a right. (See *Con-Text* on page 213.) It can also be difficult to distinguish among the many different forms of music and the variety of media in which it exists. For example, is a song that is played on the radio subject to the same copyright rules as a song that is played on a CD in a private home? ■ *Eldred* v. *Ashcroft* highlighted the complexity of questions about who owns music and controls its distribution. While representatives of media corporations praised the ruling as an important protection for songwriters and musicians, others complained that the ruling would prevent the public from enjoying the benefits of musical works. Some scholars believe that the framers of the Constitution intended copyright to encourage scientific and creative work and to ensure that such work would eventually benefit the public. But copyright law can also mean profits. It gives songwriters and musicians — and the media companies that produce and distribute their work — the right to earn money from their songs or performances, and it prevents others from profiting unfairly from copyrighted music. And the great popularity of music means that there is a great deal of money at stake. ■ Recent technological developments have added to the difficulty of sorting through these issues. The capabilities of new computer technologies have made it easier than ever for consumers to reproduce and share music. Like millions of other consumers, you might have visited Web sites where you can download, free of charge, copies of your favorite songs that someone else has made available on that site. Such capabilities raise questions about when a copy of a song is being used illegally. Is it a violation of copyright law to download a music file that was copied from a CD that another person legally purchased and then made available on a private Web site? Or is downloading a file the same thing as letting a friend borrow a CD you have purchased so that he or she can record it? The media companies supporting the decision in *Eldred* v. *Ashcroft* believe that they are losing profits whenever someone downloads a song in this way. Others argue that consumers have the right to share music through the Internet. Although the copyright to a song indicates clearly who "owns" that song, it is less clear how far that copyright extends. Must be permission be granted every time that song is played or copied, no matter what the circumstances? Such questions involve legal and economic complexities that will become even more difficult to sort out as new technologies develop. ■ But as the essays in this section indicate, controversies involving the ownership of music are not limited to legal or economic issues. Music can also be considered an expression of cultural identity. But who owns that identity? That question emerged as hip hop and rap music gained popularity in the 1980s and 1990s.

These musical forms "borrowed" from other kinds of music in the form of sampling, a practice whereby an artist incorporates or "quotes" from other songs. Some artists believe that such sampling requires payment, because parts of songs are protected by copyright law. In turn, rap music, which many consider to be a form of Black cultural expression, influenced other musicians, who then "borrowed" from rap — raising questions about whether such borrowing is simply the influence of one form of music on another or constitutes "stealing" an artist's racial or cultural identity. ■ Like certain written works, music has also been subject to censorship in the United States and elsewhere in the world. Sometimes such censorship is based on concerns about morality; sometimes it is driven by political beliefs. Whatever the case, censoring music raises questions not only about free speech but also about who has the right to control artistic expression. ■ Obviously, as such an important and widespread part of culture, music is much more than entertainment. Thus, the questions about the ownership of music raised by the essays in this section reflect important social, legal, economic, and even moral concerns that affect all of us, regardless of our musical tastes. These essays might not provide answers to the kinds of difficult questions regarding intellectual property and music that we have discussed here. But they can help us to understand the issues so that we can seek our own answers in a more informed manner.

## CON-TEXT: The Importance of Music

1 Music is a basic function of human existence, arising from the physiological, psychological, and sociological needs of human kind. As such, the value of musical pursuit derives not only from the endeavor to achieve the highest forms of the musical art according to socially accepted norms, but also from the everyday musical encounters of every person. To this end, music is a necessary, life-enhancing experience which should be nurtured in all individuals, not only in those gifted with musical aptitude.

Music is an invariant. It has been present in all cultures, at all times, and throughout the known historical development of the human species, facilitating emotional, physical, and social expression. Music satisfies the human need for aesthetic enjoyment, provides for communication of cultural ideals, integrates, and enculturates.

SOURCE: Kenneth Liske, "Philosophy of Music Education."

# ① JANIS IAN, "Free Downloads Play Sweet Music"

In the late 1990s, as digital technologies began to influence the consumer market for music, listeners began to take advantage of the capabilities of the Internet to share music with each other. With powerful new computer technologies, a consumer could purchase a CD by a favorite musician, copy a song from that CD to a computer hard drive, then send that song to a friend — and to many other people as well — through the Internet. Eventually, Web sites were established that became clearinghouses for music, usually as MP3 files, a digital format that is well suited to reproducing sound. The best-known of these Web sites was Napster, which at the height of its popularity was visited by hundreds of thousands of users each day, many of whom would download music files via Napster's peer-to-peer software. But even after a legal suit curtailed much of the file-downloading activity enabled by Napster's software in 2000, consumers have continued to find ways to share music files digitally, raising concerns among some musicians and among media companies about copyright violations and about lost profits. As media companies seek ways to prevent the exchange of music files, advocates of free speech and privacy — including some musicians, like Janis Ian — argue that music should be freely available on the Internet, even if that music is protected by copyright. In the following essay, Ian, herself an accomplished musician and recording artist who has won two Grammy awards, argues that musicians and consumers can all benefit from free music downloads; moreover, she suggests that free downloads are good for the art itself by making music more widely available. Her essay encourages us to consider some of the economic issues involving music downloads. But her argument might also be cause to wonder about who should control the distribution of music, once a song has been protected by copyright. This article appeared on *ZDNet,* an Internet technology network, in 2002. It is a shorter version of the original article, which was published in *Performing Songwriter Magazine* in 2002.

## Free Downloads Play Sweet Music
### JANIS IAN

1   When researching an article, I normally send e-mails to friends and acquaintances, who answer my request with opinions and anecdotes. But when I said I was planning to argue that free Internet downloads are good for the music industry and its artists, I was swamped.

I received over 300 replies — and every single one from someone legitimately in the music business.

Even more interesting than the

e-mails were the phone calls. I don't know anyone at the National Academy of Recording Arts & Sciences (NARAS, home of the Grammy Awards), and I know Hilary Rosen (head of the Recording Industry Association of America, or RIAA)* only in passing. Yet within 24 hours of sending my original e-mail, I'd received two messages from Rosen and four from NARAS, requesting that I call to "discuss the article."

Huh. Didn't know I was that widely read.

**5** Ms. Rosen, to be fair, stressed that she was only interested in presenting RIAA's side of the issue, and was kind enough to send me a fair amount of statistics and documentation, including a number of focus group studies RIAA had run on the matter.

However, the problem with focus groups is the same problem anthropologists have when studying peoples in the field: the moment the anthropologist's presence is known, everything changes. Hundreds of scientific studies have shown that any experimental group *wants to please the examiner*. For focus groups, this is particularly true. Coffee and donuts are the least of the payoffs.

The NARAS people were a bit more pushy. They told me downloads were "destroying sales," "ruining the music industry," and "costing *you* money."

Costing *me* money? I don't pretend to be an expert on intellectual property law, but I do know one thing. If a music industry executive claims I should agree with their agenda because it will make me more money, I put my hand on my wallet . . . and check it after they leave, just to make sure nothing's missing.

Am I suspicious of all this hysteria? You bet. Do I think the issue has been badly handled? Absolutely. Am I concerned about losing friends, opportunities, my 10th Grammy nomination, by

publishing this article? Yeah. I am. But sometimes things are just wrong, and when they're that wrong, they have to be addressed.

**10** The premise of all this ballyhoo is that the industry (and its artists) are being harmed by free downloading.

Nonsense.

Let's take it from my personal experience. My site gets an average of 75,000 hits a year. Not bad for someone whose last hit record was in 1975. When Napster was running full-tilt, we received about 100 hits a month from people who'd downloaded Society's Child or At Seventeen for free, then decided they wanted more information. Of those 100 people (and these are only the ones who let us know how they'd found the site), 15 bought CDs.

Not huge sales, right? No record company is interested in 180 extra sales a year. But that translates into $2,700, which is a lot of money in my book. And that doesn't include the people who bought the CDs in stores, or came to my shows.

RIAA, NARAS and most of the entrenched music industry argue that free

*According to its Web site, "The Recording Industry Association of America is the trade group that represents the U.S. recording industry. Its mission is to foster a business and legal climate that supports and promotes our members' creative and financial vitality. Its members are the record companies that comprise the most vibrant national music industry in the world. RIAA© members create, manufacture and/or distribute approximately 90% of all legitimate sound recordings produced and sold in the United States." The RIAA filed the lawsuit against Napster that ended Napster's online music sharing service.

## NAPSTER

An Internet service for sharing music files (in MP3 format), Napster was founded in 1999 by a college student named Shawn Fanning, who established a Web site where users could exchange their private music files. Napster quickly became an Internet phenomenon as thousands of users began to use Napster's file-sharing software to share music. As many as 60 million users were visiting the site by early 2001. In 2000, the Recording Industry Association of America (RIAA) filed suit against Napster, alleging copyright infringement, and a drawn-out court battle ensued. A court ruled in favor of the RIAA in 2000 and stopped the free exchange of copyrighted files via Napster's software, but Napster continued to operate in a more limited way until 2002, when additional court rulings finally shut it down. But the issues regarding intellectual property, copyright law, and consumer privacy that the Napster case raised generated intense debate that continued well after Napster ceased its operations.

The music industry had exactly the same response to the advent of reel-to-reel home tape recorders, cassettes, DATs, minidiscs, videos, MTV ("Why buy the record when you can tape it?") and a host of other technological advances designed to make the consumer's life easier and better. I know because I was there.

The only reason they didn't react that way publicly to the advent of CDs was because they believed CDs were uncopyable. I was told this personally by a former head of Sony marketing, when they asked me to license Between the Lines in CD format at a reduced royalty rate. ("Because it's a brand new technology.")

Realistically, why do most people download music? To hear new music, and to find old, out-of-print music — not to avoid paying $5 at the local used CD store, or taping it off the radio, but to hear music they can't find anywhere else. Face it: Most people can't afford to spend $15.99 to experiment. And an awful lot of records are out of print; I have a few myself!

downloads hurt sales. More than hurt — it's destroying the industry.

**15** Alas, the music industry needs no outside help to destroy itself. We're doing a very adequate job of that on our own, thank you.

Everyone is forgetting the main way an artist becomes successful — exposure. Without exposure, no one comes to shows, no one buys CDs, no one enables you to earn a living doing what you love. 20Again, from personal experience: In 37 years as a recording artist, I've created 25-plus albums for major labels, and I've *never* received a royalty statement that didn't show I owed *them* money. Label accounting practices are right up there with Enron. I make the bulk of my living from live touring, doing my own show. Live shows are pushed by my Web site, which is pushed by the live shows, and both are pushed by the availability of my music, for free, online.

Who gets hurt by free downloads? Save a handful of super-successes like Celine Dion, none of us. We only get helped.

Most consumers have no problem paying for entertainment. If the music industry had a shred of sense, they'd have addressed this problem seven years ago, when people like Michael Camp were trying to obtain legitimate licenses for music online. Instead, the industrywide attitude was, "It'll go away." That's the same attitude CBS Records had about rock 'n' roll when Mitch Miller was head of A&R. (And you wondered why they passed on The Beatles and The Rolling Stones.)

NARAS and RIAA are moaning about the little mom-and-pop stores being shoved out of business; no one worked harder to shove them out than our own industry, which greeted every new megamusic store with glee, and offered steep discounts to Target, WalMart, et al, for stocking their CDs. The Internet has zero

**CONTEXT**

Born in 1951, singer and songwriter Janis Ian released the first of her seventeen albums in 1967. Her 1975 hit song "At Seventeen" earned her the first of two Grammy Awards. She has recorded music for many movie soundtracks, and she has received acclaim as a jazz musician as well as for her children's music. Despite her own success, she has been an outspoken critic of many of the practices of the music industry.

to do with store closings and lowered sales.

And for those of us with major label contracts who want some of our music available for free downloading . . . well, the record companies own our masters, our outtakes, even our demos, and they won't allow it. Furthermore, they own our voices for the duration of the contract, so we can't post a live track for downloading even if we want to.

25If you think about it, the music industry should be rejoicing at this new technological advance. Here's a foolproof way to deliver music to millions who might otherwise never purchase a CD in a store. The cross-marketing opportunities are unbelievable. Costs are minimal, shipping nonexistent — a staggering vehicle for higher earnings and lower costs. Instead, they're running around like chickens with their heads cut off, bleeding on everyone and making no sense.

There is *zero* evidence that material available for free online downloading is financially harming anyone. In fact, most of the hard evidence is to the contrary.

The RIAA is correct in one thing — these are times of great change in our industry. But at a time when there are arguably only four record labels left in America (Sony, AOL Time Warner, Universal, BMG — and where is the

**COMPLICATION**

"I admit it, I love technology. Technologically speaking, I think MP3s are a great idea. But I hate music piracy.

"I believe that it is wrong to copy an artist's intellectual property (their music) without their permission. I believe the same about all intellectual property, such as computer software. I think that all intellectual property owners have the absolute right to decide how their creations are distributed.

"Because of the nature of intellectual property, stealing some of that property doesn't physically remove anything. So there's obviously nothing wrong with music piracy, right? To the contrary. Because intellectual property is just an idea or a representation of that idea, distribution rights is the only thing an intellectual property owner actually owns. In other words, downloading music when the artist doesn't give permission robs them of the only thing they actually have — the right to decide who gets to hear their music and how much it costs them." Source: Kevin Markham, "MP3s Great Technology, but Use Must Be Ethical." (2000).

RICO act when we need it?), when entire genres are glorifying the gangster mentality and losing their biggest voices to violence, when executives change positions as often as Zsa Zsa Gabor changed clothes, and "A&R" has become a euphemism for "Absent & Redundant," we have other things to worry about.

We'll turn into Microsoft if we're not careful, folks, insisting that any household wanting an extra copy for the car, the kids, or the portable CD player, has to go out and "license" multiple copies.

As artists, we have the ear of the masses. We have the trust of the masses. By speaking out in our concerts and in the press, we can do a great deal to dampen this hysteria, and put the blame for the sad state of our industry right back where it belongs — in the laps of record companies, radio programmers, and our own apparent inability to organize ourselves in order to better our own lives — and those of our fans.

30 If we don't take the reins, no one will.

## Questions for Discussion

**1.** Ian draws heavily on her own experience as a musician and a recording artist to support her position on music downloads. Evaluate her use of personal experience as evidence. How effective do you think it is? Is it adequate for her main argument? Do you think she could have used other kinds of evidence to support her argument? Explain. (In answering these questions, you might wish to review the discussion of appraising evidence on pages 76–82). **2.** Ian begins her essay by telling an anecdote about the number of messages she received from people who learned that she was writing about free music downloads. Why do you think she begins her essay in this way? Do you think this beginning is an effective way for her to introduce her subject? Explain. **3.** Ian writes, "There is *zero* evidence that material available for free online downloading is financially harming anyone. In fact, most of the hard evidence is to the contrary." To what extent do you think Ian provides such "hard evidence" in her essay? Do you think she is persuasive on this point? Why or why not? **4.** How would you describe Ian's writing style in this essay? In what ways do you think her style might make her argument more effective? What sort of persona, or *ethos* (see pages 73–75) does her style establish? How might her background and experience as a recording artist contribute to that persona? **5.** Ian devotes a considerable amount of her essay to discussing the positions of music industry people who oppose free music downloads. Why do you think she does so? Do you think she presents their concerns fairly? Explain. How does she characterize the music industry people who oppose her position? In what ways might her argument be strengthened — or weakened — by the way she characterizes these people and their interests? **6.** This essay was published in *ZDNet*, a network of Internet sites that is, according to its Web site, intended for "IT [information technology] professionals and business influencers" and "provides an invaluable perspective and resources so that users can get the most out of their investments in technology." In what ways do you think Ian addresses this audience? Do you think she does so effectively? Explain.

## ② RICHARD TARUSKIN, "Music Dangers and the Case for Control"

Efforts by governments or institutions (such as religious organizations) to ban certain kinds of music are nothing new. So when the Taliban, the Islamic group that ruled Afghanistan from 1996 to 2002, instituted severe and often brutal restrictions on music, many observers saw the move as just another example of censorship. Western critics condemned the ban as a repressive attempt by the Taliban to impose its religious views on the Afghani people, and they argued that free expression — in this case, in the form of music — is a right that should be guaranteed to all people. But is censoring or restricting music ever justified? Music professor Richard Taruskin thinks so. Although he doesn't condone repressive measures such as the Taliban instituted, Taruskin believes that governments can have a compelling — and justifiable — interest in controlling music to serve the public good. This position might seem dramatically out of step with Western values of free speech. But Taruskin argues that music, like other kinds of art, isn't just a form of artistic expression but a means of conveying ideas or beliefs as well. He contends that governments routinely try to control the distribution of certain ideas — with good reason; therefore, governments have reason to control music. Many Americans will likely disagree with Taruskin. But as you read, consider his view of what music is and why it might justifiably be controlled in the public interest. Richard Taruskin teaches music history at the University of California at Berkeley. This essay appeared in the *New York Times* in December, 2001.

## Music Dangers and the Case for Control
### RICHARD TARUSKIN

1   And on top of everything else, the Taliban hate music, too. In an interview in October with Nicholas Wroe, a columnist for the British newspaper *The Guardian,* John Baily, an ethnomusicologist on the faculty of Goldsmiths College, London, gave the details. After taking power in 1996, the Islamic fundamentalists who ruled most of Afghanistan undertook search-and-destroy missions in which musical instruments and cassette players were seized and burned in public pyres. Wooden poles were festooned with great ribbons of confiscated audio and video tape as a reminder of the ban, imposed in keeping with a maxim attributed to the prophet Muhammad warning "those who listen to music and songs in this world" that "on the Day of Judgment molten lead will be poured into their ears."

Musicians caught in the act were beaten with their instruments and imprisoned for as many as 40 days. The interdiction on professional music-making closed off yet another avenue to women's participation in public life. The only sounds on the Taliban-dominated radio that Western ears would recognize as musical were those of ritual chanting (something quite distinct from "music," both conceptually and linguistically, in Islamic thought as in many of the world's cultures).

So what else is new? Utopians, puritans and totalitarians have always sought to regulate music, if not forbid it outright. Ayatollah Ruhollah Khomeini, probably the Taliban's immediate model, banned it from Iranian radio and television in 1979, because its effects, he said, were like those of opium, "stupefying persons listening to it and making their brains inactive and frivolous."

But our own "Western" tradition is just as full of suspicion toward music, much of it religious. In the fourth century, St. Augustine confessed that as a result of his sensuous enjoyment of the melodies he heard in church, "I have become a problem unto myself." In the 12th, John of Salisbury complained that the spectacular music sung in the Paris Cathedral of Notre Dame could "more easily occasion titillation between the legs than a sense of devotion in the brain." Protestant reformers in England and Switzerland seized and burned books containing "popish ditties" with Talibanish zeal. Somewhat later, the Orthodox patriarch of Moscow ordered bonfires of musical instruments, thought to be avatars of paganism.

5 Religious distrust of music often arises out of distrust of its conduits, especially when female. St. John Chrysostom, the great Father of the Greek Orthodox Church, complained that when marriages were solemnized, "dancing, and cymbals and flutes, and shameful words and songs from the lips of painted girls" were introduced, and with them "all the Devil's great heap of garbage." Near the beginning of my career as a college music teacher, a young Hasidic man in fringes and gabardines approached me on the first day of class to inform me that he was willing to take my course, but that he would sit near the door, and I was to warn him whenever I would play a record that contained the sound of a woman's voice so that he could slip into the hall and avoid it. (Don't do me any favors, I replied.)

Secular thinkers have been no less leery of music. In a famous passage from Plato's "Republic," Socrates advocates banning most of the musical modes or scales, "because more than anything else rhythm and harmony find their way to the inmost soul and take strongest hold upon it, bringing with them and imparting grace, if one is rightly trained, and otherwise the contrary." If Plato were writing today (or less euphemistically),

## AYATOLLAH KHOMEINI AND THE TALIBAN

In 1979, exiled Islamic leader Ayatollah Ruhollah Khomeini returned to Iran after his supporters overthrew the U.S.-backed government of the Shah of Iran. Khomeini imposed a government based on his interpretation of the Koran, the holy book of Islam, and harshly criticized Western culture, especially American culture, as decadent, irreligious, and dangerous. Many scholars believed that his model of an Islamic theocracy was adopted by the Taliban when they took power in Afghanistan in 1996. By then, Khomeini had died, but the government he had established in Iran remained in power and served as an inspiration to Moslems elsewhere who shared his interpretation of the Koran. Although many Western and even some Arab nations condemned the Taliban for what they believed were repressive and brutal controls over the people of Afghanistan, some Moslems looked to the Taliban as another model for establishing an Islamic state. The Taliban were removed from power after the United States and its allies invaded Afghanistan in 2002.

arts into a delivery system for political propaganda. Here is how one of Plato's heirs, Joseph Goebbels, retorted to the conductor Wilhelm Furtwängler's plea for moderation in implementing Nazi arts policies:

"Art, in an absolute sense, as liberal democracy knows it, has no right to exist. Any attempt to further such an art could, in the end, cause a people to lose its inner relationship to art and the artist to isolate himself from the moving forces of his time, shut in the airless chambers of 'art for art's sake.' Art must be good but, beyond that, conscious of its responsibility, competent, close to the people and combative in spirit."

**10** The same kind of pronouncements and policy directives emanated from the Soviets, nominally the Nazis' enemies. Awful memories of the 1948 show trials convened by Andrei Zhdanov, Stalin's de facto cultural commissar, at which the leading Soviet composers (among them Prokofiev and Shostakovich) were humiliated for their "formalist" misdeeds, feed the current mania for vindicating the same composers, absurdly, as dissidents. The similarity of Nazi and Soviet views on the arts is only one reason political classifications nowadays tend to group the old far right and far left together, in opposition to the "liberal democracy" that appeared, until Sept. 11, to have beaten all of its opponents into submission.

he might have put body in place of soul. For surely it is the all but irresistible kinesthetic response that music evokes that makes it such a potent influence on behavior, thence on morals and belief.

That is what sets music off from literature and painting, and attracts the special attention of censors despite its relative abstractness, which might seem to exempt it from the need for political policing. Tolstoy compared its effects to those of hypnosis, linking right up with Ayatollah Khomeini's strictures. And it can only be a similar discomfort about music's affinity with our grosser animal nature that led so many musical modernists to put so much squeamish distance between their cerebral art and viscerally engaging popular culture.

In any case, Plato's mingled awe and suspicion of music's uncanny power over our minds and bodies have echoed through the ages wherever governments have tried to harness music to uphold the public order (or at least keep music from disrupting it). They found the greatest resonance in those 20th-century totalitarian states that tried to turn the

That is probably why the Taliban's ban on musical performances, while in no way an unusual historical event (and not even really news), has suddenly drawn so much comment. It symbolizes the survival of impulses we might naïvely have thought discredited for good and all — as dead, in their way, as smallpox, with whose revival we are also unexpectedly threatened in these unsettled times.

Anything that conjures up both Nazis and Soviets, and now the Taliban, can have few friends in contemporary Western society. As Mayor Giuliani found out before he became our hero, hardly anything a politician can do will elicit a more dependable outcry across the political spectrum than a move in the direction of arts censorship, even if it threatens no direct intervention in the affairs of artists but only the withholding of municipal largess from institutions (like the Brooklyn Museum of Art) that support them. There is near unanimity in the West today that when it comes to the arts, laissez-faire (coupled, perhaps illogically, with handouts) is the way to go.

But who takes art more seriously? Those who want it left alone or those who want to regulate it? Moreover, the laissez-faire position entails some serious denials. Some say that art is inherently uplifting (if it is really art). Others say that art is inherently transgressive (if it is really art). The words in parentheses, designed to discourage counterexamples and make refutation impossible, merely empty the statements of real meaning. Does such a defense really show a commitment to the value of

art or merely an unwillingness to think about it?

And what about public opinion, which sometimes demands abstentions from the performance or exhibit of artworks? Is that just another censorship tribunal? 15 The musical test case par excellence has always been the taboo on Wagner performances in Israel. Breaching it makes headlines, as the conductor Daniel Barenboim knows very well. He did it last summer to a great din of public protest and righteous indignation. But those who defended Mr. Barenboim's provocation often failed to distinguish between voluntary abstinence out of consideration for people's feelings and a mandated imposition on people's rights.

It was only a social contract that Mr. Barenboim defied, but he seemed to want credit for defying a ban. His act implied that the feelings of Holocaust survivors had been coddled long enough and that continuing to honor them was both an intolerable infringement on his career and an insult to artistic greatness. To agree with him, one had to stretch the definition of censorship way beyond that associated with Nazis, Soviets and Islamic fundamentalists, into moral terrain usually associated with forbearance or discretion or mutual respect.

Now the issue has been joined again, even more pointedly and painfully, in the aftermath of the Sept. 11 terrorist attacks. Announcing that it preferred "to err on the side of being sensitive," the management of the Boston Symphony Orchestra recently canceled its scheduled performances of choruses from "The Death of Klinghoffer," the notoriously controversial opera — masterminded by the director Peter Sellars, with a libretto by the poet Alice Goodman and a score by John Adams — that re-enacts and comments on the murder of an American Jew by Palestinian terrorists aboard the cruise ship Achille Lauro in the fall of 1985.

For thus showing forbearance and discretion, the Boston Symphony has taken some pies in the face. In an exceptionally vulgar rant that appeared in *The San Francisco Chronicle,* the arts columnist David Wiegand, enraged at what he perceived as a slight to Mr. Adams (a Bay Area luminary), wrote, "There is something deeply wrong when a nation galvanizes its forces, its men and women, its determination and its resolve, to preserve the right of the yahoos at the Boston Symphony Orchestra to decide to spare its listeners something that might challenge them or make them think." What nation had done this? And why shouldn't people be spared reminders of recent personal pain when they attend a concert?

A month earlier, Mark Swed, the chief music critic for *The Los Angeles Times,* had expressed a similar opinion, only slightly more decorously, when he boasted that, "preferring answers and understanding to comfort," he had listened to the Nonesuch recording of "Klinghoffer" the day after the World Trade Center had collapsed. But whence this quaintly macho impulse to despise comfort (women's work?) and even deny it haughtily to sufferers? And whence the idea of seeking answers and understand-

ing in an opera peopled by wholly fictional terrorists and semifictionalized victims, rather than in more relevant sources of information?
**20** Anthony Tommasini, in the *New York Times,* endorsed Mr. Adams's contention that his opera offers "the sad solace of truth." What truth? "The Death of Klinghoffer" trades in the tritest undergraduate fantasies. If the events of Sept. 11 could not jar some artists and critics out of their habit of romantically idealizing criminals, then nothing will. But isn't it time for artists and critics to grow up with the rest of us, now that the unthinkable has occurred?

## THE DEATH OF KLINGHOFFER

In 1985, armed members of the Palestine Liberation Front hijacked a commercial cruise ship called the *Achille Lauro,* which was carrying more than 400 tourists on a Mediterranean Sea cruise. The hijackers demanded that fifty Palestinians imprisoned by Israel be released, and they killed Leon Klinghoffer, a sixty-nine-year-old disabled American passenger, subsequently throwing his body and wheelchair overboard. The opera based on the incident, *The Death of Klinghoffer,* by Alice Goodman with music by John Adams, has been controversial since its premiere in 1991.

Protesting the decision of the Boston Symphony Orchestra to cancel its performance of the opera *The Death of Klinghoffer* in 2001, Anthony Tommasini wrote,

But how patronizing for the orchestra's directors to presume what audiences will or will not find offensive. Of course, art can provide solace and comfort. Yet art can also incense and challenge us, make us squirm, make us think. The Boston Symphony missed an opportunity to present an acutely relevant work. . . .

Some have found "Klinghoffer" too soft on the terrorists, too quick to caricature Jews. What do three white Westerners know about ancient conflicts in the Middle East?

Yet a few days after the [September 11, 2001 terrorist] attacks, Senator John Kerry, Democrat of Massachusetts, while calling for decisive military action, courageously suggested that we Americans have not really tried to understand why so many Muslims hate us. That is exactly what Mr. Adams and his co-creators tried to do in "Klinghoffer." Source: Anthony Tommasini, "John Adams, Banned in Boston" (2001).

If terrorism — specifically, the commission or advocacy of deliberate acts of deadly violence directed randomly at the innocent — is to be defeated, world public opinion has to be turned decisively against it. The only way to do that is to focus resolutely on the acts rather than their claimed (or conjectured) motivations, and to characterize all such acts, whatever their motivation, as crimes. This means no longer romanticizing terrorists as Robin Hoods and no longer idealizing their deeds as rough poetic justice. If we indulge such notions when we happen to agree or sympathize with the aims, then we have forfeited the moral ground from which any such acts can be convincingly condemned.

Does "The Death of Klinghoffer" romanticize the perpetrators of deadly violence toward the innocent? Its creators tacitly acknowledged that it did, when they revised the opera for American consumption after its European premieres in Brussels and Paris. In its original version, the opening "Chorus of Exiled Palestinians" was followed not by a balancing "Chorus of Exiled Jews" but by a scene, now dropped from the score, that showed the Klinghoffers' suburban neighbors gossiping merrily about their impending cruise ("The dollar's up. Good news for the Klinghoffers") to an accompaniment of hackneyed pop-style music.

That contrast set the vastly unequal terms on which the conflict of Palestinians and Jews would be perceived throughout the opera. The portrayal of suffering Palestinians in the musical language of myth and ritual was immediately juxtaposed with a musically trivial portrayal of contented, materialistic American Jews. The paired characterizations could not help linking up with lines sung later by "Rambo," one of the fictional terrorists, who (right before the murder) wrathfully dismisses Leon Klinghoffer's protest at his treatment with the accusation that "wherever poor men are gathered you can find Jews getting fat."

Is it unfair to discuss a version of the opera that has been withdrawn from publication and remains unrecorded? It would have been, except that Mr. Adams, throwing his own pie at the Boston Symphony in an interview published recently on the Andante.com Web site, saw fit to point out that the opera "has never seemed particularly shocking to audiences in Europe." He was playing the shame game, trying to make the Boston cancellation look provincial. But when one takes into account that the version European audiences saw in 1991 catered to so many of their favorite prejudices — anti-American, anti-Semitic, anti-bourgeois — the shame would seem rather to go the other way.

25 Nor have these prejudices been erased from the opera in its revised form. The libretto commits many notorious breaches of evenhandedness, but the greatest one is to be found in Mr. Adams's music. In his interview, the composer repeats the oft drawn comparison between the operatic Leon Klinghoffer and the "sacrificial victim" who is "at the heart of the Bach Passions." But his music, precisely insofar as it relies on Bach's example, undermines the facile analogy.

In the "St. Matthew Passion," Bach accompanies the words of Jesus with an aureole of violins and violas that sets him off as numinous, the way a halo would do in a painting. There is a comparable effect in "Klinghoffer": long, quiet, drawn-out tones in the highest violin register (occasionally spelled by electronic synthesizers or high oboe tones). They recall not only the Bachian aureole but also effects of limitless expanse in time or space, familiar from many Romantic scores. (An example is the beginning of Borodin's "In the Steppes of Central Asia.") These numinous, "timeless" tones accompany virtually all the utterances of the choral Palestinians or the terrorists, beginning with the opening chorus.

They underscore the words spoken by the fictitious terrorist Molqui: "We are not criminals and we are not vandals, but men of ideals." Together with an exotically "Oriental" obbligato bassoon, they accompany the fictitious terrorist Mamoud's endearing reverie about his favorite love songs. They add resonance to the fictitious terrorist Omar's impassioned yearnings for a martyr's afterlife; and they also appear when the ship's captain tries to mediate between the terrorists and the victims.

They do not accompany the victims, except in the allegorical "Aria of the Falling Body," sung by the slain Klinghoffer's remains as they are tossed overboard by the terrorists. Only after death does the familiar American middle-class Jew join the glamorously exotic Palestinians in mythic timelessness. Only as his body falls lifeless is his music ex-alted to a comparably romanticized spiritual dimension.

Why should we want to hear this music now? Is it an edifying challenge, as Mr. Wiegand and Mr. Tommasini contend? Does it give us answers that we should prefer, with Mr. Swed, to comfort? Or does it express a reprehensible contempt for the real-life victims of its imagined "men of ideals," all too easily transferable to the victims who perished on Sept. 11?

30 In a fine recent essay, the literary critic and queer theorist Jonathan Dollimore writes that "to take art seriously — to recognize its potential — must be to recognize that there might be reasonable grounds for wanting to control it." Where should control come from? Unless we are willing to trust the Taliban, it has to come from within. What is called for is self-control. That is what the Boston Symphony laudably exercised; and I hope that musicians who play to Israeli audiences will resume exercising it. There is no need to shove Wagner in the faces of Holocaust survivors in Israel and no need to torment people stunned by previously unimaginable horrors with offensive "challenges" like "The Death of Klinghoffer."

Censorship is always deplorable, but the exercise of forbearance can be noble. Not to be able to distinguish the noble from the deplorable is morally obtuse. In the wake of Sept. 11, we might want, finally, to get beyond sentimental complacency about art. Art is not blameless. Art can inflict harm. The Taliban know that. It's about time we learned.

**CONTEXT**

Andante.com describes itself as "a new type of classical music venture. Its aim is to document and preserve the world's recorded classical musical heritage and to become the definitive online resource for information about classical music and opera. . . . The mission of the andante Web site is to provide a single, convenient location for in-depth information, stimulating ideas and opinions, and exclusive performances in the world of classical music."

# Questions for Discussion

1. Taruskin asserts that Western culture "is full of suspicion toward music." What kinds of evidence does he offer to support that point? Do you think the nature and amount of his evidence are sufficient for his point? Do you find his evidence convincing? Why or why not? (In answering this question, you might refer to "Appraising Evidence" on pages 76–82.) 2. What makes music such a potentially powerful influence on behavior and belief, according to Taruskin? Why is this point important to his main argument? Do you agree with him? Explain. 3. Taruskin discusses an incident in which a conductor, Daniel Barenboim, led a performance of Richard Wagner's music in Israel in 2001, and he uses that incident to distinguish between refraining from doing something out of consideration for others ("a voluntary abstinence") and an outright ban on something. Why is this distinction important for Taruskin? How does it relate to his larger point about the control of art? 4. How does Taruskin justify his assertion that the opera *The Death of Klinghoffer* romanticizes terrorism? How convincing is his support for this assertion? Other forms of music — especially rap music in recent years — have been criticized for romanticizing violence in this way. Think of some examples of music that might do so. Do these examples strengthen or weaken Taruskin's claims, in your view? Explain. 5. In paragraphs 26 through 28, Taruskin focuses on musical elements of the opera *The Death of Klinghoffer* as well as other operas to show how operas can reflect a particular ideological viewpoint — in this case, he believes, a viewpoint that is sympathetic to the terrorists who killed Mr. Klinghoffer. Evaluate the way Taruskin uses his knowledge of musical techniques to make this point. How effective is his argument in this case? 6. Using the Toulmin model of argumentation (see pages 31–35), identify Taruskin's main reasons for his claim that music should be controlled. Also, identify his warrant for his claim. Do you think most American readers would accept Taruskin's warrant? Explain. 7. How would you describe Taruskin's tone in this essay? In what ways do you think his tone might enhance or weaken his main argument about controlling music? Cite specific passages from his essay to support your answer.

## ③ JEFFREY O.G. OGBAR AND VIJAY PRASHAD, "Black Is Back"

Arguments about intellectual property that involve rap or hip hop music usually focus on the practice of sampling, a technique that artists use to incorporate into their own songs segments, or "samples," of songs from other artists. Some critics believe that sampling violates copyright law and therefore amounts to intellectual property theft: A musician "owns" a song he or she recorded, and no one else may use that song, or even a part of it, without permission. But scholars Jeffrey Ogbar and Vijay Prashad have a different concern about the ownership of this music: They worry about who owns — or controls — the *meaning* of rap and hip hop music. If these musical styles are, as Ogbar and Prashad believe, forms of cultural expression that give voice to the concerns of Blacks, especially Black youth, then the commercialization of rap and hip hop and its popularity among mainstream groups amount to the theft of black identity as expressed in that music. If this argument seems far-fetched, consider the fact that some critics have argued that the use of folk tunes by great classical composers such as Mozart was also a kind of stealing that benefited Mozart but not the peasants whose music he used. However you feel about such arguments, Ogbar and Prashad remind us that popular music can be much more than entertainment. As a result, arguments about who controls music and how that music is used are much more than arguments about copyright. Jeffrey Ogbar, a history professor at the University of Connecticut, is also a W.E.B. Du Bois research fellow at Harvard University; Vijay Prashad, who is a professor at Trinity College (Connecticut), is the author of *Karma of Brown Folk* (2000) and *Untouchable Freedom* (2000).

## Black Is Back
### JEFFREY O.G. OGBAR AND VIJAY PRASHAD

**1** From Bogota to Beijing, hip-hop's apostles are spreading "the word," striking chords of rage and rebellion in privileged and poor kids alike, in rich countries and poor. The world, it seems, is in love with black America. But this is a treacherous affair. Back in the homeland, a war is being waged against this very same group. One of the frontlines is the prison-industrial complex — an expanding fortress, with the U.S. rate of incarceration (682 per 100,000) six to ten times higher than that of most industrialised nations. Of the two million prisoners, 49 per cent are black and 17 per cent are Latino even though they respectively represent 13 and 11 per cent of the population. Almost one in three

*Janus, a god from Roman mythology who was identified with doors, gates, and beginnings, is often represented artistically with two opposite faces.

black men between the ages of 20 and 29 are caught in the web of correctional control (incarceration, probation or parole). These men lose their right to vote, lose their place as citizens, both in the eyes of the State and in white society.

Outside of the penitentiaries, unemployment is a prison of its own. At seven per cent, the rate may seem low, but look closer and you find that this does not recognise the "disposable" part-time workers, generally composed of ethnic minorities and women. About eight per cent of African Americans are officially unemployed, but the real bombshell is reserved for black youth: almost 32 per cent cannot find a job.

Hip-hop is the "CNN of Black America", raps Chuck D of Public Enemy. Read this line with a metaphorical eye to catch a crucial but not complete reflec-tion of the world's Janus-like* attraction to rap's art of rebellion. On the one hand, CNN offers constant news coverage world-wide. In symbolic terms, we find rappers cast as reporters on the frontline, offering live updates through their music of the trials, tribulations and peculiarities of neighbourhoods and cities, from Lagos to Frankfurt. On the other hand, global media networks, like CNN, just scratch the surface and cater to mainstream political "tastes" by offering easily digestible nuggets of infotainment. Illustrating this negative side, we find a few posses of Tokyo rappers and fans, for example, literally burning their skin in tanning salons. This is an extreme example reflecting the international mantra: "Be black for a day, wigger for an afternoon!" [Wigger refers to white people who copy black fashions.]

## Contradictory impulses

Much like jazz and rock 'n' roll in the past, hip-hop has made working class U.S. youth in general and African Americans in particular a cultural hearth for the international market. Its iconic power takes many forms, depending upon the particular political goals and constraints of its practitioners. For some, hip-hop is used to attack poverty, oppression and government corruption. Other fans and musicians take aim at cultural orthodoxy by glorifying gang violence, hyper-materialism and explicit misogyny. Often these contradictory elements take shape simultaneously.

5  In the heart of advanced industrial countries, hip-hop serves as a liberation anthem for those oppressed by racism and poverty. In the disadvantaged suburbs of Paris, the lilting sounds of Senegalese MC Solaar radiate beside North African-inspired rai rap, while NTM (Nique Ta Mère — "screw your mother") besiege the fascism of Jean-Marie Le Pen's Front National party. Across the Channel, British Asian rappers Fun^Da^Mental enshrine the right to self-defence against racist attacks, while German hip-hoppers incite respect for their Turkish origins.

Yet at the same time, hip-hop is also just one of many commercial products or props used for youth rebellion against the established orders of parents. The music, dress and attitude are used to visibly divide one generation from another. In Thailand, male teens speed through the streets in swanky cars, pumped on the raw energy and anger of U.S. rap without the slightest connection to the underlying politics. In Kathmandu,[†] teens use rap's breakbeats to break with tradition, perhaps temporarily, in forging a "modern" identity.

As U.S. rapper L.L. Cool J rhymed, "there's no category, for this story. It will rock in any territory." Cuba offers an "academic's delight" in contradictions. Since 1996, the government has helped

**CONTEXT**

This essay was published in 2000 in the UNESCO *Courier*, a publication of the United Nations Educational, Scientific and Cultural Organization (UNESCO). UNESCO, which includes 188 member nations, describes its purpose as "to contribute to peace and security in the world by promoting collaboration among nations through education, science, culture and communication in order to further universal respect for justice, for the rule of law and for the human rights and fundamental freedoms which are affirmed for the peoples of the world, without distinction of race, sex, language or religion, by the Charter of the United Nations." Consider the extent to which this essay by Ogbar and Prashad is consistent with UNESCO's stated mission.

[†]**Kathmandu is the capital city of Nepal.**

As rap and hip hop have grown in popularity, the significance of these musical forms as a social and political movement has been debated. Critics have long condemned rap and hip hop music on the grounds that it expresses racist and misogynistic views and glorifies violence. But Yvonne Bynoe of Urban Think Tank, Inc. expresses the view of many observers that hip hop music has helped to spawn a broader political movement focused on Black rights and economic advancement; she advocates an even more deliberate political commitment among hip hop artists and fans:

> Serious civic engagement means that strategists from the Hip Hop generation become crucial to shifting the political current paradigm of exclusion and marginalization. Black Arts Movement writer, Larry Neal said, "artist and the political activist are one." The scholar/activist therefore must be embraced by the Hip Hop community in conversations about politics with the same fervor that the rap artist and the activist are.

Russell Simmons, the founder of Def Jam Records and one of hip hop's most influential figures, agrees with the need for broader political activism among hip hop fans but also sees the popularity of hip hop as economic power. In an interview with Africana.com, he said,

> Eighty percent of my records are sold to non-African Americans. It's important that I recognize that there's a big market out here culturally, especially since I'm working in the culture business. We have penetrated the mainstream, and if I'm using a black artist, he's not limited to black people, or black ideas that came from the black community. Black people have a take on America, they were born here.

to sponsor an annual National Hip-Hop Conference showcasing local and international stars, mostly from Latin America. According to the U.S. hip-hop magazine *The Source,* Fidel Castro "sees rap music as the existing revolutionary voice of Cuba's future." Yet hip-hop also challenges the socialist vision when fans at concerts proudly wear images of the U.S. dollar bill on their hats and shirts and scream "it's all about the Benjamins" (referring to the image of Benjamin Franklin printed on $100-bills).

Ironically, as post-Cold War hyper-materialism endangers the destiny of young people everywhere, the contradictory message of hip-hop begins to make sense. A decisive feature of the music/culture's ethic is: to "want mine", meaning a share of society's wealth. This desire operates at both the individualist and collective levels. Do you want "it" (luxury, security, etc.) for yourself, or do you want a fair share for your community or society? The urge is so complex that it's difficult, if not impossible, to find one without the other.

Take the case of South Africa, whose townships only recently produced some of the most disciplined and inspirational fighters for social justice. Now in "mixed-race" areas around Cape Town, gangs take their cue from gangsta rap, calling themselves "the Americans" and "throwing up the W", a hand signal from West Coast gangsta rappers of the U.S. The South African example shows us that hip-hop's art of rebellion does not only lead to antiracist and anti-capitalist rebellion, but it often falls victim to the pitfalls of systemic oppression against which it attempts to rebel.

10 Hip-hop alone cannot rise up to the task of political transformation — this is pop culture, not a manifesto. However, by looking at the particular political situations and aspirations of its musicians, we can trace its rise as an iconic power and its demise when the assimilationist powers of the capitalist economy flatten out the music's richness to render it a message of personal gain.

# Questions for Discussion

**1.** This essay focuses on the popularity and commercialization of rap and hip hop music, but Ogbar and Prashad begin with a discussion of the incarceration and unemployment rates of Blacks in the United States. Why do they begin their essay in this way? How effectively do you think this beginning introduces their argument? **2.** According to Ogbar and Prashad, what social and cultural purposes do rap and hip hop music serve? What similarities do Ogbar and Prashad see in how these musical forms are used in different countries? Why are these similarities important to their main argument? What purpose do they believe rap and hip hop *should* serve? (Cite specific passages from the essay to support your answer.) 3. What is the contradictory message that Ogbar and Prashad see in rap and hip hop music? Why, according to them, should we be concerned about this contradictory message? Do you think they value one side or the other of this contradictory message? Explain. **4.** How would you describe the political views of Ogbar and Prashad on the basis of this essay? In what ways do you see those views influencing their argument about rap and hip hop music? What counterarguments might you offer to their position? **5.** Do you think that the argument Ogbar and Prashad make in this essay is similar in any way to Richard Taruskin's argument in his essay (see page 219)? Explain.

④ **JENNY TOOMEY, "Empire of the Air"**

If you have had the opportunity to travel from one part of the United States to another, you probably noticed that wherever you were, you could usually find a radio station that was similar to your favorite hometown radio station. One reason for the similarities among radio stations across the country is that an increasing number of them are owned by a few large media companies. Jenny Toomey thinks that is cause for concern. She isn't worried so much that radio stations today tend to play similar music by the same artists; rather, she is concerned that such similarity reflects a concentration of control of the radio airwaves in the United States. As she points out in her essay, which appeared in the public affairs magazine *The Nation* in 2003, a majority of radio stations are now owned by a small number of media companies. According to Toomey, such a concentration of many stations in the hands of a few companies gives those companies too much control over what we hear on the radio. She argues that radio is not just a business but also a public asset. Whether or not you share Toomey's concerns, her essay asks you to consider who should have control over what we hear on the radio. A musician and leader of the band Tsunami, Jenny Toomey is the former owner of the Simple Machines record label and the founder and executive director of the Future of Music Coalition, an advocacy group that works on behalf of musicians.

# Empire of the Air
## JENNY TOOMEY

1 For too long, musicians have had too little voice in the manufacture, distribution and promotion of their music and too little means to extract fair support and compensation for their work. The Future of Music Coalition was formed in June 2000 as a not-for-profit think tank to tackle this problem, advocating new business models, technologies and policies that would advance the cause of both musicians and citizens. Much of the work the FMC has done in the past two years has focused on documenting the structures of imbalance and inequity that impede the development of an American musicians'

middle class, and translating legislative-speak into language that musicians and citizens can understand. Our most challenging work, however, and the project of which we are most proud, is our analysis of the effects of radio deregulation on musicians and citizens since the passage of the 1996 Telecommunications Act* (see page 233).

Radio is a public resource managed on citizens' behalf by the federal government. This was established in 1934 through the passage of the Communications Act, which created a regulatory body, the Federal

Communications Commission, and laid the ground rules for the regulation of radio. The act also determined that the spectrum would be managed according to a "trusteeship" model. Broadcasters received fixed-term, renewable licenses that gave them exclusive use of a slice of the spectrum for free. In exchange, they were required to serve the "public interest, convenience and necessity." Though they laid their trust in the mechanics of the marketplace, legislators did not turn the entire spectrum over to commercial broadcasters. The 1934 act included some key provisions that were designed to foster localism and encourage diversity in programming.

Although changes were made to limits on ownership and FCC regulatory control in years hence, the Communications Act of 1934 remained essentially intact until it was thoroughly overhauled in 1996 with the passage of the Telecommunications Act. But even before President Clinton signed the act into law in February 1996, numerous predictions were made regarding its effect on the radio industry:

§ The number of individual radio-station owners would decrease. Those in the industry with enough capital would begin to snatch up valuable but underperforming stations in many markets — big and small.

5   § Station owners — given the ability to purchase more stations both locally and nationally — would benefit from economies of scale. Radio runs on many fixed costs: Equipment, operations and staffing costs are the same whether broadcasting to one person or 1 million. Owners knew that if they could control more than one station in a local

market, they could consolidate operations and reduce fixed expenses. Lower costs would mean increased profit potential. This would, in turn, make for more financially sound radio stations, which would be able to compete more effectively against new media competitors: cable TV and the Internet.

§ There was a prediction based on a theory posited by a 1950s economist named Peter Steiner that increased ownership consolidation on the local level would lead to a subsequent increase in the number of radio format choices available to the listening public. (Steiner, writing in 1952, was not talking about oligopolistic control of the market by a few firms, as we have in the United States; rather, he was basing his predictions on an analysis of BBC radio, which is a nationally owned radio monopoly, not an oligopoly.) According to Steiner's theory, a single owner with multiple stations in a local market wouldn't want to compete against himself. Instead, he would program each station differently

*In 1996 Congress passed the Telecommunications Act, which was intended to update the original Communications Act of 1934 that established laws regarding broadcasting and communications. One provision of the 1996 act is "to make available, so far as possible, to all the people of the United States without discrimination on the basis of race, color, religion, national origin, or sex a rapid, efficient, nation-wide, and world-wide wire and radio communication service with adequate facilities at reasonable charges." As Jenny Toomey notes in her essay, the effects of this and related provisions of the act are still a matter of much debate.

## CLEAR CHANNEL COMMUNICATIONS

Clear Channel Communication is the largest owner of radio stations in the United States, with more than 1,200 stations of its own and 100 shows on its Radio Premier Network, which reaches an additional 6,600 stations. It claims to reach 54 percent of all people between the ages of eighteen and forty-nine in the United States. However, it has been the target of much criticism and several lawsuits as a result of its business practices. According to Eric Boehlert, who wrote a series of reports about the company for *Salon* magazine, "radio has never seen anything quite like Clear Channel, which has swallowed up nearly 1,200 radio stations while putting its unique — and some say nasty — stamp on the business. In a series of recent *Salon* reports, insiders from the radio, record and concert industries have voiced concerns about the juggernaut's unmatched power, and how the company uses it."

to meet the tastes of a variety of listeners.

But what really happened?

Well, one prediction certainly came true: The 1996 act opened the floodgates for ownership consolidation. Ten parent companies now dominate the radio spectrum, radio listenership and radio revenues, controlling two-thirds of both listeners and revenue nationwide. Two parent companies in particular — Clear Channel and Viacom — together control 42 percent of listeners and 45 percent of industry revenues.

Consolidation is particularly extreme in the case of Clear Channel. Since passage of the Telecommunications Act, Clear Channel has grown from forty stations to 1,240 stations — thirty times more than Congressional regulation previously allowed. No potential competitor owns even one-quarter the number of Clear Channel stations. With more than 100 million listeners, Clear Channel reaches more than one-third of the US population.

10 Even more bleak is the picture at the local level, where oligopolies control almost every market. Virtually every local

market is dominated by four firms controlling 70 percent of market share or greater. In smaller markets, consolidation is more extreme. The largest four firms in most small markets control 90 percent of market share or more. These companies are sometimes regional or national station groups and not locally owned.

Only the few radio-station owners with enough capital to buy additional stations have benefited from deregulation. Station owners have consolidated their operations on a local level, frequently running a number of stations out of a single building, sharing a single advertising staff, technicians and on-air talent. In some cases, radio-station groups have further reduced costs by eliminating the local component almost entirely. Local deejays and program directors are being replaced by regional directors or even by voice-tracked or syndicated programming, which explains a marked decrease in the number of people employed in the radio industry.

Prior to 1996, radio was among the least concentrated and most economically competitive of the media industries. In 1990 no company owned more than fourteen of the more than 10,000 stations nationwide, with no more than two in a single local market. But we found that local markets have now consolidated to the point that just four major radio groups control about 50 percent of the total listener audience and revenue. Clearly, deregulation has reduced competition within the radio industry.

As a result, listeners are losing. With an emphasis on cost-cutting and an effort to move decision-making out of the hands of local station staff, much of radio has become bland and formulaic. Recall Steiner's hopeful theory that an owner would not want to compete against his own company and would therefore operate stations with different programming. We found evidence to the contrary: Radio companies regularly operate two or more stations with the same format — for example, rock, country, adult contemporary, top 40 — in the same local market. In a recent *New York Times* article, "Fewer Media Owners, More Media Choices," FCC chairman Michael Powell denied this, propping up Steiner's theory by saying things like, "Common ownership can lead to more diversity — what does the owner get for having duplicative products?" But we found 561 instances of format redundancy nationwide — a parent company operating two or more stations in the same market, with the same format — amounting to massive missed opportunities for variety.

Still, from 1996 to 2000, format variety — the average number of formats available in each local market — actually increased in both large and small markets. But format variety is not equivalent to true diversity in programming, since formats with different names have similar playlists. For example, alternative, top 40, rock and hot adult contemporary are all likely to play songs by the band Creed, even though their formats are not the same. In fact, an analysis of data from charts in *Radio and Records* and *Billboard's Airplay Monitor* revealed considerable playlist overlap — as much as 76 percent — between supposedly distinct formats. If the FCC or the National Association of Broadcasters are sincerely trying to measure programming "diversity," doing so on the basis of the number of formats in a given market is a flawed methodology.

15 This final point may be the most critical one as we face an FCC that is poised to deregulate media even further in the next few months. (In September [2002], the commissioners voted unanimously to open review of the FCC's media ownership rules.) It is time to put to bed the commonly held yet fundamentally flawed notion that consolidation promotes diversity — that radio-station owners who own two stations within a marketplace will not be tempted to program both stations with the same songs. There's a clear corporate benefit in "self-competition," and it's time we made regulatory agencies admit that fact.

Even in the beginning, radio was regulated to cultivate a commercial broadcast industry that could grow to serve the greatest number of Americans possible. As the decades have passed, most calls for deregulation have come from incumbent broadcasters interested in lifting local and national ownership caps that protect against the competitive pressures of other media.

While the effects of deregulation have been widely studied and discussed, scrutiny is focused on the profitability of the radio industry. But the effect of increased corporate profitability on citizens is rarely, if ever, discussed. Radical deregulation of the radio industry allowed by the Telecommunications Act of 1996 has not benefited the public. Instead, it has led to less competition, fewer viewpoints and less diversity in programming. Substantial ethnic, regional and economic populations are not provided the services to which they are entitled. The public is not satisfied, and possible economic efficiencies of industry consolidation are not being passed on to the public in the form of improved local service. Deregulation has damaged radio as a public resource.

Musicians are also suffering because of deregulation. Independent artists have found it increasingly difficult to get airplay; in payola-like schemes, the "Big Five" music companies, through third-party promoters, shell out thousands of

CONTEXT

The 1996 Telecommunications Act is one of many efforts by U.S. lawmakers since the early 1980s to reduce federal regulation of the radio industry. In part as a response to the kinds of the concerns about deregulation that Toomey expresses in this essay, a bill titled "The Competition in Radio and Concert Industries Act of 2002" was introduced to the U.S. Senate in July 2002. The American Federation of Television and Radio Artists (AFTRA) endorsed the legislation as a way to curtail the consolidation of the radio industry, which AFTRA argued has hurt both the public and the artists whose music is played on radio stations. Supporters of deregulation maintain that the industry today is vibrant and profitable, with fierce competition for listeners in urban markets that benefits consumers by providing them with many choices addressing their listening interests. In 2003, Congress relaxed regulations on all media companies, making it easier for companies to acquire additional media outlets, including radio stations.

dollars per song to the companies that rule the airwaves. That's part of why the Future of Music Coalition undertook this research. We at the FMC firmly believe that the music industry as it exists today is fundamentally anti-artist. In addition to our radio study, our projects — including a critique of standard major-label contract clauses, a study of musicians and health insurance, and a translation of the complicated Copyright Arbitration Royalty Panel proceedings that determined the webcasting royalty rates —

were conceived as tools for people who are curious about the structures that impede musicians' ability to both live and make a living. Understanding radio deregulation is another tool for criticizing such structures. We have detailed the connections between concentrated media ownership, homogenous radio programming and restricted radio access for musicians. Given that knowledge, we hope artists will join with other activists and work to restore radio as a public resource for all people.

# NEGOTIATING DIFFERENCES

In 1999 and 2000, as the controversy over Napster intensified (see the sidebar about Napster on page 215), many universities and colleges began to prevent students on their campuses from using Napster to download music. These universities and colleges were concerned that they, too, could become the focus of lawsuits for copyright infringement if students used the schools' computer systems for downloading copyrighted music. Some critics condemned these actions, arguing that the schools were serving the interests of commercial companies rather than the public. The controversy underscored how complicated intellectual property rights issues can become

when it comes to music and when new technologies emerge for sharing music.

For this assignment, you will try to examine these complexities by looking at how students at your school use music. Your task is to write an essay in which you take and justify a position on the use of music. Your specific focus for this argument is up to you. The essays in this section provide several alternatives for you:

- You can focus on the question of digital copying of music and the downloading of music on the Internet, as Janis Ian does in her essay (page 214).

# Questions for Discussion

**1.** In the first sentence of her essay, Toomey unequivocally states her position regarding who should control music. Evaluate the effectiveness of this approach to introducing her subject. How might Toomey's introduction enhance the effectiveness of her argument? In what ways might it weaken her argument? What other strategies might she have used to introduce her argument? **2.** Why does Toomey believe that "listeners are losing" as a result of the consolidation of the radio industry? Do you agree with her? Why or why not? **3.** According to Toomey, the deregulation of the radio industry as a result of the 1996 Telecommunication Act has not benefited citizens, even though it has resulted in greater profits for companies. On what grounds does she make that claim? How convincing do you think Toomey is on this point? **4.** Toomey structures her essay around several predictions that were made about the impact of the 1996 telecommunications act on the radio industry in the United States. Do you think this approach to structuring her essay makes her argument more persuasive? Explain. **5.** Evaluate Toomey's use of statistical information as evidence for her claims. How appropriate to her argument are the kinds of statistics she cites? How do those statistics affect her argument? **6.** Toomey's essay can be considered an example of an argument based on deductive reasoning. (See pages 26–31 for an explanation of this kind of argument.) What is the basic principle or belief on which Toomey bases her argument? Does she state this principle overtly anywhere in her essay? What syllogism does her argument rest on? (See pages 28–29 for a discussion of the syllogism.)

- You can address the question of whether some kinds of music should be restricted from distribution or even banned, as Richard Taruskin argues in his essay (page 219).
- You might focus on cultural aspects of music, as Ogbar and Prashad do in their essay (page 227), perhaps addressing some of the controversies about hip hop music.
- You might address the issue of ownership of radio stations, as Jenny Toomey does (page 232]).

Whichever specific issue you choose to focus on, do some investigation to learn how other students at your university feel about the issue. You can talk informally to students you know, or you can conduct more formal research in the form of interviews or a survey. (See pages 175–177 for a discussion of these techniques for gathering information.) Then use this information, along with any relevant published materials you find (including the essays in this section) to help make your case for your position on this issue. Write your essay with the students at your school in mind as your audience. You might intend your essay as an editorial for your student newspaper, if your school has one.

**9**

# EDUCATION

EDUC

## Cluster

# HOW SHOULD WE DETERMINE WHAT OUR CHILDREN LEARN?

(1) Eleanor Martin. " 'No' Is the Right Answer"

(2) Patricia Williams, "Tests, Tracking, and Derailment"

(3) Gregory Cizek, "Unintended Consequences of High Stakes Testing"

(4) Bertell Ollman, "Why So Many Exams? A Marxist Response"

CON-TEXT
**The Report of the Committee of Ten, 1892**

A T I O N

# HOW SHOULD WE DETERMINE WHAT OUR CHILDREN LEARN?

During the 1990s many states began implementing new tests that were intended to set higher standards for both students and teachers. Many of these new standardized tests were so-called high-stakes tests — that is, students had to pass these tests to advance to the next grade or to earn a high school diploma. In the past many states allowed students to graduate or advance to the next grade level even if they did not pass the state-mandated exams, but these new high-stakes tests made that impossible in many cases. Proponents of such tests argue that setting high standards benefits students by encouraging schools to prepare all their students for the tests rather than only those students who intend to go to college. Without such tests, proponents say, struggling students or students without plans to attend college are placed in less rigorous programs than their college-bound classmates. The result is tracking: a two-tiered (or three- or four-tiered) system that favors some students and places others at a disadvantage. High-stakes tests can remedy that problem by requiring all students to meet the same high standards. ■ Of course, many critics argue just the opposite. They maintain that high-stakes tests not only harm some students, but also make tracking even more widespread. What happens, they ask, to students who complete the curriculum requirements but do not pass the standardized tests? Should they simply be sent on their way without a diploma after twelve years of schooling? And won't the curriculum itself become overly influenced by those tests so that all students will indirectly be shortchanged by teachers who must "teach to the test"? These critics argue that when high-stakes tests are mandated, the focus in schools shifts to test preparation; as a result, important aspects of student learning are ignored. ■ The increased popularity of high-stakes testing in recent years and the intensity of the debates surrounding them can make these problems seem new. In fact, however, educators, parents, students, and politicians have been wrestling with these questions about standards and assessment for many years. In the late 19th century, for example, a special panel of experts called the Committee of Ten was commissioned to look into what at the time was believed to be a crisis in education marked by low student achievement and low standards. The committee members recommended a common curriculum for all students — which is a recommendation that we continue to hear today. (See *Con-Text* on page 241.) Although much has changed since the Committee of Ten submitted its report in 1892, there is little question that concerns about what curriculum is best for students and how students should be tested have not disappeared. If anything, they have intensified, perhaps because those concerns relate to the important task of educating the nation's children. ■ The essays in this section address those concerns about curriculum and assessment. The authors of these essays offer their views on testing and tracking more than 100 years after the Committee of Ten's famous report. But in effect these authors are doing the same thing that the Committee of Ten did: trying to come to terms with how best to educate and test students. Ultimately, then, these essays reveal that arguments about testing and tracking are really arguments about what education should be.

## CON-TEXT: The Report of the Committee of Ten, 1892

1 On one very important question of general policy which affects profoundly the preparation of all school programmes, the Committee of Ten and all the Conferences are absolutely, unanimous. Among the questions suggested for discussion in each Conference were the following: —

7. Should the subject be treated differently for pupils who are going to college, for those who are going to a scientific school, and for those who, presumably, are going to neither?

8. At what age should this differentiation begin, if any be recommended?

The 7th question is answered unanimously in the negative by the Conferences, and the 8th therefore needs no answer. The Committee of Ten unanimously agree with the Conferences. Ninety-eight teachers, intimately concerned either with the actual work of American secondary schools, or with the results of that work as they appear in students who come to college, unanimously declare that every subject which is taught at all in a secondary school should be taught in the same way and to the same extent to every pupil so long as he pursues it, no matter what the probable destination of the pupil may be, or at what point his education is to cease. Thus, for all pupils who study Latin, or history, or algebra, for example, the allotment of time and the method of instruction in a given school should be the same year by year. Not that all the pupils should pursue every subject for the same number of years; but so long as they do pursue it, they should all be treated alike. It has been a very general custom in American high schools and academies to make up separate courses of study for pupils of supposed different destinations, the proportions of the several studies in the different courses being various. The principle laid down by the Conferences will, if logically carried out, make a great simplification in secondary school programmes. It will lead to each subject's being treated by the school in the same way by the year for all pupils, and this, whether the individual pupil be required to choose between courses which run through several years, or be allowed some choice among subjects year by year.

SOURCE: National Education Association. Available at The Memory Hole, http://www.blancmange.net/tmh/books/commoften/mainrpt.html.

# ① ELEANOR MARTIN, "No" Is the Right Answer

In the late 1990s Massachusetts became one of many states to implement new standardized exams for its students. Part of a nationwide trend toward higher standards and "accountability," the Massachusetts Comprehensive Assessment System (MCAS) represented a significant change for Massachusetts students because high school students who failed the test could not receive a diploma. This new high-stakes test sparked intense controversy as parents, students, and teachers worried about what would happen to students who could not pass the exam. In 1999, as the new tests were administered, a small but vocal opposition emerged. Many opponents called for students to boycott the tests. Eleanor Martin, a high school sophomore at the time, was one of twelve students at Cambridge Rindge and Latin High School who refused to take the test. In the following essay she explains why, making a case against standardized tests such as the MCAS. Although her essay focuses on the required state tests in Massachusetts, her argument addresses larger questions about standardized testing and student learning — questions that continue to stir up heated debate nationwide as more states follow the lead of Massachusetts and implement their own high-stakes tests. Martin's essay was first published in the *Boston Globe* in 1999.

## "No" Is the Right Answer
### ELEANOR MARTIN

1 On May 17, a dozen sophomores at Cambridge Rindge and Latin High School decided not to take the state-mandated Massachusetts Comprehensive Assessment Test, better known as the MCAS. I was one of them.

For weeks we had carefully researched the political and moral issues at stake. We were aware that it was going to be difficult to refuse the test. When you are a sophomore in high school, it is not easy to go against the orders of your teachers, your advisors, your school, and your state. We were not certain of the punishment that we would receive. Detention, suspension, expulsion? All had been mentioned as possibilities.

When we announced what we were going to do, we received a lot of opposition. We were told that we were going to bring down the cumulative score of our house and of the entire school. But we believed, and still do, that the reasons for fighting this test are more important than any score.

Beginning with the class of 2003, high school students who fail the MCAS test will not be able to graduate. We be-

## THE MASSACHUSETTS COMPREHENSIVE ASSESSMENT SYSTEM (MCAS)

The MCAS was developed in the late 1990s as part of the Massachusetts Education Reform Law of 1993, which mandates that all public school students, including students with disabilities and limited English proficiency, be tested in grades 4, 8, and 10 to determine whether they meet the Massachusetts state education standards. Beginning in 2003, students in grade 10 must pass the MCAS exams in English and mathematics to be eligible for a high school diploma; students will be given several opportunities to pass the exams between grade 10 and the end of their senior year. According to the Massachusetts Department of Education, "Parents may *not* legally refuse their child's participation in MCAS. Massachusetts General Laws chapter 76, Sections 2 and 4, establish penalties for truancy as well as for inducing unlawful absence of a minor from school. In addition, school discipline codes generally define local rules for school attendance and penalties for unauthorized absence from school or from a required part of the school day." The MCAS was first administered in 1998.

lieve that a single test should not determine the success and future of a student.

**5** How can four years of learning and growing be assessed by a single standardized test? There are so many things that students learn throughout high school — how to play an instrument, act, draw, paint. They learn photography, how to program a computer, fix a car engine, cook tortellini Alfredo, throw a pot, or design a set for a play. Many students say these are among the most important skills they learn in high school, yet all are skills the MCAS fails to recognize.

The MCAS test is expected to take over 20 hours of class time. No test should take that much time out of learning, especially not one whose supposed rationale is that students are not learning enough in school.

The material on the MCAS is very specific. For students to do well, teachers must redesign their curriculums to teach to the test. Districts and school administrators, eager to show high scores, have pressured teachers to create units based on the material. Because the test is based largely on memorization of facts, teachers will have to teach their students these specific facts instead of teaching for deep comprehension and understanding of the material.

Students who have been in this country for only three years are required to take the test. How can someone who has been speaking English for three years be expected to write essays with correct spelling and grammar, which is a requirement to receive a proficient score? Special needs students are also required to take this test to graduate.

Supposedly, this test will be used to evaluate teachers as well as students. However, a test like this simply measures whether a teacher teaches to the test. **10** If the MCAS test is instituted in Massachusetts, the scores will become a major consideration for parents when they choose a school for their children. Schools will therefore want their scores to be as high as possible. Programs such as Metco,* which integrates inner-city students into suburban schools, may be discouraged since it has been shown that inner-city students do not score as well as suburban students.

We are also concerned about the future of innovative programs, such as the Interactive Math Program, or IMP, which does not follow the traditional progression of algebra, geometry, trigonometry, and calculus, but integrates these throughout all four years. Therefore, a sophomore IMP student will not know the expected geometry curriculum, but will

**CONTEXT**

The MCAS exams are scored at four levels of achievement: *advanced, proficient, needs improvement,* and *failing.* In 1999, the year that Eleanor Martin refused to take the exams, 53 percent of the 10th-grade students who took the test earned a *failing* score on the math exam, and 32 percent earned a *failing* score on the English exam. However, in 2002, 25 percent of 10th-grade students failed the math exam, and 14 percent failed the English exam.

*The Metropolitan Council for Educational Opportunity (Metco) sponsors special educational programs for at-risk students in Massachusetts.

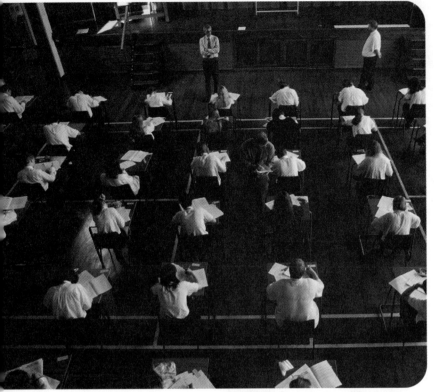

know some trigonometry and calculus that is not included on the MCAS.

Also, certain in-depth courses, such as "Bible as Literature," "The Holocaust," "Reading and Writing on Human Values," Women in Literature," and "African-American Literature" will no doubt be off-limits to freshmen and sophomores because they are not geared to the MCAS.

My humanities teacher in eighth grade used the "Facing History and Ourselves" curriculum, which spends about eight weeks teaching in incredible depth about the Holocaust. We learned about Nazi propaganda and how it compares to propaganda used today. We examined the causes of the Holocaust, confronted the difficult philosophical and moral issues it raises, and focused on what we can do to prevent it from happening again.

This is one of the best educational experiences I have ever had. Because of it, I have a deep and complex understanding of the Holocaust. All the dates and facts that I learned may not stay with me, but I feel certain that my understanding of the event will.

**15** We are worried that such innovative and respected curriculums as IMP and "Facing History" will become casualties of the MCAS test mentality.

We are not saying nothing should be done to improve public education in Massachusetts. We are simply saying that taking a paper and pencil test to graduate is not the way to amend education. Massachusetts has already spent $24 million on the MCAS test, and an estimated $14 million more is being spent this year. Roughly that same amount will be spent every year the test is given. We could use that money in better ways — for more staff developers, teacher workshops, improved bilingual education, better school supplies, and better fine arts and technical arts programs.

This is our last chance to raise awareness about getting an education that is not standardized, but meaningful, deep, and personalized. We believe an education like that is worth working for.

## Questions for Discussion

**1.** How does Martin justify her decision to boycott the MCAS? Do you find her justification convincing? Why or why not? **2.** What specific reasons does Martin provide for her opposition to the standardized test in Massachusetts that she refused to take? What do her reasons indicate about her view of what students should learn in school? **3.** What are some of the possible effects of the MCAS that concern Martin? Do you think her concerns are valid? How do they contribute to her main argument against standardized testing? **4.** Evaluate the tone of this essay. To what extent do you think the tone contributes to the essay's main argument? How does it influence your sense of Martin's credibility? **5.** Using the Toulmin model of argumentation (see pages 31–35). What do you think is Martin's central claim in her essay? What is her warrant? Do you think that most readers in Massachusetts would accept her warrant? Explain.

## ② PATRICIA WILLIAMS, "Tests, Tracking, and Derailment"

If you have gone to school in the United States, chances are that you have encountered some form of tracking: Advanced Placement or honors classes, special education programs for students with special needs, remedial courses for struggling students, enrichment programs for gifted and talented students. Even if you were not tracked into such a program, it is likely that your school's curriculum offered different options for college-bound students and students who did not intend to go to college. The purpose of all these educational tracks is to match the curriculum to students' needs and abilities. But tracking has always been controversial, in part because it is not clear that special programs or tracks serve their intended purposes. Writer Patricia Williams, for example, believes that tracking students — for whatever purpose — ultimately leads to more problems than it solves. In her essay, which was published in *The Nation* in 2002, she traces what she sees as some of those problems and argues that educational resources can be better spent to ensure that all children benefit from schooling. In one sense her essay suggests that debates about how to allocate educational monies inevitably raise larger questions about the goals of schooling. As you read, consider how Williams's sense of the purpose of education informs her argument against educational tracking.

## Tests, Tracking, and Derailment
### PATRICIA WILLIAMS

**1** As state budgets around the country are slashed to accommodate the expense of the war on terror, the pursuit of educational opportunity for all seems ever more elusive. While standardized tests are supposed to be used to diagnose problems and facilitate individual or institutional improvement, too often they have been used to close or penalize precisely the schools that most need help; or, results have been used to track students into separate programs that benefit the few but not the many. The implementation of gifted classes with better student-teacher ratios and more substantial resources often triggers an unhealthy and quite bitter competition for those unnaturally narrowed windows of opportunity. How much better it would be to have more public debate about why the pickings are so slim to begin with. In any event, it is no wonder there is such intense national anxiety just now, a fantastical hunger for children who speak in complete sentences by the age of six months.

A friend compares the tracking of students to the separation of altos from sopranos in a choir. But academic ability and/or intelligence is both spikier and more malleably constructed than such an analogy allows. Tracking students by separating the high notes from the low only works if the endgame is to teach all children the "Hallelujah Chorus." A system that teaches only the sopranos because no parent wants their child to be less than a diva is a system driven by the shortsightedness of narcissism. I think we make a well-rounded society the same way we make the best music: through the harmonic combination of differently pitched, but uniformly well-trained voices.

A parsimony of spirit haunts education policy, exacerbated by fear of the extremes. Under the stress of threatened budget cuts, people worry much more about providing lifeboats for the very top and containment for the "ineducable" rock bottom than they do about properly training the great masses of children, the vibrant, perfectly able middle who are capable of much more than most school systems offer. In addition, discussions of educational equality are skewed by conflation of behavioral problems with IQ,* and learning disabilities with retardation. Repeatedly one hears complaints that you can't put a gifted child in a class full of unruly, noisy misfits and expect anyone to benefit. Most often it's a plea from a parent who desperately wants his or her child re-

moved from a large oversubscribed classroom with a single, stressed teacher in an underfunded district and sent to the sanctuary of a nurturing bubble where peace reigns because there are twelve kids in a class with two specialists and everyone's riding the high of great expectations. But all children respond better in ordered, supportive environments; and all other investments being equal, gifted children are just as prone to behavior problems — and to learning disabilities — as any other part of the population. Nor should we confuse exceptional circumstances with behavior problems. The difficulty of engaging a child who's just spent the night in a homeless shelter, for example, is not productively treated as chiefly an issue of IQ.

The narrowing of access has often resulted in peculiar kinds of hairsplitting. When I was growing up, for example, Boston's Latin School was divided into two separate schools: one for boys and one for girls. Although the curriculum was identical and the admissions exam

*IQ, or intelligence quotient, is a measure of intelligence based partly on the ideas of 19th century French psychologist Alfred Binet. Drawing on his observations of children with and without various disabilities, Binet developed a test to measure a child's "mental age." His test was adapted by several American psychologists and used by the U.S. Army to measure the intelligence levels of its recruits during World War I. IQ tests have long been criticized as inaccurate and unfair, and criticisms of the tests as racially biased intensified in the 1960s and 1970s.

CONTEXT

In 1972, in response to a state law ending gender-based discrimination in Massachusetts schools, Girls' Latin Academy was changed to Boston Latin Academy and began accepting boys. That same year, girls were accepted into Boston Latin School, which describes itself as the oldest school in America, founded in 1635.

the same, there were some disparities: The girls' school was smaller and so could admit fewer students; and the science and sports facilities were inferior to those of the boys.

## THE INTERNATIONAL BACCALAUREATE CURRICULUM (IBO)

This curriculum is based on guidelines from the International Baccalaureate Organization, founded in Geneva, Switzerland, in 1968. According to its Web site, the IBO "grew out of international schools' efforts as early as 1924 to establish a common curriculum and university entry credential. The schools were also motivated by an idealistic vision. They hoped that critical thinking and exposure to a variety of points of view would encourage intercultural understanding by young people." The IBO diploma program is a rigorous curriculum of six academic subjects based on well-established criteria for assessing students' knowledge of those subjects. As of 2002, there were 1,376 authorized IB schools in 114 countries.

**5** There was a successful lawsuit to integrate the two schools about twenty years ago, but then an odd thing happened. Instead of using the old girls' school for the middle school and the larger boys' school for the new upper school, as was originally suggested, the city decided to sever the two. The old boys' school retained the name Boston Latin, and the old girls' school — smaller, less-equipped — was reborn as Boston Latin Academy. The entrance exam is now administered so that those who score highest go to Boston Latin; the next cut down go to what is now, unnecessarily, known as the "less elite" Latin Academy.

One of the more direct consequences of this is that the new Boston Latin inherited an alumni endowment of $15 million dollars, much of it used to provide college scholarships. Latin Academy, on the other hand, inherited the revenue of the old Girls' Latin alumni association — something under $200,000. It seems odd: Students at both schools are tremendously talented, the cutoff between them based on fairly insignificant scoring differences. But rather than pool the resources of the combined facilities — thus maximizing educational opportunity, in particular funding for college — the resolution of the pre-existing gender inequality almost purposefully reinscribed that inequality as one driven by wealth and class.

There are good models of what is possible. The International Baccalaureate curriculum, which is considered "advanced" by most American standards, is administered to a far wider range of students in Europe than here, with the result that their norm is considerably higher than ours in a number of areas. The University of Chicago's School Mathematics Project, originally developed for gifted students at the Chicago Lab School, is now recommended for all children — all children, as the foreword to its textbooks says, can "learn more and do more than was thought to be possible ten or twenty years ago." And educator Marva Collins's widely praised curriculum for inner-city elementary schools includes reading Shakespeare.

Imparting higher levels of content requires nothing exceptional but rather normal, more-or-less stable children, taught in small classes by well-trained, well-mentored teachers who have a sophisticated grasp of mathematics and literature themselves. It will pay us, I think, to stop configuring education as a battle of the geniuses against the uncivilized. We are a wealthy nation chock-full of those normal, more-or-less stable children. The military should not be the only institution that teaches them to be all that they can be.

CONTEXT

According to its Web site, "The Nation will not be the organ of any party, sect, or body. It will, on the contrary, make an earnest effort to bring to the discussion of political and social questions a really critical spirit, and to wage war upon the vices of violence, exaggeration, and misrepresentation by which so much of the political writing of the day is marred." Founded in 1865, The Nation is a respected magazine of political affairs that is generally considered to espouse a liberal viewpoint. In what ways does Patricia Williams's argument against tracking reflect the editorial slant of this magazine and its expressed purpose?

## Questions for Discussion

**1.** Williams compares tracking to separating the singers in a choir. How effectively do you think this comparison helps Williams to make her point about the disadvantages of tracking? What does this comparison reveal about her beliefs about the purposes of schooling? **2.** Williams refers to "the great masses of children, the vibrant, perfectly able middle who are capable of much more than most school systems offer." What evidence does she offer to support this assertion? Do you think she is right? Why or why not? **3.** What point does Williams use the example of the Boston Latin School to illustrate? How effectively does this example help her to make her point? How does it contribute to her main argument about tracking? **4.** In her final paragraph Williams argues that we should not think of education "as a battle of the geniuses against the uncivilized." To what extent do you think Bertell Ollman and Gregory Cizek, whose essays appear later in this chapter, would agree with Williams? Cite specific passages from their essays to support your answer.

**5.** Williams's essay might be considered an essay based on inductive reasoning (see pages 25–26). How effective do you think her essay is as such an argument? How persuasively does she compile evidence to reach her conclusion?

③ GREGORY CIZEK, **"Unintended Consequences of High Stakes Testing"**

As author Gregory Cizek himself notes, the title of the following essay is misleading. We tend to think of "unintended consequences" as negative. But Cizek makes a vigorous case in favor of standardized testing, arguing that high-stakes tests lead to a number of important and beneficial consequences for students, schools, and teachers alike. Like many proponents of such tests, Cizek believes that carefully constructed standardized tests are a crucial element in efforts to improve public education. As you read through his discussion of the benefits of testing, consider what his list of these benefits reveals about his view of the purpose of formal education. Consider, too, the extent to which his fundamental beliefs about education match — or diverge from — the views of the other writers in this section. Gregory Cizek is an associate professor of education at the University of North Carolina and the author of *Detecting and Preventing Classroom Cheating* (1999). This essay originally appeared in 2002 at EducationNews.org, an online news service devoted to educational issues.

# Unintended Consequences of High Stakes Testing
## GREGORY CIZEK

**\*Eschatology is a branch of theology concerned with the end of the world or of humankind.**

**1**  It's eschatological.\* In one tract after another, the zealous proclaim that there is a dire threat posed by the anti-Christ of postmodern education: testing. To be more precise, the Great Satan does not comprise *all* testing, only testing *with consequences* — consequences such as grade retention for students, salaries for educators, or the futures of (in particular) low-performing schools. In this fevered and frenzied battle, what is clear is that any sort of high-stakes test is the beast. On the side of the angels are those who take the path of beast-resistance.

As I reflect on my own writing here, I wondered if I would need to make a confession for the sin of hyperbole. Then I re-read some of the sacred texts.

According to Alfie Kohn in a recent issue of the *Kappan,* we must "make the fight against standardized tests our top priority . . . until we have chased this monster from our schools."[1] A companion article in the same issue discussed high-stakes testing in an article titled "the authentic standards movement and its evil twin."[2] Still another canonized a list of 22 martyrs and described their sacrifices of resistance to testing.[3] I concluded that there was no need for me to repent.

In addition to the zealotry, there is also heresy. This article is one example. Testifying to the truth of that label, I confess that the very title of this article is somewhat deceptive. Perhaps many readers will, like me, recall having reviewed several articles with titles like the one used here. In those epistles the faithful are regaled with the travails of students who were denied a diploma as a result of a high-stakes test. They illustrate how testing narrows the curriculum, frustrates our best teachers, produces gripping anxiety in our brightest students, and makes young children vomit or cry, or both. This article will not repeat any of those parables, either in substance or perspective. We now turn to the apocrypha.

### Reports from the Battlefield

If nothing else, published commentary concerning high-stakes testing has been remarkable for its uniformity. The conclusion: high-stakes tests are uniformly bad. A recent literature search to locate information about the effects of high-stakes tests turned up 59 entries over the last 10 years. A review of the results revealed that only 2 of the 59 could even remotely be categorized as favorably inclined toward testing. The two entries included a two-page, 1996 publication in a minor source, which bore the straightforward title, "The Case for National Standards and Assessments."[4] The other nominally favorable article simply reviewed surveys of public opinion about high-stakes tests and concluded that broad support for such tests persists.[5] The other 57 entries reflected the accepted articles of faith concerning high-stakes tests. Examples of the titles of these articles include:

"Excellence in Education versus High-stakes Testing"[6] (which carries the obvious implication that testing is antithetical to high-quality education);

"The Distortion of Teaching and Testing: High-stakes Testing and Instruction"[7] (ditto);

"Burnt at the High-Stakes"[8] (no explanation required);

"Judges Ruling Effectively Acquits High-stakes Test: To the Disadvantage of Poor and Minority Students in Texas"[9] (personally, I thought that the less equivocal title, "Analysis Reveals High-quality Test: Everyone Gets the Shaft" could have been used); and

"I Don't Give a Hoot If Somebody is Going to Pay Me $3600: Local School District Reactions to Kentucky's High-stakes Accountability Program."[10]

### The Roots of All Evil

5   There have always been high-stakes tests. Testing history buffs have traced high-stakes testing to civil service examinations of 200 B.C., military selection dating to 2000 B.C., and Biblical accounts of the Gilead guards. Mehrens and Cizek relate the story of the minimum competency exam that took place when the Gilead Guards challenged the fugitives from the tribe of Ephraim who tried to cross the Jordan river.

"Are you a member of the tribe of Ephraim?" they asked. If the man replied that he was not, then they demanded, "Say Shibboleth." But if he couldn't pronounce the H and said Sibboleth instead of Shibboleth he was dragged away and killed. So forty-two thousand people of Ephraim died there."[11]

In the scriptural account of this assessment, nothing is reported concerning the professional and public debates that may have occurred regarding: what competencies should have been tested; how to measure them; how minimally-proficient performance should be defined; whether paper/pencil testing might have been cheaper and more reliable than performance assessment; whether there was any adverse impact against the people of Ephraim; or what remediation should be provided for those judged to be below the standard. Maybe the Gilead Guards should have abandoned their test altogether because it was unclear whether Ephraimites really had the opportunity to learn to pronounce "shibboleth" correctly, because the burden of so many oral examinations was a top-down mandate, or because listening to all those Ephraimites try to say "shibboleth" reduced the valuable instructional time available for teaching young members of the tribe of Gilead the real-life skills of sword fighting and tent making.[12]

While it is certain that high-stakes testing as been around for some time, it is curious that current high-stakes tests in American education face such an inquisition from, primarily, educators. Ironically, for this, too, we should blame those in the field of testing. Those who know and make high-stakes tests have done the least to make known the purposes and benefits of testing. The laws of physics apply: for every action in opposition to tests, there has been and equal and opposite silence.

### A Revelation

One assumption underlying high-stakes testing has received particularly scant attention: the need to make decisions. There is simply no way to escape making decisions about students. These decisions, by definition, create categories. If, for example, some students graduate from high school and others do not, a categorical decision has been made, even if a graduation test was not used. (The decisions were, presumably, made on *some* basis.) High school music teachers make decisions such as who should be first chair for the clarinets. College faculties make decisions to tenure (or not) their colleagues. We embrace decision making regarding who should be licensed to practice medicine. All of these kinds of decisions are unavoidable; each should be based on sound information; and the information should be combined in some deliberate, considered fashion.

**10** It is currently fashionable to talk as if high-stakes tests are the *single* bit of in-

formation used to make categorical decisions that wreak hellacious results on both people and educational systems. But simple-minded slogans like "high stakes are for tomatoes" are, well, simple-minded. One need only examine the context in which high-stakes tests are given to see that they are almost never the single bit of information used to make decisions. In the diploma example, multiple sources of information are used to make decisions, and success on each of them is necessary. For instance: So many days of attendance are required. Just one too few days?: No diploma. 2) There are course requirements. Didn't take American Government?: No diploma. 3) There are credit hour requirements. Missing one credit?: No diploma. 4) And, increasingly, there are high-stakes tests. Miss one too many questions on a test?: No diploma. Categorical decisions are made on each of these four criteria. It makes as much sense to single out a single test as the sole barrier as it does to single out a student's American Government examination as "the single test used to make the graduation decision."

We could, of course, not make success on each of the elements essential. One could get a diploma by making success on, say, three out of the four. But which three? Why three? Why not two? The same two for everyone? That seems unfair, given that some people would be denied a diploma simply on the basis of the arbitrary two that were identified. Even if all other criteria were eliminated, and all that remained was a requirement that students must attend at least 150 out of 180 days in their senior year to get a diploma, then what about the student who attends 149 and is a genius? In the end, as long as any categorical decisions must be made, there is going to be subjectivity involved. If there is going to

be subjectivity, most testing specialists — and most of the public — simply favor coming clean about the source and magnitude of the subjectivity, and trying to minimize it.

In the end, it cannot be that high-stakes tests themselves are the cause of all the consternation. It is evident that categorical decisions will be made with or without tests. The real reasons are two-fold. One reason covers resistance to high-stakes testing within the education profession; the second explains why otherwise well-informed people would so easily succumb to simplistic rhetoric centering on testing. On the first count, the fact that high-stakes tests are increasingly used as part of accountability systems provides a sufficient rationale for resistance. Education is one of the few (only?) professions for which advancement, status, compensation, longevity, and so on are not related to personal performance. The entire accountability movement — of which testing has been the major element — has been vigorously resisted by many in the profession. The rationale is rational when there is a choice between being accountable for performance or maintaining a status quo without accountability.

**Two Tables of Stone**
There is much to be debated about professionalization of teaching and its relationship to accountability. My primary focus here, however, is on the second count — the debate about testing. As mentioned previously, those who know the most about testing have been virtually absent from the public square when any criticism surfaces. In response to 57 bold articles nailed to the cathedral door, 2 limp slips of paper are slid under it. The benefits of high-stakes tests have been assumed, unrecognized, or unarticulated. The following paragraphs present

10 unanticipated consequences of high-stakes testing — consequences that are actually *good* things that have grown out of the increasing reliance on test data concerning student performance.[13]

*I. Professional Development*   I suspect that most educators painfully recall what passed as professional development in the not-too-distant past. Presentations with titles like the following were all-too-common:

- Vitamins and Vocabulary: Just Coincidence that Both Begin with "V"?
- Cosmetology across the Curriculum
- Horoscopes in the Homeroom
- The Geometry of Rap: 16 Musical Tips for Pushing Pythagoras
- Multiple Intelligences in the Cafeteria

In a word, much professional development was spotty, hit-or-miss, of questionable research base, of dubious effectiveness, and thoroughly avoidable. 15 But professional development is increasingly taking a new face. Much of it is considerably more focussed on what works, curriculum-relevant, and results-oriented. Driven by the demands of high-stakes tests, the press toward professional development that helps educators hone their teaching skills and content area expertise is clear.

*II. Accommodation*   Recent federal legislation enacted to guide the implementation of high-stakes testing has been a catalyst for increased attention to students with special needs. Describing the impact of that legislation, researchers Martha Thurlow and James Ysseldyke observe that, "Both Goals 2000* and the more forceful IASA indicated that high standards were to apply to *all* students. In very clear language, these laws defined "all students" as including students with disabilities and students with limited English proficiency."[14]

Because of these regulations applied to high-stakes tests, states across the US are scurrying to adapt those tests for all students, report disaggregated results for subgroups, and implement accommodations so that tests more accurately reflect the learning of all students. The result has been a very positive diffusion of awareness. Increasingly, at the classroom level, educators are becoming more sensitive to the needs and barriers faced by special needs students when they take tests — even the ordinary assessments they face in the classroom. If not forced by the context of once-per-year, high-stakes tests, it is doubtful that such progress would have been witnessed in the daily experiences of many special needs learners.

*III. Knowledge about Testing*   For years, testing specialists have documented a lack of knowledge about assessment on the part of many educators. The title of a 1991 *Kappan* article bluntly asserted educators' "Apathy toward Testing and Grading."[15] Other research has chronicled the chronic lack of training in assessment for teachers and principals and has offered plans for remediation.[16] Unfortunately, for the most part, it has been difficult to require assessment training for pre-service teachers or administrators, and even more difficult to wedge such training into graduate programs in education.

Then along came high-stakes tests. What faculty committees could not enact has been accomplished circuitously. Granted, misperceptions about tests persist (for example, in my state there is a lingering myth that "the green test form" is harder than "the red one"), but I am discovering that more educators know more about testing than ever before. Because many tests now have stakes associated with them, it has become *de rigeur* for educators to inform themselves about their content, construction, and consequences. Increasingly, teachers can tell you the difference between a norm-referenced and a criterion-reference tests; they can recognize, use, or develop a high-quality rubric; they can tell you how their state's writing test is scored, and so on. In this case, necessity has been the mother of intervention.

20 *IV and V. Collection and Use of Information*   Because pupil performance on high-stakes tests has become of such prominent and public interest, there has been an intensity of effort directed toward data collection and quality control that is unparalleled. As many states mandate the collection and reporting of this information (and more), unparalleled access has also resulted. Obtaining information about test performance,

graduation rates, per-pupil spending, staffing, finance, and facilities is, in most states, now just a mouse-click away. How would you like your data for secondary analysis: Aggregated or disaggregated? Single year or longitudinal? PDF or Excel? Paper or plastic? Consequently, those who must respond to state mandates for data collection (i.e., school districts) have become increasingly conscientious about providing the most accurate information possible — sometimes at risk of penalties for inaccuracy or incompleteness.

This is an unqualified boon. Not only is more information about student performance available, but it is increasingly used as part of decision making. At a recent teacher recruiting event, I heard a recruiter question a teacher about how she would be able to tell that her students were learning. "I can just see it in their eyes," was the reply. Sorry, you're off the island. Increasingly, from the classroom to the school board room, educators are making use of student performance data to help them refine programs, channel funding, and identify roots of success. If the data weren't so important, it is unlikely that this would be the case.

*VI. Educational Options*   Related to the increase in publicly-available information about student performance and school characteristics is the spawning of greater options for parents and students. Complementing a hunger for information, the public's appetite for alternatives has been whetted. In many cases, schools have responded. Charter schools, magnet schools, home schools, and increased offerings of honors, IB and AP courses,[†] have broadened the choices available to parents. And, research is slowly accumulating which suggests that the presence of choices has not spelled doom for traditional options, but has largely raised all boats.[17] It is almost surely the case

*Goals 2000 and IASA. Goals 2000 refers to the Educate America Act, passed by the U.S. Congress in 1994 and intended to promote coherent educational standards for K–12 schools by supporting efforts in individual states to set standards for student learning. IASA, or the Improving America's Schools Act, which was also passed in 1994, is broad legislation that provided funding and other kinds of support for various initiatives, including improving services for students with disabilities, enhancing basic educational programs, upgrading technology, and strengthening substance abuse prevention efforts.

†IB refers to International Baccalaureate programs, which are described in the sidebar on page 248. AP refers to Advanced Placement programs, which are rigorous high school courses that can lead to college credit. Founded in 1955, the AP program standards are set by the College Board, which also administers the AP exams that students who complete AP courses must usually take to earn college credit.

that legislators' votes and parents' feet would not be moving in the direction of expanding alternatives if not for the information provided by high-stakes tests — the same tests are being used to gauge the success or failure of these emerging alternatives.

*VII. Accountability Systems*   No one would argue that current accountability systems have reached a mature state of development. On the contrary, nascent systems are for the most part crude, cumbersome, embryonic endeavors. Equally certain, though, is that even rudimentary accountability systems would not likely be around if it weren't for high-stakes tests. For better or worse, high-stakes tests are often the foundation upon which accountability systems have been built. This is not to say that this relationship between high-stakes tests and accountability is right, noble, or appropriate. It simply recognizes the reality that current accountability systems were enabled by an antecedent: mandated, high-stakes tests.

To many policy makers, professionals, and the public, however, the notion of introducing accountability — even just acknowledging that accountability is a *good* innovation — is an important first step. That the camel's nose took the form of high-stakes tests was (perhaps) not recognized or (almost certainly) viewed as acceptable. Debates continue about the role of tests and the form of accountability.

**25** A memory that has helped me to understand both sides of accountability debates involves high school sports physicals. I have vivid memories evoked to this day whenever I drive by a marquee outside a high school on which the notice appears: Boys' Sports Physicals Next Tuesday. As an adolescent male trying out for a high-school baseball team, I recall that event as one at which

dozens of similarly situated guys would line up mostly naked and be checked over by a hometown physician, who volunteered his time to poke, prod, and probe each potential player. The characteristics of the event included that it was: a) somewhat embarrassing; b) performed by an external person; c) somewhat invasive; d) and had the possibility of denying individuals access to an opportunity. I think that these same four characteristics help explain the reaction of many educators to high-stakes tests.

But the analogy can be extended. At the time — and still — I can see that the physicals were necessary to identify small problems, and to prevent potentially bigger problems. But here's the big difference with high-stakes tests: if one of the players was found to have a heart murmur, it was acknowledged that he had a problem and something was done about it. In education, if a student fails a high-stakes test, we assail the test. Now, we all know that achievement tests aren't perfect, but neither are medical tests. Pregnancy tests are often wrong; blood pressure readings are subjective and variable within an individual; even with DNA tests, experts can only say things like "there is 99.93% chance that the DNA is a match." Yet nobody reports their blood pressure as 120/80 with an associated standard error. Maybe I don't really have high blood pressure. Maybe my pressure is 120/80 plus or minus 17.

People seem inclined to accept medical measurements as virtually error-free because there's no finger pointing, only therapy. Maybe his blood pressure is high because he failed to heed the physician's orders to lay off the salt and lose some weight. Maybe her pregnancy test was positive because she was sexually active. Who should be held accountable for the results of the pregnancy test or blood pressure but the person? We seem resigned to accountability in this context.

Don't get me wrong. When a defective medical measuring device is identified, it gets pulled by the FDA. If there were intolerable error rates in home pregnancy test kits, it would create a stir, and the product would be improved, or fall out of use. In education, however, if a pupil doesn't pass a high-stakes test, there are a lot of possible (and confounded) explanations: lack of persistence, poor teaching, distracting learning environment, inadequate resources, lack of prerequisite skills, poorly-constructed test, dysfunctional home situation, and so on. We know that all of these (and more) exist to greater or lesser extents in the mix. Who should be accountable? The teacher for the quality of instruction? I think so. The student for effort and persistence? Yes, again. Administrators for providing safe learning environment? Yep. Assessment specialists for developing sound tests? Bingo. Communities for providing adequate resources? Sure. Parents for establishing a supportive home environment? Yessirree. The key limitation is that, we can only make policies and products to address those factors that are legitimately under governmental control. And, in education, we understand that intervention may or may not prove effective.

Thus, although high-stakes tests have made a path in the wilderness, the controversy clearly hinges on accountability itself. The difficult fits and starts of developing sound accountability systems may actually cause some hearts to murmur. Understanding the importance, complexity, and difficulties as the accountability infant matures will be surely be trying. How — or if — high-stakes tests will fit into the mature version is hard to tell, and the devil will be in the details. But it is evident that the presence of high-stakes tests have at least served as a conversation-starter for a policy dialogue that may not have taken place in their absence.

**30** *VIII. Educators' Intimacy with Their Disciplines* Once a test has been mandated in, say, language arts, the first step in any high-stakes testing program is to circumscribe the boundaries of what will be tested. The almost universal strategy for accomplishing this is to empanel groups of (primarily) educators who are familiar with the ages, grades, and content to be tested. These groups are usually large, selected to be representative, and expert in the subject area. The groups first study relevant documentation (e.g. the authorizing legislation, state curriculum guides, content standards). They then begin the arduous, time-consuming task of discussing among themselves the nature of the content area, the sequence and content of typical instruction, learner characteristics and developmental issues, cross-disciplinary relationships, and relevant assessment techniques.

These extended conversations help shape the resulting high-stakes tests, to be sure. However, they also affect the discussants, and those with whom they interact when they return to their districts, buildings, and classrooms. As persons with special knowledge of the particular high-stakes testing program, the participants are sometimes asked to replicate those disciplinary and logistic discussions locally. The impact of this trickling-down is just beginning to be noticed by researchers — and the effects are beneficial. For example, at one session of the 2000 American Educational Research Association conference, scholars reported on the positive effects of a state testing program in Maine on classroom assessment practices[18] and on how educators in Florida were assimilating their involvement in large-scale testing activities at the local level.[19]

These local discussions mirror the large scale counterparts in that they provide educators with an opportunity to become more intimate with the nature and structure of their own disciplines, and to contemplate interdisciplinary relationships. As Martha Stewart would say: it's a good thing. And the impulse for this good thing is clearly the presence of a high-stakes test.

*IX. Equity*    There is a flip-side to the common concern that high-stakes tests result in the homogenizing of education. The flip-side is that high-stakes tests promote greater homogeneity of education. Naturally, we should be vigilant about the threat posed by common *low* standards that could be engendered, and it is right to worry about gravitating to the lowest common denominator.[20] On the other hand, there is something to be said for increased equity in expectations and experiences for all students. As a result of schools' aligning their curricula and instructional focus more closely to outcomes embodied in high-stakes tests, the experiences of and aspirations for children in urban, suburban, and rural districts within a state are more comparable than they have been in the recent past.

Surely, inequalities — even savage ones — persist. However, some movement toward greater consistency is perceptible. And, the press toward more uniformity of expectation and experience may be particularly beneficial in an increasingly mobile society. The seamlessness with which a student can move from one district to another — even one school to another within a district — may well translate into incremental gains in achievement sufficient enough to spell the difference between promotion and graduation, or retention and dropping out.

**35** *X. Quality of Tests*    The final benevolent consequence is the profoundly positive effect that the introduction of high-stakes consequences has had on the tests themselves. Along with more serious consequences has come heightened scrutiny. The high-stakes tests of today are surely the most meticulously developed, carefully constructed, and rigorously reported. Many criticisms of tests are valid, but a complainant who suggests that today's high-stakes tests are "lower-order" or "biased" or "not relevant" are most likely unfamiliar with that which they purport to critique.

If only for its long history and ever-present watch-dogging, high-stakes tests have evolved to a state of being: highly reliable; free from bias; relevant and age appropriate; higher order; tightly related to important, public goals; time and cost efficient; and yielding remarkably consistent decisions. It is fair to say that one strains the gnat in objecting to the characteristics of high-stakes tests, when the characteristics of those tests is compared to what a child will likely experience in his or her classroom the other 176 days of the school year. It is not an overstatement to say that, at least on the grounds just articulated, the high-stakes, state test that a student takes will, by far, be the best assessment that student will see all year.

A secondary benefit of the quality of typical high-stakes tests is that, because of their perceived importance, they become mimicked at lower levels. It is appropriate to abhor teaching to the test. However, it is also important to recognize the beneficial effects of exposing educators to high-quality writing prompts, document-based questions, constructed-response formats, and even challenging multiple-choice items. It is not cheating, but the highest form of praise when educators then rely on these exemplars to enhance their own assessment practices.

## Keepin' It Real

It would be foolish to ignore the short-comings and undesirable consequences of high-stakes tests. Current discussions and inquiries are essential, productive, and encouraging. However, amidst the consternation about high-stakes tests, it is equally inappropriate to fail to consider the unanticipated positive consequences, or to fail to incorporate these into any cost-benefit calculus that should characterize sound policy decisions.

Vigorous debates about the nature and role of high-stakes tests and accountability systems are healthy and needed. To these frays, the protestants may bring differing doctrinal starting points and differing conceptions of the source of salvation. It is an exhilarating time of profound questioning. High-stakes tests: we don't know how to live with them; we can't seem to live without them. The oft-quoted first sentence of Charles Dickens' *A Tale of Two Cities* ("It was the best of times, it was the worst of times") seems especially relevant to the juncture at which we find ourselves. The remainder of Dickens' opening paragraph merely extends the piquant metaphor:

> **40** It was the age of wisdom, it was the age of foolishness, it was the epoch of belief, it was the epoch of incredulity, it was the season of Light, it was the season of Darkness, it was the spring of hope, it was the winter of despair, we had everything before us, we had nothing before us, we were all going direct to Heaven, we were all going direct the other way.[21]

## Notes

1. Alfie Kohn, "Fighting the Tests: A Practical Guide to Rescuing Our Schools," *Phi Delta Kappan*, vol. 82, 2001, p. 349.
2. Scott Thompson, "The Authentic Testing Movement and Its Evil Twin," *Phi Delta Kappan,* vol. 82, 2001, pp. 358–362.
3. Susan Ohanian, "News from the Test Resistance Trail," *Phi Delta Kappan,* vol. 82, 2001, p. 365.
4. Diane Ravitch, "The Case for National Standards and Assessments," *The Clearing House,* vol. 69, 1996, pp. 134–135.
5. Richard Phelps, "The demand for standardized student testing," *Educational Measurement: Issues and Practice,* vol. 17, no. 3, 1998, pp. 5–23.
6. Asa Hilliard, "Excellence in Education versus High-Stakes Testing," *Journal of Teacher Education,* vol. 51, 2000, pp. 293–304.
7. George Madaus, "The Distortion of Teaching and Testing: High-stakes Testing and Instruction," *Peabody Journal of Education,* vol. 65, 1998, pp. 29–46.
8. Alfie Kohn, "Burnt at the High Stakes," *Journal of Teacher Education,* vol. 51, 2000, pp. 315–327.
9. Karin Chenoweth, "Judge's Ruling Effectively Acquits High-stakes Test: To the Disadvantage of Poor and Minority Students," *Black Issues in Higher Education,* vol. 51, 2000, p. 12.
10. Patricia Kannapel and others, "I Don't Give a Hoot If Somebody Is Going to Pay Me $3600: Local School District Reaction to Kentucky's High-stakes Accountability System." Paper presented at the Annual Meeting of the American Educational Research Association, New York, April 1996 (ERIC Document No. 397 135).
11. Judges 12:5–6, *The Living Bible;* cited in William Mehrens and

CONTEXT

A web portal devoted to education news, EducationNews.org describes itself as "the Internet's leading source of education news." It claims to provide more balanced coverage of education issues than more traditional media, and it seeks to use Internet technologies "to increase interest and subsequent involvement in education reform."

Gregory Cizek, "Standard Setting and the Public Good: Benefits Accrued and Anticipated," in G. J. Cizek (Ed.), *Setting Performance Standards: Concepts, Methods, and Perspectives,* (Mahwah, NJ: Lawrence Erlbaum, 2001).

**12.** Mehrens and Cizek, pp. 477–478.

**13.** Ordinarily, the 10 items should probably be presented with appropriate recognition of their downsides, disadvantages, etc. However, for the sake of clarity, brevity, and because most readers are probably already all too aware of the counter arguments, I have chosen to avoid any facade of balanced treatment.

**14.** Martha Thurlow and James Ysseldyke, "Standard Setting Challenges for Special Populations," in G. J. Cizek (Ed.), *Setting Performance Standards: Concepts, Methods, and Perspectives,* (Mahwah, NJ: Lawrence Erlbaum, 2001), p. 389.

**15.** John Hills, "Apathy toward Testing and Grading," *Phi Delta Kappan,* vol. 72, 1991, pp. 540-545.

**16.** See, for example, Rita O' Sullivan and Marla Chalnick, "Measurement-related Course Requirements for Teacher Certification and Recertification," *Educational Measurement: Issues and Practice,* vol. 10, 1991, pp. 17-19, 23; Richard Stiggins, "Assessment Literacy," *Phi Delta Kappan,* vol. 72, 1991, pp. 534-539; James Impara and Barbara Plake, "Professional Development in Student Assessment for Educational Administrators,"

*Educational Measurement: Issues and Practice,"* vol. 15, 1996, pp. 14-20.

**17.** Chester Finn, Jr., Bruno V. Manno, and Gregg Vanourek, *Charter Schools in Action: Renewing Public Education* (Princeton, N.J.: Princeton University Press, 2000).

**18.** Jeff Beaudry, "The Positive Effects of Administrators and Teachers on Classroom Assessment Practices and Student Achievement." Paper presented at the annual meeting of the American Educational Research Association, April 2000, New Orleans, LA.

**19.** Madhabi Banerji, "Designing District-level Classroom Assessment Systems." Paper presented at the annual meeting of the American Educational Research Association, April 2000, New Orleans, LA.

**20.** Actually, the concern about low expectations may have passed and, if the experiences of states like Washington, Arizona, and Massachusetts are prescient, the concern may be being replaced by a concern that content or performance expectations (or both) are too high and coming too fast. See http://seattletimes. nwsource.com/news/ local/html98/test_19991010.html ; http://www.edweek.org/ew/ ewstory.cfm?slug=13ariz.h20; and Donald C. Orlich, "Education Reform and Limits to Student Achievement," *Phi Delta Kappan,* vol. 81, 2000 pp. 468–472.

**21.** Charles Dickens, *A Tale of Two Cities* (New York: Dodd, Mead, and Company, 1925), p. 3.

# Questions for Discussion

**1.** Examine the way in which Cizek opens this essay, noting especially his use of religious metaphors. How, specifically, does he introduce his subject and establish his own stance toward it? How does he set the tone for his argument? How effective do you think his introduction is in setting up his argument? In your answer, cite specific words and phrases from his introductory paragraphs. **2.** Cizek devotes much of his essay to summarizing and responding to the arguments of those who are opposed to testing. Evaluate his use of his references to his opponents. How effective are these references in helping him to make his own argument in favor of standardized testing? Do you think he represents his opponents fairly? Explain. **3.** In paragraph 25, Cizek recalls his own experience as a student to introduce an analogy in which he compares high school physical exams to standardized testing. What point does Cizek use this analogy to make? How effectively do you think this analogy helps Cizek to make his point? Would the analogy have been less effective if Cizek had not referred to his own experience as a student? Explain. **4.** In many ways, Cizek's writing style is unusual for a scholarly essay, especially his use of figurative language. How would you describe Cizek's writing style? In what ways do you think it strengthens or weakens his argument? Cite specific passages from his essay in your answer. **5.** Cizek describes the way in which curriculum standards are typically set by panels of experts who determine the appropriate content for specific grade levels in specific subjects. He declares this to be a "good thing." What are some pros and cons that you see in this approach to developing curriculum? Do you think Cizek's discussion of this process enhances his argument? Explain. **6.** Near the end of his essay, Cizek states that vigorous debates about testing "are healthy and needed" and that it is an "exhilarating time of profound questioning" about testing. Do you agree? Why or why not? To what extent do you think Cizek's essay contributes positively to this ongoing debate?

## ④ BERTELL OLLMAN, "Why So Many Exams? A Marxist Response"

Complaints about public education in the United States are so common that the view that schools are in crisis seems to be almost universal. Rarely does anyone describe the schools as working. Critic Bertell Ollman is someone who does. But he doesn't think that's a good thing. Ollman believes that despite constant criticism of schools and calls for reform, public education in the United States effectively serves the basic economic system on which American society is based: capitalism. In his view, the many problems that are typically associated with schools actually reflect of the needs of capitalism rather than the needs of individual students. More specifically, standardized testing is necessary to prepare students for their roles in a capitalist system, and as long as that system remains in place, neither standardized tests nor the problems associated with schooling will go away. Whether or not you agree with Ollman's view of capitalism or his position on testing, his essay is a good example of an argument that reflects a specific theory or political ideology (in this case, Marxism). It suggests as well that educational issues such as testing are related in complex ways to our political and economic lives. Bertell Ollman is a professor of political science at New York University. A well-known Marxist scholar, he has written many books and essays about political and social issues, including *Dialectical Investigations* (1993) and *How to Take an Exam . . . and Remake the World* (2001). The following essay was published in 2002 in *Z Magazine*.

# Why So Many Exams? A Marxist Response
## BERTELL OLLMAN

1 Psychologist Bill Livant, has remarked, "When a liberal sees a beggar, he [sic] says the system isn't working. When a Marxist does, he [sic] says it is." The same insight could be applied today to the entire area of education. The learned journals, as well as the popular media, are full of studies documenting how little most students know and how fragile are their basic skills. The cry heard almost everywhere is "The system isn't working."

Responding to this common complaint, conservatives — starting (but not ending) with the Bush administration — have offered a package of reforms in which increased testing occupies the central place. The typical liberal and even radical response to this has been to demonstrate that such measures are not likely to have the "desired" effect. The assumption, of course, is that we all want more or less the same thing from a system of education and that conservatives have made an error in the means they have chosen to attain our common end. But what if students are already receiving — more or less — the kind of education that conservatives favor? This would cast their proposals for "reform" in another light. What if, as Livant points out in the case of beggars, the system is working?

Before detailing what young people learn from their forced participation in this educational ritual, it may be useful to dispose of a number of myths that surround exams and exam taking in our society.

(1) *Exams are a necessary part of education.* Education, of one kind or another has existed in all human societies, but exams have not; and the practice of requiring frequent exams is a very recent innovation and still relatively rare in the world.

5 (2) *Exams are unbiased.* In 1912, Henry Goddard, a distinguished psychologist, administered what he claimed were "culture free" IQ* tests to new immigrants on Ellis Island and found that 83 percent of Jews, 80 percent of Hungarians, 79 percent of Italians, and 87 percent of Russians were "feebleminded," adding that "all feebleminded are at least potential criminals." IQ* tests have gotten better since then, but given the character of the testing process, the attitudes of those who make up any test, and the variety of people — coming from so many different backgrounds — who take it, it is impossible to produce a test that does not have serious biases

(3) *Exams are objectively graded.* Daniel Stark and Edward Elliot sent two English essays to 200 high school teachers for grading. They got back 142 grades. For one paper, the grades ranged from 50 to 99; for the other, the grades went from 64 to 99. But English is not an "objective" subject, you say. Well, they did the same thing for an essay an-swer in mathematics and got back grades ranging from 28 to 95. Though most of the grades they received in both cases fell in the middle ground, it was evident that a good part of any grade was the result of who marked the exam and not of who took it.

(4) *Exams are an accurate indication of what students know and of intelligence in general.* But all sorts of things, including luck in getting (or not getting) the questions you hoped for and one's state of mind and emotions the day of the exam, can have an important effect on the result.

(5) *All students have an equal chance to do well on exams,* that even major differences in their conditions of life have a negligible impact on their performance. There is such a strong correlation between students' family income and their test scores, however, that the radical educational theorist, Ira Shor, has suggested (tongue-in-cheek) that college applications should ignore test scores altogether and just ask students to enter their family income. The results would be the same — with relatively few exceptions, the same people would get admitted into college, but then, of course, the belief that there is equality of opportunity in the classroom would stand forth as the myth that it is.

(6) *Exams are the fairest way to distribute society's scarce resources* to the young, hence the association of exams with the ideas of meritocracy and equality of opportunity. But if some students consistently do better on exams because of the advantages they possess and other students do not outside of school, then directing society's main benefits to these same people compounds the initial inequality.

10 (7) *Exams, and particularly the fear of them, are necessary in order to motivate students to do their assignments.* Who can

*See the sidebar on IQ tests on page 247.

ams work. They know, for example, that exams don't only involve reading questions and writing answers. They also involve forced isolation from other students, prohibition on talking and walking around and going to the bathroom, writing a lot faster than usual, physical discomfort, worry, fear, anxiety, and often guilt.

They are also aware that exams do a poor job of testing what students actually know. But it is here that most of their criticisms run into a brick wall, because most students don't know enough about society to understand the role that exams — especially taking so many exams — play in preparing them to take their place in it.

But if exams are not what most people think they are, then what are they? The short answer is that exams have less to do with testing us for what we are supposed to know than teaching us what the other aspects of instruction cannot get at (or get at as well). To understand what that is we must examine what the capitalist class require from a system of education.\* Here, it is clear that capitalists need a system of education that provides young people with the knowledge and skills necessary for their businesses to function and prosper. But they also want schools to give youth the beliefs, attitudes, emotions, and associated habits of behavior that make it easy for capitalists to tap into this store of knowledge and skills. They need all this not only to maximize their profits, but to help reproduce the social, economic, and even political con-

doubt that years of reacting to such threats have produced in many students a reflex of the kind depicted here? The sad fact is that the natural curiosity of young people and their desire to learn, develop, advance, master, and the pleasure that comes from succeeding — which could and should motivate all studying — has been progressively replaced in their psyches by a pervasive fear of failing. This needn't be. For the rest, if the only reason a student does the assignments is that he/she is worried about the exam, he/she should not be taking that course in the first place.

(8) *Exams are not injurious, socially, intellectually, and psychologically.* Complaining about exams may be most students' first truly informed criticism about society because they are its victims and know from experience how ex-

*\*The term **capitalism** can be used to refer to an economic system based on a free market in which supply and demand dictate the movement of goods and services. The term can be used more broadly to refer to a social system based on the ideas of individual rights and free choice.*

ditions and accompanying processes that allow them to extract profits. Without workers, consumers and citizens who are well versed in and accepting of their roles in these processes, the entire capitalist system would grind to a halt. It is here — particularly as regards the behavioral and attitudinal prerequisites of capitalist rule — that the culture of exams has become indispensable. So what do exams "teach" students?

(1) The crush of tests gets students to believe that one gets what one works for, that the standards by which this is decided are objective and fair, and therefore that those who do better deserve what they get; and that the same holds for those who do badly. After a while, this attitude is carried over to what students find in the rest of society, including their own failures later in life, where it encourages them to "blame the victim" (themselves or others) and feel guilty for what is not their fault.

15 (2) By fixing a time and a form in which they have to deliver or else, exams prepare students for the more rigorous discipline of the work situation that lies ahead.

(3) In forcing students to think and write faster than they ordinarily do, exams get them ready mentally, emotionally, and also morally for the speed-ups they will face on the job.

(4) The self-discipline students acquire in preparing for exams also helps them put up with the disrespect, personal abuse, and boredom that awaits them on the job.

(5) Exams are orders that are not open to question — "discuss this," "outline that," etc. — and taking so many exams conditions students to accept unthinkingly the orders that will come from their future employers.

(6) By fitting the infinite variety of answers given on exams into the strait-jacket of A, B, C, D, and F, students get accustomed to the standardization of people as well as of things and the impersonal job categories that will constitute such an important part of their identity later on.

20 (7) Because passing an exam is mainly good for enabling students to move up a grade so they can take a slightly harder exam, which — if they pass — enables them to repeat the exercise *ad infinitum,* they begin to see life as an endless series of ever more complicated exams, where one never finishes being judged and the need for being prepared and respectful of the judging authorities only grows.

(8) Because their teachers know all the right answers to the exams, students tend to assume that those who are above them in other hierarchies also know much more than they do.

(9) Because their teachers genuinely want them to do well on exams, students also mistakenly assume that those in relation of authority over them in other hierarchies are also rooting for them to succeed, that is, have their best interests at heart.

(10) Because most tests are taken individually, striving to do well on a test is treated as something that concerns students only as individuals. Cooperative solutions are equated with cheating, if considered at all.

(11) Because one is never quite ready for an exam, there is always something more to do, students often feel guilty for reading materials or engaging in activities unrelated to the exam. The whole of life, it would appear, is but preparation for exams or doing what is required in order to succeed (as those in charge define "success").

25 (12) With the Damocles[†] sword of a failing (or for some a mediocre) grade hanging over their heads throughout

[†]According to Roman myth, Damocles was a courtier in Syracuse, Greece, in the 4th century B.C.E. who envied the life of his ruler Dionysius. Given the chance to experience that life, Damocles agreed until he realized that, once seated in the ruler's throne, a large sword was suspended over his head by a single horse hair. The experience prompted him to reevaluate his beliefs about what constitutes a good life.

their years in school (including university), the inhibiting fear of swift and dire punishment never leaves students, no matter their later situation.

(13) Coupled with the above, because there is always so much to be known, exams — especially so many of them — tend to undermine students' self-confidence and to raise their levels of anxiety, with the result that most young people remain unsure that they will ever know enough to criticize existing institutions and become even physically uncomfortable at the thought of trying to put something better in their place.

(14) Exams also play a key role in determining course content, leaving little time for material that is not on the exam. Among the first things to be omitted in this "tightening" of the curriculum are students' own reactions to the topics that come up, collective reflection on the main problems of the day, alternative points of view and other possibilities generally, the larger picture (where everything fits), explorations of topics triggered by individual curiosity, and anything else that is likely to promote creative, cooperative, or critical thinking.

(15) Exams also determine the form in which most teaching goes on, since for any given exam there is generally a best way to prepare for it. Repetition and forced memorization, even learning by rote, and frequent quizzes (more exams) leave little time for other more imaginative approaches to conveying, exchanging and questioning facts and ideas.

(16) Multiple exams become one of the main factors determining the character of the relation between students (with students viewing each other as competitors for the best grades), the relation between students and teachers (with most students viewing their teachers as examiners and graders first, and most teachers viewing their students largely in terms of how well they have done on exams), also the relation between teachers and school administrators (since principals and deans now have an "objective" standard by which to measure teacher performance), and even the relation between school administrations and various state bodies (since the same standard is used by the state to judge the work of schools and school systems). Exams mediate all social relations in the educational system in a manner similar to the way money mediates relations between people in the larger society with the same dehumanizing results.
**30** While exams have been with us for a long time, socializing students in all the ways that I have outlined above, it is only recently that the mania for exams has begun to affect government policies. Why now? Globalization, or whatever it is one chooses to call this new stage, has arrived. But to which of its aspects is the current drive for more exams a carefully fashioned response? The proponents of such educational "reform" point to the intensified competition between industries and workers worldwide and the in-

## GLOBALIZATION

The term *globalization* has been used to refer to a complex set of political, social, and economic developments in the last decade or so that have made nations, societies, and regions of the world more interdependent. Commerce, communication, and travel between various regions of the world have increased, and international trade agreements have facilitated economic and social contacts across national borders. According to journalist Thomas Friedman, whose 1999 book *The Lexus and the Olive Tree* examines the effects of globalization, "Globalization is not a phenomenon. It is not just some passing trend. Today it is an overarching international system shaping the domestic politics and foreign relations of virtually every country, and we need to understand it as such." Whether or not globalization is a good thing is intensely debated. You can find a sampling of the debate at http://globalization.about.com/library/weekly/aa080701a.htm. (Also see Chapter 13 for essays on issues associated with globalization.)

creasingly rapid pace at which economic changes of all kinds are occurring. To survive in this new order requires people, they say, who are not only efficient, but also have a variety of skills (or can quickly acquire them) and the flexibility to change tasks whenever called upon to do so. Thus, the only way to prepare our youth for the new economic life that awaits them is to raise standards of education, and that entails, among other things, more exams.

A more critical approach to globalization begins by emphasizing that the intensification of economic competition worldwide is driven by capitalists' efforts to maximize their profits. It is this that puts all the other developments associated with globalization into motion. It is well known that, all things being equal, the less capitalists pay their workers and the less money they spend on improving work conditions and reducing pollution, the more profit they make. Recent technological progress in transportation and communication, together with free trade and the abolition of laws restricting the movement of capital, allow capitalists to consider workers all over the world in making their calculations. While the full impact of these developments is yet to be felt, we can already see two of its most important effects in the movement of more and more companies (and parts of companies) out of the U.S. and a roll-back of modest gains in wages, benefits, and work conditions that American workers have won over the last 50 years.

The current rage for more exams needs to be viewed as part of a larger strategy that includes stoking patriotic fires and chipping away at traditional civil liberties (both rationalized by the so-called war on terrorism), the promotion of "family values," restrictions on sexual freedom (but not, as we see, on sexual hypocrisy), and the push for more prisons and longer prison sentences for a whole range of minor crimes.

Is there a connection between exams and the privatization of public education? They appear to be separate, but look again. With new investment opportunities failing to keep up with the rapidly escalating surpluses in search of them (a periodic problem for a system that never pays its workers enough to consume all the wealth they produce), the public sector has become the latest "last" frontier for capitalist expansion. Given its size and potential for profit, what are state prisons or utilities or transport or communication systems or other social services next to public education? But how to convince the citizenry that companies whose only concern is with the bottom line can do a better job educating our young than public servants dedicated to the task? What seems impossible could be done if somehow education were redefined to emphasize the qualities associated with business and its achievements. Then — by definition — business could do the "job" better than any public agency.

Enter exams. Standardization, easily quantifiable results, and the willingness to reshape all intervening processes to obtain them characterize the path to success in both exams and business. When that happens (and to the extent it has already happened), putting education in the hands of businesspeople who know best how to dispense with "inessentials" becomes a perfectly rational thing to do.

35 What should students do about all this? Well, they shouldn't refuse to take exams (unless the whole class gets in-volved) and they shouldn't drop out of school. Given the relations of power inside education and throughout the rest of society, that would be suicidal and suicide is never good politics. Rather, they should become better students by learning more about the role of education, and exams in particular, in capitalism. Nowhere does the contradiction between the selfish and manipulative interests of our ruling class and the educational and developmental interests of students stand out in such sharp relief as in the current debate over exams. Students of all ages need to get involved in this debate in order to raise the consciousness of young people regarding the source of their special oppression and the possibility of uniting with other oppressed groups to create a truly human society. Everything depends on the youth of today doing better on this crucial test than my generation did, because the price for failure has never been so high. Will they succeed? Can they afford to fail?

# NEGOTIATING DIFFERENCES

As a student, you have undoubtedly had direct experiences with standardized tests as well as the many other kinds of tests given in schools. Like every student, you know from those experiences how great the impact of testing can be.

But testing affects others as well: teachers, parents, school administrators, and politicians, to name a few. In many states, if students perform poorly on standardized tests, school funding can be affected, and teachers' and administrators' jobs can be at stake. The consequences of testing are great indeed. And given the trend in the United States toward more rather than fewer high-stakes tests, the debates about testing and its consequences are likely to intensify in the coming years.

With that in mind, and drawing on your own experiences, write an essay in which you state your own position about the need for and use of standardized tests. Imagine that your audience is a general audience of students, educators, and parents who have some direct interest in testing and in education generally.

**1.** Ollman discusses eight "myths" that he believes surround testing in the United States. Evaluate his discussion of these "myths." How widespread do you think the eight beliefs he calls "myths" really are? How effectively does he dispel each of these beliefs? To what extent does his discussion of these beliefs — and his description of them as "myths" — enhance or weaken his argument? How does his discussion of these "myths" compare to Gregory Cizek's discussion of the ten benefits of standardized testing (see pages 250–261)?

**2.** Ollman asserts that "most students don't know enough about society to understand the role that exams . . . play in preparing them to take their place in it." How does this point contribute to his main argument about testing? How might it reflect his Marxist perspective? Do you agree with him? **3.** Ollman claims that a capitalist system requires citizens with certain beliefs, attitudes, and skills who also accept specified roles in American society. He then offers a list of sixteen ways in which testing teaches students what they need to know to serve the capitalist system. How persuasive do you find this list? What responses might you offer to Ollman's lessons? Do you think Ollman expects most Americans to reject his list? **4.** Why does Ollman believe that globalization is an important factor influencing standardized testing? What evidence does he offer in support of this position? Evaluate the effectiveness of that evidence. Do you agree with Ollman about the connection between globalization and testing? Why or why not? **5.** Ollman offers advice to students about what they should do about standardized tests. In what ways do you think this advice might enhance the effectiveness of his argument? How realistic do you think his advice is? **6.** Ollman's essay can be described as an argument based on deductive reasoning (see pages 26–31). What is the basic premise of his argument? Do you think most Americans would agree with him? Explain. **7.** Using the Toulmin Model of Argumentation (see pages 31–35), identify Ollman's central claim and the warrant (or warrants) on which that claim is based. Do you think most Americans would accept his warrant(s)? Explain.

If you live in a state where standardized tests are mandated, such as New York or California, consider using your experiences with your state tests to help make your argument. You can also draw on the essays in this section to support your position. As you formulate your argument, keep in mind the different reasons for — or against — the use of testing, such as Eleanor Martin, Patricia Williams, Gregory Cizek, and Bertell Ollman have discussed in their arguments in this section. In stating and justifying your own position on testing, try to address the concerns of others who have a legitimate interest in the kinds of standardized tests that you have had to take as a student — for example, the administrators and teachers at your school or members of the community where you live.

Alternatively, construct a Web site intended to present your position on testing. Be sure to design your Web site in a way that will present your position effectively to a specific audience that you wish to address.

# 10

## ENVIRONMENTS

ENVIRO

## Cluster
### HOW DO WE DESIGN COMMUNITIES?

(1) David Plotz. "A Surburb Grown Up and All Paved Over"

(2) Virginia Postrel, "Misplacing the Blame for Our Troubles on 'Flat, Not Tall' Spaces"

(3) Donella Meadows, "So What Can We Do — Really Do — About Sprawl?"

(4) Robert Wilson, "Enough Snickering. Suburbia Is More Complicated and Varied Than We Think"

CON-TEXT
**A Beautiful Place
Made Ugly**

N M E N T S

# HOW DO WE DESIGN COMMUNITIES?

Visitors to Washington, D.C., sometimes complain about how difficult it can be to drive in that city. The streets seem to be laid out in a confusing pattern, with several main thoroughfares cutting across otherwise parallel streets at odd angles. It might surprise those visitors to learn that Washington, D.C. was originally designed from scratch by French architect Pierre L'Enfant, who was commissioned by President Washington in 1791. If you look at a street map of the city, you can make out the main features of that original design. For instance, those angled thoroughfares radiate from the central location of the Capitol Building; the famous Mall in front of the Capitol reflects L'Enfant's vision for a wide, central avenue. L'Enfant's original design was changed in several ways even as the city was being built, and in the years since it was constructed, the city, like many American cities, has grown dramatically. The confusing street patterns partially reflect the lack of planning and regulation as the city has grown; other oddities have occurred as builders and city leaders have tried to accommodate to the original design. For example, some buildings, such as the FBI Building and the East Building of the National Gallery of Art, are not square or rectangular but have unusual angles (such as a trapezoid) to fit into the odd-shaped city blocks created by those radiating thoroughfares. If you live in a city or town that has experienced recent growth, you might have seen the same phenomenon. ■ The growth of cities and towns tends to be seen as a good thing. But as the example of Washington, D.C., indicates, growth can create problems too. As cities and towns expand, new residents and businesses require more services, which lead to even more growth. There is an increasing need for more energy and more space. Not surprisingly, such growth often occurs at the edges of cities, where farmland and rural communities once existed. Despite the economic benefits, residents sometimes resist growth because it inevitably changes the quality of life in their communities. Famous architect Frank Lloyd Wright, whose building designs reflected his belief that our structures should be part of the natural environment where they are located, once scolded the people of Miami about the unnatural way in which their city developed (see *Con-Text* on page 273). Wright's argument was really a call to create livable communities that foster a certain kind of quality of life. But "quality of life" might not be the same for all people, and that is where conflicts can arise. Ultimately, growth raises questions about the kinds of communities we want. And how do we determine what kinds of communities we should have? ■ In a sense, all the essays in this section address that question. Ostensibly, these essays are about the problems associated with the growth of our communities. A few of the writers discuss "sprawl," which is the rapid and seemingly unchecked growth of cities and towns into surrounding rural areas. Others describe the "smart growth" movement that emerged in the 1990s, partly as a reaction to sprawl. In making their arguments, these writers offer their respective visions for the kinds of communities we should have. Their essays remind us that when we argue about practical problems such as sprawl, we are really addressing deeper — and often more difficult — questions about how we should live together.

## CON-TEXT: "A Beautiful Place Made Ugly"

1 We were coming in on the plane looking over this great, marvelous and very beautiful plateau and what do we see? Little tiny subdivisions of squares, little pigeonholes, little lots, everything divided up into little lots, little boxes on little lots, little tacky things.

And you come downtown and what's happening? Plenty of skyscrapers. You call them hotels. You can't tell whether they're hotels or office buildings or something in a cemetery. They have no feelings, no richness, no sense of this region.

And that, I think is happening to the country. It's not alone your misfortune. . . .

You want to live in a way becoming to human beings with your spirit and a devotion to the beautiful, don't you? Well, why don't you? Why would you accept this sort of thing? Why would you let them put it over on you? You say because of economic reasons.

Well, if that's what this country talks about as the highest standard of living in the world, then I think it isn't at all the highest,

it's only biggest — and quite ignorant.

Nature must be ashamed of these hotels that you're building down here. Nature must be ashamed of the way this place has been laid out and patterned after a checkerboard and parceled out in little parcels where you stand on each other's toes, face the sidewalk, your elbows in the next neighbor's ribs. . . .

SOURCE: Frank Lloyd Wright, public address, Miami, Florida (1955).

## ① DAVID PLOTZ, "A Suburb Grown Up and All Paved Over"

The tension between individual rights and the interests of the state is an old one in American society. And it often emerges in the form of controversies about the rights of property owners to determine how to use their land. In the following essay, journalist Dave Plotz describes one such controversy: a law prohibiting homeowners in Fairfax County, Virginia, one of the wealthiest counties in the country, from paving their yards. At first glance, the purpose of the law, reasonably enough, seems to be to protect property values and preserve the character of a community. But Plotz argues that much more is involved. He traces the origins of the law to concerns about growth, development, and especially immigration — longstanding issues that have often caused conflict among Americans. In his essay, which was published in the *New York Times* in 2002, Plotz raises questions about the social effects of economic development. He also prompts us to consider what kinds of communities we wish to have. Plotz is the Washington bureau chief of Slate.com, an online public affairs magazine.

## A Suburb Grown Up and All Paved Over
### DAVID PLOTZ

CONTEXT

As Plotz notes in his essay, Fairfax County, Virginia, is one of the richest counties in the United States. With about one million residents, it is more populous than seven states. The county's median annual household income in 2001 was $84,683, with 20 percent of households earning $150,000 or more annually.

1 The first commandment of the suburbs used to be Not in My Back Yard. Apparently now it is Not in Your Front Yard — at least here in Fairfax County, Va., just over the Potomac from Washington.

Earlier this month the county council passed a law forbidding homeowners from paving over their front yards to create extra parking spaces. This legislation is directed not at the mansion-owners of Reston, who have ample room for their fleets of Beemers, but at the immigrants sardined into houses in the county's less tony neighborhoods, like Groveton. There has apparently been a rash of yard-paving: the owners of these houses have asphalted the lawn so they have a place to put the three, four or six cars that their sisters and husbands and cousins need to get to work.

Fairfax isn't the only jurisdiction that is fighting yard-paving; Boston and San Francisco are, too. But there is something absurd in the idea of Fairfax trying to limit car ownership. Like most suburbs, Fairfax County owes not just its existence but its prosperity to the automobile. Its major landmarks are intersections (Bailey's Crossroads, Tysons Corner, Seven Corners and so on). And there's something equally silly in the notion that stopping pave-overs somehow preserves Fairfax's natural beauty — as if any remained. One councilwoman said she supported the bill because pave-overs had "nibbled away" at Fairfax's green space.

Nibbled is right: When you add up the malls and highways and condos and office parks and malls and malls, what's left is enough greenery for a side salad. Every neighborhood in Fairfax is named after the nature that was destroyed to build it: Rose Hill, Blueberry Farm, Sycamore Lakes — every place but Money's Corner.

**5** The paving regulation stems partly, of course, from the usual paranoia about property values. Grass sells better than asphalt. But the regulation may succeed only in moving cars from the front lawn to the front curb. As soon as the pave-over law passed, at least one resident griped that it would encourage people to park on the street. No doubt the council will be weighing street parking bans next.

The true cause of the pave-over law, however, is not parking. It's Fairfax's midlife crisis. Fairfax County, which strutted and preened through the 1990's, is having some bad years. America Online, which was born and raised here, married Time Warner and moved its headquarters to New York City. Michael Saylor, Fairfax County's very own Internet billionaire, has become a pariah, his crippled company, Microstrategy, a symbol of all that was wrong with the tech bubble. The richest county in America according to the 1990 census, Fairfax discovered a few weeks ago that it has now dropped to No. 2.

Yet the roots of the crisis here go even deeper. Since the 1970's, Fairfax

has morphed from a bucolic exurb into its own metropolis, a hotbed of industry and commerce. The typical lazy comforts of the distant suburb have vanished; the

## U.S. POVERTY RATE

The U.S. Bureau of Labor Statistics determines the U.S. poverty rate, or the percentage of poor people in the United States, by calculating the number of households below the poverty line. That line varies according to the number of people in a household. In 2002 a family of four fell below the poverty line if its total income was less than $18,104. A single person was considered poor if he or she earned less than $9,044 a year. In 2001 only 4.6 percent of the residents met these criteria in Fairfax County, Virginia; by contrast, the U.S. national poverty rate in 2001 was 11.7 percent.

## COMPLICATION

Gerald Gordon, president of the Fairfax County Economic Development Authority, responded to Plotz's essay by pointing out that 11,500 jobs were created in Fairfax County in 2001. He also noted that "the county has more than 30,000 acres of dedicated parkland, including a national wildlife refuge established to protect bald eagles and one of the largest urban marshes on the east coast." (See an excerpt from his letter in Chapter 2, page 24.)

danger and disorder of the city always seem to be encroaching. The county's population will top a million any day now — nearly twice that of Washington itself.

Growth is not new to the county, but immigrants are. The number of immigrants in Fairfax jumped 86 percent in the 90's, to nearly a quarter of the population. (Essentially all the population growth came from immigrants and their children.) A third of county residents now speak a language other than English at home, more than twice the national average.

Fairfax is the very model of the benefits of immigration. Southeast Asians, Indians, Arabs, Pakistanis, West Africans, East Africans and Latin Americans have all settled here in huge numbers, but the county remains wonderfully mixed up. It lacks ethnic enclaves. Immigration has accomplished the impossible in Fairfax: it has made the county interesting, with the area's best and oddest ethnic restaurants and stores.

10 Fairfax's high-tech industry has relied heavily on highly educated foreign workers. At the same time, though without the same eagerness, Fairfax has accepted tens of thousands of low-skill immigrants. They are the backbone of the county's service sector. Working-class immigrants move to Fairfax because that is where the jobs are. They pack houses because rents and home prices are so high they can't afford to live in less cramped conditions. They buy cars because that's the only way they can get to the jobs that everyone wants them to do. And so they pave driveways.

Poverty rates have climbed with the arrival of these immigrants, and middle-class neighbors feel squeezed. The pave-over bill is only the most recent manifestation of their worry. Last year a state senator from Fairfax introduced a bill to the Virginia Legislature that would forbid Virginians from sleeping in living rooms, dining rooms, kitchens and closets. The measure was withdrawn immediately after loud complaints from civil libertarians and immigrant groups.

Fairfax is growing up faster than its residents can adjust. Like many sprawled suburbs, it has consumed its youthful vim and isn't quite sure what to do now. In the space of a generation, Fairfax lost its rural character and its middle-class white identity. In exchange it has won jobs, businesses and bustling, hustling immigrants.

The pave-over battle is a small rearguard action to preserve some vision of a Fairfax past, and in a way it's oddly encouraging. It signals the success of the American melting pot: Fairfax County has undergone great change, causing enormous upheaval, and all anyone can find to fight about is parking.

# Questions for Discussion

**1.** To what extent is social class relevant to the conflicts that Plotz describes in Fairfax County, Virginia? In your experience, does social class determine what people expect from government regulations about housing and zoning? Should government set different standards for different neighborhoods based on the value of property? **2.** On what grounds does Plotz criticize the Fairfax County law that prevents homeowners from paving their lawns? Do you think most people would agree with him? Do you? Why or why not? **3.** Plotz writes that Fairfax Country "lacks ethnic enclaves" and that races within the county are "wonderfully mixed up." What do these statements reveal about his values? Do you think residents of Fairfax County are likely to agree that the lack of ethnic enclaves is a benefit? Explain. **4.** How would you describe the tone of Plotz's essay? In what ways do you think his tone affects his main argument? Given his broad audience (this essay was published in the *New York Times,* a widely circulated newspaper), do you think his tone is appropriate. Explain, citing specific words and phrases from his essay in your answer. **5.** Is Fairfax County a special case? Or is rapid growth causing conflicts in a county in your own state? What do your answers to these questions indicate about the validity of Plotz's argument? What indication can you find in the essay that Plotz sees Fairfax County as one example of a larger problem?

## ② VIRGINIA POSTREL, "Misplacing the Blame for Our Troubles on 'Flat, Not Tall' Spaces"

In 1999 Vice President Al Gore announced a federal "smart growth" initiative. It was intended to help cities and towns combat the effects of unchecked development and to manage their growth to create more livable communities. Gore's smart growth initiative reflected a belief in the possibility of sustaining economic growth while maintaining healthy communities and protecting the environment. Writer Virginia Postrel calls this possibility a myth. Contemporary life, she suggests in the following essay, requires tradeoffs; our lifestyle choices will have both positive and negative consequences, she says. Postrel is making what seems to be a common-sensical argument, one that might match your own experience. But Postrel's argument addresses a much larger matter: What kinds of communities do we really wish to live in? Proponents of smart growth, she suggests, embrace a vision of community that differs from the lifestyle that many suburbanites consciously seek. She suggests that "smart-growthers" wish to impose their vision on others. Although Postrel's starting point for her argument is a 1999 speech by former Vice President Al Gore, a champion of smart growth, the issues that she addresses remain timely and intensely debated today. In late 2002, for example, the New Jersey state legislature was debating a proposed law that would severely restrict suburban sprawl by implementing measures that are based on the idea of smart growth. Whether or not you agree with such measures — or with Postrel — might depend upon your own vision of the ideal community. Postrel is the author of *The Future and Its Enemies* (Free Press, 1998) and a columnist whose essays about business and culture have appeared in the *New York Times, Forbes,* and *D Magazine.* This essay was published in the *Los Angeles Times* in 1999.

## Misplacing the Blame for Our Troubles on 'Flat, Not Tall' Spaces
### VIRGINIA POSTREL

1 If Al Gore denounced soccer moms, told us everything was better in the good old days and demanded that we let his friends redesign our lives to fit their morality, you might think he'd gone over to the religious right. You'd be wrong, however.

Welcome to the war on sprawl, otherwise known as the suburbs.

Gore describes the problem this way: "Acre upon acre of asphalt have transformed what were once mountain clearings and congenial villages into little more than massive parking lots. The ill-thought-out sprawl hastily developed around our nation's cities has turned what used to be friendly, easy suburbs into lonely cul-de-sacs, so distant from the city center that if a family wants to buy an affordable house they have to drive so far that a parent gets home too late to read a bedtime story."

This tale raises many questions: How did those houses in "easy suburbs" catapult themselves to become "lonely cul-de-sacs" reachable only by hours on the road? Why did that transformation make housing more expensive? How early do those kids go to bed?

**5** Gore is clearer on one thing. The problem is that "we've built flat, not tall," putting houses and offices on inexpensive outlying land instead of packing them tighter and tighter in crowded, expensive cities. "Flat, not tall" is the definition of "sprawl." The anti-sprawl critique is that houses with yards and businesses with ample parking are ruining the country.

If you listen only to Gore's speeches, you'd think that the anti-sprawl crusade is about magically making all the nasty trade-offs in life go away. Abandon "ill-planned and ill-coordinated development," and houses will be cheap everywhere. No one will ever sit in traffic. We will all enjoy "livability."

It's a myth, of course. But attacking "sprawl" is a way of blaming an impersonal force for the trade-offs individuals have made in their lives, notably the decisions to work long hours and buy elbow room. The anti-sprawl campaign simultaneously indulges baby boomers' guilt and excuses their life choices, treating them as victims rather than actors. It tells voters that they're bad parents who are destroying the Earth, but then says that it's not their fault.

Harried commuters just want fewer traffic jams. But anti-sprawl technocrats

have something more grandiose in mind. They want everyone to live the way I do: in an urban townhouse off a busy street, with no yard but plenty of shops and restaurants within walking distance. Their "smart growth" planning means confining family life to crowded cities so that the countryside can be left open for wildlife, recreation and a few farmers. They crave "density," which they believe is more efficient and more interesting.

Thus a study highlighted on the Sierra Club's Web site celebrates multi-unit housing: "Sharing walls shares and saves heat. . . . The

### COMPLICATION

Postrel points out that higher populations and housing densities can have negative consequences, such as an increase in traffic. Proponents of "smart growth" argue that the matter is more complicated and that higher densities, together with regional planning, can actually reduce traffic. According to one group of researchers:

Building smart-growth neighborhoods that are more compact can reduce traffic, too. Transportation research indicates that each doubling of average neighborhood density is associated with a decrease in per-household vehicle use of 20–40 percent, with a corresponding decline in emissions. This is one of the reasons that European cities typically exhibit only one-fourth the per-person emissions of carbon dioxide and other pollutants from transportation that are typical of American cities. Source: Benfield, Raimi, and Chen, *Once There Were Greenfields: How Urban Sprawl Is Undermining America's Environment, Economy and Social Fabric* (1999).

single-family houses consume four times as much land for streets and roads and 10 times as much for the houses themselves. The single-family houses use nearly six times as much metal and concrete, the mining of which threatens many of our natural areas."

**10** The ideal is San Francisco's densities of 50 to 100 units per acre. Crowding is good. Density means more traffic — more cars in a smaller space, plus no new road construction. Given enough pain, anti-sprawlers hope to get people out of their cars. They favor inflexible rail systems and other mass transit. "As traffic congestion builds, alternative travel modes will become more attractive" is how Minnesota's Twin Cities Metropolitan Council justified a decision not to build any more roads for the next 20 years.

"Smart-growthers" have no sympathy for suburban family life, which they find wasteful and sterile. And they have no patience for the way contemporary cities have evolved to spread out jobs and houses, to build "flat not tall" in response to the desire for privacy and personal space. They disapprove not merely of the congestion generated when people flock to a new area, but of the reduction in congestion in the city created at the same time.

The anti-sprawl campaign seeks to impose a static, uniform future through nostalgic appeals to an idealized past. It does indeed have much in common with the least tolerant elements of the religious right. It is just less honest.

# Questions for Discussion

**1.** Postrel first published this argument in 1999, when Al Gore was Vice President of the United States and campaigning for the Democratic nomination for the presidency. How would that context explain why she chose to tie her defense of "sprawl" to a critique of Gore? How do you think that writing decision affects her argument today? **2.** Postrel writes, "Harried commuters just want fewer traffic jams." What evidence does Postrel offer for this statement? Do you think she needs to support this statement in any way? Explain. What purpose do you think this statement serves in Postrel's main argument? **3.** What is the purpose of paragraph 9? How does citing the Sierra Club help Postrel's case? What does it suggest to you about Postrel's values? How did you respond to this paragraph? What might your response to it reveal about your own values? **4.** Postrel suggests that the Twin Cities Metropolitan Council's decision not to build new roads for the next twenty years reflects the inflexibility of smart-growth proponents when it comes to problems such as traffic congestion. You can read an introduction to the study commissioned by the Council at www.me3.org/sprawl/bckgrnd.pdf. Review that introduction and assess how Postrel represents the position of the council. Is her representation fair? Explain, citing passages from the study in your answer. **5.** The opening and concluding paragraphs of this argument link opponents of urban sprawl to the religious right. What do you think Postrel means by "the religious right?" What could it have in common with opponents of urban sprawl? In what ways might Postrel's strategy of linking "smart-growthers" and the religious right strengthen or weaken her argument?

③ DONELLA MEADOWS, "So What Can We Do —
Really Do — About Sprawl?"

Debates about sprawl — a term that refers to the spread of housing developments, strip malls, and office buildings into rural areas — often focus on concerns about quality of life and environmental damage. But Donella Meadows demonstrates that sprawl is also a public policy issue. She is clearly an opponent of unchecked development, but she refuses simply to criticize developers. "We can't blame those who make the money," she writes. "They're playing the game according to the rules." For Meadows combating sprawl means understanding — and changing — those rules, which include tax laws and zoning ordinances. Meadows refuses to reduce the problem of sprawl to a pro-versus-con debate. All of us, she suggests, benefit from municipal services and economic development, no matter how fervently we might support environmental protection. So we cannot simply say that we are for or against development. Her argument encourages us to think about protecting the environment and enhancing our quality of life in terms of such mundane (and perhaps dull) matters as taxes and zoning. In doing so, we might also think about our own responsibilities — as consumers and as citizens of a town or city — for the problems caused by sprawl. In this sense her essay is an effort to address a complex problem by understanding it rather than by opposing those who might disagree with her. Donella Meadows, who died in 2001, was the director of the Sustainability Institute and an adjunct professor of environmental studies at Dartmouth College. Author or co-author of nine books, including the best-selling *Limits to Growth* (1972), she was an internationally known voice for an environmentally conscious lifestyle. This essay appeared in her weekly "Global Citizen" column in 1999.

## So What Can We Do — Really Do — About Sprawl
### DONELLA MEADOWS

1 In my mind St. Louis is the poster city for sprawl (see photo on page 283). It has a glittering, high-rise center where fashionable people work, shop and party. Surrounding the center are blocks and blocks of empty lots, abandoned buildings, dying stores, a sad wasteland through which the fashionable people speed on wide highways to the suburbs. In the suburbs the subdivisions and shopping centers expand rapidly outward onto the world's best farmland.

When I imagine the opposite of sprawl, I think of Oslo, Norway (see photo on page 284). Oslo rises halfway up the hills at the end of a fjord and then abruptly stops. What stops it is a huge public park, in which no private entity is allowed to build anything. The park is full of trails, lakes, playgrounds, picnic tables, and scattered huts where you can stop for a hot drink in winter or cold drink in summer. Tram lines radiate from the city to the park edges, so you can ride to the end of a line, ski or hike in a loop to the end of another line and ride home.

That is a no-nonsense urban growth boundary. It forces development inward. There are no derelict blocks in Oslo. Space no longer useful for one purpose is snapped up for another. Urban renewal goes on constantly everywhere. There are few cars, because there's hardly any place to park and anyway most streets in the shopping district are pedestrian zones. Trams are cheap and frequent and go everywhere. The city is quiet, clean, friendly, attractive and economically thriving.

How could we make our cities more like Oslo and less like land-gulping, energy-intensive, half-empty St. Louis? There is a long list of things we could do. Eben Fodor, in his new book "Better Not Bigger" (the most useful piece of writing on sprawl control I've seen) organizes them under two categories: taking the foot off the accelerator and applying the brake.

5 The accelerator part comes from widespread public subsidies to sprawl. Fodor lists ten of them, which include:

go up to provide public services for new residents.)

- Tax breaks, grants, free consulting services, and other handouts to attract new businesses. (There's al-

- Free or subsidized roads, sewer systems, water systems, schools, etc. (Instead charge development impact fees high enough to be sure the taxes of present residents don't

### BETTER NOT BIGGER

"Our cities and towns keep growing and growing. 'To what end?' you might ask. Are big cities so much better than small cities that we should strive to convert every small city into a bigger one? It seems clear from looking at many of the world's largest cities that we have little reason to envy them. Maybe there is some ideal size where all the best qualities of a community come together to reach an optimal state of urban harmony? If there is such a size, would we know when we've reached it? Would we be less able to stop growing once we were there? The reality is that we just grow and grow, regardless of our community's size or whether further growth is good or bad for us. Endless growth is the only plan on the table." Source: Eben Fodor, *Better Not Bigger* (1999).

most never a good reason for the public to subsidize a private business, especially not in a way that allows it to undercut existing businesses.)

- Waiving environmental or land-use regulations. (Make the standards strong enough to protect everyone's air, water, views and safety and enforce those standards firmly and evenly.)
- Federally funded road projects. (The Feds pay the money, but the community puts up with the sprawl. And where do you think the Feds get the money?)

Urban growth accelerators make current residents pay (in higher taxes, lower services, more noise and pollution and traffic jams) for new development. There is no legal or moral reason why they should do that. Easing up on the accelerator should at least guarantee that growth pays its own way.

Applying the brake means setting absolute limits. There are some illegal reasons for wanting to do this: to protect special privilege, to keep out particular kinds of persons; to take private property for public purpose without fair compen-

sation. There are also legal reasons: to protect watersheds or aquifers or farmland or open space, to force growth into places where public services can be efficiently delivered, to slow growth to a rate at which the community can absorb it, to stop growth before land, water, or other resources fail.

Fodor tells the stories of several communities that have limited their growth and lists many techniques they have used to do so. They include:

- Growth boundaries and green belts like the one around Oslo.
- Agricultural zoning. Given the world food situation, not another square inch of prime soil should be built upon anywhere.
- Infrastructure spending restrictions. Why should a Wal-Mart that sucks in traffic force the public to widen the road? Let Wal-Mart do it, or let the narrow road limit the traffic.
- Downzoning. Usually met with screams of protest from people whose land values are reduced, though we never hear objections when upzoning increases land values.
- Comprehensive public review of all aspects of a new development, such as required by Vermont's Act 250.
- Public purchase of development rights.
- Growth moratoria, growth rate limits, or absolute caps on municipal size, set by real resource limitations.

Boulder, Colorado, may be the American town that has most applied growth controls, prompted by a sober look at the "build-out" implications of the city's zoning plan. Boulder voters approved a local sales tax used to acquire greenways around the city. A building height limitation protects mountain views. Building permits are limited in number, many can be used only in the city center, and 75 percent of new housing permits must be allocated to affordable housing. Commercial and industrial land was downzoned with the realization that if jobs grow faster than housing, commuters from other towns will overload roads and parking facilities.

**10** All that and more is possible in any city. But controlling growth means more than fiddling at the margins, "accommodating" growth, "managing" growth. It means questioning myths about growth, realizing that growth can bring more costs than benefits. That kind of growth makes us poorer, not richer. It shouldn't be celebrated or welcomed or subsidized or managed or accommodated; it should be stopped.

We have planning boards. We have zoning regulations. We have urban growth boundaries and "smart growth" and sprawl conferences. And we still have sprawl. Between 1970 and 1990 the population of Chicago grew by four percent; its developed land area grew by 46 percent. Over the same period Los Angeles swelled 45 percent in population, 300 percent in settled area.

Sprawl costs us more than lost farmland and daily commutes through landscapes of stunning ugliness. It costs us dollars, bucks straight out of our pockets, in the form of higher local taxes. That's because our pattern of municipal growth, especially land-intensive city-edge growth, consistently costs more in public services than it pays in taxes.

In his new book "Better Not Bigger," Eben Fodor cites study after study showing how growth raises taxes. In Loudon County, Virginia, each new house on a quarter-acre lot adds $705 per year to a town budget (in increased garbage collection, road maintenance, etc. minus increased property tax). On a five-acre lot a new house costs the community $2232 per year. In Redmond, Washington, single-family houses pay 21 percent of property tax but account for 29 percent of the city budget. A study in California's Central Valley calculated that more compact development could save municipalities 500,000 acres of farmland and $1.2 billion in taxes.

There are dozens of these studies. They all come to the same conclusion. New subdivisions reach into the pockets of established residents to finance additional schools and services. Commercial and industrial developments sometimes pay more in taxes than they demand in services, but the traffic and pollution they generate reduces nearby property value. New employees don't want to live near the plant or strip, so they build houses and raise taxes in the NEXT town. Large, well-organized companies such as sports teams and Wal-Mart, push city governments to widen roads, provide free water or sewage lines, offer property tax breaks, even build the stadium.

**15** Given all the evidence to the contrary, it's amazing how many of us still believe the myth that growth reduces taxes. But then, every myth springs from a seed of truth. Municipal growth does benefit some people. Real estate agents get sales, construction companies get jobs, banks get more depositors and borrowers, newspapers get higher circulations, stores get more business (though they also get more and tougher competition). Landowners who sell to developers can make big money; developers can make even bigger money.

> ### COMPLICATION
>
> Boulder, Colorado, is sometimes listed among America's most desirable cities, but it has also developed a reputation for being an expensive place to live. A 1998 study of the cost of living in Colorado found that Boulder County had an above-average cost-of-living index, which measures the cost of household expenditures for various common items. It ranked seventeenth among Colorado's fifty-six counties in overall cost-of-living. However, housing costs in Boulder County did not have as large an influence on cost of living as the sixteen counties with higher cost-of-living indexes.

## PYRAMID SCHEMES

A pyramid scheme is a fraudulent way of making money through which someone creates the illusion of a profitable business by attracting new investment through false claims. Any "profits" are the result of new investment, not because the company is succeeding in producing or selling anything. New investment eventually dries up, and the pyramid collapses. To use a simple analogy, you might use a chain letter to convince five people to give you $1.00 each, promising that they will each receive $5.00 back once they recruit five more investors at a $1.00 apiece as the chain letter continues. Sooner or later, people stop writing back. For more information, visit http://skepdic.com/pyramid.html.

Those folks are every town's growth promoters. Eben Fodor calls them the "urban growth machine" and cites an example of how the machine is fueled. Imagine a proposed development that will cost a community $1,000,000 and bring in $500,000 in benefits. The $500,000 goes to ten people, $50,000 apiece. The $1,000,000 is charged to 100,000 people as a $10 tax increase. Who is going to focus full attention on this project, be at all the hearings, bring in lawyers, chat up city officials? Who is going to believe sincerely and claim loudly that growth is a good thing?

Fodor quotes Oregon environmentalist Andy Kerr, who calls urban growth, "a pyramid scheme in which a relatively few make a killing, some others make a living, but most [of us] pay for it." As long as there is a killing to be made, no tepid "smart-growth" measures are going to stop sprawl. We will go on having strips and malls and cookie-cutter subdivisions and traffic jams and rising taxes as long as someone makes money from them.

We can't blame those who make the money. They're playing the game according to the rules, which are set mainly by the market, which rewards whomever is clever enough to put any cost of doing business onto someone else. They get the store profits, we build the roads. They hire the workers (paying as little as they can get away with, because the market requires them to cut costs), we sit in traffic jams and breathe the exhaust. They get jobs building the subdivision, we lose open lands, clean water, and wildlife. Then we subsidize them with our taxes. That, the tax subsidy, is not the market, it's local politics. Collectively we set out pots of subsidized honey at which they dip. We can't expect them not to dip; we can only expect them to howl if the subsidy is taken away.

The "we-they" language in the previous paragraph isn't quite right. They may profit more than we do, but we flock to the stores with the low prices. We buy dream homes in the ever-expanding suburbs. We use the services of the growth machine. (With some equally amateur friends I'm trying to create a 22-unit eco-development, and I'm learning to appreciate the skills needed and the risks borne by developers.) We want our local builders and banks and stores and newspapers to thrive.

20 So what can we do about this spreading mess, which handsomely rewards a few, which turns our surroundings into blight, which most of us hate but in which most of us are complicit — and which we subsidize with our tax dollars?

Concrete answers to that question take a long chapter in Fodor's book and will take another column here. The general answer is clear. Don't believe the myth that all growth is good. Ask hard questions. Who will benefit from the next development scheme and who will pay? Are there better options, including undeveloped, protected land? How much growth can our roads, our land, our waters and air, our neighborhoods, schools and community support? Since we can't grow forever, where should we stop?

# Questions for Discussion

**1.** In her opening paragraphs, Meadows contrasts St. Louis and Oslo. How effective is this contrast? To what extent does her argument as a whole depend on comparison or contrast? **2.** Meadows devotes much of her space to summarizing the work of Eben Fodor. Evaluate her use of Fodor's ideas. Does she tell you enough about his work that you can understand the principles he advocates? Does Meadows inspire sufficient confidence as a writer for you to believe that her summary of Fodor is accurate? In what ways do you think her argument about sprawl is strengthened or weakened by her use of Fodor's ideas? **3.** Drawing on Eben Fodor's work, Meadows uses the metaphors of growth accelerators and brakes to explain her concerns about sprawl. How effectively does this strategy enable her to review her concerns? Do you think the metaphors of accelerators and brakes are appropriate in this case? Explain. **4.** Meadows asserts that there is "no legal or moral reason" why current residents of an area should be compelled to pay for new development of that area. What does this assertion reveal about Meadows's fundamental beliefs and assumptions about communities and development? Do you agree with her? Why or why not? **5.** Meadows cites various statistics related to development and growth, and she cites several studies as well. How persuasive is her use of such evidence to support her claims? **6.** According to Meadows, who is responsible for urban sprawl? Do you agree? Why or why not? **7.** Meadows ends her argument with a series of questions. How effectively do you think her questions conclude her argument? In what sense might they be appropriate, given her main argument about sprawl? **8.** Meadows asserts that the problem of sprawl is not really a "we-they" problem. In other words, it is not possible to reduce the issue to two sides: one in favor and one against. She encourages us to consider how everyone involved has some responsibility for the problem. In this regard, her argument might be considered a Rogerian argument. Drawing on the explanation of Rogerian argument on pages 19–21, evaluate Meadows's essay as a Rogerian argument. Do you think it can justifiably be described as a Rogerian argument? Explain. How effective do you think it is as such an argument?

## ④ ROBERT WILSON, "Enough Snickering. Suburbia Is More Complicated and Varied Than We Think"

When people debate about sprawl, they usually talk about suburbs, since the growth that creates sprawl tends to occur there. But just what do we mean by the term *suburb*? Robert Wilson seeks to answer that question. He argues that we need to understand suburbs in part because they reflect our values and our visions for the lives we wish to have. In the following essay, Wilson explores not only what suburbs are, but also what they mean to our sense of ourselves as Americans. He reveals that although he is not a big fan of the way suburbs have evolved since the early 20th century, he also sees suburbs as an important part of American culture. Furthermore, he points out, many people love them. Notice that Wilson approaches his subject from the perspective of a journalist and citizen who is deeply interested in preserving American culture. At the time this essay was published in the *Architectural Record* in 2000, he was the editor of *Preservation*, the magazine of the National Trust for Historical Preservation, which is devoted to preserving historically and culturally significant buildings and places.

## Enough Snickering. Suburbia Is More Complicated and Varied Than We Think
### ROBERT WILSON

*Award-winning novelist John Updike is especially known for a series of novels focused on a character named Harry "Rabbit" Angstrom, who responds with mixed results to the opportunities and challenges of suburban, middle-class life.*

**1** As the editor of *Preservation* magazine, a publication that sees itself as being about place, I've realized recently that we have been overlooking a pretty significant subject: suburbia, the place where half of Americans live. We have run stories about sprawl and the New Urbanism and made the usual condescending references to cookie-cutter houses and placeless places. But we have failed to look at the suburbs with the same curiosity and courtesy that we've shown to Dubrovnik, say, or Sioux Falls or Paducah. "Why is that?" I now wonder. Snobbery is part of the answer. Nothing can be less hip than suburbia. At a time when our cities are showing new signs of life and our open space is still being chewed up at an exponential rate, whose imagination is going to catch fire over the problems of the suburbs? Part of the answer is also linguistic. The s-word itself has become so ubiquitous and so baggage-laden that it barely means anything anymore. There is a paradox lurking here. The word suburbia has been used to describe the increasingly varied places where more and more of us live — gritty inner suburbs that share many of the problems of their urban neighbors, immigrant neighborhoods at every economic level, and new greenfield developments sporting one McMansion bigger than the next. Yet our definition of the word remains fixed in a former time, decades ago, when women worked at home and men commuted to work. The biggest problem with suburbia is that we are all so certain that we know what it means. We watched *Father Knows Best* and read our Updike,* and even a recent film like the Oscar-laden *American Beauty* confirms what we think we know: suburbia is a dull, sterile, unhappy place.

### A Persistent Bias

As this suggests, the problem is also cultural. For the most part, American culture and opinion are still created, even in the Internet age, in cities at either edge of the continent. City dwellers, whether native born or the still more unforgiving recent converts, think of the suburbs as a mediocre place for mediocre people, a place where they will never venture or from which they have happily escaped. Even those who work in cities and live in suburbs (many of which now offer more urban amenities than nine-to-five cities) share this antisuburban frame of mind. If intellectuals do deign to look at the suburbs — whether cleverly in a film like *American Beauty* or clumsily, as in another recent film, the ugly paranoid fantasy *Arlington Road* — they assume that so much banality must be hiding something deeply evil.

### Beyond the Movies

I'm really not here to defend suburbia, only to suggest that it is a more complicated, more various, and more quickly evolving place than we think. Two writers

**CONTEXT**

Many critics saw the Academy Award–winning film *American Beauty*, released in 1999, as a comment on life in white suburbia. In contrast to the seemingly healthy and happy suburban families portrayed in television shows such as *Father Knows Best* or *Ozzie and Harriet*, the family in *American Beauty* displays dysfunction and deep dissatisfaction with their apparently normal lives.

I admire, Witold Rybczynski and Joel Garreau, have helped me reach this state of cautious curiosity. The former, in his recent biography of Frederick Law Olmsted[†] and elsewhere, has reminded me that the suburb was a noble idea that was often, in the first decades of its existence, nobly executed. Many of these places, such as Chevy Chase near Washington, D.C., continue to function admirably well. Garreau's insight is that Venice didn't become Venice the instant it was built, but developed over a period of centuries. If we remember that the suburbs, especially the postwar suburbs over which we do most of our hand-wringing, are still relatively new places, the question becomes not "Why are they so bad?" but, "What is the next step to making them better?"

### Who's to Blame?

As a journalist, I am naturally filled with righteous indignation about the subject. My instincts are first to find someone to blame and second to flatter myself that I know the solution. So, here goes: One reason that the suburbs are not better is that the best minds in architecture abandoned them. Once, not just Olmsted but Frank Lloyd Wright, Le Corbusier, Clarence Stein,[‡] and others considered, in an urgent and serious way, the questions of where and how people might live if they didn't live in cities or on farms. Am I wrong in believing that between the Garden City movement of the 1910s and 1920s and the New Towns of the 1960s there was a wasteland of ideas beyond the city limits — just as the suburbs

[†]**Frederick Law Olmsted (1822–1903)** is widely considered one of our country's most important landscape architects. With his partner Calvert Vaux, he created the winning design for the creation of Central Park in New York City. He also designed the grounds for the U.S. Capitol, among many other projects of national significance.

[‡]**Frank Lloyd Wright (1869–1959), Le Corbusier (1887–1967),** and **Clarence Stein (1882–1975)** were influential architects in the early twentieth century. Stein, in particular, is associated with the Garden City Movement, which sought to create beautifully landscaped communities within easy access of major cities.

Andres Duany, Elizabeth Plater-Zyberk, and Jeff Speck frankly admit and defend their suburban focus. Whether they helped create the slow-growth, sustainable-growth, antisprawl movements that have captured the imagination of so many voters in recent elections at all levels of government, or whether they merely capitalized on these movements, their book seems timely. In a recent front-page article, the *New York Times* reported that academics have suddenly taken an urgent interest in suburbia. Other major newspapers across the country have latched on to the subject, perhaps as an outgrowth of the widening interest in sprawl.

began to lay waste to vast portions of the American landscape? And that there was precious little between the New Towns and the New Urbanists? Isn't this why the design and execution of suburbs have been so disappointing, because the field was abandoned to the merely avaricious? For anyone who is irritated by how much attention the New Urbanists get, here is the simple answer to their popularity with the media: However retrograde their ideas, however short their accomplishments to date might fall, at least they have an idea and at least they have acted upon it.

**5** The New Urbanists spent a certain amount of time reacting to Vincent Scully's suggestion that they should really be thought of as the New Suburbanists, but in their new book, *Suburban Nation: The Rise of Sprawl and the Decline of the American Dream,*

Recent stories in *Preservation,* beginning with a cover story on the new suburban immigrants, have not thrilled hardcore preservationists, for whom suburbia has always been a particular bete noire. For me, this resistance is only a speed bump on the road to the movement's democratization.

Do I foresee the wholesale preservation of postwar suburbs? Probably not. Rapid evolution would be far more desirable. Still, alarms were sounded recently in Houston, where a whole neighborhood of brick ranch houses was under siege. The truth is that most people love their suburban homes and neighborhoods and will fight to save them. And if preservationists have learned anything in the last century or so, it is that the notion of what is worth preserving changes. Just recall how Victorian buildings were despised as recently as a few decades ago.

Perhaps the split-level will be the retro rage in 2050.

### Design Creeps in

As money and newly sophisticated consumers pour into the suburbs, good design and architecture are beginning to follow. In my neck of suburbia, northern Virginia, where even a determined electorate has had trouble slowing sprawl, there are nonetheless hopeful signs that good ideas are arriving — from town-center schemes for shopping and living to interesting and appealing buildings for churches, college campuses, and office complexes.

Most welcome of all, perhaps, is the improved architecture for public buildings, including schools, which were the most bereft places we allowed to be built in the bad old days just ending. May all of you who read these words enthusiastically enter the fray, enriching yourselves even as you enrich a vast part of our landscape that urgently needs you.

## NEW TOWNS AND THE NEW URBANISTS

The New Towns movement in regional planning gained popularity in the United States in the 1920s. It focused on carefully designed and largely residential communities that were located away from urban centers. These New Towns, also called "Garden Cities," sometimes developed into large suburban areas. The New Urbanism, which emerged in the 1990s, is a reaction to the New Town idea of community planning. As an alternative to sprawl, New Urbanism emphasizes the integration of housing, workplaces, businesses, and recreation into small neighborhoods that are connected by public transportation. According to Ute Angleki Lehrer, a professor of urban and regional planning at the State University of New York at Buffalo, "By establishing specific rules for land use and building design, the architects of New Urbanism believe that they can create diversity and density in neighborhoods of both new suburban development and revitalization projects in existing urban areas."

## Questions for Discussion

**1.** Wilson opens his argument by establishing that he is editor of *Preservation* magazine. To what extent does this information make him a credible source? When considering his argument as a whole, how would you evaluate his credibility? **2.** On what grounds might preservationists try to protect suburban neighborhoods that some critics find ugly? Do you think Wilson does justice to a more positive view of suburban communities? Explain. **3.** Wilson suggests in this essay that suburbs can be better. What exactly does he mean? What does his position reveal about his own beliefs regarding the ideal community? Do you agree with him? Why or why not? **4.** Notice the many references Wilson makes in his essay to films, literature, historical developments, and social movements. What do these references suggest about the audience Wilson is addressing in this essay? Does that audience include you? Explain. **5.** Wilson's essay raises questions about how we think about the communities we live in. How does his argument affect the way you think communities should be designed? Do you think he wishes to challenge conventional views about community design? Explain, citing specific passages from his essay to support your answer.

# NEGOTIATING DIFFERENCES

Several of the authors included in this section express concern about the effects of sprawl on open space such as farmland. But urban sprawl can also damage inner cities as people move to distant suburbs and eventually also work and shop many miles from the city center. Moreover, sprawl can also affect older suburbs located at the inner ring around a city. According to one expert, "These are the patterns that many cities in the Rust Belt are carving out — entire rings spreading outward relentlessly, or pie-shaped pieces doing the same. Left behind are devastated neighborhoods in formerly industrial cities. So natural landscapes aren't the only victims of the public policies and private preferences that have suburbanized America. They've also taken a toll on aging built landscapes and the people remaining in them" (Deron Lovass, "Shrinking Cities, Growing Populations").

So sprawl can affect most Americans: city dwellers, suburbanites, and anyone living in a rural area within commuting distance of a metropolitan region.

Imagine now that you are at a public meeting at which a developer is seeking permission to build new housing on 500 acres of farmland an hour's drive from the center of the largest city in your state. This meeting has attracted environmentalists who are concerned about the consequences of development, commuters who are worried that highways are already overcrowded, and residents from the city and older suburbs who believe that continued growth will damage the areas in which they live. Other voices are also heard at this meeting, however. Several people speak about an urgent need for safe, affordable housing, and others insist that additional development is essential for the economic well-being of the metropolitan area as a whole. Finally, someone else points out that new developments do not have to be ugly. On the contrary, they can be well designed and built in an environmentally responsible way.

With this scenario in mind, write an essay in which you advocate a specific plan for the land in question. In your essay, discuss what you see as the primary goals for the community that will be built — and for the use of such land in general. Also try to account for the various perspectives of people who are concerned about how that land will be used. Taking these matters into account, make an argument for what you believe should be done with the land. Ideally, your argument will address the various concerns expressed at the meeting, even if all parties involved would not agree with your proposal.

Alternatively, focus your essay on an actual controversy involving sprawl or development in the area where you live. Follow the same guidelines described in the previous paragraph, but focus on the specific situation in your area.

**11**

# AMERICAN NATIONAL IDENTITY

AMERICAN NAT

## Cluster

# WHAT KIND OF POWER SHOULD WE GIVE OUR GOVERNMENT?

(1) Martin Luther King, Jr., "Letter From a Birmingham Jail"

(2) Michael Kelly, "Liberties Are a Real Casualty of War"

(3) Heather Green, "Databases and Security vs. Privacy"

(4) Alan M. Dershowitz, "Why Fear National ID Cards?"

CON-TEXT
The Declaration
of Independence

ONAL IDENTITY

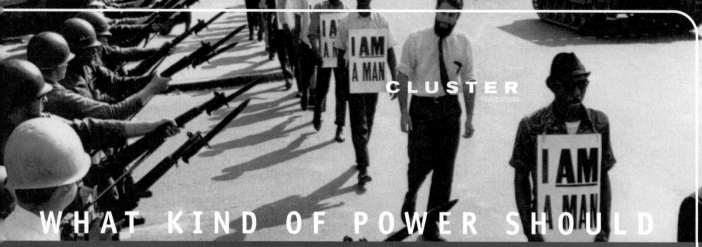

# WHAT KIND OF POWER SHOULD
# WE GIVE OUR GOVERNMENT?

Americans consider the Declaration of Independence to be a sacred document (see *Con-Text* on page 297). American children learn in school that the Declaration, written mostly by Thomas Jefferson, was a catalyst for the American Revolutionary War. Its presentation to King George III of England made it clear that the American colonists were rejecting the British government that had ruled them. What students often overlook is how radical a step the colonists had taken. In the 18th century the idea that citizens, rather than governments, ultimately hold political power was almost unheard of — an idea that flew in the face of the established order, under which people were viewed as the *subjects* of their rulers. But in the Declaration of Independence, Jefferson and his cosigners stated unequivocally that it should be the other way around: Leaders served at the behest of citizens; if those leaders should compromise the inherent rights of the citizens, then citizens were legally and morally justified in removing those leaders. Power to the people. ■ In this sense the founding of the United States ushered in a new era in which the whole idea of government was redefined, but it also created a new set of questions about the relationship between a government and its citizens. If political power ultimately resides in the people, then what is the role of government? How is that role determined? And how much power should a government have over citizens? These questions are not answered in the Declaration of Independence except in the abstract. Jefferson and his cosigners famously declared that government exists to secure the rights of citizens to "Life, Lliberty, and the pursuit of Happiness," but they left it up to later generations to define exactly what "life, liberty, and the pursuit of happiness" means. And each generation has wrestled with the question of how much power government should have to fulfill that purpose. ■ The essays in this section reveal some of the ways in which Americans have confronted this question. In his famous "Letter from a Birmingham Jail," Martin Luther King, Jr., refers directly to the Declaration of Independence to make his argument that citizens are morally justified — and even obligated — to disobey laws that are unjust. The entire Civil Rights Movement of the 1960s, in which King was such an important figure, rested largely on that very idea. After September 11, 2001, Americans revisited some of the same questions that Civil Rights activists and protesters against the Vietnam War raised about granting government too much power over individual citizens. In the wake of the 9/11 terrorist attacks, the U.S. government took several actions to protect the nation against additional attacks. But many Americans believed that the government overstepped its legal powers and compromised the rights of its own citizens. Fierce debates ensued about how much freedom citizens should give up so that their government could better protect them. The essays in this section reveal the complexity and intensity of those debates. ■ As a group, these essays provide various perspectives on the relationship between a government and its citizens. They also suggest that Americans are still trying to answer the same question about government power that Thomas Jefferson and the cosigners of the Declaration of Independence posed more that 225 years ago.

## CON-TEXT: "The Declaration of Independence"

**1** When in the Course of human events, it becomes necessary for one people to dissolve the political bands which have connected them with another, and to assume among the powers of the earth, the separate and equal station to which the Laws of Nature and of Nature's God entitle them, a decent respect to the opinions of mankind requires that they should declare the causes which impel them to the separation.

We hold these truths to be self-evident, that all men are created equal, that they are endowed by their Creator with certain unalienable Rights, that among these are Life, Liberty and the pursuit of Happiness. That to secure these rights, Governments are instituted among Men, deriving their just powers from the consent of the governed. That whenever any Form of Government becomes destructive of these ends it is the Right of the People to alter or to abolish it, and to institute new Government, laying its foundation on such principles and organizing its powers in such form, as to them shall seem most likely to effect their Safety and Happiness. Prudence, indeed, will dictate that Governments long established should not be changed for light and transient causes; and accordingly all experience has shown, that mankind are more disposed to suffer, while evils are sufferable, than to right themselves by abolishing the forms to which they are accustomed. But when a long train of abuses and usurpations, pursuing invariably the same Object evinces a design to reduce them under absolute Despotism, it is their right, it is their duty, to throw off such Government, and to provide new Guards for their future security. Such has been the patient sufferance of these Colonies; and such is now the necessity which constrains them to alter their former Systems of Government. . . .

# ① MARTIN LUTHER KING, JR., "Letter From a Birmingham Jail"

Martin Luther King, Jr. (1929–1968), was the most important leader of the movement to secure civil rights for black Americans during the mid-twentieth century. Ordained a Baptist minister in his father's church in Atlanta, Georgia, King became the founder and director of the Southern Christian Leadership Conference, an organization he continued to lead until his assassination in 1968. He first came to national attention by organizing a boycott of the buses in Montgomery, Alabama (1955–1956) — a campaign that he recounts in *Stride Toward Freedom: The Montgomery Story* (1958). An advocate of nonviolence who was jailed fourteen times in the course of his work for civil rights, King was instrumental in helping to secure the passage of the Civil Rights Bill in 1963. His efforts on behalf of civil rights led to many awards, most notably the Nobel Peace Prize in 1964. "Letter From a Birmingham Jail" was written in 1963, when King was jailed for eight days as the result of his campaign against segregation in Birmingham, Alabama. In the letter, King responds to white clergymen who had criticized his work and blamed him for breaking the law. But "Letter From a Birmingham Jail" is more than a rebuttal of criticism; it is a well-reasoned and carefully argued defense of civil disobedience as a means of securing civil liberties. In justifying his refusal to obey what he believed were unjust laws, King invokes a high moral standard by which to judge a government's actions. His famous essay thus prompts us to consider the limits of governmental power and the responsibilities of citizens in supporting or opposing that power.

## Letter From a Birmingham Jail
### MARTIN LUTHER KING, JR.

April 16, 1963
My Dear Fellow Clergymen:

**1** While confined here in the Birmingham city jail, I came across your recent statement calling my present activities "unwise and untimely." Seldom do I pause to answer criticism of my work and ideas. If I sought to answer all the criticisms that cross my desk, my secretaries would have little time for anything other than such correspondence in the course of the day, and I would have no time for constructive work. But since I feel that you are men of genuine good will and that your criticisms are sincerely put forth, I want to try to answer your statement in what I hope will be patient and reasonable terms.

I think I should indicate why I am here in Birmingham, since you have been influenced by the view which argues against "outsiders coming in." I have the honor of serving as president of the Southern Christian Leadership Conference, an organization operating in every southern state, with headquarters in Atlanta, Georgia. We have some eighty-five affiliated organizations across the South, and one of them is the Alabama Christian Movement for Human Rights. Frequently we share staff, educational, and financial resources with our affiliates. Several months ago the affiliate here in Birmingham asked us to be on call to engage in a nonviolent direct-action program if such were deemed necessary. We readily consented, and when the hour came we lived up to our promise. So I, along with several members of my staff, am here because I was invited here. I am here because I have organizational ties here.

But more basically, I am in Birmingham because injustice is here. Just as the prophets of the eighth century B.C. left their villages and carried their "thus saith the Lord" far beyond the boundaries of their home towns, and just as the Apostle Paul left his village of Tarsus and carried the gospel of Jesus Christ to the far corners of the Greco-Roman world, so am I compelled to carry the gospel of freedom beyond my own home town. Like Paul, I must constantly respond to the Macedonian call for aid.

Moreover, I am cognizant of the interrelatedness of all communities and states. I cannot sit idly by in Atlanta and not be concerned about what happens in Birmingham. Injustice anywhere is a threat to justice everywhere. We are caught in an inescapable network of mutuality, tied in a single garment of des-

tiny. Whatever affects one directly, affects all indirectly. Never again can we afford to live with the narrow, provincial, "outside agitator" idea. Anyone who lives inside the United States can never be considered an outsider anywhere within its bounds.

**5** You deplore the demonstrations taking place in Birmingham. But your statement, I am sorry to say, fails to express a similar concern for the conditions that brought about the demonstrations. I am sure that none of you would want to rest content with the superficial kind of social analysis that deals merely with effects and does not grapple with underlying causes. It is unfortunate that demonstrations are taking place in Birmingham, but it is even more unfortunate that the city's white power structure left the Negro community with no alternative.

In any nonviolent campaign (see "Nonviolence" on page 300), there are four basic steps: collection of the facts

## NONVIOLENCE

Inspired by the ideas of Mahatma Gandhi, whose nonviolent movement helped to end the British rule of India, Martin Luther King, Jr., developed a philosophy of nonviolent resistance based on the Christian ideal of brotherly love. In an essay published in 1960, King wrote that "the Christian doctrine of love operating through the Gandhian method of nonviolence was one of the most potent weapons available to oppressed people in their struggle for freedom." In a related essay, King responded to a critique of pacifism by Christian philosopher Reinhard Neibuhr by arguing that "pacifism is not unrealistic submission to evil power, as Niebuhr contends. It is rather a courageous confrontation of evil by the power of love." King's philosophy was put to the test in 1956 during the bus boycott in Montgomery, Alabama, during which Blacks and civil rights activists were harrassed and sometimes physically attacked. In the end, King's nonviolent protest movement resulted in a Supreme Court decision that declared segregation on public buses unconstitutional.

to determine whether injustices exist; negotiation; self-purification; and direct action. We have gone through all these steps in Birmingham. There can be no gainsaying the fact that racial injustice engulfs this community. Birmingham is probably the most thoroughly segregated city in the United States. Its ugly record of brutality is widely known. Negroes have experienced grossly unjust treatment in courts. There have been more unsolved bombings of Negro homes and churches in Birmingham than in any other city in the nation. These are the hard, brutal facts of the case. On the basis of these conditions, Negro leaders sought to negotiate with the city fathers. But the latter consistently refused to engage in good-faith negotiation.

Then, last September, came the opportunity to talk with leaders of Birmingham's economic community. In the course of the negotiations, certain promises were made by the merchants — for example, to remove the stores' humiliating racial signs. On the basis of these promises, the Reverend Fred Shuttlesworth and the leaders of the

Alabama Christian Movement for Human Rights agreed to a moratorium on all demonstrations. As the weeks and months went by, we realized that we were the victims of a broken promise. A few signs, briefly removed, returned; the others remained.

As in so many past experiences, our hopes had been blasted, and the shadow of deep disappointment settled upon us. We had no alternative except to prepare for direct action, whereby we would present our very bodies as means of laying our case before the conscience of the local and the national community. Mindful of the difficulties involved, we decided to undertake a process of self-purification. We began a series of workshops on nonviolence, and we repeatedly asked ourselves: "Are you able to accept blows without retaliating?" "Are you able to endure the ordeal of jail?" We decided to schedule our direct-action program for the Easter season, realizing that except for Christmas, this is the main shopping period of the year. Knowing that a strong economic-withdrawal program would be the byproduct of direct action, we felt that this would be the best time to bring pressure to bear on the merchants for the needed change.

Then it occurred to us that Birmingham's mayoral election was coming up in March, and we speedily decided to postpone action until after election day. When we discovered that the Commissioner of Public Safety, Eugene "Bull" Connor, had piled up enough votes to be in the run-off, we decided again to postpone action until the day after the run-off so that the demonstrations could not be used to cloud the issues. Like many others, we waited to see Mr. Connor defeated, and to this end we endured postponement after postponement. Having aided in this community need, we felt that our direct-action program could be delayed no longer.

**10** You may well ask, "Why direct action? Why sit-ins, marches, and so forth? Isn't negotiation a better path?" You are quite right in calling for negotiation. Indeed, this is the very purpose of direct action. Nonviolent direct action seeks to create such a crisis and foster such a tension that a community which has constantly refused to negotiate is forced to confront the issue. It seeks so to dramatize the issue that it can no longer be ignored. My citing the creation of tension as part of the work of the nonviolent resister may sound rather shocking. But I must confess that I am not afraid of the word "tension." I have earnestly opposed violent tension, but there is a type of constructive, nonviolent tension which is necessary for growth. Just as Socrates felt that it was necessary to create a tension in the mind so that individuals could rise from the bondage of myths and half-truths to the unfettered realm of creative analysis and objective appraisal, so must we see the need for nonviolent gadflies to create the kind of tension in society that will help men rise from the dark depths of prejudice and racism to the majestic heights of understanding and brotherhood.

The purpose of our direct-action program is to create a situation so crisis-packed that it will inevitably open the door to negotiation. I therefore concur with you in your call for negotiation. Too long has our beloved Southland been bogged down in a tragic effort to live in monologue rather than dialogue.

One of the basic points in your statement is that the action that I and my associates have taken in Birmingham is untimely. Some have asked: "Why didn't you give the new city administration time to act?" The only answer that I can give to this query is that the new Birmingham administration must be prodded about as much as the outgoing one, before it will act. We are sadly mistaken if we feel that the election of Albert Boutwell as mayor will bring the millennium to Birmingham. While Mr. Boutwell is a much more gentle person than Mr. Connor, they are both segregationists, dedicated to maintenance of the status quo. I have hoped that Mr. Boutwell will be reasonable enough to see the futility of massive resistance to desegregation. But he will not see this without pressure from devotees of civil rights. My friends, I must say to you that we have not made a single gain in civil rights without determined legal and nonviolent pressure. Lamentably, it is an historical fact that privileged groups seldom give up their privileges voluntarily. Individuals may see the moral light and voluntarily give up their unjust posture; but, as Reinhold Niebuhr* has reminded us, groups tend to be more immoral than individuals.

We know through painful experience that freedom is never voluntarily given by the oppressor; it must be demanded by the oppressed. Frankly, I have yet to engage in a direct-action campaign that was "well timed" in the view of those who have not suffered unduly from the disease of segregation. For years now I have heard the word "Wait!" It rings in the ear of every Negro with piercing familiarity. This "Wait" has almost always meant "Never." We must come to see, with one of our distinguished jurists, that "justice too long delayed is justice denied."

We have waited for more than 340 years for our constitutional and God-given rights. The nations of Asia and Africa are moving with jetlike speed toward gaining political independence, but we still creep at horse-and-buggy pace toward gaining a cup of coffee at a lunch counter. Perhaps it is easy for those who have never felt the stinging darts of segregation to say, "Wait." But when you have seen vicious mobs lynch your mothers and fathers at will and drown your sisters and brothers at whim; when you

*Reinhold Neibuhr (1892–1971) was a Protestant theologian who explored how Christianity related to modern politics and diplomacy (see www. newgenevacenter. org/biography/ niebuhr2.htm).

have seen hate-filled policemen curse, kick, and even kill your black brothers and sisters; when you see the vast majority of your twenty million Negro brothers smothering in an airtight cage of poverty in the midst of an affluent society; when you suddenly find your tongue twisted and your speech stammering as you seek to explain to your six-year-old daughter why she can't go to the public amusement park that has just been advertised on television, and see tears welling up in her eyes when she is told that Funtown is closed to colored children, and see ominous clouds of inferiority beginning to form in her little mental sky, and see her beginning to distort her personality by developing an unconscious bitterness toward white people; when you have to concoct an answer for a five-year-old son who is asking, "Daddy, why do white people treat colored people so mean?"; when you take a cross-country drive and find it necessary to sleep night after night in the uncomfortable corners of your automobile because no motel will accept you; when you are humiliated day in and day out by nagging signs reading "white" and "colored"; when your first

name becomes "nigger," your middle name becomes "boy" (however old you are) and your last name becomes "John," and your wife and mother are never given the respected title "Mrs."; when you are harried by day and haunted by night by the fact that you are a Negro, living constantly at tiptoe stance, never quite knowing what to expect next, and are plagued with inner fears and outer resentments; when you are forever fighting a degenerating sense of "nobodiness" — then you will understand why we find it difficult to wait. There comes a time when the cup of endurance runs over, and men are no longer willing to be plunged into the abyss of despair. I hope, sirs, you can understand our legitimate and unavoidable impatience.

**15** You express a great deal of anxiety over our willingness to break laws. This is certainly a legitimate concern. Since we so diligently urge people to obey the Supreme Court's decision of 1954 outlawing segregation in the public schools, at first glance it may seem rather paradoxical for us consciously to break laws. One may well ask: "How can you advocate breaking some laws and obeying others?" The answer lies in the fact that there are two types of laws; just and unjust. I would be the first to advocate obeying just laws. One has not only a legal but a moral responsibility to obey just laws. Conversely, one has a moral responsibility to disobey unjust laws. I would agree with St. Augustine that "an unjust law is no law at all."

Now, what is the difference between the two? How does one determine whether a law is just or unjust? A just law is a man-made code that squares with the moral law or the law of God. An unjust law is a code that is out of harmony with the moral law. To put it in the terms of St. Thomas Aquinas: An unjust law is a human law that is not rooted in

eternal law and natural law. Any law that uplifts human personality is just. Any law that degrades human personality is unjust. All segregation statutes are unjust because segregation distorts the soul and damages the personality. It gives the segregator a false sense of superiority and the segregated a false sense of inferiority. Segregation, to use the terminology of the Jewish philosopher Martin Buber, substitutes an "I–it" relationship for an "I–thou" relationship and ends up relegating persons to the status of things. Hence segregation is not only politically, economically, and sociologically unsound, it is morally wrong and sinful. Paul Tillich has said that sin is segregation. Is not segregation an existential expression of man's tragic separation, his awful estrangement, his terrible sinfulness? Thus it is that I can urge men to obey the 1954 decision of the Supreme Court, for it is morally right; and I can urge them to disobey segregation ordinances, for they are morally wrong.

Let us consider a more concrete example of just and unjust laws. An unjust law is a code that a numerical or power majority group compels a minority group to obey but does not make binding on itself. This is *difference* made legal. By the same token, a just law is a code that a majority compels a minority to follow and that it is willing to follow itself. This is *sameness* made legal.

Let me give another explanation. A law is unjust if it is inflicted on a minority that, as a result of being denied the right to vote, had no part in enacting or devising the law. Who can say that the legislature of Alabama which set up that state's segregation laws was democratically elected? Throughout Alabama all sorts of devious methods are used to prevent Negroes from becoming registered voters, and there are some counties in

## BROWN V. THE *TOPEKA* BOARD OF EDUCATION

On May 17, 1954, Chief Justice Earl Warren read the decision of the unanimous U.S. Supreme Court in the case of *Brown* v. *The Board of Education of Topeka, Kansas*, which overturned the previous policy of providing "separate but equal" education for Black children:

> We come then to the question presented: Does segregation of children in public schools solely on the basis of race, even though the physical facilities and other "tangible" factors may be equal, deprive the children of the minority group of equal educational opportunities? We believe that it does. . . . We conclude that in the field of public education the doctrine of 'separate but equal' has no place. Separate educational facilities are inherently unequal. Therefore, we hold that the plaintiffs and others similarly situated for whom the actions have been brought are, by reason of the segregation complained of, deprived of the equal protection of the laws guaranteed by the Fourteenth Amendment.

which, even though Negroes constitute a majority of the population, not a single Negro is registered. Can any law enacted under such circumstances be considered democratically structured?

Sometimes a law is just on its face and unjust in its application. For instance, I have been arrested on a charge of parading without a permit. Now, there is nothing wrong in having an ordinance which requires a permit for a parade. But such an ordinance becomes unjust when it is used to maintain segregation and to deny citizens the First-Amendment privilege of peaceful assembly and protest.

**20** I hope you are able to see the distinction I am trying to point out. In no sense do I advocate evading or defying the law, as would the rabid segregationist. That would lead to anarchy. One who breaks an unjust law must do so openly, lovingly, and with a willingness to accept the penalty. I submit that an individual who breaks a law that conscience tells him is unjust, and who willingly accepts the penalty of imprisonment in order to

*Nebuchadnezzar, King of Babylon, destroyed the temple at Jerusalem and brought the Jewish people into captivity. He set up a huge image in gold and commanded all to worship it. Shadrach, Meshach, and Abednego refused and were thrown into a fiery furnace from which they emerged unscathed. (See *Daniel* 3.)

†In 1956 Hungarian citizens temporarily overthrew the communist dictatorship in their country. Unwilling to confront the Soviet Union, Western democracies stood by when the Red Army suppressed the revolt by force.

arouse the conscience of the community over its injustice, is in reality expressing the highest respect for law.

Of course, there is nothing new about this kind of civil disobedience. It was evidenced sublimely in the refusal of Shadrach, Meshach, and Abednego to obey the laws of Nebuchadnezzar,* on the ground that a higher moral law was at stake. It was practiced superbly by the early Christians, who were willing to face hungry lions and the excruciating pain of chopping blocks rather than submit to certain unjust laws of the Roman Empire. To a degree, academic freedom is a reality today because Socrates practiced civil disobedience. In our own nation, the Boston Tea Party represented a massive act of civil disobedience.

We should never forget that everything Adolf Hitler did in Germany was "legal" and everything the Hungarian freedom fighters did in Hungary† was "illegal." It was "illegal" to aid and comfort a Jew in Hitler's Germany. Even so, I am sure that, had I lived in Germany at the time, I would have aided and comforted my Jewish brothers. If today I lived in a Communist country where certain principles dear to the Christian faith are suppressed, I would openly advocate disobeying that country's anti-religious laws.

I must make two honest confessions to you, my Christian and Jewish brothers. First, I must confess that over the past few years I have been gravely disappointed with the white moderate. I have almost reached the regrettable conclusion that the Negro's great stumbling block in his stride toward freedom is not the White Citizen's Counciler or the Ku Klux Klanner, but the white moderate, who is more devoted to "order" than to justice; who prefers a negative peace which is the absence of tension to a positive peace which is the presence of justice;

who constantly says, "I agree with you in the goal you seek, but I cannot agree with your methods of direct action"; who paternalistically believes he can set the timetable for another man's freedom; who lives by a mythical concept of time and who constantly advises the Negro to wait for a "more convenient season." Shallow understanding from people of good will is more frustrating than absolute misunderstanding from people of ill will. Lukewarm acceptance is much more bewildering than outright rejection.

I had hoped that the white moderate would understand that law and order exist for the purpose of establishing justice and that when they fail in this purpose they become the dangerously structured dams that block the flow of social progress. I had hoped that the white moderate would understand that the present tension in the South is a necessary phase of the transition from an obnoxious negative peace, in which the Negro passively accepted his unjust plight, to a substantive and positive peace, in which all men will respect the dignity and worth of human personality. Actually, we who engage in nonviolent direct action are not the creators of tension. We merely bring to the surface the hidden tension that is already alive. We bring it out in the open, where it can be seen and dealt with. Like a boil that can never be cured so long as it is covered up but must be opened with all its ugliness to the natural medicines of air and light, injustice must be exposed, with all the tension its exposure creates, to the light of human conscience and the air of national opinion, before it can be cured. 25 In your statement you assert that our actions, even though peaceful, must be condemned because they precipitate violence. But is this a logical assertion? Isn't this like condemning a robbed man because his possession of money precipitated the evil act of robbery? Isn't this like condemning Socrates because his unswerving commitment to truth and his philosophical inquiries precipitated the act by the misguided populace in which they made him drink hemlock? Isn't this like condemning Jesus because his unique God-consciousness and never-ceasing devotion to God's will precipitated the evil act of crucifixion? We must come to see that, as the federal courts have consistently affirmed, it is wrong to urge an individual to cease his efforts to gain his basic constitutional rights because the quest may precipitate violence. Society must protect the robbed and punish the robber.

I had also hoped that the white moderate would reject the myth concerning time in relation to the struggle for freedom. I have just received a letter from a white brother in Texas. He writes: "All Christians know that the colored people will receive equal rights eventually, but it is possible that you are in too great a religious hurry. It has taken Christianity almost two thousand years to accomplish what it has. The teachings of Christ take time to come to earth." Such an attitude stems from a tragic misconception of time, from the strangely irrational notion that there is something in the very flow of time that will inevitably cure all ills. Actually, time itself is neutral; it can be used either destructively or constructively. More and more I feel that the people of ill will have used time much more effectively than have the people of good will. We will have to repent in this generation not merely for the hateful words and actions of the bad people, but for the appalling silence of the good people. Human progress never rolls in on wheels of inevitability; it comes through the tireless efforts of men willing to be coworkers with God, and without this hard work, time itself becomes an ally of the forces of social stagnation. We must use time creatively, in the knowledge that the time is always ripe to do right. Now is the time to make real the promise of democracy and transform our pending national elegy into a creative psalm of brotherhood. Now is the time to lift our national policy from the quicksand of racial injustice to the solid rock of human dignity.

You speak of our activity in Birmingham as extreme. At first I was rather disappointed that fellow clergymen would see my nonviolent efforts as those of an extremist. I began thinking about the fact that I stand in the middle of two opposing forces in the Negro community. One is a force of complacency, made up in part of Negroes who, as a result of long years of oppression, are so drained of self-respect and a sense of "somebodiness" that they have adjusted to segregation; and in part of a few middle-class Negroes who, because of a degree of academic and economic security and because in some ways they profit by segregation, have become insensitive to the problems of the masses. The other force is one of bitterness and hatred, and it comes perilously close to advocating violence. It is expressed in the various black nationalist groups that are springing up across the nation, the largest and best-known being Elijah Muhammad's Muslim movement. Nourished by the Negro's frustration over the continued existence of racial discrimination, this movement is made up of people who have lost faith in America, who have absolutely repudiated Christianity, and who have concluded that the white man is an incorrigible "devil."

I have tried to stand between these two forces, saying that we need emulate neither the "do-nothingism" of the complacent nor the hatred and despair of the black nationalist. For there is the more excellent way of love and nonviolent protest. I am grateful to God that, through the influence of the Negro church, the way of nonviolence became an integral part of our struggle.

If this philosophy had not emerged, by now many streets of the South would, I am convinced, be flowing with blood. And I am further convinced that if our white brothers dismiss as "rabble-rousers" and "outside agitators" those of us who employ nonviolent direct action, and if they refuse to support our nonviolent efforts, millions of Negroes will, out of frustration and despair, seek solace and security in black-nationalist ideologies — a development that would inevitably lead to a frightening racial nightmare.

30 Oppressed people cannot remain oppressed forever. The yearning for freedom eventually manifests itself, and that is what has happened to the American Negro. Something within has reminded him of his birthright of freedom, and something without has reminded him that it can be gained. Consciously or unconsciously, he has been caught up by the *Zeitgeist,* and with his black brothers of Africa and his brown and yellow brothers of Asia, South America, and the Caribbean, the United States Negro is moving with a sense of great urgency toward the promised land of racial justice. If one recognizes this vital urge that has engulfed the Negro community, one should readily understand why public demonstrations are taking place. The Negro has many pent-up resentments and latent frustrations, and he must release them. So let him march; let him make prayer pilgrimages to the city hall; let him go on freedom rides — and try to understand why he must do so. If his repressed emotions are not released in nonviolent ways, they will seek expression through violence; this is not a threat but a fact of history. So I have not said to my people, "Get rid of your discontent." Rather, I have tried to say that this normal and healthy discontent can be channeled into the creative outlet of nonviolent direct action. And now this approach is being termed extremist.

But though I was initially disappointed at being categorized as an extremist, as I continued to think about the matter I gradually gained a measure of satisfaction from the label. Was not Jesus an extremist for love: "Love your enemies, bless them that curse you, do good to them that hate you, and pray for them which despitefully use you, and persecute you." Was not Amos an extremist for justice: "Let justice roll down like waters and righteousness like an everflowing stream." Was not Paul an extremist for the Christian gospel: "I bear in my body the marks of the Lord Jesus." Was not Martin Luther an extremist: "Here I stand; I cannot do otherwise, so help me God." And John Bunyan: "I will stay in jail to the end of my days before I make a butchery of my conscience." And Abraham Lincoln: "This nation cannot survive half slave and half free." And Thomas Jefferson: "We hold these truths to be self-evident, that all men are created equal. . . ." So the question is not whether we will be extremists, but what kind of extremists we will be. Will we be extremists for hate or for love? Will we be extremists for the preservation of injustice or for the extension of justice? In that dramatic scene on Calvary's hill three men were crucified. We must never

**COMPLICATION**

King describes a number of revered historical figures, including Thomas Jefferson, Abraham Lincoln, and even Jesus, as "extremists" for love and justice. In 1964, a year after King wrote this letter, Arizona Senator Barry Goldwater, then running for nomination as the Republican Party's candidate for president, said in a speech at the Republican Party's national convention, "Extremism in the defense of liberty is no vice" — a statement for which he was severely criticized by many. In 2001 the men who carried out the attacks on the United States on September 11th were routinely described in the press and by U.S. government officials as "extremists." To what extent are all these uses of the term *extremist* similar? To what extent are they different? To what extent is the effectiveness of King's use of this term dependent on the time in which he wrote his essay?

forget that all three were crucified for the same crime — the crime of extremism. Two were extremists for immorality, and thus fell below their environment. The other, Jesus Christ, was an extremist for love, truth, and goodness, and thereby rose above his environment. Perhaps the South, the nation, and the world are in dire need of creative extremists.

I had hoped that the white moderate would see this need. Perhaps I was too optimistic; perhaps I expected too much. I suppose I should have realized that few members of the oppressor race can understand the deep groans and passionate yearnings of the oppressed race, and still fewer have the vision to see that injustice must be rooted out by strong, persistent, and determined action. I am thankful, however, that some of our white brothers in the South have grasped the meaning of this social revolution and committed themselves to it. They are still all too few in quantity, but they are big in quality. Some — such as Ralph McGill, Lillian Smith, Harry Golden, James McBride Dabbs, Ann Braden, and Sarah Patton Boyle — have written about our struggle in eloquent and prophetic terms. Others have marched with us down nameless streets of the South. They have languished in filthy, roach-infested jails, suffering the abuse and brutality of policemen who view them as "dirty nigger-lovers." Unlike so many of their moderate brothers and sisters, they have recognized the urgency of the moment and sensed the need for powerful "action" antidotes to combat the disease of segregation.

Let me take note of my other major disappointment. I have been so greatly disappointed with the white church and its leadership. Of course, there are some notable exceptions. I am not unmindful of the fact that each of you has taken some significant stands on this issue. I commend you, Reverend Stallings, for your Christian stand on this past Sunday, in welcoming Negroes to your worship service on a nonsegregated basis. I commend the Catholic leaders of this state for integrating Spring Hill College several years ago.

But despite these notable exceptions, I must honestly reiterate that I have been disappointed with the church. I do not say this as one of those negative critics who can always find something wrong with the church. I say this as a minister of the gospel, who loves the church; who was nurtured in its bosom; who has been sustained by its spiritual blessings and who will remain true to it as long as the cord of life shall lengthen. **35** When I was suddenly catapulted into the leadership of the bus protest in Montgomery, Alabama, a few years ago, I felt we would be supported by the white church. I felt that the white ministers, priests, and rabbis of the South would be among our strongest allies. Instead, some have been outright opponents, refusing to understand the freedom movement and misrepresenting its leaders; all too many others have been more cautious than courageous and have remained silent behind the anesthetizing security of stained-glass windows.

In spite of my shattered dreams, I came to Birmingham with the hope that the white religious leadership of this community would see the justice of our cause and, with deep moral concern, would serve as the channel through which our just grievances could reach the power structure. I had hoped that each of you would understand. But again I have been disappointed.

There was a time when the church was very powerful — in the time when the early Christians rejoiced at being deemed worthy to suffer for what they believed.

In those days the church was not merely a thermometer that recorded the ideas and principles of popular opinion; it was a thermostat that transformed the mores of society. Whenever the early Christians entered a town, the people in power became disturbed and immediately sought to convict the Christians for being "disturbers of the peace" and "outside agitators." But the Christians pressed on, in the conviction that they were "a colony of heaven," called to obey God rather than man. Small in number, they were big in commitment. They were too God-intoxicated to be "astronomically intimidated." By their effort and example they brought an end to such ancient evils as infanticide and gladiatorial contests.

Things are different now. So often the contemporary church is a weak, ineffectual voice with an uncertain sound. So often it is an archdefender of the status quo. Far from being disturbed by the presence of the church, the power structure of the average community is consoled by the church's silent — and often even vocal — sanction of things as they are.

But the judgment of God is upon the church as never before. If today's church does not recapture the sacrificial spirit of the early church, it will lose its authenticity, forfeit the loyalty of millions, and be dismissed as an irrelevant social club with no meaning for the twentieth century. Every day I meet young people whose disappointment with the church has turned into outright disgust.

40 Perhaps I have once again been too optimistic. Is organized religion too inextricably bound to the status quo to save our nation and the world? Perhaps I must turn my faith to the inner spiritual church, the church within the church, as the true *ekklesia** and the hope of the world. But again I am thankful to God

that some noble souls from the ranks of organized religion have broken loose from the paralyzing chains of conformity and joined us as active partners in the struggle for freedom. They have left their secure congregations and walked the streets of Albany, Georgia, with us. They have gone down the highways of the South on torturous rides for freedom. Yes, they have gone to jail with us. Some have been dismissed from their churches, have lost the support of their bishops and fellow ministers. But they have acted in the faith that right defeated is stronger than evil triumphant. Their witness has been the spiritual salt that has preserved the true meaning of the gospel in these troubled times. They have carved a tunnel of hope through the dark mountain of disappointment.

I hope the church as a whole will meet the challenge of this decisive hour. But even if the church does not come to the aid of justice, I have no despair about the future. I have no fear about the outcome of our struggle in Birmingham, even if our motives are at present misunderstood. We will reach the goal of freedom in Birmingham and all over the nation, because the goal of America is freedom. Abused and scorned though we may be, our destiny is tied up with America's destiny. Before the pilgrims landed at Plymouth, we were here. Before the pen of Jefferson etched the majestic words of the Declaration of Independence across the pages of history, we were here. For more than two centuries our forebears labored in this country without wages; they made cotton king; they built the homes of their masters while suffering gross injustice and shameful humiliation — and yet out of a bottomless vitality they continued to thrive and develop. If the inexpressible cruelties of slavery could not stop us, the

*Ekklesia* is a Greek word meaning assembly, congregation, or church.

opposition we now face will surely fail. We will win our freedom because the sacred heritage of our nation and the eternal will of God are embodied in our echoing demands.

Before closing I feel impelled to mention one other point in your statement that has troubled me profoundly. You warmly commended the Birmingham police force for keeping "order" and "preventing violence." I doubt that you would have so warmly commended the police force if you had seen its dogs sinking their teeth into unarmed, nonviolent Negroes. I doubt that you would so quickly commend the policemen if you were to observe their ugly and inhumane treatment of Negroes here in the city jail; if you were to watch them push and curse old Negro women and young Negro girls; if you were to see them slap and kick old Negro men and young boys; if you were to observe them, as they did on two occasions, refuse to give us food because we wanted to sing our grace together. I cannot join you in your praise of the Birmingham police department.

It is true that the police have exercised a degree of discipline in handling the demonstrators. In this sense they have conducted themselves rather "nonviolently" in public. But for what purpose? To preserve the evil system of segregation. Over the past few years I have consistently preached that nonviolence demands that the means we use must be as pure as the ends we seek. I have tried to make clear that it is wrong to use immoral means to attain moral ends. But now I must affirm that it is just as wrong, or perhaps even more so, to use moral means to preserve immoral ends. Perhaps Mr. Connor and his policemen have been rather nonviolent in public, as was Chief Pritchett in Albany, Georgia, but they have used the moral means of nonviolence to maintain the immoral end of racial injustice. As T. S. Eliot has said, "The last temptation is the greatest treason: To do the right deed for the wrong reason."

I wish you had commended the Negro sit-inners and demonstrators of Birmingham for their sublime courage, their willingness to suffer, and their amazing discipline in the midst of great provocation. One day the South will recognize its real heroes. They will be the James Merediths,[†] with the noble sense of purpose that enables them to face jeering and hostile mobs, and with the agonizing loneliness that characterizes the life of the pioneer. They will be old, oppressed, battered Negro women, symbolized in a seventy-two-year-old woman in Montgomery, Alabama, who rose up with a sense of dignity and with her people decided not to ride segregated buses, and who responded with ungrammatical profundity to one who inquired about her weariness: "My feets is tired, but my soul is at rest." They will be the young high school and college students, the young ministers of the gospel and a host of their elders, courageously and nonviolently sitting in at lunch counters and willingly going to jail for conscience's sake. One day the South will know that when these disinherited children of God sat down at lunch counters, they were in reality standing up for what is best in the American dream and for the most sacred values in our Judeo-Christian heritage, thereby bringing our nation back to those great wells of democracy which were dug deep by the founding fathers in their formulation of the Constitution and the Declaration of Independence.

45 Never before have I written so long a letter. I'm afraid it is much too long to take your precious time. I can assure you that it would have been much shorter if I

[†]In the fall of 1962 James Meredith became the first black student to enroll at the University of Mississippi. His act, which sparked riots on the university's campus that resulted in two deaths, is widely considered an important event in the Civil Rights Movement.

had been writing from a comfortable desk, but what else can one do when he is alone in a narrow jail cell, other than write long letters, think long thoughts, and pray long prayers?

If I have said anything in this letter that overstates the truth and indicates an unreasonable impatience, I beg you to forgive me. If I have said anything that understates the truth and indicates my having a patience that allows me to settle for anything less than brotherhood, I beg God to forgive me.

I hope this letter finds you strong in the faith. I also hope that circumstances will soon make it possible for me to meet each of you, not as an integrationist or a civil-rights leader but as a fellow clergyman and a Christian brother. Let us all hope that the dark clouds of racial prejudice will soon pass away and the deep fog of misunderstanding will be lifted from our fear-drenched communities, and in some not too distant tomorrow the radiant stars of love and brotherhood will shine over our great nation with all their scintillating beauty.

Yours for the cause of Peace
and Brotherhood,
Martin Luther King, Jr.

## Questions for Discussion

**1.** What reason does King give for writing this letter? What justification does he provide for its length? In what ways might these explanations strengthen his argument? **2.** One of the many charges brought against King at the time of his arrest was that he was an "outsider" who had no business in Birmingham. How does he justify his presence in Birmingham? How convincing do you think his justification is? **3.** What does King mean by nonviolent "direct action"? Why did he believe that such action was necessary in Birmingham? How does he build his case for the nonviolent campaign in Birmingham? Do you think he does so convincingly? Why or why not? **4.** Examine the images that King invokes in paragraph 14. What does he accomplish with these images? How do they contribute to his overall argument? Do you think he is intentionally making an emotional appeal there? **5.** How does King distinguish between a just and an unjust law? Why is this distinction important for his main argument? What evidence does King provide to support his contention that unjust laws must be broken? Do you think King's original audience of White ministers would have found his argument on this issue convincing? Explain. **6.** What specific features of King's letter reveal that it was written originally for an audience of White Christian ministers? What strategies does King employ that might be effective for such an audience? Do you think King intended his letter *only* for that audience? Explain. **7.** At one point in his essay King explains that one purpose of the campaign in Birmingham was "to create a situation so crisis-packed that it will inevitably open the door to negotiation." Do you think King's letter itself is intended to lead to negotiation? Explain, citing specific passages in his letter to support your answer.
**8.** King had much experience as a preacher when he wrote this famous letter. Is there anything about its style that reminds you of oratory? How effective would this letter be if delivered as a speech?

## ② MICHAEL KELLY, "Liberties Are a Real Casualty of War"

Americans have long debated the extent to which individual liberties can be compromised when issues of national security or public safety are at stake. After September 11, 2001, those debates were renewed as the U.S. government began to vigorously pursue terrorists and take measures that were intended to prevent new attacks like those that occurred on September 11th. In times of war or crisis Americans are often willing to give up some of the freedoms guaranteed by the Constitution. But some critics caution that allowing government to supercede individual rights is a dangerous path that can even lead to the elimination of Constitutional protections that most Americans take for granted. Indeed, some critics argue that it is precisely in times of crisis that Americans must guard their constitutional rights most jealously, for it is the guarantee of those rights that makes America what it is. In the following essay syndicated columnist Michael Kelly discusses such concerns as they emerged after September 11th. He refers to the case of Abdullah al Muhajir (formerly José Padilla), an American citizen who was held as a terrorist without formal charges, without a lawyer, and without a trial, on the grounds that he was plotting a terrorist attack — a case that, according to critics, illustrated the dangers of too much government power over individual rights. Kelly understands such criticisms. But his priorities are clear: National security sometimes means sacrificing individual liberties. That's fine with him. The question his argument raises for us is whether such a sacrifice is warranted or whether it represents a government overstepping the constitutional limits of its power. Kelly's essay was published in June 2002.

## Liberties Are a Real Casualty of War
### MICHAEL KELLY

**The FBI is now telling the American people, "You no longer have to do anything unlawful to get that knock on the door. You can be doing a perfectly legal activity like worshiping or talking in a chat room and they can spy on you anyway."**

— Laura Murphy, of the American Civil Liberties Union, as quoted in *The Washington Post,* May 30, 2002.

1   Murphy was referring specifically to new rules promulgated by the FBI that will give federal investigators far greater latitude than in the past to monitor — oh, all right, spy upon — private conversations in such venues as libraries, Internet sites and religious institutions. But her complaint may be taken beyond

*According to its Web site, "The ACLU's mission is to fight civil liberties violations wherever and whenever they occur. Most of our clients are ordinary people who have experienced an injustice and have decided to fight back. The ACLU is also active in our national and state capitals, fighting to ensure that the Bill of Rights will always be more than a 'parchment barrier' against government oppression and the tyranny of the majority" (See www.aclu.org/about/aboutmain.cfm).

its specifics as a fair example of a rising chorus of worry and woe concerning the threat to civil liberties posed by the increasingly hard-nosed security measures being adopted by a nation at war. We have not heard the last of Murphy on this subject. There is not much in life that is certain, but one thing we can be sure of is that the creation of a $37 billion, 22-agency, super-colossal Department of Homeland Security will not usher in a new era of civil liberties sensitivity, and that the ACLU* will find this objectionable.

As traditional as the cries from the once-again-wounded hearts of once-again-outraged liberals is the governmental response in such circumstances: It isn't so. No liberties are at risk, or not much anyway. All safeguards are being taken. This administration stands second to none in its concern for the sacred rights of all Americans, etc.

The whole thing is ritual. When Attorney Gen. John Ashcroft announced new regulations requiring the fingerprinting and photographing of foreign visitors from all nations deemed to harbor anti-

American terrorism, Sen. Ted Kennedy was, of course, "deeply disappointed" in a plan that would "further stigmatize innocent Arab and Muslim visitors." White House press secretary Ari Fleischer was of course quick to assure that President Bush was acting "fully in accordance with protecting civil rights and civil liberties."

Would it be too much to ask that we cut this out? The United States is at war — its first utterly unavoidable war since World War II and its first war since the Civil War in which the enemy has been able to significantly bring the conflict onto American soil. This war must be successfully prosecuted and success in war pretty much always requires the violation of civil liberties.

5 As a generally liberties-minded friend notes, war in itself constitutes the grossest imaginable violation of liberties. In war, the state may choose to say to its citizens: We are exercising our collective right to deprive you of the most fundamental of your individual rights — your liberty and quite possibly life (don't even mention your pursuit of happiness). We are taking you away, putting you in a uniform, subjecting you to a wholly dictatorial order — and, we are sending you off to very likely die. If you run away, we will ourselves shoot you. The proper response to complaints such as those voiced by Murphy and Kennedy is: Yes, it is true, this action will indeed hurt or at least insult some innocent people, and we are sorry about that. And this action does represent an infringement of the rights and liberties enjoyed not just by Americans but by visitors to America, and we are sorry about that, too. But we must do everything we can to curtail the ability of the enemy to attack us. This is necessary.

Right now, there sits in a jail cell an American citizen named Abdullah al Muhajir, formerly José

## ABDULLAH AL MUHAJIR (JOSÉ PADILLA)

Abdullah al Muhajir was taken into custody by the United States on May 8, 2002. U.S. officials claimed that he had connections with Al Qaeda, the terrorist organization that carried out the attacks on the United States on September 11, 2001; they also claimed that he was planning to detonate a "dirty bomb" that would release radiation in the United States. Though an American citizen, al Muhajir was declared an "enemy combatant" by the U.S. government, a status that enabled the government to hold him indefinitely without charge and without access to the legal protections and due process to which American citizens are entitled. His detention sparked controversy. Critics charged that al Muhajir was being held illegally; some argued that the case suggested that the rights of all Americans were being put at risk. In September 2002 the American Civil Liberties Union filed a legal challenge to the U.S. government's detention of al Muhajir, arguing that the government did not have the right to detain an American citizen without formally charging him with a crime.

Padilla. He was arrested at O'Hare International Airport in Chicago on a sealed warrant after arriving on a flight from Zurich on May 8. He is accused, based on what is believed to be credible intelligence, of plotting to explode a radioactive bomb in the United States. He was seized as a material witness and has not been charged with a crime, apparently because the U.S. government does not think it possesses evidence sufficient to charge him. Instead, he is being held as "an enemy combatant," which means that the U.S. military can keep him locked up for as long as it wants, with no jury trial. No one outside the government really knows what the evidence is against al Muhajir. The government didn't even reveal his arrest until a scheduled court hearing forced the revelation.

Now, that is what I call a violation of civil liberties. I am sorry about it, and I will be even sorrier in the unlikely event that al Muhajir is innocent and should not have been locked away. But I wouldn't have it any other way.

## Questions for Discussion

**1.** Note how Kelly refers to liberals in this essay. What do these references reveal about Kelly's own politics? How might your own political views influence your reaction to his argument? **2.** Describe Kelly's style and tone in this essay. Do you think they are appropriate for his argument? Explain. In what ways do you think his style and tone make his argument more or less effective? **3.** Kelly asserts that "success in war pretty much always requires the violation of civil liberties." What evidence does he offer for that assertion? Do you agree with him? Why or why not? **4.** Kelly ends his essay by discussing the case of Abdullah al Muhajir, also known as José Padilla (see the sidebar on page 312), and he raises the possibility that al Muhajir might be innocent and therefore jailed unjustly. How does Kelly's raising this possibility contribute to his argument? Do you think this is an effective strategy on his part? Explain. **5.** We might describe Kelly's argument as one based on deductive reasoning (see pages 26–31). What fundamental principle does he based his argument on? Do you think he builds an effective argument on that principle?

③ **HEATHER GREEN, "Databases and Security vs. Privacy"**

Concerns about threats to their country's — and their personal — security after September 11, 2001, led many Americans to reexamine an idea that has been debated in the United States for many years: the establishment of a national identification card system. Such a system would, in effect, require all Americans to carry an authorized identification card to be used for important but routine transactions, such as withdrawing money from a bank account; paying a bill; visiting a doctor; boarding an airplane or train; entering a government building; and purchasing a variety of items, including medications, alcohol, ammunition, knives, or fertilizer. To an extent, some kind of official identification is already required for many of these activities. For example, when you withdraw money from your bank account, you usually must present a photo ID such as a driver's license. A national ID card system, however, would centralize this process and place it in the hands of the federal government. That worries many critics, including business reporter Heather Green, who sees in such ID cards the potential for the abuse of the privacy of individual Americans. As Green points out in the following essay, which was first published in *Business Week* in 2002, the debate over national ID cards is really a broader debate about the extent to which Americans are willing to sacrifice some of their rights to privacy for greater security in a dangerous world. In this respect, the controversy about ID cards is also part of a debate about how much power the government should have over its citizens.

## Databases and Security vs. Privacy
### HEATHER GREEN

**1** The debate about whether or not the U.S. should or would adopt a national identification-card system has emerged with a jolting intensity. Jolting because even through world wars and a cold war, in which the U.S. feared an enemy within the country as much as the armies outside, Americans resisted the creation of a national ID that they would carry to prove their citizenship. Now, however, public surveys, congressional speeches, and remarks by high-profile CEOs are bringing the issue to the forefront, causing everyone to consider whether America is ready to adopt a card ID system — like those widely used in other countries — at the expense of our privacy.

The problem is, the debate over trading security provided by card IDs for a lower standard of privacy focuses on the wrong issue. The federal government and law enforcement don't need national ID cards. Indeed, the Bush Administration stated publicly last month that it had no intention of pushing for cards. Instead, law-enforcement and intelligence agencies can achieve many of the same goals of an ID card by increasing the collection and sharing of data among federal and state agencies, banks, transportation authorities, and credit-card companies.

People concerned about balancing privacy and security need to focus on this point and not get caught up in the red herring* debate around the ID cards themselves.

*Robust Resource:* After all, the U.S. already is a database nation. In the corporate world, the push to gather, store, and trade information about individuals' daily lives, habits and tastes, families, purchases, health, and financial standing has steadily increased as database software and hardware, data-mining technology, and computer networks have become cheaper to run and connect.

**5** The FBI, Central Intelligence Agency, Federal Aviation Administration, Immigration & Naturalization Service, port authorities, and state motor vehicle departments could possibly take a page from Corporate America. By creating data-gathering systems in the background that pull together information about people — including their travel plans, frequent-flier info, license certification, border crossings, and financial records — law-enforcement and intelligence agencies can run a robust national ID system without the card itself.

Two questions: Would government in the U.S. really be able to implement a system of databases, and why have other countries avoided this path? First, commercial databases are a particularly American heritage. We're concerned about privacy, but not urgently. Most believe that if we personally think it's important, we can set limits on how our information

is used: We can call a number provided by the Direct Marketing Assn., say, to get ourselves off catalog lists. And we accept that some benefits and efficiency come from providing data to companies, including health insurers, credit-card issuers, and airlines. So a huge system of commercial databases has been created.

*Highly Protected:* Second, Europe has a different, more tragic historical perspective. The Nazis used personal information culled from commercial and government files, including telephone and bank records, to track down Jews, communists, resistance fighters, and the mentally ill. As a direct result of that experience, privacy is very highly protected in countries such as Germany and France.

That doesn't mean these countries aren't interested in protecting security. It simply means that instead of amassing huge amounts of information in databases, these countries favor national ID cards. According to privacy group Privacy International, most of the Western European countries that have strict controls protecting the privacy of personal information — including Germany, France, Belgium, Greece, Luxembourg, Portugal, and Spain — have compulsory national ID systems. (See "ID Cards in Europe" on page 316.)

So, Americans need to get more sophisticated and realize that, in the interest of security, law-enforcement and intelligence agencies are likely to start beefing up their databases on citizens. We need to be on guard and informed about this eventuality. Despite how difficult it might be to make these

*A red herring is something that distracts attention from the real issue at hand. The term comes from an old practice of dragging a smoked, or "red," herring across a trail to confuse hunting dogs.*

## COMPLICATION

Established in 1917, the Direct Marketing Association (DMA) claims to be the oldest and largest trade association for direct marketing. It provides a service by which consumers can ask to have their names removed from the lists used by DMA member businesses to market directly to consumers through telephone calls and mailings. In 1995 DMA was the focus of a lawsuit challenging its practice of distributing names of consumers among its member businesses. Documents filed in that case indicated that as of 1995, DMA had more than 3.2 million names of consumers in its databases. The suit led to several bills in Congress that were intended to protect consumers from direct marketing practices that they believe violate their rights to privacy by sharing information about them without permission.

## ID CARDS IN EUROPE

As of 2002, citizens in eleven of the fifteen countries in the European Union were required to carry ID cards issued by their national governments. In some countries these cards are used in addition to other forms of identification, such as drivers' licenses; in other countries national ID cards can be used in place of these other forms of identification. Despite a long tradition of such cards (dating back to 1919), Europeans continue to debate whether these cards unnecessarily violate individual privacy or are essential for security. In 2002 citizens of Great Britain were debating a proposal to establish a national ID card system there. During that same year some polls indicated that 70 percent of Americans favored such ID cards.

databases work effectively, you have to believe that security officials view networked databases as key to their war on terrorism.

**10** *Overstepped Boundaries:* Facing this likelihood, citizens need to know and make clear what the rules are under which people land in these databases and are flagged as suspects, who gets to look at the information, and what protections can be established so that information collected for one purpose isn't used for another without some kind of oversight. America needs clear definitions about what terrorism is, so that someone who is protesting against U.S. policies isn't labeled a terrorist out of hand. This is where the true privacy vs. security battlefield will be in the future.

After September 11, it's only natural that the nation would search for ways to increase its security. But law enforcement has overstepped the boundaries of acceptable surveillance of Americans in the past. Widespread wiretapping of civil-rights leaders, including Martin Luther King, as well as Vietnam war dissidents including Jane Fonda and John Lennon during the 1960s and early 1970s led to stricter controls over the kind of information intelligence agencies could gather and the type of broad investigations they could conduct.

Just because we depend on the government to protect us doesn't mean that it will always respect our individual rights. That's the contest that has always been waged in a democracy: the rights of individuals against the safety of the community. Individuals have a duty to be aware of the steps a security-focused government will contemplate and to fight for the protection of rights that they believe are the foundation of a democracy. Privacy is a civil liberty worthy of protection.

## Questions for Discussion

**1.** Why does Green believe that the debate about national ID cards focuses on the wrong issue? On what point, according to Green, should Americans focus instead? **2.** Green calls the United States a "database nation." What does she mean by that phrase? What evidence does she offer to support that statement? Do you agree with her? Why or why not? **3.** What is the main difference between European countries where ID cards are in use and the United States when it comes to information privacy, in Green's view? Why is this difference important to her main argument? **4.** What is Green's primary concern regarding the use of a national ID card in the United States? What evidence does she present that such a concern is justified? Do you find this evidence persuasive? Why or why not? **5.** How does the fact that Heather Green is a business reporter — and that her essay was published in a business journal — affect your reaction to her argument? Do you think her identity as a business reporter enhances her credibility in making this argument? Explain.

# ④ ALAN M. DERSHOWITZ, "Why Fear National ID Cards?"

The right to individual liberty is guaranteed to U.S. citizens by the Constitution. But that right is more than a legal one; it also reflects a belief in individual freedom that runs deep in American culture. Perhaps that is one reason that the debate about national ID cards has been so intense in the United States. Any proposal that seems to compromise individual rights tends to make Americans suspicious. But balancing the rights of individuals with the well-being of all Americans is a challenge, in part because of the great diversity of the United States and in part because of the enormous difficulties of protecting citizens from harm. If, like Alan M. Dershowitz, you prefer "a system that takes a little bit of freedom from all to one that takes a great deal of freedom and dignity from the few," then perhaps you will agree with him that a national ID card is a worthwhile tradeoff. On the other hand, you might share the concerns of many Americans about the danger of giving up any of your freedoms to your government. As you read the following essay by this well-known lawyer and activist, consider how your own views about individual liberties influence your reaction to his argument. Alan M. Dershowitz is also a columnist and the author of many books on legal issues, including *Why Terrorism Works* (2002).

## Why Fear National ID Cards?
### ALAN M. DERSHOWITZ

**CONTEXT**

This essay was originally published in October 2001 on the editorial page of the *New York Times*, which has one of the largest national circulations of any publication in the United States. What audience do you think Dershowitz primarily intended to address with this essay? Do you think he addressed this audience effectively?

**1**  At many bridges and tunnels across the country, drivers avoid long delays at the toll booths with an unobtrusive device that fits on a car's dashboard. Instead of fumbling for change, they drive right through; the device sends a radio signal that records their passage. They are billed later. It's a tradeoff between privacy and convenience: the toll-takers know more about you — when you entered and left Manhattan, for instance — but you save time and money.

An optional national identity card could be used in a similar way, offering a similar kind of tradeoff: a little less anonymity for a lot more security. Anyone who had the card could be allowed to pass through airports or build-ing security more expeditiously, and anyone who opted out could be examined much more closely.

As a civil libertarian,* I am instinctively skeptical of such tradeoffs. But I support a national identity card with a chip that can match the holder's fingerprint. It could be an effective tool for preventing terrorism, reducing the need for other law-enforcement mechanisms — especially racial and ethnic profiling — that pose even greater dangers to civil liberties.

I can hear the objections: What about the specter of Big Brother?† What about fears of identity cards leading to more intrusive measures? (The National Rifle Association, for example, worries that a government that registered people might also decide to register guns. See "Complication" on page 320.) What about fears that such cards would lead to increased deportation of illegal immigrants? 5 First, we already require photo ID's for many activities, including flying, driving, drinking and check-cashing. And fingerprints differ from photographs only in that they are harder to fake. The vast majority of Americans routinely carry photo ID's in their wallets and pocketbooks. These ID's are issued by state motor vehicle bureaus and other public and private entities. A national card would be uniform and difficult to forge or alter. It would reduce the likelihood that someone could, intentionally or not, get lost in the cracks of multiple bureaucracies.

The fear of an intrusive government can be addressed by setting criteria for any official who demands to see the card. Even without a national card, people are always being asked to show identification. The existence of a national card need not change the rules about when ID can properly be demanded. It is true that the card would facilitate the deportation of illegal immigrants. But President Bush has proposed giving legal status to many of the illegal immigrants now in this country. And legal immigrants would actually benefit from a national ID card that could demonstrate their status to government officials.

Finally, there is the question of the right to anonymity. I don't believe we can afford to recognize such a right in this age of terrorism. No such right is hinted at in the Constitution. And though the Supreme Court has identified a right to privacy, privacy and anonymity are not the same. American taxpayers, voters and drivers long ago gave up any right of anonymity without loss of our right to engage in lawful conduct within zones of privacy. Rights are a function of experience, and our recent experiences teach that it is far too easy to be anonymous — even to create a false identity — in this large and decentralized country. A national ID card would not prevent all threats of terrorism, but it would make it more difficult for potential terrorists to hide in open view, as many of the Sept. 11 hijackers apparently managed to do.

A national ID card could actually enhance civil liberties by reducing the need for racial and ethnic stereotyping. There would be no excuse for hassling someone merely because he belongs to a particular racial or ethnic group if he presented a card that matched his print and that permitted

*A civil libertarian generally supports individual rights as opposed to state control. In the United States, civil libertarians are usually defenders of the specific rights guaranteed by the U.S. Constitution, including the right to free speech and protection against unreasonable search and seizure. The American Civil Liberties Union, the best known such organization, describes its mission as "fighting to ensure that the Bill of Rights will always be more than a 'parchment barrier' against government oppression and the tyranny of the majority."

†"Big Brother" refers to the totalitarian government in George Orwell's novel 1984. The term is generally used to describe an omnipotent and oppressive government or institution.

## COMPLICATION

According to the National Rifle Association, "The language and intent of the framers of the Second Amendment were perfectly clear two centuries ago. Based on English Common Law, the Second Amendment guaranteed against federal interference with the citizen's right to keep and bear arms for personal defense. Also, the revolutionary experience caused the Founding Fathers to address a second concern — the need for the people to maintain a citizen-militia for national and state defense without adopting a large standing army, which was viewed as the bane of liberty."

his name to be checked instantly against the kind of computerized criminal-history retrieval systems that are already in use. (If there is too much personal information in the system, or if the information is being used improperly, that is a separate issue. The only information the card need contain is name, address, photo and print.) From a civil liberties perspective, I prefer a system that takes a little bit of freedom from all to one that takes a great deal of freedom and dignity from the few — especially since those few are usually from a racially or ethnically disfavored group. A national ID card would be much more effective in preventing terrorism than profiling millions of men simply because of their appearance.

# NEGOTIATING DIFFERENCES

In his famous "Letter From a Birmingham Jail," Martin Luther King, Jr., argues on moral grounds that citizens are justified and even obligated to resist their government if that government imposes unjust laws on them. Many people who resisted the military draft during the Vietnam War made the same argument, asserting that their government was forcing them to fight in an unjust war, so they were justified in defying the laws that required them to submit to the military draft. In a sense, the arguments about U.S. government actions in response to the terrorist attacks on September 11, 2001, focus on the same basic question of the moral responsibility of citizens to disobey their government's laws if they determine that those laws are immoral or unjust. For most Americans these arguments about government power and moral responsibility can seem abstract. But they can become real when the government takes action that directly affects the lives of citizens, as the military draft did during the Vietnam War. Americans who have never faced such a situation might wonder, "What would *I* do?"

In 2003 the possibility that some Americans would have to answer that question arose in the form of a war with Iraq. If the United States were to find itself in a protracted war — with Iraq or any other nation — young men and women might eventually be subject to the military draft. They would, in effect, be asked to

## Questions for Discussion

**1.** Notice the images Dershowitz describes in his opening paragraph. How do these images help him to establish his position in the debate about national ID cards? Do you think the use of these images is a good strategy for introducing his argument? Explain. **2.** Dershowitz describes himself as a "civil libertarian." Why do you think he does so? How might describing himself in this way affect his readers' response to his argument? **3.** In his essay Dershowitz addresses several possible objections to his position on ID cards What are those objections? Do you think Dershowitz answers them effectively? Explain. Evaluate the extent to which Dershowitz strengthens or weakens his argument by including these possible objections. **4.** Dershowitz makes a distinction between the right to privacy and the right to anonymity. Why is this distinction important to his argument? **5.** How does Dershowitz support his point that national ID cards could enhance civil liberties? Do you agree with him on this point? Why or why not? What counterarguments might you offer in response to this point?

---

sacrifice their own safety and liberty for the sake of their government and other citizens.

What would you do in such a case? In an essay in which you draw on the readings in this chapter (and any other appropriate sources), put forth your position on the question of the government's authority to ask you to sacrifice your life for your country. Under what circumstances do you think the government is justified in compelling young men and women to serve in the military and possibly go to war? When is it acceptable for a government to ask you to sacrifice your health and maybe your life? When is it not acceptable? To what extent are you justified in blatantly disobeying the laws that would require you to

serve in the military? On what moral or legal or philosophical grounds would you do so? And do Americans have any special obligations to serve their country because of its history? In other words, how does your idea of America figure into your answer to these questions?

These are some of the question you should try to address in your essay. In effect, you are writing a position paper on the military draft in which you make an argument about the extent and the limits of your government's power over you and other citizens.

Alternatively, you may make your argument about the use of national ID cards or other security measures that were proposed after 9/11.

**12**

**FREE ENTERPRISE**

## Cluster
### WHAT DOES IT MEAN TO BE A CONSUMER?

(1) Ian Frazier, "All-Consuming Patriotism: American Flag: $19.95. New Yacht: $75,000. True Patriotism: Priceless."

(2) James Deacon, "The Joys of Excess"

(3) Norman Solomon, "Mixed Messages Call for Healthy Skepticism"

(4) Peter Singer, "The Singer Solution to World Poverty"

CON-TEXT
**Conspicuous Consumption**

E R P R I S E

# WHAT DOES IT MEAN
## TO BE A CONSUMER?

In the 1980s a popular television show called *Lifestyles of the Rich and Famous* featured celebrities in their spectacular homes or in other locations such as their yachts or vacation homes. In the 1990s a similar show on the MTV network called *Cribs* focused on the expensive homes of well-known musicians, actors, and athletes. The astronomically expensive homes featured on these shows are out of reach of the vast majority of Americans, but perhaps the popularity of the shows reflects the dreams and desires of that majority. If so, then we might think of "conspicuous consumption" as a good thing. ■ *Conspicuous consumption* is a term coined in 1899 by American economist and social critic Thorstein Veblen (1857–1929) to describe the spending of money as a way to display wealth (see *Con-Text* on page 325). In other words, a person spends conspicuously, so that others can see his or her wealth. Veblen originally used the term in reference to what he called "the leisure class," which was made up of well-to-do businesspeople, property owners, professionals, and others in "non-industrial" occupations. But in the decades since Veblen first published his theory, the term *conspicuous consumption* has taken on a larger meaning. Today we tend to use it to refer to anyone's "conspicuous" spending, especially if that spending can be considered unnecessary. For example, someone of very modest means who buys an extremely expensive sports car can be said to be engaged in conspicuous consumption. Just as the celebrities in *Lifestyles of the Rich and Famous* or *Cribs* do not really need such enormous and expensive homes for their basic shelter, neither does the person who bought the expensive sports car truly need such a vehicle for basic transportation. Yet many people would defend that person's right to buy such a car, whether or not it is necessary — and whether or not that person can afford it. ■ Conspicuous consumption of this kind raises questions about the decisions individuals make in spending their money. Do we really have the right to spend our money in any way we please, without regard to possible consequences? Is the kind of excessive consumption featured on television shows such as *Cribs* something that people should aspire to in a society that includes some people who are desperately poor? In other words, what responsibilities, if any, do consumers have in deciding how to spend their money? ■ The essays in this cluster reveal that there are many different answers to such questions. A few of these authors argue that consumers do not make their decisions in isolation and therefore must sometimes face ethical considerations when deciding how to spend their money. Such arguments seem to fly in the face of mainstream American attitudes about individual choice and free markets. Indeed, some critics argue that it is patriotic to be a consumer, since consumption can contribute to a strong U.S. economy. Yet other critics offer warnings about how consumers can fall prey to business practices that seek to maximize profits at the expense of individual consumers. ■ All these arguments suggest that buying things as consumers might not be as straightforward as we might think. The essays in this cluster might therefore deepen your appreciation for the ways in which our choices as consumers — conspicuous or not — are connected to many other aspects of our lives.

# CON-TEXT: "Conspicuous Consumption"

**1** Conspicuous consumption of valuable goods is a means of reputability to the gentleman of leisure. As wealth accumulates on his hands, his own unaided effort will not avail to sufficiently put his opulence in evidence by this method. The aid of friends and competitors is therefore brought in by resorting to the giving of valuable presents and expensive feasts and entertainments. Presents and feasts had probably another origin than that of naive ostentation, but they required their utility for this purpose very early, and they have retained that character to the present; so that their utility in this respect has now long been the substantial ground on which these usages rest. Costly entertainments, such as the potlatch or the ball, are peculiarly adapted to serve this end. The competitor with whom the entertainer wishes to institute a comparison is, by this method, made to serve as a means to the end. He consumes vicariously for his host at the same time that he is witness to the consumption of that excess of good things which his host is unable to dispose of single-handed, and he is also made to witness his host's facility in etiquette.

SOURCE: Thorstein Veblen, *Theory of the Leisure Class* (1899).

# ① IAN FRAZIER, "All-Consuming Patriotism: American Flag: $19.95. New Yacht: $75,000. True Patriotism? Priceless"

Shortly after the terrorist attacks of September 11, 2001, fears about the potential damage of those attacks to the U.S. economy prompted President George W. Bush to urge Americans to carry on as usual. In particular, President Bush suggested, Americans should patronize businesses as they normally would, and maybe even take their families on vacation. The idea was that spending money was good for the economy and therefore good for the country. In other words, it would be patriotic to be a consumer. Some critics scoffed at President Bush's comments, but the idea that it is patriotic to consume is not far-fetched for many Americans. In the 1980s, as some U.S. industries seemed to be losing ground in the marketplace to expanding Japanese companies, there were calls for American consumers to "buy American" as a way to keep the U.S. economy strong in the face of foreign competition. And during the economic downturn in the first few years of the 21st century, some economists indicated that the buying habits of Americans were keeping the economy from an even more serious recession. Such news prompted some political leaders to suggest that consumers were actually doing their **patriotic duty** by buying goods at a time when the U.S. economy was weak. In the following essay, writer Ian **Frazier** examines this connection between consumption and patriotism. Although he pokes fun at the idea that consumption is patriotic, Frazier is making a serious point about what it means to be a consumer and a patriot. As you read his essay, which was published in 2002 in *Mother Jones* magazine, consider what it might say about the role of consumers in American society.

## All-Consuming Patriotism: American Flag: $19.95. New Yacht: $75,000. True Patriotism? Priceless.

### IAN FRAZIER

1  I think of myself as a good American. I follow current events, come to a complete stop at stop signs, show up for jury duty, vote. When the government tells me to shop, as it's been doing recently, I shop. Over the last few months, patriotically, I've bought all kinds of stuff I have no use for. Lack of money has been no obstacle; years ago I could never get a credit card, due to low income and lack of a regular job, and then one day for no reason credit cards began tumbling on me out of the mail. I now owe more to credit card companies than the average family of four earns in a year. So when buying something I don't want or need, I simply take out my credit card. That part's been easy; for me, it's the shop-

ping itself that's hard. I happen to be a bad shopper — nervous, uninformed, prone to grab the first product I see on the shelf and pay any amount for it and run out the door. Frequently, trips I make to the supermarket end with my wife shouting in disbelief as she goes through the grocery bags and immediately transfers one wrongly purchased item after another directly into the garbage can.

It's been hard, as I say, but I've done my duty — I've shopped and then shopped some more. Certain sacrifices are called for. Out of concern for the economy after the terror attacks, the president said that he wanted us to go about our business, and not stop shopping. On a TV commercial sponsored by the travel industry, he exhorted us to take the family for a vacation. The treasury secretary, financial commentators, leaders of industry — all told us not to be afraid to spend. So I've gone out of my comfort zone, even expanded my purchasing patterns. Not long ago I detected a look of respect in the eye of a young salesman with many piercings at the music store as he took in my heavy middle-aged girth and then the rap music CD featuring songs of murder and gangsterism that I had selflessly decided to buy. My life is usually devoid of great excitement or difficulty, knock wood and thank God, and I have nothing to cry about, but I've also noticed in the media recently a strong approval for uninhibited public crying. So now, along with the shopping, I've been crying a lot, too. Sometimes I cry and shop at the same time.

As I'm pushing my overfull shopping cart down the aisle, sobbing quietly, moving a bit more slowly because of the extra weight I've lately put on, a couple of troubling questions cross my mind. First, I start to worry about the real depth of my shopping capabilities. So far I have more or less been able to keep up

with what the government expects of me. I'm at a level of shopping that I can stand. But what if, God forbid, events take a bad turn and the national crisis worsens, and more shopping is required? Can I shop with greater intensity than I am shopping now? I suppose I could eat even more than I've been eating, and order additional products in the mail, and go on costlier trips, and so on. But I'm not eager, frankly, to enter that "code red" shopping mode. I try

to tell myself that I'd be equal to it, that in a real crisis I might be surprised by how much I could buy. But I don't know.

My other worry is a vague one, more in the area of atmospherics, intangibles. I feel kind of wrong even mentioning it in this time of trial. How can I admit that I am worried about my aura? I worry that my aura is not . . . well, that it's not what I had once hoped it would be. I can explain this only by comparison, obliquely. On the top shelf of my book-case, among the works vital to me, is a book called *Trials and Triumphs: The Record of the Fifty-Fifth Ohio Volunteer Infantry,* by Captain Hartwell Osborn. I've read this book many times and studied it to the smallest detail, because I think the people in it are brave and cool and admirable in every way.

5 The Fifty-Fifth was a Union Army regi-ment, formed in the Ohio town of Norwalk, that fought throughout the Civil War. My great-great-grandfather served in the regiment, as did other relatives. The book lists every mile the regiment marched and every casualty it suffered. I like reading about the soldiering, but I can't really identify with it, having never been in the service myself. I identify more with the soldiers' wives and moth-ers and daughters, whose home-front struggles I can better imagine, *Trials and Triumphs* devotes a chapter to them, and to an organization they set up called the Soldiers' Aid Society.

The ladies of the Soldiers' Aid Society worked for the regiment almost con-stantly from the day it began. They sewed uniforms, made pillows, held ice-cream sociables to raise money, scraped lint for bandages, emptied their wedding chests of their best linen and donated it all. To provide the men with antiscorbu-tics* while on campaign, they pickled everything that would pickle, from onions to potatoes to artichokes. Every other

day they were shipping out a new order of homemade supplies. Some of the women spent so much time stooped over while packing goods in barrels that they believed they had permanently affected their postures. When the war ended the ladies of the Soldiers' Aid said that for the first time in their lives they under-stood what united womanhood could ac-complish. The movements for prohibition and women's suffrage that grew powerful in the early 1900s got their start among those who'd worked in similar home-front organizations during the war.

I don't envy my forebears, or wish I'd lived back then. I prefer the greater speed and uncertainty and complicated-ness of now. But I can't help thinking that in terms of aura, the Norwalk ladies have it all over me. I study the pages with their photographs, and admire the plainness of their dresses, the set of their jaws, the expression in their eyes. Next to them my credit card and I seem a sorry spectacle indeed. Their sense of purpose shames me. What the country needed from those ladies it asked for, and they provided, straightforwardly; what it wants from me it somehow can't come out and ask. I'm asked to shop more, which really means to spend more, which eventually must mean to work more than I was working before. In pre-vious wars, harder work was a civilian sacrifice that the government didn't hesi-tate to ask. Nowadays it's apparently un-willing to ask for any sacrifice that might appear to be too painful, too real.

But I want it to be real. I think a lot of us do. I feel like an idiot with my tears and shopping cart. I want to par-ticipate, to do something — and shop-ping isn't it. Many of the donors who contributed more than half a billion dol-lars to a Red Cross fund for the families of terror attack victims became angry when they learned that much of the

*The term *antiscorbu-tics* refers to herbal medicines that provide vitamin C.

money would end up not where they had
intended but in the Red Cross bureau-
cracy. People want to express themselves
with action. In New York City so many
have been showing up recently for jury
duty that the courts have had to turn
hundreds away; officials said a new surplus of civic consciousness was responsible for the upsurge. I'd be glad if I were
asked to — I don't know — drive less or
turn the thermostat down or send in
seldom-used items of clothing or collect
rubber bands or plant a victory garden
or join a civilian patrol or use fewer disposable paper products at children's
birthday parties. I'd be willing, if asked,
just to sit still for a day and meditate
on the situation, much in the way that
Lincoln used to call for national days of
prayer.

A great, shared desire to do something is lying around mostly untapped.
The best we can manage, it seems, is to
show our U.S.A. brand loyalty by putting
American flags on our houses and cars.
Some businesses across the country even
display in their windows a poster on
which the American flag appears as a
shopping bag, with two handles at the
top. Above the flag-bag are the words
"America: Open for Business." Money and
the economy have gotten so tangled up
in our politics that we forget we're citizens of our government, not its consumers. And the leaders we elect, who
got where they are by selling themselves
to us with television ads, and who often
are only on short loan from the corporate
world anyway, think of us as customers
who must be kept happy. There's a
scarcity of ideas about how to direct all
this patriotic feeling because usually the
market, not the country, occupies our
minds. I'm sure it's possible to transform
oneself from salesman to leader, just as
it is to go from consumer to citizen. But
the shift of identity is awkward, without

## THE RED CROSS AND 9-11

"In the hours after the Sept. 11 attacks, a record-breaking amount of donations started pouring into more than 1,000 local American Red Cross chapters.

"What donors didn't know was that some of the chapters entrusted with
all that money had been identified by Red Cross headquarters just a few
weeks before for having poor accounting procedures, inaccurate financial
reports and for keeping national disaster contributions that should have
been sent to headquarters in Washington. That according to internal documents obtained by CBS news. . . .

"According to documents obtained by CBS News, a dozen of the Red
Cross chapters audited were marking, or 'coding', donations as local funds.
This means chapters like San Diego, Southwest Florida, and Gateway Area,
Iowa would keep the money instead of sending it in for Sept. 11 victims."
Source: Sharyl Attkisson, "Red Faces at the Red Cross." CBSNews.com
(July 2002).

many precedents, not easily done. In between the two — between selling and
leading, between consuming and being
citizens — is where our leaders and the
rest of us are now.

**10** We see the world beyond our immediate surroundings mostly through televi-

sion, whose view is not much wider than that of a security peephole in a door. We hear over and over that our lives have forever changed, but the details right in front of us don't look very different, for all that. The forces fighting in Afghanistan are in more danger than we are back home, but perhaps not so much more; everybody knows that when catastrophe comes it could hit anywhere, most likely someplace it isn't expected. Strong patriotic feelings stir us, fill us, but have few means of expressing themselves. We want to be a country, but where do you go to do that? Surely not the mall. When Mayor Giuliani left office at the end of 2001, he said he was giving up the honorable title of mayor for the more honorable title of citizen. He got that right. Citizen is honorable; shopper is not.

## Questions for Discussion

**1.** How would you summarize Frazier's main argument in this essay? Identify the passage or passages in the essay that you think most clearly state his main point. **2.** According to Frazier, why is it difficult for Americans to determine how to express their patriotic feelings? Do you agree with him? Why or why not? **3.** The tone of Frazier's essay might be described as tongue-in-cheek — an attempt to poke fun at the idea that it is patriotic for Americans to spend money on consumer goods. What features of his writing style create this tongue-in-cheek approach to his subject? Cite specific passages from the essay to support your answer. **4.** Frazier devotes considerable space in his essay to discussing *Trials and Triumphs*, a book about a Civil War infantry unit, and the men and women described in that book. What purpose does this discussion serve in Frazier's essay? How does this discussion relate to his main argument about consumption? Do you find this discussion effective? Explain. **5.** This essay was originally published in *Mother Jones* magazine, which generally reflects a left-leaning political viewpoint that is often critical of the U.S. government. In what ways does Frazier's essay reflect the editorial viewpoint of *Mother Jones*? Do you think Frazier's argument would be effective for a wider audience than readers of *Mother Jones*? Explain, citing specific passages from the essay to support your answer.

## ② JAMES DEACON, "The Joys of Excess"

Americans are sometimes criticized for excessive buying habits as consumers. But as James Deacon makes clear in the following essay, Americans are not the only people who might be guilty of conspicuous consumption. (For a discussion of conspicuous consumption, see the introduction to this cluster on page 324; see also *Con-Text* on page 325.) Deacon describes some of the spending habits of wealthier citizens of his own country, Canada, a nation whose economy and culture are in many ways similar to those of the United States. But although Deacon is critical of what he believes is excessive spending on consumer goods by many Canadians, he avoids simply judging consumers; rather, he is interested in understanding why consumers engage in conspicuous consumption. His essay raises questions about the implications of such consumption — especially when it involves items that can obviously damage the environment, such as fuel-inefficient SUVs. In asking why such consumption occurs, Deacon helps us to explore the complicated issue of what it means to be a consumer. His essay was published in 2002 in *MacLean's* magazine.

# The Joys of Excess
## JAMES DEACON

*Canadian lawyer J.J. Robinette is well known throughout Canada for having argued a number of high-profile cases before the Canadian Supreme Court. *Barrister* is another term for lawyer.

1  Back in 1904, a banker named James Breckenridge moved his family into a gorgeous new red-brick home on one of the most sought-after streets in Rosedale, a leafy enclave in the centre of Toronto. Over the years, the rambling, three-story classic was home to a couple of other families, including famed barrister J.J. Robinette,* his wife and their three children. But the home isn't there anymore. The next-door neighbours bought it and tore it down so they could put an addition on their already substantial home. They also bought and demolished two even bigger houses immediately behind them for yet more additions that are currently under construction.

As conspicuous consumption goes, that's tough to beat. But nowadays, even with the uncertainties of the stock market, the competition is fierce. Just two blocks away, someone bought a pair of century-old homes on vast, side-by-side lots, ripped them down and is erecting what, at a projected 7,500 square feet, can only loosely be termed a single-family dwelling. It will not only be the biggest house on the block; it will tower over the elementary school directly across the street. Still, that place is puny compared to the $16-million, 48,500-

**CONTEXT**

According to the U.S. Census Bureau, the relative share of income declined for 80 percent of all Americans between 1970 and 1998; in that same time period the wealthiest 20 percent of Americans saw their share of income increase from 43 percent to 49 percent. In other words, as of 1998, nearly half of total wealth in the United States was owned by the richest 20 percent of the population. More recent census data indicate little change in those figures.

The relative distribution of incomes in Canada has changed less noticeably. For example, in 1980 the wealthiest 20 percent of Canadians accounted for 42 percent of total income; in 1996 that figure increased to 44 percent.

Have the rich gone mad? The numbers shout yes, but the experts who track such things say no. In the last two decades, while low- and middle-income paycheques remained static or declined, the country's top earners saw their incomes more than double. (That was partly due to companies' generous outlay of stock options, a practice that, in the post-Enron world, is in retreat). At any rate, all they're doing now is spending at comparably lavish levels. And if you believe Adam Smith, the noted 18th-century Scottish economist, the ravenous craving for ultra-luxurious goods is actually a good thing. It was Smith 200-odd years ago who suggested that the pursuit of individual self-interest would ultimately produce gains for society as a whole. Free markets create wealthier economies, he argued, and free-spending puts more cash in more pockets.

**5** Many wealthy people are discreet about it, but there have always been those who are willing to throw money around like confetti. The term "conspicuous consumption,"* in fact, was coined more than a century ago by an eccentric University of Chicago economist named Thorstein Veblen, and the practice has likely been going on forever. And as in the past, the current luxury-goods craze has boosted, as Smith promised, the fortunes of countless car dealers and retailers and tradesmen and architects.

But others argue that there are costs that don't get paid by the conspicuous consumers, and that undercut whatever benefits free-spending offers. Humongous boats and SUVs are fearsome gas-guzzlers that deplete resources and release far more pollutants into waterways and the atmosphere than do smaller cars and boats. There is enormous waste when one monster home replaces two, three or even four pre-existing houses: in many cases, more people are forced to com-

square-foot lakeside home that a businessman has planned for himself, his wife and their one child in suburban Oakville. And so on — in Calgary, Montreal, Vancouver, wherever, the stories are the same. Bigger is better, and spare no expense. Heck, someone recently paid $10 million for a lakeside chalet in Whistler, B.C., which begs the question: how many hot tubs do you get for 10 million bucks?

And it's not just monster homes. It's monster cars, too. One-upmanship in the sports-utility market has prompted automotive companies to produce vehicles with the square footage and creature comforts of two-storey condos. Luxury car manufacturers such as Mercedes-Benz Canada, BMW Canada and Infiniti have all reported record sales in the first months of 2002. There's hot demand for mega-yachts and money's-no-object holiday packages, and there seems no limit on what people will spend for big-screen home-entertainment units. You've got to fill those vast basements with something.

mute, and a street loses some diversity. And that kind of creeping neighbourhood imperialism can tear at local heritage and destroy historically significant architecture. More practically for people nearby, demolition and construction projects produce months and sometimes years of aggravating noise, dirt and disruption.

Look-at-me displays of wealth may seem vulgar to some, but for those in the dough, it's all relative. For example, Bill Gates' 65,000-square-foot home sounds positively Versailles-like, but it's still smaller (by nearly 10,000 square feet) than the behemoth built for another Microsoft exec, Paul Allen. Perhaps Mr. Allen was thinking of having his football team, the Seattle Seahawks, play their home games at, well, home. Anyway, from that perspective, your neighbour's renovation suddenly appears restrained.

All of the excess would be less problematic if it weren't for the desire of others to keep up. Not everyone is driven by the consumer urge, but there's still a ton of house envy (or car or boat or you-name-it) out there, and that's the insidious downside of conspicuous consumption, says Robert Frank, a Cornell University economics professor and author of *Luxury Fever: Money and Happiness in an Era of Excess.* As the luxury bar gets set so much higher, he says, it tends to make less affluent people feel that they're falling behind — their circumstances may not have declined, but the gap between them and the rich is greater.

And while baby-boomers may once have seen themselves as anti-consumerism Woodstockers, they got over it while watching *Dynasty* and *Lifestyles of the Rich and Famous.* Most can't compete with the big-mansion set, but they're doing their best to transform their 25-foot lots. The average square footage of a North American home has increased by

more than 50 per cent in the last 30 years. That means more expensive mortgages and property taxes, and higher costs for everything from utilities to yard care. And you're supporting a life that's in keeping with others nearby — the car, the schools, the built-in fridge. "How do you afford it?" Frank asks. "Well, you have both parents working, you commute longer distances, you work longer hours, you save less and you borrow more." And that's led mainly by the spending at the top. "When everyone else builds bigger," he adds, "the main effect of that is to make you feel that you need to build bigger, too."

10 And for what? It bears asking because while conspicuous consumption may well enhance the economy, it's of no use to the people doing the spending if they're working too hard to enjoy the bigger houses and cars and TVs. And the money that's being spent keeping up could be used in other ways — everything from longer family holidays to charitable contributions — that enhance both domestic and community affairs. "The resources that it takes to build bigger," Frank says, "could be used for other things that, on objective grounds, would make more of a difference." Less of the good life to make a better life? It's a lovely concept, but not everyone's buying it.

*See *Con-Text* on page 325.

## CONTEXT

Figures from the U.S. Environmental Protection Agency from 2000 indicate that average fuel economy for all vehicles (various passenger cars, vans, light trucks, SUVs) was 23.6 miles per gallon. For vehicles classified as SUVs, vans, and pickup trucks, the figure was 18 miles per gallon. The five models with the lowest fuel economy were all SUVs. A report by the National Research Council indicates that increasing fuel efficiency results in lower consumption of oil and decreases emissions that contribute to greenhouse gases.

## LUXURY FEVER

"[T]he spending of the superrich, though sharply higher than in decades past, still constitutes just a small fraction of total spending. Yet their purchases are far more significant than might appear, for they have been the leading edge of pervasive changes in spending patterns of middle- and even low-income families. The runaway spending at the top has been a virus, one that's spawned a luxury fever that, to one degree or another, has all of us in its grip." Source: Robert H. Frank, *Luxury Fever: Money and Happiness in an Era of Excess* (2000).

# Questions for Discussion

**1.** Deacon discusses both benefits and drawbacks of conspicuous consumption. What are some of these benefits and drawbacks? Do you think Deacon presents a fair picture of conspicuous consumption? Why or why not? **2.** According to Deacon, what is the effect of the excessive consumption of the wealthy on less affluent people? What evidence does he provide to support this claim about the effect of such consumption? How persuasive do you find this evidence? **3.** On the basis of this essay, what do you think is Deacon's idea of "the good life"? What role should consumption play in that life, in Frank's view? Do you think Frank expects that most readers will agree with him on this point? Explain, citing specific passages from the essay to support your answer. **4.** This essay might be considered an example of an argument based on inductive reasoning (see pages 25–26). How effectively do you think Deacon leads us to his conclusion about conspicuous consumption?

③ NORMAN SOLOMON, **"Mixed Messages Call for Healthy Skepticism"**

Writer Norman Solomon has a very specific answer to the question of what it means to be a consumer: It means being skeptical. In the following essay Solomon examines what he sees as the contradictory messages conveyed by the news media, especially when it comes to issues such as health. For Solomon, who writes a syndicated column on media and politics, these contradictory messages are not just a reason for consumers to be skeptical of media reports; these contradictory messages also reflect a more fundamental problem in the media industry. As Solomon sees it, the media help to create the very health problems they report on, in large part because they support products that are unhealthy and environmentally destructive. In making his argument, Solomon encourages us to cast a skeptical eye on the news media. But perhaps more important, he may prompt us to reexamine our own habits and our beliefs about what it means to be a consumer. Solomon is coauthor (with Reese Erlich) of *Target Iraq: What the News Media Didn't Tell You* (2003). The following essay appeared in his syndicated column in 2003.

## Mixed Messages Call for Healthy Skepticism
### NORMAN SOLOMON

**1** A special issue of *Time,* the nation's biggest newsmagazine, was filled with health information in mid-January, offering plenty of encouragement under the rubric of medical science with an ethereal twist: "How Your Mind Can Heal Your Body."

The spread on "The Power of Mood" begins with this teaser: "Lifting your spirits can be potent medicine. How to make it work for you." An article about "Mother Nature's Little Helpers" is a discussion of alternative remedies. Other pieces probe techniques of psychotherapy, investigate high-tech ways of scanning the brain, and ponder "Are Your Genes to Blame?"

Of course, more than altruism is at work here. While the Jan. 20 issue of *Time* contains page after page of informative journalism, it also includes dozens of lucrative full-color ads pegged to the theme of health. There are elaborate pitches for laxative capsules, a purple pill for heartburn, over-the-counter sinus medication, and prescription drugs for allergies and Alzheimer's. On a preventative note, there's even a full-page ad for an inhaler that "helps you beat cigarette cravings one at a time" and another for a "stop smoking lozenge."

While all this was going on inside *Time* magazine, the same kind of advertising appeared in *Newsweek* to harmo-

nize with its cover's keynote: "What Science Tells Us About Food and Health."
**5** We may feel that it's nice of America's largest-circulation news weeklies to print so much healthful information. But if you picked up the previous week's *Time* and turned past the cover, the first thing you saw was a two-page layout for Camels, with the heading "Pleasure to Burn." Like the multi-entendre slogan, the ad's graphic is inviting; a handsome guy, presumably quite debonaire as he stands next to a liquor shelf, lights up a cigarette as he eyes the camera.

And so it goes. Many big media outlets tell us how to make ourselves healthy while encouraging us to make ourselves sick. They offer us tips and new scientific data on how to maximize longevity. But overall complicity with the lethal cigarette industry — whether through glamorization or silence — is widespread and ongoing.

The media's mixed messages about health are unabashedly self-contradictory, but they're also customary to such an extent that they're integral to a media cycle that never quits. The same news organizations that produce innumerable downbeat stories about obesity in America are beholden to huge quantities of ad revenue from fast food — and usually wink at the most popular artery-clogging chains. If most people are ignorant of the deep-fried dangers posed by McDonald's and Burger King, they can thank the news media for dodging the matter.

With television, radio and print media now devoting plenty of coverage to health concerns, and with aging baby boomers serving as a massive demographic target, the media emphasis is tilted toward high-end health expectations. But we need much more than news about the latest theories and scientific findings on preventative measures, palliatives and cures.

## FAST FOOD ADVERTISING

"White Castle is credited with being the first fast-food chain, opening the doors to its first restaurant in 1921. Eleven years later, the home of the square, steamed hamburger inaugurated another lasting trend — fast-food advertising — placing coupons in local newspapers.

"Columbus, Ohio–based White Castle has grown to 327 restaurants and $418 million in sales. Restaurant advertising has had its own, even more remarkable growth, topping $3 billion last year. Though the White Castle concept has changed little since 1932, restaurant advertising has become an increasingly sophisticated and high-stakes game.

"Oak Brook, Ill.–based McDonald's Corp. was the single most heavily advertised brand — in any product category — in 1998, according to Competitive Media Reporting, New York, even though the chain's total spending declined 1.2% to $569.2 million. The second most heavily advertised single brand last year also was a fast-food chain, Miami-based Burger King Corp. It, too, cut spending in 1998, reporting a 4.4% drop to $404.6 million.

"In third place was Taco Bell ($202.8 million), followed by Wendy's ($187.3 million) and KFC ($161.6 million).

"Together, these five restaurant chains accounted for nearly 2% of the $79.3 billion in consumer ad spending logged by all U.S. companies in all media, according to CMR data." Source: Paul O'Connor, "Getting the Message," *Restaurants and Institutions* magazine (1999).

**SENSE OF PLACE**

"I doubt that we will ever get the motion out of the Americans, for everything in his culture of opportunity and abundance has, up to now, urged motion on him as a form of virtue. Our tradition of restlessness will not be outgrown in a generation or two, even if the motives for restlessness are withdrawn. But after all, in a few months it will be half a millennium since Europeans first laid eyes on this continent. At least in geographical terms, the frontiers have been explored and crossed. It is probably time we settled down. It is probably time we looked around us instead of looking ahead. We have no business, any longer, in being impatient with history. We need to know our history in much greater depth, even back to geology, which, as Henry Adams said, is only history projected a little way back from Mr. Jefferson." **Source: Wallace Stegner, "The Sense of Place." (1986).**

Until news outlets shift their commitments, they will continue to undermine public health as well as promote it. The present-day contradictions are severe: Journalists do not equivocate about cancer; we all understand that there's nothing good about the disease. Yet journalists routinely go easy on proven causes of cancer, such as cigarettes and an array of commercially promoted chemicals with carcinogenic effects.

**10** Air pollution from gas-guzzling vehicles certainly qualifies as cancer-causing. But for every drop of ink that explores such causality, countless gallons are devoted to convincing Americans that they should own air-fouling trucks or SUVs. While the health-oriented front covers of *Time* and *Newsweek* now on the stands are similar, the back covers are identical

— an advertisement for Chevy's Silverado diesel truck. The headline trumpets the appeal: "A Sledgehammer in a Ballpeen World."

In a 1986 essay, the American writer Wallace Stegner wrote: "Neither the country nor the society we built out of it can be healthy until we stop raiding and running, and learn to be quiet part of the time, and acquire the sense not of ownership but of belonging."

Such outlooks are antithetical to the functional precepts of the media industry. It is largely dedicated to "raiding and running." It perceives quiet as dead air and squandered space. It portrays ownership as the essence of success and human worth. How healthy can such operative values be?

C O N T E X T

This essay appeared in 2003 on the Web site for Fairness and Accuracy in Reporting (FAIR), a national media watch group that describes itself as an anticensorship and progressive organization that "believes that structural reform is ultimately needed to break up the dominant media conglomerates, establish independent public broadcasting and promote strong non-profit sources of information. . . . We maintain a regular dialogue with reporters at news outlets across the country, providing constructive critiques when called for and applauding exceptional, hard-hitting journalism. We also encourage the public to contact media with their concerns, to become media activists rather than passive consumers of news." Consider the extent to which Solomon's essay is consistent with the purpose and perspective of FAIR.

## Questions for Discussion

**1.** Solomon opens this essay with descriptions of the contents and advertising of two issues of *Time* and *Newsweek,* two large and well-known newsmagazines. How effectively do you think these examples illustrate Solomon's claim that "the media's mixed messages about health are unabashedly self-contradictory"?

**2.** What does Solomon mean by his assertion that the media's mixed messages about health are "integral to a media cycle that never quits"? What exactly is the media cycle to which he refers? Why does it concern Solomon? Do you think his concern is justified? Explain. **3.** On the basis of this essay, identify what you think are Solomon's own views about a healthy lifestyle. Cite specific passages from his essay to support your answer. **4.** This essay originally appeared on a Web site maintained by Fairness and Accuracy in Reporting, a media watch group (see "Context" above). In what ways do you think this essay is addressed to the kind of readers who might visit the FAIR Web site? Do you think the essay makes an effective argument for a more general audience as well? Why or why not?

## ④ PETER SINGER, "The Singer Solution to World Poverty"

Do relatively comfortable consumers have any responsibility for people living in poverty? If so, what exactly is that responsibility? Well-known ethicist and philosopher Peter Singer has a very specific and provocative answer to those questions: Singer believes that people who are economically comfortable do indeed have a responsibility for the economic plight of others who may be less fortunate; moreover, he has calculated exactly what that responsibility is in dollar figures. He does so by examining how much money an average person in the United States must have to provide for basic needs. Any additional money, he asserts, is unnecessary and should be used to alleviate the pressing problem of world poverty. Singer's argument will no doubt raise a few eyebrows — especially among readers in the United States, where the consumption of goods is viewed almost as a fundamental right of all Americans. But although you might find Singer's views too extreme or idealistic, his essay challenges us to think about the responsibilities consumers have for others who share our planet. Singer addresses the matter of consumption as an overtly ethical issue. He surely knows that most consumers don't see it that way, and he understands that few Americans will take his advice and willingly give up such a substantial portion of their money to the poor. But he also believes that we must all accept our responsibility for each other. As you read, consider how far you believe that responsibility extends. Peter Singer is the Ira. W. DeCamp Professor of Bioethics at Princeton University and the author of many books about ethics, including *Animal Rights* (1975), *Practical Ethics* (1979), and *One World: The Ethics of Globalization* (2002). The following essay was published in the *New York Times Sunday Magazine* in 1999.

## The Singer Solution to World Poverty
### PETER SINGER

**1** In the Brazilian film *Central Station,* Dora is a retired schoolteacher who makes ends meet by sitting at the station writing letters for illiterate people. Suddenly she has an opportunity to pocket $1,000. All she has to do is persuade a homeless 9-year-old boy to follow her to an address she has been given. (She is told he will be adopted by wealthy foreigners.) She delivers the boy, gets the money, spends some of it on a television set and settles down to enjoy her new acquisition. Her neighbor spoils the fun, however, by telling her that the boy was too old to be adopted — he will be killed and his organs sold for transplantation. Perhaps Dora knew this all along, but after her neighbor's plain speaking, she spends a troubled night. In the morning Dora resolves to take the boy back.

Suppose Dora had told her neighbor that it is a tough world, other people have nice new TV's too, and if selling the kid is the only way she can get one, well, he was only a street kid. She would then have become, in the eyes of the audience, a monster. She redeems herself only by being prepared to bear considerable risks to save the boy.

At the end of the movie, in cinemas in the affluent nations of the world, people who would have been quick to condemn Dora if she had not rescued the boy go home to places far more comfortable than her apartment. In fact, the average family in the United States spends almost one-third of its income on things that are no more necessary to them than Dora's new TV was to her. Going out to nice restaurants, buying new clothes because the old ones are no longer stylish, vacationing at beach resorts — so much of our income is spent on things not essential to the preservation of our lives and health. Donated to one of a number of charitable agencies, that money could mean the difference between life and death for children in need.

All of which raises a question: In the end, what is the ethical distinction between a Brazilian who sells a homeless child to organ peddlers and an American who already has a TV and upgrades to a better one — knowing that the money could be donated to an organization that

would use it to save the lives of kids in need?

5 Of course, there are several differences between the two situations that could support different moral judgments about them. For one thing, to be able to consign a child to death when he is standing right in front of you takes a chilling kind of heartlessness; it is much easier to ignore an appeal for money to help children you will never meet. Yet for a utilitarian philosopher* like myself — that is, one who judges whether acts are right or wrong by their consequences — if the upshot of the American's failure to donate the money is that one more kid dies on the streets of a Brazilian city, then it is, in some sense, just as bad as selling the kid to the organ peddlers. But one doesn't need to embrace my utilitarian ethic to see that, at the very least, there is a troubling incongruity in being so quick to condemn Dora for taking the child to the organ peddlers while, at the

*Utilitarianism is a school of philosophy that is concerned with identifying the values and actions that will result in the greatest benefit for the most people.

**CONTEXT**

Originally organized in 1946 as the United Nations International Children's Emergency Fund to aid children who had been affected by World War II, UNICEF became a permanent part of the United Nations in 1953. Its primary mission is to work with governments and non-governmental organizations to address the plight of children living in poverty worldwide. Oxfam America offers financial and technical aid to grassroots organizations around the world in an effort to alleviate poverty, hunger, and injustice.

same time, not regarding the American consumer's behavior as raising a serious moral issue.

In his 1996 book, *Living High and Letting Die,* the New York University philosopher Peter Unger presented an ingenious series of imaginary examples designed to probe our intuitions about whether it is wrong to live well without giving substantial amounts of money to help people who are hungry, malnourished or dying from easily treatable illnesses like diarrhea. Here's my paraphrase of one of these examples:

Bob is close to retirement. He has invested most of his savings in a very rare and valuable old car, a Bugatti, which he has not been able to insure. The Bugatti is his pride and joy. In addition to the pleasure he gets from driving and caring for his car, Bob knows that its rising market value means that he will always be able to sell it and live comfortably after retirement. One day when Bob is out for a drive, he parks the Bugatti near the end of a railway siding and goes for a walk up the track. As he does so, he sees that a runaway train, with no one aboard, is running down the railway track. Looking farther down the track, he sees the small figure of a child very likely to be killed by the runaway train. He can't stop the train and the child is too far away to warn of the danger, but he can throw a switch that will divert the train down the siding where his Bugatti is parked. Then nobody will be killed — but the train will destroy his Bugatti. Thinking of his joy in owning the car and the financial security it represents, Bob decides not to throw the switch. The child is killed. For many years to come, Bob enjoys owning his Bugatti and the financial security it represents.

Bob's conduct, most of us will immediately respond, was gravely wrong.

Unger agrees. But then he reminds us that we, too, have opportunities to save the lives of children. We can give to organizations like UNICEF or Oxfam America. How much would we have to give one of these organizations to have a high probability of saving the life of a child threatened by easily preventable diseases? (I do not believe that children are more worth saving than adults, but since no one can argue that children have brought their poverty on themselves, focusing on them simplifies the issues.) Unger called up some experts and used the information they provided to offer some plausible estimates that include the cost of raising money, administrative expenses and the cost of delivering aid where it is most needed. By his calculation, $200 in donations would help a sickly 2-year-old transform into a healthy 6-year-old — offering safe passage through childhood's most dangerous years. To show how practical philosophical argument can be, Unger even tells his readers that they can easily donate funds by using their credit card and calling one of these toll-free numbers: (800) 367-5437 for Unicef; (800) 693-2687 for Oxfam America.

Now you, too, have the information you need to save a child's life. How should you judge yourself if you don't do it? Think again about Bob and his Bugatti. Unlike Dora, Bob did not have to look into the eyes of the child he was sacrificing for his own material comfort. The child was a complete stranger to him and too far away to relate to in an intimate, personal way. Unlike Dora, too, he did not mislead the child or initiate the chain of events imperiling him. In all these respects, Bob's situation resembles that of people able but unwilling to donate to overseas aid and differs from Dora's situation.

**10** If you still think that it was very wrong of Bob not to throw the switch that would have diverted the train and saved the child's life, then it is hard to see how you could deny that it is also very wrong not to send money to one of the organizations listed above. Unless, that is, there is some morally important difference between the two situations that I have overlooked.

Is it the practical uncertainties about whether aid will really reach the people who need it? Nobody who knows the world of overseas aid can doubt that such uncertainties exist. But Unger's figure of $200 to save a child's life was reached after he had made conservative assumptions about the proportion of the money donated that will actually reach its target.

One genuine difference between Bob and those who can afford to donate to overseas aid organizations but don't is that only Bob can save the child on the tracks, whereas there are hundreds of millions of people who can give $200 to overseas aid organizations. The problem is that most of them aren't doing it. Does this mean that it is all right for you not to do it?

Suppose that there were more owners of priceless vintage cars — Carol, Dave, Emma, Fred and so on, down to Ziggy — all in exactly the same situation as Bob, with their own siding and their own switch, all sacrificing the child in order to preserve their own cherished car. Would that make it all right for Bob to do the same? To answer this question affirmatively is to endorse follow-the-crowd ethics — the kind of ethics that led many Germans to look away when the Nazi atrocities were being committed. We do not excuse them because others were behaving no better.

We seem to lack a sound basis for drawing a clear moral line between Bob's situation and that of any reader of this article with $200 to spare who does not donate it to an overseas aid agency. These readers seem to be acting at least as badly as Bob was acting when he chose to let the runaway train hurtle toward the unsuspecting child. In the light of this conclusion, I trust that many readers will reach for the phone and donate that $200. Perhaps you should do it before reading further.

**15** Now that you have distinguished yourself morally from people who put their vintage cars ahead of a child's life, how about treating yourself and your partner to dinner at your favorite restaurant? But wait. The money you will spend at the restaurant could also help save the lives of children overseas! True, you weren't planning to blow $200 tonight, but if you were to give up dining out just for one month, you would easily save that amount. And what is one month's dining out, compared to a child's life? There's the rub. Since there are a lot of desperately needy children in the world, there will always be another child whose life you could save for another $200. Are you therefore obliged to keep giving until you have nothing left? At what point can you stop?

Hypothetical examples can easily become farcical. Consider Bob. How far past losing the Bugatti should he go? Imagine that Bob had got his foot stuck in the track of the siding, and if he diverted the train, then before it rammed the car it would also amputate his big toe. Should he still throw the switch? What if it would amputate his foot? His entire leg?

As absurd as the Bugatti scenario gets when pushed to extremes, the point it

COMPLICATION

According to a 1998 report from the American Institute of Philanthropy (AIP), only 26 percent of money donated to charities is actually used for the intended charitable purposes; the other 74 percent goes to cover the costs of fund raising. The AIP report continues, "When a charity that you have never supported or contacted is soliciting you through the mail or by phone, you should realize that most of the money sent in response to the solicitation will likely go to the cost of the solicitation campaign. Only through resolicitations, and in some cases by selling your name to other charities and businesses, will there be money left for charitable purposes."

CONTEXT

According to the National Restaurant Association, in 1999 the average American household spent $2116 on food while away from home, which works out to $846 per capita spending per year.

*Although there is no universally accepted definition of *middle class*, many economists use income figures to define the term, grouping the middle class around the national income average. For example, one measure sets middle-class annual income in the United States as ranging from about $25,000 to $65,000 per household, which would account for about 70 percent of all Americans. Another measure sets the range as $25,000 to $45,000, which would include about 25 percent of the U.S. population. Some economists and scholars define middle class by using other criteria, such as educational level and the kind of job a person holds or by setting a ratio of income to needs.

raises is a serious one: only when the sacrifices become very significant indeed would most people be prepared to say that Bob does nothing wrong when he decides not to throw the switch. Of course, most people could be wrong; we can't decide moral issues by taking opinion polls. But consider for yourself the level of sacrifice that you would demand of Bob, and then think about how much money you would have to give away in order to make a sacrifice that is roughly equal to that. It's almost certainly much, much more than $200. For most middle-class Americans,* it could easily be more like $200,000.

Isn't it counterproductive to ask people to do so much? Don't we run the risk that many will shrug their shoulders and say that morality, so conceived, is fine for saints but not for them? I accept that we are unlikely to see, in the near or even medium-term future, a world in which it is normal for wealthy Americans to give the bulk of their wealth to strangers. When it comes to praising or blaming people for what they do, we tend to use a standard that is relative to some conception of normal behavior. Comfortably off Americans who give, say, 10 percent of their income to overseas aid organizations are so far ahead of most of their equally comfortable fellow citizens that I wouldn't go out of my way to chastise them for not doing more. Nevertheless, they should be doing much more, and they are in no position to criticize Bob for failing to make the much greater sacrifice of his Bugatti.

At this point various objections may crop up. Someone may say: "If every citizen living in the affluent nations contributed his or her share I wouldn't have to make such a drastic sacrifice, because long before such levels were reached, the resources would have been there to save

the lives of all those children dying from lack of food or medical care. So why should I give more than my fair share?" Another, related, objection is that the Government ought to increase its overseas aid allocations, since that would spread the burden more equitably across all taxpayers.

**20** Yet the question of how much we ought to give is a matter to be decided in the real world — and that, sadly, is a world in which we know that most people do not, and in the immediate future will not, give substantial amounts to overseas aid agencies. We know, too, that at least in the next year, the United States Government is not going to meet even the very modest United Nations–recommended target of 0.7 percent of gross national product; at the moment it lags far below that, at 0.09 percent, not even half of Japan's 0.22 percent or a tenth of Denmark's 0.97 percent. Thus, we know that the money we can give beyond that theoretical "fair share" is still going to save lives that would otherwise be lost. While the idea that no one need do more than his or her fair share is a powerful one, should it prevail if we know that others are not doing their fair share and that children will die preventable deaths unless we do more than our fair share? That would be taking fairness too far.

Thus, this ground for limiting how much we ought to give also fails. In the world as it is now, I can see no escape from the conclusion that each one of us with wealth surplus to his or her essential needs should be giving most of it to help people suffering from poverty so dire as to be life-threatening. That's right: I'm saying that you shouldn't buy that new car, take that cruise, redecorate the house or get that pricey new suit.

After all, a $1,000 suit could save five children's lives.

So how does my philosophy break down in dollars and cents? An American household with an income of $50,000 spends around $30,000 annually on necessities, according to the Conference Board, a nonprofit economic research organization. Therefore, for a household bringing in $50,000 a year, donations to help the world's poor should be as close as possible to $20,000. The $30,000 required for necessities holds for higher incomes as well. So a household making $100,000 could cut a yearly check for $70,000. Again, the formula is simple: whatever money you're spending on luxuries, not necessities, should be given away.

Now, evolutionary psychologists tell us that human nature just isn't sufficiently altruistic to make it plausible that many people will sacrifice so much for strangers. On the facts of human nature, they might be right, but they would be wrong to draw a moral conclusion from those facts. If it is the case that we ought to do things that, predictably, most of us won't do, then let's face that fact head-on. Then, if we value the life of a child more than going to fancy restaurants, the next time we dine out we will know that we could have done something better with our money. If that makes living a morally decent life extremely arduous, well, then that is the way things are. If we don't do it, then we should at least know that we are failing to live a morally decent life — not because it is good to wallow in guilt but because knowing where we should be going is the first step toward heading in that direction.

When Bob first grasped the dilemma that faced him as he stood by that railway switch, he must have thought how extraordinarily unlucky he was to be placed in a situation in which he must choose between the life of an innocent child and the sacrifice of most of his savings. But he was not unlucky at all. We are all in that situation.

## Questions for Discussion

**1.** Singer opens this essay with a summary of a Brazilian film entitled *Central Station*. How effectively do you think this summary introduces the issue of poverty that Singer wishes to address? In what ways do you think the example of the film *Central Station* is appropriate for Singer's main argument? Does it matter whether you have seen the film? Explain. **2.** Examine the kinds of items and activities that Singer describes as unnecessary in this essay. What does his description of such things as unnecessary indicate about his values? Do you think most American readers would share those values? Do you think Singer expects that most of his readers would share his values? Explain, citing specific passages from his essay to support your answer. **3.** At one point in his essay, Singer poses the question, "What is the ethical distinction between a Brazilian who sells a homeless child to organ peddlers and an American who already has a TV and upgrades to a better one — knowing that the money could be donated to an organization that would use it to save the lives of kids in need?" How does he answer that question? How would you answer it? **4.** What issues does Singer use the hypothetical example of "Bob" to raise (see paragraphs 7–9)? How effective do you find this

# NEGOTIATING DIFFERENCES

As a group, the essays in this cluster raise several complicated questions about what it means to be a consumer. To a degree, though, all of these essays ask you to consider the implications of the choices you make as a consumer in a free market economy. This assignment asks you to explore the implications of your specific decisions as a consumer.

In an essay intended for an audience made up primarily of people who live in your region of the country, examine the effects of a decision to buy a specific item that is commonly available to consumers. For example, in their essays, James Deacon and Peter Singer mention

SUVs as questionable choices for consumers who are buying an automobile. You might consider other common items: entertainment equipment such as a television, certain kinds of clothing, services such as wireless telephone service, transportation such as airline travel. Once you have selected the item you wish to focus on, closely examine the reasons that you — or any consumer — might choose to buy that item. Look at the specific choices available for that item — for example, the different kinds of cars you could choose from if you were going to buy a car. Examine as well the possible effects that purchasing that item might have on the local economy, the environ-

example in raising these issues and in supporting Singer's main argument? Would some other kind of example be more effective, in your view? Explain. **5.** Singer addresses his readers directly as "you" throughout this essay, posing ethical dilemmas for his readers to consider. Evaluate the effectiveness of this strategy in helping Singer make his argument. What does he accomplish by addressing readers in this way? What potential drawbacks do you see in this strategy? Do you think Singer intends to make his readers uncomfortable by addressing them in this way? Explain, citing passages from his essay to support your answer. **6.** How does Singer arrive at the specific amount of money that he believes middle-class Americans should contribute to the poor? What purposes do you think his numerical calculations serve in supporting his argument? Do you think Singer is serious about the specific amount of money he believes Americans should give to the poor? Cites specific passages in the essay to support your answer. **7.** What counterarguments could you offer to Singer's proposal?

ment, your health, and the well-being of your neighbors or community. You might have to do some research to learn about such effects, and you might consider interviewing people who have made such a purchase. Once you have explored these matters, write an essay in which you make an argument about your responsibilities as a consumer. Use the item you have selected as an example to help make your argument.

Alternatively, select one of the essays in this cluster and write an argument in response to it. In your response, summarize the main argument of the essay you are responding to, identify the central issue that is being ad-

dressed in that essay, and explain why you think that the essay does not adequately address that issue. Offer an alternative approach to addressing the issue. For example, you might disagree with Peter Singer that contributing a significant portion of your income to the poor is an adequate way to address poverty. In responding to Singer, identify what you see as the central problem to be solved, and offer an alternative to his proposal. Be sure to justify your alternative on practical and ethical grounds.

# 13

**GLOBALIZATION**

GLOBAL

(1) Daniel Yergin, "Giving Aid to World Trade"

(2) Helena Norberg-Hodge, "The March of the Monoculture"

(3) Vandana Shiva, "The Living Democracy Movement: Alternatives to the Bankruptcy of Globalisation"

(4) Bjorn Skorpen Claeson, "Singing for the Global Community"

CON-TEXT
**The Marshall Plan**

ZATION

# IS GLOBALIZATION

# PROGRESS?

I n 1947, as the world was recovering from the appalling devastation of World War II, U.S. Secretary of State George C. Marshall outlined an expansive economic initiative to help Europe recover from the war. In a commencement speech at Harvard University, Marshall identified the need for nations to work together to rebuild the ruined European economies, and he claimed a leading role for the United States in doing so. (See *Con-Text* on page 351.) This initiative, which became known as the Marshall Plan, pumped millions of dollars of economic aid into Europe — money that was essential for those nations to return to economic health. But the Marshall Plan did more than help Europe rebuild its economy; it also reshaped the world economic map. Even as the Cold War that pitted the United States and its allies against the Soviet Union was starting up, the Marshall Plan was laying the foundation for a new global economy that would emerge decades later in the late 1980s when the Soviet Union broke apart. In this sense we can think of the Marshall Plan as an important step in the process that we now call globalization. ■ Globalization is a tricky term to define, but it refers to a general trend toward more numerous and intimate connections among nations around the world. For many, globalization is primarily an economic phenomenon. Since the 1980s the economies of individual nations have become more integrated, as developments such as the North America Free Trade Agreement (NAFTA) or the General Agreement of Trade and Tariffs (GATT) have facilitated international trade. But although globalization might be fueled by economic developments, it is not exclusively an economic phenomenon. Globalization also refers to the rapid increase of cross-cultural exchange, driven in part by powerful new communications technologies and media, including the Internet, and by increased international travel made possible by cheaper and more accessible transportation. With these new technologies both time and space become lesser obstacles to social and cultural interactions. The kind of exchange that was once rare, if not impossible — between, say, an American engineer from Seattle and a village leader in a remote region in Nepal — can now occur quite easily via the Internet. The frequency of such interactions, together with the expansion of broadcast media into previously isolated regions, have made the world a smaller place. In the process, the boundaries between cultures have become blurred, and some critics now describe a global consumer culture that is replacing what was once an extensive network of distinct and diverse cultures. (See Chapter 12 for readings on consumer culture.) American travelers might no longer be surprised to see a resident of a tiny village in Central Asia wearing Nike running shoes or a T-shirt emblazoned with the New York Yankees baseball team logo. It is perhaps more surprising to realize how much larger and separate the world seemed when George C. Marshall gave his famous commencement address in 1947. His statement that "the people of this country are distant from the troubled areas of the earth" no longer seems true. ■ For many globalization represents great opportunity and progress. It means that the villager in Nepal can have access to the same consumer goods as a shopper in New York City. It means that an immigrant from Ukraine living in Fort Worth, Texas, can read the news of his homeland in his native language by buying a Ukrainian newspaper at his local newsstand or by visiting a Ukrainian Web site. But globalization has a growing number of critics. In the early years of the 21st century, as world economies became more integrated, large-scale protests against globalization became common at meetings of international organizations such as the World Bank and the World Trade Organization. For some critics globalization represents not opportunity but the growing power of multinational corporations and the dominance of American consumer culture at the expense of local cultures. It means that people have less control as more and more aspects of their lives seem to be determined by distant economic and cultural forces. ■ The essays in this cluster highlight these complexities. Each one makes an argument about some aspect of globalization: economic, cultural, political, social. In the process, these essays remind us why globalization can be so difficult to define and understand. They also remind us that this process that we now call globalization is perhaps the most important development of our time — perhaps even more important than the Marshall Plan proved to be in post–World War II Europe. For that reason alone, arguments about globalization are increasingly important.

## CON-TEXT: The Marshall Plan

1 I need not tell you gentlemen that the world situation is very serious. That must be apparent to all intelligent people. I think one difficulty is that the problem is one of such enormous complexity that the very mass of facts presented to the public by press and radio make it exceedingly difficult for the man in the street to reach a clear appraisement of the situation. Furthermore, the people of this country are distant from the troubled areas of the earth and it is hard for them to comprehend the plight and consequent reactions of the long-suffering peoples, and the effect of those reactions on their governments in connection with our efforts to promote peace in the world. . . .

There is a phase of this matter which is both interesting and serious. The farmer has always produced the foodstuffs to exchange with the city dweller for the other necessities of life. This division of labor is the basis of modern civilization. At the present time it is threatened with breakdown. The town and city industries are not producing adequate goods to exchange with the food-producing farmer. Raw materials and fuel are in short supply. Machinery is lacking or worn out. The farmer or the peasant cannot find the goods for sale which he desires to purchase. So the sale of his farm produce for money which he cannot use seems to him an unprofitable transaction. He, therefore, has withdrawn many fields from crop cultivation and is using them for grazing. He feeds more grain to stock and finds for himself and his family an ample supply of food, however short he may be on clothing and the other ordinary gadgets of civilization. Meanwhile people in the cities are short of food and fuel. So the governments are forced to use their foreign money and credits to procure these necessities abroad. This process exhausts funds which are urgently needed for reconstruction. Thus a very serious situation is rapidly developing which bodes no good for the world. The modern system of the division of labor upon which the exchange of products is based is in danger of breaking down.

The truth of the matter is that Europe's requirements for the next three or four years of foreign food and other essential products — principally from America — are so much greater than her present ability to pay that she must have substantial additional help or face economic, social, and political deterioration of a very grave character.

The remedy lies in breaking the vicious circle and restoring the confidence of the European people in the economic future of their own countries and of Europe as a whole. The manufacturer and the farmer throughout wide areas must be able and willing to exchange their products for currencies the continuing value of which is not open to question.

SOURCE: George C. Marshall, U.S. Secretary of State, Commencement Address, Harvard University, June 5, 1947.

# ① DANIEL YERGIN, "Giving Aid to World Trade"

One of the most persistent criticisms of economic globalization is that it contributes to poverty, particularly in developing nations whose populations are already poor. Some critics point out that as multinational corporations take advantage of relaxed international trade policies to increase their business in developing nations, they exploit resources at the expense of local populations. Daniel Yergin, a leading proponent of globalization, argues that such criticisms miss the point. In the following essay, which appeared in the summer of 2002 as members of the Group of Eight, a powerful international trade organization, were meeting in Canada, he maintains that globalization offers opportunities for poorer nations to reap the same benefits that wealthier nations enjoy. The key, according to Yergin, is greater access to international trade, so that developing nations can become successful participants in the world marketplace. Their success, in turn, will lead to prosperity for their citizens. In acknowledging that this process is not necessarily easy, Yergin implicitly reminds us that economic progress, which we tend to think of as a good thing, is never simple and can sometimes result in losers as well as winners in the marketplace. His essay might encourage you to examine some of the tradeoffs we may all face as global markets evolve. Daniel Yergin is coauthor of *The Commanding Heights: The Battle for the World Economy* (1998) and the author of *The Prize: The Epic Quest for Oil, Money and Power* (1991), for which he received the Pulitzer Prize. This essay was first published in the *New York Times*.

## Giving Aid to World Trade
### DANIEL YERGIN

1 By meeting in an idyllic retreat in the Canadian Rockies, leaders of the Group of 8, a conference of the leading industrial powers plus Russia, may succeed in avoiding the critics of globalization. But they will hardly be getting away from the question of global poverty. Confronting Africa's appalling economic distress is at the top of their agenda.

One of the great tests for globalization will be its inclusiveness — what it does to improve the plight of the terribly poor in developing countries. Sept. 11 has pushed the question even more to the fore, as is evident in the 50 percent increase in foreign aid — reaching a level of $15 billion in three years — proposed by the Bush administration in March.

But the debate is often upside down, with critics of globalization contending that it causes poverty. On the contrary,

globalization — in the form of expanded trade and investment — offers the most significant means for reducing poverty. Foreign aid can play a very important role in relieving hardship and helping poor countries improve health, education and national infrastructure. It can also help build legal and lending institutions, making it possible for the poor to participate in market economies and poor countries to participate in the global economy. Such improvements can attract long-term foreign investment that creates jobs and encourages transfers of technologies to poorer nations.

It is trade, however, that is the primary engine for economic development. The best proof is from some nations in Asia. Four decades ago, Asian countries were among the poorest in the world. They varied widely in their political systems, but the common theme among the economically successful countries was their engagement with the world trading system. The results have been extraordinary. In 1960 South Korea was as poor as India. Today its per capita income is 20 times higher than India's.

**5** In the last decade, India has also moved to participate more actively in the world economy through trade. Within India, this engagement has stimulated growth rates, and now India is on its way to becoming a force in the world economy. It's hard to imagine the Internet as we know it without India and Indian technologists.

Singapore provides an even more dramatic example. In the late 1960's, it was so poor that its very survival was problematic. Today its per capita income is higher than Britain's.

For developing countries to benefit from trade, the first requirement is better access to markets in developed countries and increased flows of investment. That was the message of the developing countries that was lost in the din of the

*In 1999 the meeting of the World Trade Organization (WTO) in Seattle was the focus of large protests by a number of advocacy groups and nongovernmental organizations opposed to the policies of the WTO. Thousands of protesters gathered in the streets of Seattle during the WTO meetings, sometimes clashing with police. The event became known as the "Battle in Seattle."

World Trade Organization meeting in Seattle in 1999.*

What would expanding trade mean for poorer nations? Sub-Saharan Africa, hit by falling commodity prices, poorly governed and unable to attract even much domestic investment, missed out on the manufacturing-led trade boom of the late 20th century. But if it were simply to regain the share of the world's non-oil exports that it held in 1980, it would have earned $161 billion in 2000 — not the $69 billion it actually earned.

Developing countries need to work to make themselves, as Singapore's senior minister, Lee Kuan Yew, has put it, "relevant" to the world economy in terms of education, skills, legal systems and economic culture.

**10** At the same time, industrialized countries need to reduce barriers to imports from the poorest countries, a principle that has been increasingly recognized by the United States and the European Union. But it's a principle that needs to be put into practice.

For expanded market access to work, it must be accompanied by adjustment mechanisms in the industrial countries for workers that are adversely affected. But it would be a great error to think that giving poorer countries a share of global trade means a loss for the industrial countries.

In the 1990's, world trade, American imports and American exports all doubled. In that same decade, 17 million new jobs, on a net basis, were created in the United States. By any calculation, that's a pretty good deal, and one well worth remembering in these troubled economic times.

---

### COMPLICATION

"As Yergin noted, expanded trade has indeed fueled startling economic development in Asia over the past four decades. What he didn't mention was that the three countries he cited as examples — South Korea, India, and Singapore — have been among the world's worst mercantilists and interventionists. Does Yergin really want the rest of the third world to follow this example? Could global economic stability possibly tolerate this?" Source: Alan Tonelson, "Follies: Yergin-Nonsense, Not Yergin-omics," TradeAlert.org (2002).

### COMPLICATION

Arguments about trade and globalization often involve statistical information, such as Daniel Yergin uses in this essay. But there is often disagreement about how to measure such things as income and economic output; moreover, economists often disagree on what these figures mean. In paragraph 6 Yergin states that Singapore had a higher per capita income than Britain's in 2002. However, according to the World Bank, per capita income in Britain in 2001 was $24,230 (U.S. dollars). At the same time the government of Singapore reported that per capita income in that country was approximately $23,000. It is possible that Singapore's per capita income surpassed Britain's in 2002. It is also possible that Yergin used different figures, which might have reflected different formulas for calculating per capita income. Such subtle differences in statistics like these underscore the need to examine statistical evidence carefully in an argument. (See also the discussion of evidence on pages 76–81.)

# Questions for Discussion

**1.** On what basis does Yergin make his claim that trade is the primary engine for the economic development of poor nations? How effective is Yergin's evidence for this claim? **2.** Much of Yergin's essay is devoted to discussion of examples of countries that he believes have evolved from poverty into economic successes. How convincing do you think these specific examples are in helping Yergin make his argument? Do you think these examples will make sense to most readers? Explain. (Keep in mind that Yergin's essay was originally published in the *New York Times*, which has a large national and international readership.) **3.** Examine Yergin's use of statistical information in this essay. What kinds of statistics does he provide? How relevant are these statistics to his claims? Do you think most readers would find these statistics to be persuasive? Why or why not? (See "Complication" on page 354.) **4.** Yergin wrote this essay just as representatives from the Group of Eight were meeting in western Canada to discuss trade-related issues, including poverty in developing nations. In what ways is Yergin's argument specifically connected to this event? Do you think his main argument would be relevant even if it were not connected to the G-8 meeting? Explain. **5.** Yergin's essay might be considered an example of an essay based on inductive reasoning. How effectively do you think his approach helps him make his argument? (In answering this question, you might wish to refer to the discussion of arguments based on inductive reasoning on pages 25–26.)

② HELENA NORBERG-HODGE, **"The March of the Monoculture"**

As Helena Norberg-Hodge points out in the following essay, globalization not only results in economic change, but can also have a profound and devastating impact on local cultures. Where many advocates of globalization see great benefits in the increased availability of consumer goods in remote places, Norberg-Hodge sees the loss of distinctive and vibrant ways of life. In this sense, she suggests, the costs of globalization might far outweigh its benefits. Moreover, she argues that the ideal of the "global village" might reflect Western values that are not shared by other cultures. But what is most troubling to Norberg-Hodge is that although the global consumer culture that is replacing many local cultures might bring more material goods for consumers, it might not result in greater well-being for individuals. In other words, this emerging global monoculture could make our lives less happy, less satisfying, less fulfilling. This is a disconcerting view of globalization. Even if you do not share her view, Norberg-Hodge's essay might prompt you to consider the implications of globalization for the kind of life you hope to have. Helena Norberg-Hodge is the director of the International Society for Ecology and Culture, a nonprofit organization promoting local culture and biodiversity.

# The March of the Monoculture
## HELENA NORBERG-HODGE

**1** Around the world, the pressure to conform to the expectations of the spreading, consumer monoculture is destroying cultural identity, eliminating local economies and erasing regional differences. As a consequence the global economy is leading to uncertainty, ethnic friction, and collapse, where previously there had been relative security and stability.

For many, the rise of the global economy marks the final fulfillment of the great dream of a 'Global Village'. Almost everywhere you travel today you will find multi-lane highways, concrete cities and a cultural landscape featuring grey business suits, fast-food chains, Hollywood films and cellular phones. In the remotest corners of the planet, Barbie, Madonna and the Marlboro Man are familiar icons. From Cleveland to Cairo to Caracas, Baywatch is entertainment and CNN news.

The world, we are told, is being united by virtue of the fact that everyone will soon be able to indulge their innate human desire for a Westernised, urbanised consumer lifestyle. West is best, and joining the bandwagon brings closer a harmonious union of peaceable, rational, democratic consumers 'like us'.

This world-view assumes that it was the chaotic diversity of cultures, values and beliefs that lay behind the chaos and conflicts of the past: that as these differences are removed, so the differences between us will be resolved.

5 As a result, all around the world, villages, rural communities and their cultural traditions, are being destroyed on an unprecedented scale by the impact of globalising market forces. Communities that have sustained themselves for hundreds of years are simply disintegrating. The spread of the consumer culture seems virtually unstoppable.

## Consumers R Us: The Development of the Global Monoculture

Historically, the erosion of cultural integrity was a conscious goal of colonial developers. As applied anthropologist Goodenough explained: "The problem is one of creating in another a sufficient dissatisfaction with his present condition of self so that he wants to change it. This calls for some kind of experience that leads him to reappraise his self-image and re-evaluate his self-esteem."[1] Towards this end, colonial officers were advised that they should:

"1: Involve traditional leaders in their programmes.

2: Work through bilingual, acculturated individuals who have some knowledge of both the dominant and the target culture.

3: Modify circumstances or deliberately tamper with the equilibrium of the traditional culture so that change will become imperative.

4: Attempt to change underlying core values before attacking superficial customs."[2]

It is instructive to consider the actual effect of these strategies on the well-being of individual peoples in the South. For example, the Toradja tribes of the Poso district in central Celebes (now Sulawesi, Indonesia) were initially deemed completely incapable of 'development' without drastic intervention. Writing in 1929, A.C. Kruyt reported that the happiness and stability of Toradja society was such that "development and progress were impossible" and that they were "bound to remain at the same level".[3]

Toradja society was cashless and there was neither a desire for money nor the extra goods that might be purchased with it. In the face of such contentment, mission work proved an abject failure as the Toradjas had no interest in converting to a new religion, sending their children to school or growing cash crops. So, in 1905 the Dutch East Indies government decided to bring the Poso region under firm control, using armed force to crush all resistance. As a result of relocation and continual government harassment, mortality rates soared among the Toradjas. Turning to the missionaries for help, they were "converted" and began sending their children to school. Eventually they began cultivating coconut and coffee plantations and began to acquire new needs for oil lamps, sewing machines, and 'better' clothes. The self-sufficient tribal economy had been superseded, as a result of deliberate government action.

In many countries, schooling was the prime coercive instrument for changing "underlying core values" and proved to be a highly effective means of destroying self-esteem, fostering new 'needs', creating dissatisfactions, and generally disrupting traditional cultures. An excerpt from a French reader designed in 1919 for use by French West African schoolchildren gives a flavour of the kinds of pressure that were imposed on children:

"It is . . . an advantage for a native to work for a white man, because the

Whites are better educated, more advanced in civilisation than the natives. . . . You who are intelligent and industrious, my children, always help the Whites in their task. That is a duty."[4]

### The Situation Today: Cultural Erosion

**10** Today, as wealth is transferred away from nation states into the rootless casino of the money markets, the destruction of cultural integrity is far subtler than before. Corporate and government executives no longer consciously plan the destruction they wreak — indeed they are often unaware of the consequences of their decisions on real people on the other side of the world. This lack of awareness is fostered by the cult of specialisation and speed that pervades our society — the job of a public relations executive is confined to producing business-friendly soundbites — time pressures and a narrow focus prevent a questioning of the overall impact of corporate activity. The tendency to undermine cultural diversity proceeds, as it were, on 'automatic pilot' as an inevitable consequence of the spreading global economy.

But although the methods employed by the masters of the 'Global Village', are less brutal than in colonial times, the scale and effects are often even more devastating. The computer and telecommunications revolutions have helped to speed up and strengthen the forces behind the march of a global monoculture, which is now able to disrupt traditional cultures with a shocking speed and finality which surpasses anything the world has witnessed before.

### Preying on the Young

Today, the Western consumer conformity is descending on the less industrialised parts of the world like an avalanche. 'Development' brings tourism, Western films and products and, more recently, satellite television to the remotest corners of the Earth. All provide overwhelming images of luxury and power. Adverts and action films give the impression that everyone in the West is rich, beautiful and brave, and leads a life filled with excitement and glamour.

In the commercial mass culture which fuels this illusion, advertisers make it clear that Westernised fashion accessories equal sophistication and 'cool'. In diverse 'developing' nations around the world, people are induced to meet their needs not through their community or lo-

cal economy, but by trying to 'buy in' to the global market. People are made to believe that, in the words of one US advertising executive in China, "imported equals good, local equals crap".

Even more alarmingly, people end up rejecting their own ethnic and racial characteristics — to feel shame at being who they are. Around the world, blonde-haired blue-eyed Barbie dolls and thin-as-a-rake 'cover girls' set the standard for women. Already now, seven-year-old girls in Singapore are suffering from eating disorders. It is not unusual to find east Asian women with eyes surgically altered to look more European, dark-haired southern European women dying their hair blonde, and Africans with blue- or green-coloured contact lenses aimed at 'correcting' dark eyes.

**15** The one-dimensional, fantasy view of modern life promoted by the Western media, television and business becomes a slap in the face for young people in the 'Third World'. Teenagers, in particular, come to feel stupid and ashamed of their traditions and their origins. The people they learn to admire and respect on television are all 'sophisticated' city dwellers with fast cars, designer clothes, spotlessly clean hands and shiny white teeth. Yet they find their parents asking them to choose a way of life that involves working in the fields and getting their hands dirty for little or no money, and certainly no glamour. It is hardly surprising, then, that many choose to abandon the old ways of their parents for the siren song of a Western material paradise.

For millions of young people in rural areas of the world, modern Western culture appears vastly superior to their own. They see incoming tourists spending as much as $1,000 a day — the equivalent of a visitor to the US spending about $50,000 a day. Besides promoting the il-

lusion that all Westerners are multi-millionaires, tourism and media images also give the impression that we never work — since for many people in 'developing' countries, sitting at a desk or behind the wheel of a car does not constitute work.

People are not aware of the negative social or psychological aspects of Western life so familiar to us: the stress, the loneliness and isolation, the fear of growing old alone, the rise in clinical depression and other 'industrial diseases' like cancer, stroke, diabetes and heart problems. Nor do they see the environmental decay, rising crime, poverty, homelessness and unemployment. While they know their own culture inside out, including all of its limitations and imperfections, they only see a glossy, exaggerated side of life in the West.

## Ladakh: The Pressure to Consume

My own experience among the people of Ladakh or 'Little Tibet', in the trans-Himalayan region of Kashmir, is a clear, if painful, example of this destruction of traditional cultures by the faceless consumer monoculture. When I first arrived in the area 23 years ago, the vast majority of Ladakhis were self-supporting farmers, living in small scattered settlements in the high desert. Though natural resources were scarce and hard to obtain, the Ladakhis had a remarkably high standard of living — with beautiful art, architecture and jewellery. Life moved at a gentle pace and people enjoyed a degree of leisure unknown to most of us in the West. Most Ladakhis only really worked for four months of the year, and poverty, pollution and unemployment were alien concepts. In 1975, I remember being shown around the remote village of Hemis Shukpachan by a young Ladakhi called Tsewang. It seemed to me, a newcomer, that all the

CONTEXT

Situated in mountainous northern India, Ladakh is part of the arid Tibetan plateau. Once nearly isolated from outside societies, Ladakh remains remote and sparsely populated, though it has seen Western-style economic development in the form of tourism and trade in locally made arts and crafts. In recent years, as travel and communication have connected it more intimately with the rest of India, Ladakh has been affected by the sometimes violent tensions among Muslims, Hindus, and Buddhists in the Indian state of Kashmir, of which Ladakh is part.

houses I saw were especially large and beautiful, and I asked Tsewang to show me the houses where the poor lived. He looked perplexed for a moment, then replied, "We don't have any poor people here."

In recent years external forces have caused massive and rapid disruption in Ladakh. Contact with the modern world has debilitated and demoralised a once-proud and self-sufficient people, who today are suffering from what can best be described as a cultural inferiority complex. When tourism descended on Ladakh some years ago, I began to realise how, looked at from a Ladakhi perspective, our modern, Western culture appears much more successful, fulfilled and sophisticated than we find it to be from the inside.

**20** In traditional Ladkhi culture, virtually all basic needs — food, clothing and shelter, were provided without money. Labour was free of charge, part of an intricate and long-established web of human relationships. Because Ladakhis had no need for money, they had little or none. So when they saw outsiders — tourists and visitors — coming in, spending what was to them vast amounts of cash on inessential luxuries, they suddenly felt poor. Not realising that money was essential in the West — that without it, people often go homeless or even starve — they didn't realise its true value. They began to feel inadequate and backward. Eight years after Tsewang had told me that Ladakhis had no poverty, I overheard him talking to some tourists. "If you could only help us Ladakhis," he was saying, "we're so poor."

Tourism is part of the overall development which the Indian government is promoting in Ladakh. The area is being integrated into the Indian, and hence the global, economy. Subsidised food is imported from the outside, while local farmers who had previously grown a variety of crops and kept a few animals to provide for themselves have been encouraged to grow cash crops. In this way they are becoming dependent on forces beyond their control huge transportation networks, oil prices, and the fluctuations of international finance. Over the course of time, financial inflation obliges them to produce more and more, so as to secure the income that they now need in order to buy what they used to grow themselves. In political terms, each Ladakhi is now one individual in a national economy of 800 million, and, as part of a global economy, one of about six billion.

As a result of external investments, the local economy is crumbling. For generation after generation Ladakhis grew up learning how to provide themselves with clothing and shelter; how to make shoes out of yak skin and robes from the wool of sheep; how to build houses out of mud and stone. As these building traditions give way to 'modern' methods, the plentiful local materials are left unused, while competition for a narrow range of modern materials — concrete, steel and plastic — skyrockets. The same thing happens when people begin eating identical staple foods, wearing the same clothes and relying on the same finite energy sources. Making everyone dependent on the same resources creates efficiency for global corporations, but it also creates an artificial scarcity for consumers, which heightens competitive pressures.

As they lose the sense of security and identity that springs from deep, long-lasting connections to people and place, the Ladakhis are starting to develop doubts about who they are. The images they get from outside tell them to be different, to own more, to buy more and to thus be 'better' than they are. The previously strong, outgoing women of Ladakh have been replaced by a new generation — unsure of themselves and desperately concerned with their appearance. And as their desire to be 'modern' grows, Ladakhis are turning their backs on their traditional culture. I have seen Ladakhis wearing wristwatches they cannot read, and heard them apologising for the lack of electric lighting in their homes — electric lighting which, in 1975, when it first appeared, most villagers laughed at as an unnecessary gimmick. Even traditional foods are no longer a source of pride; now, when I'm a guest in a Ladakhi village, people apologise if they serve the traditional roasted barley, ngamphe, instead of instant noodles.

Ironically, then, modernisation — so often associated with the triumph of individualism — has produced a loss of individuality and a growing sense of personal insecurity. As people become self-conscious and insecure, they feel pressured to conform, and to live up to an idealised image. By contrast, in the traditional village, where everyone wore essentially the same clothes and looked the same to the casual observer, there was more freedom to relax. As part of a close-knit community, people felt secure enough to be themselves.

**25** In Ladakh, as elsewhere, the breaking of local cultural, economic and political ties isolates people from their locality and from each other. At the same time, life speeds up and mobility increases — making even familiar relationships more superficial and brief. Competition for scarce jobs and political representation within the new centralised structures increasingly divides people. Ethnic and religious differences began to take on a political dimension, causing bitterness and enmity on a scale hitherto unknown. With a desperate irony, the monoculture — instead of bringing people together, creates divisions that previously did not exist.

As the fabric of local interdependence fragments, so do traditional levels of tolerance and co-operation. In villages near the capital, Leh, disputes and acrimony within previously close-knit communities, and even within families, are increasing. I have even seen heated arguments over the allocation of irrigation water, a procedure that had previously been managed smoothly within a co-operative framework. The rise in this kind of new rivalry is one of the most painful divisions that I have seen in Ladakh. Within a few years, growing competition has actually culminated in violence (see "Complication" on page 362) — and this in a place where, previously, there had been no group conflict in living memory.

## Deadly Divisions

The rise of divisions, violence and civil disorder around the world are the consequence of attempts to incorporate di-

## TENSIONS IN LADAKH

Norberg-Hodge refers to political and ethnic tensions that have emerged in recent years in Ladakh. Those tensions relate to longstanding religious and ethnic conflicts in India, of which Ladakh is part. In 2001 *The Indian Express* reported on one Ladakhi leader, Lama Lobzang, who attempted to find solutions to these conflicts, which had worsened in nearby regions of Kashmir. Here is part of that report:

A key campaigner for separate Union Territory status for Ladakh region, Lama Lobzang, has said that autonomy for Jammu and Kashmir could be the best solution possible for the state's problems, if it is coupled with trifurcation of the state. The Lama, also a member of the Scheduled Castes and Scheduled Tribes Commission, said trifurcation was the only realistic solution to the Kashmir tangle within the ambit of the Constitution. Speaking to *The Indian Express*, the Lama said Ladakhis were "disturbed with the hobnobbing between the Centre and the J-K government over autonomy package." Ladakhis, he said, foresaw a bleak future for themselves if more political powers were given to Jammu and Kashmir without giving cognisance to the feelings of the people of the other two regions. . . . Ladakh's problem, the Lama said, was a gradual encroachment upon their land and political powers by the Kashmiri-speaking people. He alleged it was being done under a design and with the blessings from the National Conference government. Moreover, the state was communalising the situation in the border region by brazenly favouring Muslims in admissions to professional colleges and jobs against Buddhists. Source: Aasha Khosa, "Autonomy with trifurcation is the answer: Ladakh leader."

verse cultures and peoples into the global monoculture. These divisions often deepen enough to result in fundamentalist reaction and ethnic conflict. Ladakh is by no means an isolated example.

In Bhutan, where different ethnic groups had also lived peaceably together for hundreds of years, two decades of economic development have resulted in the widespread destruction of decentralised livelihoods and communities — unemployment, once completely unknown, has reached crisis levels. Just like in Ladakh, these pressures have created intense competition between individuals and groups for places in schools, for jobs, for resources. As a result, tensions between Buddhists and Bhutanese Hindus of Nepalese origin have led to an eruption of violence and even a type of 'ethnic cleansing'.

Elsewhere, Nicholas Hildyard has written of how, when confronted with the horrors of ethnic cleansing in Yugoslavia or Rwanda, it is often taken for granted that the cause must lie in ingrained and ancient antagonisms. The reality, however, as Hildyard notes, is different: **30** "Scratch below the surface of interethnic civil conflict, and the shallowness and deceptiveness of 'blood' or 'culture' explanations are soon revealed. 'Tribal hatred' (though a real and genuine emotion for some) emerges as the product not of 'nature' or of a primordial 'culture', but of a complex web of politics, economics, history, psychology and a struggle for identity."[5]

In a similar vein, Michel Chossudovsky, Professor of Economics at the University of Ottawa, argues that the current Kosovo crisis has its roots at least partly in the macro-economic reforms imposed by Belgrade's external creditors such as the International Monetary Fund (IMF). Multi-ethnic Yugoslavia was a regional industrial power with relative economic success. But after a decade of Western economic ministrations and five years of disintegration, war, boycott, and embargo, the economies of the former Yugoslavia are in ruins. Chossudovsky writes:

"In Kosovo, the economic reforms were conducive to the concurrent impoverishment of both the Albanian and Serbian populations contributing to fuelling ethnic tensions. The deliberate manipulation of market forces destroyed economic activity and people's livelihood creating a situation of despair."[6]

It is sometimes assumed that ethnic and religious strife is increasing because modern democracy liberates people, allowing old, previously suppressed, prejudices and hatreds to be expressed. If there was peace earlier, it is thought it was the result of oppression. But after more than twenty years of first-hand experience on the Indian subcontinent, I am convinced that economic 'development' not only exacerbates existing tensions but in many cases actually creates them. It breaks down human-scale structures, it destroys bonds of reciprocity and mutual dependence, while encouraging people to substitute their own culture and values with those of the media. In effect this means rejecting one's own identity — rejecting one's self.

Ultimately, while the myth makers of the 'Global Village' celebrate values of togetherness, the disparity in wealth between the world's upper income brackets and the 90 per cent of people in the poor countries represents a polarisation far more extreme than existed in the 19th century. Use of the word 'village' — intended to suggest relative equality, belonging and harmony — obscures a reality of high-tech islands of privilege and wealth towering above oceans of impoverished humanity struggling to survive. The global monoculture is a dealer in illusions — while it destroys traditions, local economies and sustainable ways of living, it can never provide the majority

CONTEXT

Helena Norberg-Hodge directs the International Society for Ecology and Culture (ISEC). According to its Web site, ISEC promotes "locally based alternatives to global consumer culture." Based in Great Britain, ISEC is "a non-profit organisation concerned with the protection of both biological and cultural diversity. Our emphasis is on *education for action:* moving beyond single issues to look at the more fundamental influences that shape our lives." Norberg-Hodge was involved in an ISEC project in Ladakh that began the 1970s. Consider the extent to which her long experience in that region might influence her credibility as author of this essay.

with the glittering, wealthy lifestyle it promised them. For what it destroys, it provides no replacement but a fractured, isolated, competitive and unhappy society.

## References:

1. Quoted, John Bodley, Victims of Progress, Mayfield Publishing, 1982, pp. 111–112.
2. Ibid., p. 112.
3. Ibid., p. 129.
4. Ibid., p. 11.
5. N. Hildyard, Briefing 11 — Blood and Culture: Ethnic Conflict and the Authoritarian Right, The Cornerhouse, 1999.
6. M. Chossudovsky, Dismantling Yugoslavia, Colonising Bosnia, Ottawa, 1996, p. 1.

## Questions for Discussion

**1.** Near the beginning of her essay, Norberg-Hodge asserts that "we are told" that the world is being united in a global, Western-style consumer culture. Who is the "we" to whom she refers here? Why do you think Norberg-Hodge begins her essay in this fashion? What advantages do you see to such a beginning? What disadvantages? **2.** Early in her essay Norberg-Hodge refers to the ideas of an anthropologist about the impact of colonial power on local culture. What point does she use these ideas to make? How is this point related to her main argument about globalization? **3.** Norberg-Hodge cites several historical examples of non-Western societies becoming "converted" to Western values and economic practices. What do these examples illustrate, in her view? Do you find these examples persuasive? Why or why not? Do you think they strengthen or weaken her argument? Explain. **4.** According to Norberg-Hodge, what are the differences between the destruction of local cultures by the current process of globalization and the destruction caused by colonialization in previous eras? Why is this difference important to her main argument? **5.** Evaluate Norberg-Hodge's use of the example of Ladakh to help her make her main argument. What points does she use this example to make? What specific details about Ladakh does she include in making these points? How effective do you think this example is in supporting her main argument? **6.** Throughout her essay Norberg-Hodge challenges the view that a Western-style consumer culture is good for all people. She claims that such a consumer culture reflects values that not all cultures share. On the basis of your reading of this essay, what values regarding lifestyle and community do you think Norberg-Hodge holds? Do you think most Western readers share these values? Cite specific passages from her essay to support your answer. **7.** How does Norberg-Hodge support her claim that consumer culture does not lead to a better life? What specific kinds of evidence does she cite? How convincing is this evidence, in your view? Do you think she presents a fair picture of consumer culture and its possible benefits and disadvantages? Why or why not?

**8.** How would you describe the tone of this essay? Do you think the tone is appropriate to the subject matter? Explain. In what ways might the tone enhance or weaken the main argument?

③ VANDANA SHIVA, "The Living Democracy Movement: Alternatives to the Bankruptcy of Globalisation"

In 1999, when thousands of anti-globalization activists gathered in Seattle to protest the policies of the World Trade Organization (WTO), the press labeled the event "The Battle in Seattle." Press reports during the protests sometimes focused on the unusually diverse nature of the protesters: environmentalists, animal rights activists, trade unionists and advocates for workers rights, civil libertarians, even anarchists. Many very different people, it seemed, had a wide range of concerns that were somehow connected to the process of globalization. Some critics suggested that this diversity of concerns indicated a lack of a clear purpose to the antiglobalization movement; according to such critics, that was why so many different interests were represented among the protesters. But the following essay by human rights and environmental activist Vandana Shiva suggests another explanation: So many different concerns were expressed by the protesters because globalization involves so much more than economic policy. Shiva, a physicist who has become one of the world's foremost critics of globalization, argues that the policies of international organizations such as the WTO are not only economic measures, but also reflect philosophical, political, and ecological beliefs that are not shared by the world population. For Shiva the process of globalization that is fueled by such policies is bankrupt because it reduces the complex needs of human beings to commodities. In rejecting globalization, Shiva transforms the issue from an economic one to a human one. Her argument is challenging, but it reminds us that the growing debates about globalization are intense precisely because the stakes are so high. Vandana Shiva founded the Research Foundation for Science, Ecology, and Technology, which supports biodiversity and indigenous foods and local cultures. The following essay was originally delivered as an address to the World Social Forum in 2002.

## The Living Democracy Movement: Alternatives to the Bankruptcy of Globalisation
### VANDANA SHIVA

### The Bankruptcy of Globalisation

**1** Globalisation was projected as the next great leap of human evolution in a linear forward march from tribes to nations to global markets. Our identities and context were to move from the national to the global, just as in the earlier phase of state driven globalisation, it was supposed to have moved from the local to the global.

Deregulated commerce and corporate

**5** The dominant political and economic order has a number of features that are new, which increase injustice and non-sustainability on scales and at rates that the earth and human community have not experienced.

1. It is based on enclosures of the remaining ecological commons — biodiversity, water and air, and the destruction of local economies on which people's livelihoods and economic security depends.
2. The commodification of water and biodiversity is ensured through new property rights built into trade agreements like the WTO which are transforming people's resources into corporate monopolies viz. TRIPs and trade in environmental goods and services.
3. The transformation of commons to commodities is ensured through shifts in governance with decisions moving from communities and countries to global institutions, and rights moving from people to corporations through increasingly centralised and unaccountable states acting on the principle of eminent domain* — the absolute sovereignty of the ruler.

rule was offered as the alternative to the centralised bureaucratic control under communist regimes and state dominated economies. Markets were offered as an alternative to states for regulating our lives, not just our economies.

As the globalisation project has unfolded, it has exposed its bankruptcy at the philosophical, political, ecological and economic levels. The bankruptcy of the dominant world order is leading to social, ecological, political and economic non-sustainability, with societies, ecosystems, and economies disintegrating and breaking down.

The philosophical and ethical bankruptcy of globalisation was based on reducing every aspect of our lives to commodities and reducing our identities to merely that of consumers on the global market place. Our capacities as producers, our identity as members of communities, our role as custodians of our natural and cultural heritage were all to disappear or be destroyed. Markets and consumerism expanded. Our capacity to give and share were to shrink. But the human spirit refuses to be subjugated by a world view based on the dispensability of our humanity.

This in turn led to political bankruptcy and anti-democratic formations and constellations. Instead of acting on the public trust doctrine and principles of democratic accountability and subsidiarity, globalisation led to governments usurping power from parliaments, regional and local governments, and local communities.

For example the TRIPs agreement was based on central governments hijacking the rights to biodiversity and knowledge from communities and assigning them as exclusive, monopolistic rights to corporations.

*Eminent domain is a principle by which a government can acquire private property for public use, such as parks, public transportation, or defense. Usually, laws require governments to compensate private citizens or businesses that lose property to eminent domain.

The Agreement on Agriculture was based on taking decisions away from farming communities and regional governments.

The General Agreement on Trade in Services (GATS) takes decisions and ownership over water from the local and public domain to the privatised, global domain. This undemocratic process of privatisation and deregulation led to increased political bankruptcy and corruption and economic bankruptcy.

A decade of corporate globalisation has led to major disillusionment and discontentment. Democracy has been eroded, livelihoods have been destroyed. Small farmers and businesses are going bankrupt everywhere. Even the promise of economic growth has not been delivered. Economic slow down has been the outcome of liberalising trade. Ironically some corporations that led the process of trade liberalisation and globalisation have themselves collapsed.
10 Enron[†] which came to India as the "Flagship" project of globalisation with the full force of backing and blackmail by the U.S. Trade Representative has gone bankrupt and is steeped in scandals of corruption. Chiquita, which forced the banana wars on Europe through a U.S./Europe W.T.O. dispute has also declared bankruptcy.

First South East Asia, now Argentina have exposed how vulnerable and volatile current economic arrangements are.

The non-sustainability and bankruptcy of the ruling world order is fully evident. The need for alternatives has never been stronger.

## Creating Alternatives to Corporate Globalisation
During the last decade of the 20th century, corporate driven globalisation shook up the world and the economic and polit-ical structures that we have shaped to govern us.

In December 1999, citizens of the world rebelled against the economic to-talitarianism of corporate globalisation. Social and economic justice and ecological sustainability became the rallying call for new movements for citizen freedoms and liberation from corporate control.
15 September 11th 2001 shut down the spaces that people's movements had opened up. It also brought back the focus on the intimate connection between violence, inequality and non-sustainability and the indivisibility of peace, justice and sustainability. Doha[‡] was rushed through in the shadow of global militarisation in response to the terror attacks.

As we face the double closure of spaces by corporate globalisation and militarised police states, by economic facism aided by political facism, our challenge is to reclaim our freedoms and the freedoms of our fellow beings. Reclaiming and recreating the indivisible freedom of all species is the aim of the Living Democracy Movement. The living democracy movement embodies two indivisibilities and continuums. The first is the continuum of freedom for all life on earth, and all humans without discrimination on the basis on gender, race, religion, class and species. The second is the continuum between and indivisibility of justice, peace and sustainability — without sustainability and just share of the earth's bounties there is no justice, and without justice three can be no peace.

Corporate globalisation ruptures these continuities. It establishes corporate rule through a divide and rule policy, and creates competition and conflict between different species and peoples and between different aims. It transforms diversity and multiplicity into oppositional differences both by breeding fundamentalisms through spreading insecurity and

[†]A large U.S. energy-trading corporation, Enron was beset by accounting scandals in 2002.

[‡]Doha, Qatar, was the site of the Fourth World Trade Organization Ministerial Conference, in November 2001.

CONTEXT

TRIPs, GATS, and the Agreement on Agriculture, international agreements negotiated by the World Trade Organization, all relax barriers to various kinds of trade and thus contribute to economic globalization. TRIPs, the Agreement On Trade-Related Aspects of Intellectual Property Rights, governs international copyright and related issues. GATS, the General Agreement on Trade in Services, sets international trade policies on such services as telecommunications and transportation. The Agreement on Agriculture is intended to open national agricultural markets to international competition by reducing agricultural subsidies that governments often provide for their farmers. These three agreements, along with the General Agreement on Trade and Tariffs, form the foundation of the international economic policies of the WTO and are often the focus of protest and criticism.

then using these fundamentalisms to shift humanities focus and preoccupation from sustainability and justice and peace to ethnic and religious conflict and violence.

We need a new paradigm to respond to the fragmentation caused by various forms of fundamentalism. We need a new movement which allows us to move from the dominant and pervasive culture of violence, destruction and death to a culture of non-violence, creative peace and life. That is why in India we started the living democracy movement.

### Creative Resistance

Seattle was a watershed for citizens movements.* People brought an international trade agreement and W.T.O. the institution that enforces it to a halt by mobilising globally against corporate globalisation. Seattle was the success of a strategy focussing on the global level and on protest. It articulated at the international level what citizens do not want. Corporations and governments responded quickly to Seattle's success. They killed protest possibilities by moving to venues like Doha where thousands could not gather. And they started to label protest and dissent of any kind as "terrorism".

20 The Biotech industry (*Economist,* Jan 12th, 18th, p. 62) has called on governments to use anti-terror laws against groups like Greenpeace and Friends of the Earth and groups critical of the industry.

Mr. Zoellick, the US Trade Representative has called the anti-globalisation movement terrorist.

A different strategy is needed post September 11/post Doha. Massive protests at global meetings can no longer be the focus on citizen mobilisation. We need international solidarity and autonomous organising. Our politics needs

to reflect the principle of subsidiarity. Our global presence cannot be a shadow of the power of corporations and Bretton Woods institutions.[†] We need stronger movements at local and national levels, movements that combine resistance and constructive action, protests and building of alternatives non-cooperation with un-just rule and cooperation within society. The global, for us, must strengthen the local and national, not undermine it. The two tendencies that we demand of the economic system needs to be central to people's politics — localisation and al-

*Seattle was the site of meetings of the World Trade Organization in 1999 that drew thousands of protestors. See the sidebar on page 354 in this cluster.

†In July 1944, representatives of nations from around the world met at a resort called Bretton Woods in New Hampshire to discussion international economic and monetary policy. The agreement that was adopted at Bretton Woods established the International Bank for Reconstruction and Development, a precursor to the World Bank.

## COMPLICATION

Robert Zoellick, the U.S. Trade Representative, spoke out about the importance of economic globalization in the wake of the terrorist attacks of September 11, 2001. According to a press release by the U.S. Department of State in September, 2001,

The U.S. trade representative also challenged the anti-globalization movement. "We will not be intimidated by those who have taken to the streets to blame trade — and America — for the world's ills," he said. Erecting new barriers to trade won't help the poor, but open markets will, he said. Zoellick noted that per capita income for globalizing developing countries has grown at more than 5 percent annually compared to 1 percent a year for non-globalizing countries. The absolute poverty rates for globalizing developing countries, he added, have fallen sharply over the past 20 years.

Zoellick further argued that trade liberalization will add stability to skittish global financial markets by providing important stimulus for global economic recovery.

ternatives. Both are not just economic alternatives they are democratic alternatives. Without them forces for change cannot be mobilised in the new context.

At the heart of building alternatives and localising economic and political systems is the recovery of the commons and the reclaiming of community. The living democracy movement is reclaiming people's sovereignty and community rights to natural resources.

Rights to natural resources are natural rights. They are not given by States, nor can they be extinguished by States, the W.T.O, or by corporations, even though under globalisation, attempts are being made to alienate people's rights to vital resources of land water and biodiversity.
**25** Globalisation has relocated sovereignty from people to corporations, through centralising, militarising States. Rights of people are being appropriated by States to carve out monopoly rights of corporations over our land, our water, our biodiversity, our air. States acting on the principle of eminent domain or absolute sovereignty of the State are undermining people's sovereign rights and their role as trustees of people's resources on the public trust doctrine. State sovereignty, by itself, is therefore not enough to generate countervailing forces and processes to corporate globalisation.

The reinvention of sovereignty has to be based on the reinvention of the state so that the state is made accountable to the people. Sovereignty cannot reside only in centralised state structures, nor does it disappear when the protective functions of the state with respect to its people start to wither away. The new partnership of national sovereignty needs empowered communities which assign functions to the state for their protec-

tion. Communities defending themselves always demand such duties and obligations from state structures. On the other hand, TNCs and international agencies promote the separation of the community interests from state interests and the fragmentation and divisiveness of communities.

## The Living Democracy Movement

We started the living democracy movement to respond to the enclosures of the commons that is at the core of economic globalisation. The living democracy movement is simultaneously an ecology movement, an anti-poverty movement, a recovery of the commons movement, a deepening of democracy movement, a peace movement. It builds on decades of movements defending people's rights to resources, the movements for local, direct democracy, our freedom movements gifts of Swadeshi (economic sovereignty),

Swaraj (self-rule) and Satyagraha (non-cooperation with unjust rule). It seeks to strengthen rights enshrined in our Constitution.

The living democracy movement in India is a movement to rejuvenate resources, reclaim the commons and deepen democracy. It relates to the democracy of life in three dimensions.

Living democracy refers to the democracy of all life, not just human life. It is about earth democracy not just human democracy.

30 Living democracy is about life, at the vital everyday level, and decisions and freedoms related to everyday living — the food we eat the clothes we wear, the water we drink. It is not just about elections and casting votes once in 3 or 4 or 5 years. It is a permanently vibrant democracy. It combines economic democracy with political democracy.

Living democracy is not dead, it is alive. Under globalisation, democracy even of the shallow representative kind is dying. Governments everywhere are betraying the mandates that brought them to power. They are centralising authority and power, both by subverting democratic structures of constitutions and by promulgating ordinances that stifle civil liberties. The September 11 tragedy has become a convenient excuse for anti-people legislation worldwide. Politicians everywhere are turning to xenophophic and fundamentalist agendas to get votes in a period when economic agenda have been taken away from national levels and are being set by World Bank, IMF, W.T.O. and global corporations.

The living democracy movement is about living rather that dead democracy. Democracy is dead when governments no longer reflect the will of the people but are reduced to anti-democratic unaccountable instruments of corporate rule under the constellation of corporate globalisation as the Enron and Chiquita case make so evident. Corporate globalisation is centered on corporate profits.

Living democracy is based on maintaining life on earth and freedom for all species and people.

Corporate globalisation operates to create rules for the global, national and local markets which privilege global corporations and threaten diverse species, the livelihoods of the poor and small, local producers and businesses.

35 Living democracy operates according to the ecological laws of nature, and limits commercial activity to prevent harm to other species and to people.

Corporate globalisation is exercised through centralising, destructive power.

Living democracy is exercised through decentralised power and peaceful coexistence.

## CHIQUITA BANANA DISPUTE

In 1993 the European Union (EU) imposed stiff new tariffs on bananas imported to Europe from countries that were not members of the EU or territories of EU nations. Chiquita Brands International, Inc., a U.S. company, challenged the EU policy, charging that it discriminated against bananas produced in Latin American nations, where Chiquita operated. The dispute continued throughout the 1990s, during which time the World Trade Organization (WTO) issued several rulings on the case. In 1999 the United States, frustrated by developments in the case, retaliated by imposing new tariffs on several kinds of imports from European nations. In 2001 the EU agreed to a new policy, to be implemented by 2006, that would effectively open European markets to banana imports from countries that have been subject to its high tariffs. This agreement between the European Union and the United States generally conformed to WTO rulings on the issue. Although some criticized the ruling, it was generally seen as the end of the dispute.

Corporate globalisation globalises greed and consumerism. Living democracy globalises compassion, caring and sharing.

Democracy emptied of economic freedom and ecological freedom becomes a potent breeding ground for fundamentalism and terrorism.

**40** Over the past two decades, I have witnessed conflicts over development and conflicts over natural resources mutate into communal conflicts, culminating in extremism and terrorism. My book *Violence of the Green Revolution* was an attempt to understand the ecology of terrorism. The lessons I have drawn from the growing but diverse expressions of fundamentalism and terrorism are the following:

Nondemocratic economic systems that centralize control over decision making and resources and displace people from productive employment and livelihoods create a culture of insecurity. Every policy decision is translated into the politics of "we" and "they." "We" have been unjustly treated, while "they" have gained privileges.

Destruction of resource rights and erosion of democratic control of natural resources, the economy, and means of production undermine cultural identity. With identity no longer coming from the positive experience of being a farmer, a craftsperson, a teacher, or a nurse, culture is reduced to a negative shell where one identity is in competition with the "other" over scarce resources that define economic and political power.

Centralized economic systems also erode the democratic base of politics. In a democracy, the economic agenda is the political agenda. When the former is hijacked by the World Bank, the IMF, or the WTO, democracy is decimated. The only cards left in the hands of politicians eager to garner votes are those of race, religion, and ethnicity, which subsequently give rise to fundamentalism. And fundamentalism effectively fills the vacuum left by a decaying democracy. Economic globalisation is fueling economic insecurity, eroding cultural diversity and identity, and assaulting the political freedoms of citizens. It is providing fertile ground for the cultivation of fundamentalism and terrorism. Instead of integrating people, corporate globalization is tearing apart communities.

The survival of people and democracy are contingent on a response to the double facism of globalization — the economic facism that destroys people's rights to resources and the fundamentalist facism that feeds on people's displacement, dispossession, economic insecurities, and fears. On September 11, 2001, the tragic terrorist attacks on the World Trade Center and at the Pentagon unleashed a "war against terrorism" promulgated by the US government under George W. Bush. Despite the rhetoric, this war will not contain terrorism because it fails to address the roots of terrorism — economic insecurity, cultural subordination, and ecological dispossession. The new war is in fact creating a chain reaction of violence and spreading the virus of hate. And the magnitude of the damage to the earth caused by "smart" bombs and carpet bombing remains to be seen.

**45** Living Democracy is true freedom of all life forms to exist on this earth.

Living Democracy is true respect for life, through equitable sharing of the earth's resources with all those who live on the planet.

Living Democracy is the strong and continual articulation of such democratic principles in everyday life and activity.

The constellation of living democracy is people's control over natural resources, and a just and sustainable utilisation of land, water, biodiversity, communities having the highest sovereignty and delegating power to the state in its role as trustee. The shift from the principle of eminent domain to the public trust doctrine for functions of the State is key to localisation, to recovery of the commons and the fight against privatisation and corporate take over of land, water and biodiversity.

This shift is also an ecological imperative. As members of the earth family, Vasudhaiva Kutumbhakam, we have a share in the earth's resources. Rights to natural resources for needs of sustenance are natural rights. They are not given or assigned. They are recognised or ignored. The eminent domain principle inevitably leads to the situation of "all for some" — corporate monopolies over biodiversity through patents, corporate monopolies on water through privatisation and corporate monopolies over food through free trade.

50 The most basic right we have as a species is survival, the right to life. Survival requires guaranteed access to resources. Commons provide that guarantee. Privatisation and enclosures destroy it. Localisation is necessary for recovery of the commons. And living democracy is the movement to relocate our minds, our production systems and consumption patterns from the poverty creating global markets to the sustainability and sharing of the earth community. This shift from global markets to earth citizenship is a shift of focus from globalisation to localisation of power from corporations to citizens. The living democracy movement is a movement to establish that a better world is not just possible, it is necessary.

## Questions for Discussion

**1.** What specifically does Shiva mean by "the bankruptcy of globalisation"? How does she establish that globalization is "bankrupt"? Cite specific passages from her essay to support your answer. **2.** According to Shiva, what do we lose when markets and consumerism grow? Do you think she is right? Why or why not? **3.** What is the "dominant political and economic order," as Shiva sees it? What features of this dominant order does she identify? Why are these features important, in her view? How does her discussion of these features fit into her main argument? **4.** How would you describe the style and tone of this essay? Identify specific words and phrases that you think contribute to this style. In what ways do you think the style and tone are appropriate for the argument Shiva makes in this essay? **5.** At one point in her essay Shiva writes, "The non-sustainability and bankruptcy of the ruling world order is fully evident. The need for alternatives has never been stronger." What evidence does Shiva offer for this claim? What kinds of evidence does she offer for her claims about globalization in general? Do you think her use of evidence strengthens or weakens her essay? Explain. **6.** As an alternative to globalization, Shiva proposes what she calls the Living Democracy Movement. What exactly is this movement, as Shiva describes it? What are its primary characteristics and goals? In what specific ways does it differ from globalization? Do you think the goals and principles of this movement are widely shared? Explain. **7.** On what fundamental rights or beliefs does Shiva base her argument? To what extent do you think these rights or beliefs strengthen or weaken her argument?

④ **BJORN SKORPEN CLAESON, "Singing for the Global Community"**

In the late 1990s and the first years of the 21st century, large-scale protests against globalization became almost commonplace. Each meeting of the World Trade Organization or the World Bank seemed to attract thousands of protesters followed by hundreds of journalists, whose articles and television reports often focused on the number of protesters and sometimes on clashes between protesters and security forces. The irony of such large-scale events is that they seemed to obscure the very same individuals whom the protesters claimed are most negatively affected by globalization. In the following essay, Bjorn Skorpen Claeson tries to keep those individuals in view by putting a human face on the concerns that are so often heard in protests against globalization. He describes a different kind of event that occurred in Bangor, Maine, in the summer of 2002: a concert and fair that were intended not only to publicize the plight of the workers whose lives have been harmed by globalization, but also to celebrate these same workers and the global community we are all part of. In comparison to the weighty and sometimes angry arguments that focus on the political and economic aspects of globalization, Claeson's essay might strike you as idealistic and perhaps even romantic. But his argument about what it means to be part of a world that is increasingly interdependent is not so easy to dismiss. As you read, consider the values that lie at the heart of Claeson's concerns for the people he describes. To what extent might his values represent a realistic vision for the global community to which we all contribute in some way? Bjorn Skorpen Claeson is an organizer with Peace through Interamerican Community Action (PICA). This essay was published in the Bangor (Maine) *Daily News* in 2002.

## Singing for the Global Community
### BJORN SKORPEN CLAESON

*Well-known folk singer Pete Seeger (b. 1919) has also been a political activist whose views made him a target during the anticommunist campaigns of the 1950s. Among the many songs he composed are "If I Had a Hammer" and "Where Have All the Flowers Gone."

1 Imagine 50 children from across the globe, arm in arm, singing out: "Drop the gun! Drop the gun!" That promises to be a highlight of the Concert for Our Future, Thursday, July 11, at the Bangor City Waterfront Park.

Eleven-year-olds from Brazil, Chile, El Salvador, Mexico, the United States, Canada, Norway, Sweden, Finland, Germany, Italy and India living together in an international month-long children's summer village in Old Town will join members of the St. Mary's youth choir to open the concert with Pete Seeger's* latest song, "Take It From Doctor King." Written in response to Sept. 11 and intended for children to teach adults, the song carries an important message: Let's expand our sense of community across boundaries of nation, language, race and class for, surely, a semi-permanent state of war is not a solution with which most people can live.

We hard-to-convince hardened adults might do well to memorize the song's refrain: "Don't say it can't be done. The battle's just begun. Take it from Doctor King. You too can learn to sing!"

The children, the concert and the immediately preceding Clean Clothes Fair speak to us of international community, a notion that is increasingly rare in the versions of the globalization story that most of us today are living to some extent.

5 In one such version there are two main sorts of characters. First there are the consumers who are painted as passive, atomized and disengaged from workers by complicated corporate chains of production. They are more or less economically secure but feel powerless to make change since the market, rather than human beings, is in control. Confined into an artificially safe and insulated universe, consumers' ability to do good rests on their ability to buy. According to this version of globalization, consumers might even be called upon to make a sacrifice by buying products made in poor countries: the more we buy, the better for them.

The other main set of characters are the disposables: the anonymous, the nobodies, the forgotten, the excluded. They are not only in the Southern Hemisphere, or in poor, developing countries. In Bangor, they are, for example, laid-off shoe workers who receive a fraction of what they need to survive in unemployment insurance, while the companies that once employed them now make the very same shoes in China for a fraction of Maine wages and higher profits. "To be considered disposable by the country we so dearly love is intolerable," says one.

In China, they are, for example, the shoe workers who toil 14 to 16 hours a day, seven days a week, in an environment of intense heat and stinging odor.

They are an expendable, short-term source of labor to be used until worn out. These are the people whom Thomas Friedman, in his celebrated telling of this story of globalization, "The Lexus and the Olive Tree," calls "turtles" (see page 376): They simply don't run fast enough in the fast world and are desperately trying to avoid becoming road kill. In this fashion the gap between the consumers and the disposables grows ever wider.

In another now often-told version of this globalization story this gap has become charged with hostility and danger. It's a world of "us and them," people lumped into mutually exclusive categories who are for or against, good or evil, black or white.

Differences, middle grounds and alternatives have gone the way of dialogue, diplomacy and understanding. Believing "it can't be done," we suspend ourselves in a state of "yellow alert," a neverending conflict without borders.
10 The Concert for Our Future and the Clean Clothes Fair help us break the artificial isolation imposed by consumerism and the new go-at-italone mentality. At the fair the workers behind the labels are real human beings whose lives are woven into the very clothes we wear. Come and meet Hathaway shirt workers from Waterville selling the

CONTEXT

The Clean Clothes Fair is part of the Clean Clothes Campaign, which is an effort to publicize the poor conditions of workers in the garment industry. According to the Web site for the Campaign, "the purchasing power of consumers is being mobilized on the issue of working conditions in the garment industry." Through publications, rallies, and the Internet the Campaign tries to educate consumers, particularly young people, about the origins of the clothes they buy. (See www.cleanclothes.org/campaign.htm.)

## THE LEXUS AND THE OLIVE TREE

"The defining economists of the globalization system are Joseph Schumpeter and former Intel CEO Andy Grove, who prefer to unleash capitalism. Schumpeter, a former Austrian Minister of Finance and Harvard Business School professor, expressed the view in his classic work, *Capitalism, Socialism and Democracy*, that the essence of capitalism is the process of "creative destruction" — the perpetual cycle of destroying the old and less efficient product or service and replacing it with new, more efficient ones. Andy Grove took Schumpeter's insight that "only the paranoid survive" . . . and made it in many ways the business model of globalization capitalism. Grove helped to popularize the view that dramatic, industry-transforming innovations are taking place today faster and faster. Thanks to these technological breakthroughs, the speed by which your latest invention can be made obsolete or turned into a commodity is now lightning quick. Therefore, only the paranoid, only those who are constantly looking over their shoulders to see who is creating something new that will destroy them and then staying just one step ahead of them, will survive. Those countries that are most willing to let capitalism quickly destroy inefficient companies, so that money can be freed up and directed to more innovative ones, will thrive in the era of globalization. Those which rely on their governments to protect them from such creative destruction will fall behind in this era." Source: Thomas L. Friedman, *The Lexus and the Olive Tree* (1999).

products they make. Come and hear the stories of immigrant Mexican workers in Los Angeles who have found respect and dignity as union workers making the new SweatX label. Learn about artisans in West Africa, Nepal, Thailand, El Salvador and Peru from local small businesses committed to fair trade without middle-men. Meet local Native American artisans who tell the stories of their lives and histories in their crafts. Hear music from West Africa, the Andes and local indigenous people. The people without voice will be speaking loud and clear.

Perhaps because either-or choices don't come naturally to children, or because their curiosity and imagination defy the artificial limits of consumerism, our children can teach us a story of globalization where our sense of community is as global as our economy. We should be all ears.

# NEGOTIATING DIFFERENCES

Part of the challenge of negotiating the debates about globalization is understanding just what is meant by the term *globalization*. As the essays in this cluster suggest, participants in these debates define the term in different ways and focus on different aspects of globalization: social, cultural, economic, political, and philosophical. If we are to make arguments that can lead to viable solutions to the problems associated with globalization, then we must understand just what globalization is. This assignment encourages you to do so.

Imagine that you are participating in an international conference of college students who are concerned about globalization. Your task is to write a position statement on globalization for the conference. If your teacher allows it, consider working with a group of your classmates to complete this assignment.

To accomplish this task will require two steps. First, you will need to do some research on globalization to gain an understanding of what people mean by that term and what the most important concerns about globalization are. You might start with the four essays in this cluster, but you might also wish to consult additional sources. There are many very good sources, and part of your challenge will be

# Questions for Discussion

**1.** What are the two versions of the "globalization story" that Claeson describes in his essay? What is his purpose in describing these two versions? How do they contribute to his main argument? **2.** What is the vision of a global community that Claeson offers? On what values or beliefs is his vision based? Do you think most people would share his vision? **3.** Examine Claeson's descriptions of the workers who he claims are most directly affected by globalization. What specific details does he provide about these workers? What kind of picture do these details paint? How effectively does this picture contribute to his main argument?

**4.** Claeson claims that globalization has been framed in public discussion as a debate about how "the consumers" can deal with "the disposables." He asserts that the children's concert addresses globalization in a way that avoids such "either-or" thinking. Examine the articles in this cluster and determine whether you see this kind of either-or thinking. Visit the Clean Clothes Campaign, Rugmark and SweatX Web sites. Do these organizations provide the kind of exploration of "differences" and "middle ground" that Claeson believes is important? **5.** Claeson's essay is connected to a specific event that occurred in Maine in 2002. In what ways does that specific context influence his argument? In what ways might his description of that event enhance or weaken his main argument about globalization? **6.** Claeson's appeal in this essay is both an announcement for an event and an argument about workers' rights. After reading this article, would you be inclined to attend the event he is announcing?

sorting through the wide range of available sources. You might begin by visiting this Web site: www.globalisationguide.org/01.html.

Once you have gained a better understanding of globalization, draft your position statement. Your statement should clearly define the issues associated with globalization that you (and your classmates) consider to be most important. These issues can be related to jobs, poverty, the environment, politics, or any other concerns you see as important. Your statement should also present a position on these issues and justify that position. Ideally, your position should address the concerns of many

other people about globalization. In other words, your position statement can make an argument that is a step toward solving the problems associated with globalization.

Alternatively, consider organizing a student forum to address the issues that you and your classmates have identified as important. This forum can be limited to members of your class, but you might also consider a larger forum involving students and faculty at your school as well as community members. In organizing this forum, develop a flyer that explains the purpose of the forum and its intended outcome.

TEXT
CREDITS

**Chapter 4, pp. 106–107**
From online discussion at http://groups.google.com. Reprinted by permission.

**Figure 6.3**
From www.google.com. Reprinted by permission.

**Figure 6.4**
From www.google.com. Reprinted by permission.

**Figure 6.6**
Reprinted by permission of OCLC Online Computer Library Center, Inc. and the H.W. Wilson Co.

**Figure 6.7**
Reprinted by permission of OCLC Online Computer Library Center, Inc. and the H.W. Wilson Co.

**Figure 6.8**
Reprinted by permission of OCLC Online Computer Library Center, Inc. and the H.W. Wilson Co.

**Figure 6.9**
From web.lexis-nexis.com.

**Figure 6.10**
From web.lexis-nexis.com.

**Figure 6.11**
Reprinted by permission of University Libraries, University at Albany, SUNY.

**Andante**
From www.andante.com. Reprinted by permission.

**Harvey Araton**
"Mixed Doubles in a World Gone Mad" by Harvey Araton from THE NEW YORK TIMES, July 2, 2002. Copyright © 2002 The New York Times Co. Reprinted by permission.

**Pamela Bailey**
Letter to editor by Pamela G. Bailey from CLEVELAND PLAIN DEALER, September 4, 2002.

**Filip Bondy**
"Ronaldo Earns His Glory" by Filip Bondy as appeared in the ALBANY TIMES UNION, July 1, 2002. Reprinted by permission of Tribune Media Services.

**John F. Borowski**
From "Is the Trend of Trashing Textbooks in Texas Going National?" by John F. Borowski from COMMON-DREAMS.org, August 27, 2002.

**CBS**
"Red Faces at the Red Cross." Copyright © 2002 CBS Worldwide Inc. All Rights Reserved. Originally broadcast on The Evening News with Dan Rather on July 30, 2002 over the CBS Television Network.

**Gregory Cizek**
"Unintended Consequences of High Stakes Testing" by Gregory Cizek from EducationNews.org. Reprinted by permission of the author.

**Bjorn Claeson**
"Singing for the Global Community" by Bjorn Claeson from BANGOR DAILY NEWS, July 9, 2002. Reprinted by permission of the author.

**James Deacon**
"Monster Homes, SUVs, TVs, Yachts: Bigger Is Better—Or Is It?" by James Deacon from MACLEAN'S, August 5, 2002, p. 34. Reprinted by permission from Maclean's Magazine.

# PHOTO CREDITS

# INDEX

# A

Abstracting services, 173
Academic writing, 14
*Achille Lauro*, 223
Adams, John, 223, 224
*Ad hominem* argument, 37
Adirondack Mountains, 78–79
Adolescent topics, 63–64
Advanced Placement (AP) programs, 255
Adversarial nature of argument, 5
Advertising
    American flag in, 83–85
    assertive argument, 12
    character in, 44–45
    cigarette manufacturers, 336
    Evian water images, 85–86
    fast food, 337
    sound, use of, 110–111
    television, integrating text, 93–94
Africa, 353
Afterword, MLA bibliography style, 194
Age
    beauty, changing ideas of, 61
    culture and, 63–64
AIDS epidemic, 75
Al Muhajir, Abdullah, 312–313
Alternatives, presenting false dilemma, 40
Ambitious language, 39
*American Beauty* (movie), 289
American flag, 83–85
*American Flag: $19.95. New Yacht: $75,000. True Patriotism? Priceless* (Frazier), 326–330
American national identity, 296–320
American Psychological Association. *See* APA style
Analogy, arguing by, 37
Analyzing. *See also* reading critically
    arguments, 7
    audience for rhetorical situation, 55–56
    claims, 33–35
    evidence, 133
    Internet resources, 165
Andante.com, 225
Annotating
    note taking versus, 160
    reading critically, 154–155
Anonymous work, APA bibliography style, 206

Anthology
    documentation notes, 180
    MLA bibliography style, 194
Anticorbustics, 328
AP. *See* Advanced Placement (AP) programs
APA (American Psychological Association) style
    bibliography references, 199–207
    content notes, 184
    endnotes, 185
    guidebooks to, 184
    parenthetical documentation, 185, 188–190
    quotations, 183
Appraising evidence, 76–80
Appropriateness, 65–66
Arab culture, considering in argument, 60
Araton, Harvey
    article on tennis players, 46–48
    culture, considering in argument, 60
    historical context, 65
Argument
    constructing, 113–148
    contexts, 53–67
    defined, 4–6
    importance of learning to write effective, 6–7
    media, 69–111, 70–111, 146
    purposes, 9–21
    strategies, 23–51
*Argumentation on the Web* (Formato), 100–103
Aristotle
    character, 44
    logic relying on two premises (enthymeme), 30
    rhetoric, 23, 24, 145
Art as visual argument, 89–93
Articles
    APA bibliography style, 199, 204
    author, previewing, 153
    documentation notes, 180
    finding on Internet, 167–170
    MLA bibliography style, 195–196
    newspaper, researching, 172–173
    summary of current, 173
    titles, underlining versus italicizing, 190
Asia, 354
Assertion, 11–13
Association, attributing guilt by, 38
Asynchronous online discussion forums, 105–109

Audience
    circumstances, influence on, 57–58
    concessions, making, 118–119
    evidence, effect on, 133
    expectations, 119
    facts, choosing, 77
    identifying, 117–118
    imagining for rhetoric, 56–58
    language, effective use of, 146
    misjudging, 121
    online discussion forums, 108, 109
    radio and television, 110
    rhetorical situation, 55–56
    sample student essay addressing, 119–124
    support and need for additional evidence, 145
    tone, 148
    Toulmin model, 140
    written argument, 72
Authority
    backfiring claims, 50–51
    character and, 44
    evidence, 79–80
Authors
    anonymous work, APA bibliography style, 206
    articles, MLA bibliography style, 195
    bibliography style, MLA, 191
    corporate
        APA bibliography style, 204
        APA parenthetical documentation, 189–190
        MLA parenthetical documentation, 186–187
    multiple
        APA bibliography style, 204, 205
        APA parenthetical documentation, 189
        MLA bibliography style, 193–194
        MLA parenthetical documentation, 186
    multiple works by same, MLA parenthetical documentation, 187
    single
        APA bibliography style, 199–200, 203
        APA parenthetical documentation, 188–189
        MLA bibliography style, 193
        MLA parenthetical documentation, 186
    of work, previewing, 153–154

Automobile purchases, 10
*Autonomy with trifurcation is the answer: Ladakh leader* (Khosa), 362

## B

Background, statement of, 126
Bailey, Pamela G., 48–49
*A Beautiful Place Made Ugly* (Wright), 273
Beauty, changing ideas of, 61–62
Begging the question, 38–39
Beliefs
    differing, ability to understand, 3
    as flaw in logical system, 29–30
    reliance on fundamental, 28
Benefits statement, Rogerian argument, 128
Bias, summarizing, 157
Bibliography
    APA style, 199–207
    MLA style, 191–199
    organizing, 190–207
    preliminary, 180
    previewing material, 154
    sources, citing, 183
*Bigger, Not Better* (Foder), 283
Birkerts, Sven, 25–26
*Black Is Back* (Ogbar and Prashad), 227–230
Blacks, cultural context, 59
Bolter, Jay David *(Writing Space)*, 14–15
Bondy, Filip, 42–43
Books
    author, previewing, 153–154
    in bibliographies
        APA, 199, 203–205
        MLA style, 193–194
    documentation notes, 180
    finding, 173–175
    MLA parenthetical documentation, 186–188
    titles, underlining versus italicizing, 190
Boolean operators, 168–169
Borowski, John, 146–147
Boston Latin School, 248
Boulder, Colorado, 285
Brainstorming, 139
Bretton Woods, 368
Broadening topic, 163
Brooklyn Museum of Art, 222
Browning, Frank *(A Queer Geography)*, 64–65
Brownmiller, Susan *(Femininity)*, 62–63

*Brown v. The Topeka Board of Education*, 303
Brubaker, Kristen, 140–145
Bush, George W.
    attitude toward following September 11, 2001, 65–66
    visual media, use of, 82–84
Business issues
    corporate greed and unethical behavior, 56–57
    economic growth, ecological damage and, 79–80
    globalization
        defined, 266
        progress and, 350–377
    growth and development, 24
    meat-processing plant, building, 139–144
Bynoe, Yvonne, 230

## C

Call number, library book, 174
Canada, 331–334
Capitalism, 264
Car purchases, 10
Cartoons, 94
Catalogs, library, 174–175
Causes, attributing false, 38
CD-ROM
    MLA bibliography style, 197
    research on, 175
Chapters, APA style, 199
Character
    argument, strategy for, 43–51
    attacking opponent's, 37
    visual elements, 85
Charitable appeals, 36
Charities, funding spent by, 343
Chat rooms, 109–110
Children, cultural view of, 30–31, 64
Chiquita Banana, 370
Cicero *(De Oratore)*, 126
Cigarette marketing, 336
Circular reasoning, 38–39
Circumstances, influence on audience, 57–58
Citing sources. *See also* APA style; MLA style
    styles, described, 183
    when to, 182–183
Civil libertarian, 319
Civil rights, 303

Cizek, Gregory *(Unintended Consequences of High Stakes Testing)*, 250–260
Claesen, Bjorn Skorpen *(Singing for the Global Community)*, 374–376
Claim
    evaluating, 33–35
    evidence, evaluating support, 78
    online discussion forums, 108
    questioning, deemed impolite in certain cultures, 60–61
    rhetorical context, 35
    supporting and presenting evidence, 144–145
    Toulmin model, 31–35, 138, 139
Class discussions, 13
Classical logic, 30, 126–127
Clean Clothes Campaign, 375
Clear Channel Communications, 234
Climbing equipment article, 72–73
CMS (Chicago Manual of Style), 183
Coe, Richard *(Form and Substance)*, 127–128
Coincidences, 38
Cole, Thomas, 90
Color
    persuasive power, 88
    posters, 91, 92–93
    visual media, 87–89
Community design, 274–276, 288–291
Concessions, making, 118–119
Conclusion
    classical arrangement, 126
    deductive reasoning, 134
    drawing based on specific evidence (inductive reasoning), 25–26, 37, 132–133
    jumping to, 39
    resting on two premises (syllogism), 28–30, 32
*Confirmatio*, 126
Conspicuous Consumption, 325
Conspiracy theory, 38
Constructing arguments
    audience, 117–124
    as inquiry, 114–115
    language, effective use of, 145–148
    proceed, how to, 113–114
    structure, 125–132
    supporting claims and presenting evidence, 144–145
    terms, 124–125
    topic, 115–116

Consumers
described, 325
marketing messages, 336–339
patriotic spending, 326–330
responsibilities to poor, 340–345
spending in Canada, 331–334
Content notes, 184
Context
described, 53–54
facts, choosing, 77
historical, 65–67
rhetorical situation, 54–58
statement in Rogerian argument, 128
Controversial issues, 41–43
Conversational tone
design reinforcing, 89
ethos, 74
writing style, 73
Copyright, 212–213
Corporate author
APA bibliography style, 204
parenthetical documentation
APA, 189–190
MLA, 186–187
*Courier* (UNESCO), 229
Credibiity, writer's. *See* ethos
Credibility
online discussion forums, 108–109
questioning, deemed impolite in certain
cultures, 60–61
Credit card debt, 327
Crime issues, 10–11, 50
Critical reading. *See* reading critically
Culture
age, 63–64
considering in argument, 60–61
differences and deductive reasoning,
30–31
gender, 61–63
sexual orientation, 64–65
understanding, 58–60
Curriculum
college versus non-college bound, 241
consequences of high-stakes testing,
250–260
Marxist response to exams, 262–268
tracking, 246–249

**D**

Damocles, 265
Data, Toulmin model, 31, 138

Database, in bibliographies
online, APA style, 203
periodically published, MLA style,
196–197
printed publication, MLA style, 197
*Databases and Security vs. Privacy* (Green),
314–316
Date, publication, 175
Deacon, James *(The Joys of Excess),*
331–334
*The Death of Klinghoffer* (Goodman and
Adams), 223, 224
The Declaration of Independence, 297
annotations, sample, 155, 156
deductive reasoning in, 26
historical context, 66
Deductive reasoning, 26–31, 134–138
Defining terms, 124–125
Democracy, globalization and,
365–372
Dershowitz, Alan M. *(Why Fear National
ID Cards?),* 318–320
Design, visual media, 87–89
Desktop publishing software, 82
Dictionary, 124
Differences
ability to understand, 3
ethos, importance of, 75
irreconcilable, 21, 118
negotiating, 2, 6, 19–21
Digital Freedom Network Web site,
104–105
Digital technology, 175
Dilemma, false, 40, 121
Direct Marketing Association (DMA),
315
Discussion forums
electronic media, 105–110
MLA bibliography style, 199
Disputable major premise, 29–30
DMA. *See* Direct Marketing Association
Documenting sources
citations, 182–207
integrating into paper, 181–182
notes, taking, 180
organizing, 180–181
Doha, Qatar, 367
Dominating, 16–18
Do-not-call list, 315
Draft, final, 207–208
Driving habits, 81–82
Drug articles, 10–11, 50

**E**

Eating out, money spent on, 343
*Ecological Literacy* (Orr), 79–80
Economic growth, ecological damage and,
79–80
Edited book, APA bibliography,
204
Editions subsequent to first, in
bibliographies
APA style, 204
MLA style, 194
Editor, letters to. *See* letters to the editor
Editorials
MLA bibliography style, 196
Pledge of Allegiance, 27–28
Editorial support, print versus resources,
165
Editorial tone, newspapers, 72
Ekklesia, 308
Electronic communication, reliance on,
25–26
Electronic media
Internet, 97–99
online discussion forums, 105–110
radio and television, 110–111
Web sites, 99–105
Electronic resources
documentation notes, 180
MLA parenthetical documentation,
188
Electroshock therapy, letter to *Newsweek* in
response to, 57
Ellipsis (...), 182
Email discussion lists, 97–98
Eminent domain, 366
Emotion
arguments, 41–43
evoking visually, 43, 86
language heavy in, 64
Empathetic listening. *See* Rogerian
argument
*Empire of the Air* (Toomey), 232–236
Encyclopedia article, MLA bibliography
style, 194–195
Endnotes
APA style, 185
MLA style, 184–185
Ends, leading to undesirable, 40–41
*Enough Snickering. Suburbia Is More
Complicated Than We Think*
(Wilson), 288–291

Enron, 367
Entertainment, 5
Enthymeme, 30
Environment, community, 272–293
Environmental issues
awareness, raising through art, 90
car purchases, 10
economic growth, 79–80
gasoline boycott article, 34–35
schoolbooks, 146–147
Equivocating, 39
Eschatology, 250
Ethics, 2, 9
Ethnic background. *See* culture
Ethos
defined, 44
online discussion forums, 108
print media, 73–75
EU. *See* European Union
Europe
The Marshall Plan, 351
per capita income, 354
European Union (EU)
Chiquita Banana dispute, 370
ID cards, 316
Evaluating. *See* analyzing
Evian water images, 85–86
Evidence
authority, 79–80
commonly used types, 76
developing in Toulmin model, 140
drawing conclusion based on specific,
25–26, 37, 132–133
facts, 76–78
personal experience, 78–79
presenting, 144–145
print media, 76–80
Toulmin model of argumentation, 31,
138
values, 80–81
visual, 81–82
Exclamation point, simple annotating with,
155
*Exordium*, 126
Expectations, 119
Experience, writer's, 75
Expertise, 44
Expert opinion, 32

**F**

Facts, 32, 76–78
Fairfax County, Virginia, 274–276

Fairness and Accuracy in Reporting (FAIR),
339
Fallacies
analogy, arguing by, 37
begging the question, 38–39
character, attacking opponent's, 37
eliminating in sample student essay, 123
equivocating, 39
false causes, attributing, 38
false dilemma, presenting, 40
guarding against, 35–36
guilt by association, attributing, 38
ignoring the question, 39
jumping to conclusions, 39
pity, appeals to, 36
prejudice, appeals to, 36
reasoning that does not follow, 40
slippery slope, 40–41
straw man, opposing, 39–40
tradition, appeals to, 37
False causation, 35, 38
False dilemma, 40, 121
Family, meaning of, 64
Fascism, 91
Fast food advertising, 337
Faulty reasoning, 29–30
Fay, Brian, 59–60
*Femininity* (Brownmiller), 62–63
Feminism, 19
Figurative language, 147–148
Final draft, 207–208
Flag, American, 83–85
Flame wars, 98, 109
Foder, Eben, 283
Footnotes, MLA (Modern Language
Association) style, 184–185, 185
Foreman, Gary, 34–35
Foreword, MLA bibliography style, 194
Formal language, 146
Formal logic. *See* classical logic
*Form and Substance* (Coe), 127–128
Formato, Tom ("Argumentation on the
Web"), 100–103
Formatting manuscript, 208
Forms, written argumentation, 3
Fourteenth Amendment, 303
Frazier, Ian (*American Flag: $19.95. New
Yacht: $75,000. True Patriotism?
Priceless*), 326–330
*Free Downloads Play Sweet Music* (Ian),
214–218
Free enterprise, 324–345
French State Railways poster, 90–91

Friedman, Milton, 49
Friedman, Thomas L., 376

**G**

G-8. *See* Group of Eight
Gasoline boycott article, 34–35
Gender, 61–63
General Agreement on Tariffs and Trade
(GATT), 367
Generalization, 134
General Motors automobile factory poster,
92–93
*Getting the Message* (O'Connor), 337
Giuliani, Rudolf, 222
*Giving Aid to World Trade* (Yergin), 352–354
Globalization
defined, 266
progress and, 350–377
Global warming, 4–5
Goals, 114
Goals 2000, 255
Goldwater, Barry, 306
Goodman, Alice, 223, 224
Google, 165–166
Gordon, Gerald, 24, 276
Government power
civil liberties, 311–313
"The Declaration of Independence"
(Jefferson), 297
ID cards, 318–320
King, Martin Luther Jr. on, 298–310
Government publication, in bibliographies
APA style, 206
MLA style, 195
Goya, Francisco José, 89–90
Graham, Mary, 33–34
Graph, 81–82, 94–95
Graphics, 82, 87
Greek theory, 65
Green, Heather (*Databases and Security vs.
Privacy*), 314–316
Group of Eight (G-8), 352
Growth and development in Fairfax County
Virginia, 24
Guetter, Rachel
essay "A Reasonable Approach to Gay
Adoption," 129–132
footnotes and endnotes, 184–185
quotation, integrating into essay, 182
sample source citation, 183
Guilt by association, attributing, 38
Gun control article, 41–42

## H

Hadad, Amir, 46–48
Health and Human Services department, 168
Hernandez, Daisy (*The Laments of Commuting*), 74
Highlighting, 155
Hip hop music, 227–230
Historical contexts of argument, 65–67
Home page, personal, MLA bibliography style, 198
Household credit card debt, 327
Hudson Valley School, 90
Humanities sources, citing. *See* MLA
Hungary, Soviet Union in, 304
Hypertextual Web sites, 99–103

## I

Ian, Janis (*Free Downloads Play Sweet Music*), 214–218
IASA. *See* Improving America's Schools Act
IB. *See* International Baccalaureate programs
IBO. *See* International Baccalaureate Curriculum
ID cards, 316
Identifying audience, 117–118
Ignoring the questions, 39
Image, twisting to make point, 87
Imagining audience for rhetorical situation, 56–58
IM (instant messaging), 109–110
Import, historical context and, 66
Improving America's Schools Act (IASA), 255
Income, per capita, 354
Indexes, periodical, 167–170
Inductive leap, 133
Inductive reasoning
    analogy, arguing by, 37
    described, 25–26
    logic, 132–133
Informal logic. *See* enthymeme
InfoTrac, 168
Inquiry, arguments as, 13–16, 114–115
Instant messaging. *See* IM
Intellectual theft, 161
Intelligence quotient (IQ), 247
Interdependence of world, 374–376
Interlibrary loan, 175
International Baccalaureate Curriculum (IBO), 248

International Baccalaureate programs (IB), 255
International Society for Ecology and Culture (ISEC), 363
Internet
    chat rooms, appeal of, 63–64
    documentation notes, 180
    evaluating resources, 165
    music downloads, 214–218
    newspaper articles, researching, 170, 172–173
    online discussion groups, 97–99
    paper-selling services, 161
    research, 164–167
Internet downloads, 214–218
Interpretation of evidence, 133
Interview
    in bibliographies
        APA style, 206
        MLA style, 198–199
    conducting, 175–176
Introduction
    classical arrangement, 126
    MLA bibliography style, 194
    Rogerian argument, 127
Invention, 23
IQ. *See* intelligence quotient
Irreconcilable positions, 21, 118
ISEC. *See* International Society for Ecology and Culture
Italicizing titles, 190
Italy, 91

## J

Janus, 228
Japan, 59, 60–61
Jefferson, Thomas, 26, 28, 66, 297
Jordan, Michael, 44
Journal article
    in bibliographies
        APA, 201, 205, 206
        MLA, 195
    finding, 167–170
    online versions, 167
    titles, underlining versus italicizing, 190
*The Joys of Excess* (Deacon), 331–334
Judgment, opinions as, 116
Jumping to conclusions, 39

## K

*Kairos*, 65
Kathmandu, 229

Kelly, Michael (*Liberties Are a Real Casualty of War*), 311–313
Key points, identifying, 152
Key words
    Internet searches, 165–166, 168–169
    library books, finding, 174
Khomeini, Ayatollah, 220
Khosa, Aasha (*Autonomy with trifurcation is the answer: Ladakh leader*), 362
King, Martin Luther, Jr. (*Letter From a Birmingham Jail*), 80–81, 298–310
Klinghoffer, Leon, 223
Knowledge, writer's, 75
Kohn, Alfie, 251
Koran, University of North Carolina policy on reading, 45

## L

Ladakh, 359–362
*The Laments of Commuting* (Hernandez), 74
Language
    effective use of, 145–148
    emotionally charged, 64
    neutrality in Rogerian argument, 19
    technical, 58
    vague or ambitious, 39
Law
    character in, 44–45
    warrant, 34
Length
    of paragraphs, 154
    of summaries, 157
    of work, 153, 175
*Letter from a Birmingham Jail* (King), 80–81, 298–310
Letters to the editor
    about Mike Myers, 74–75
    changing ideas of beauty, 61–62
    corporate greed and unethical behavior, 56–57
    electroshock therapy, 57
    growth and development in Fairfax County Virginia, 24
    medical technology, 48–49
Lexis-Nexis, 170, 172–173
*The Lexus and the Olive Tree* (Friedman), 376
*Liberties Are a Real Casualty of War* (Kelly), 311–313
Library
    catalogs, 174–175
    loans from other, 175

Listening in Rogerian argument, 19
Listing, 181
Listserv, 97–98
*The Living Democracy Movement: Alternatives to the Bankruptcy of Globalisation* (Shiva), 365–372
Lobzang, Lama, 361
Local culture, 356–363
Logic
  deductive reasoning, 26–31, 134–138
  fallacy, 35
  inductive reasoning, 25–26, 132–133
  main premise, validity of, 24–25
  multiple methods, use of, 144
  objectivity and, 24
  Toulmin model, 31–35, 138–144
  visual elements, 85
Lopresti, Mike, 147–148

## M

Magazine article
  author, previewing, 153
  bibliography style
    APA, 205
    MLA, 195–196
  finding, 167–170
  online versions, 167
  titles, underlining versus italicizing, 190
Mailing list, MLA bibliography style, 199
Main clause, subordinate clause not related to, 40
Major (main) premise
  disputable, 29–30
  flawed, 32
  syllogism, 28–29
  validity, 24–25
Mandela, Nelson, 20
Manuscript form, 208
Mapping, 181
*The March of the Monoculture* (Norberg-Hodge), 356–363
Marketing messages, 336–339
Markham, Kevin (*MP3s Great Technology, but Use Must Be Ethical*), 217
Marshall, George C., 351
Martin, Eleanor (*"'No'" Is the Right Answer*), 242–244
Massachusetts Comprehensive Assessment System (MCAS), 243
Matthiessen, Peter (*Tigers in the Snow*), 96
MCAS. *See* Massachusetts Comprehensive Assessment System

McLuhan, Marshall, 111
Meadows, Donella (*So What Can We Do — Really Do — About Sprawl*), 282–286
Meaning, historical context, 66
Meat eating, argument against, 135–138
Meat-processing plant, building, 139–144
Media
  electronic, 97–111
  language use, 146
  print, 70–82
  visual, 82–97
Medical issues
  AIDS epidemic, 75
  electroshock therapy, 57
  technology, 48–49
Meredith, James, 309
*Microform*, 175
Middle class, 344
Minnesota Public Radio Web site, 104
Misjudging audience, 121
*Misplacing the Blame for Our Troubles on 'Flat, Not Tall' Spaces* (Postrel), 278–280
*Mixed Messages Call for Healthy Skepticism* (Solomon), 336–339
MLA (Modern Language Association) style
  bibliography style, 191–199
  footnotes or endnotes, 184–185
  parenthetical documentation, 185, 186–188
  publications outlining, 184
  quotation, citing source, 183
  when to use, 183
Montgomery, Kristen, 135–138
Moore, Michael, 65–66
Moral values, 2, 80–81
Mother figures, 86
Mount Rushmore, 82–83
MP3, 217
*MP3s Great Technology, but Use Must Be Ethical* (Markham), 217
MUDs (multi-user domains), 109–110
Muhammad, Elijah, 305
Multimedia, 103
Multiple authors
  bibliography style
    APA, 204, 205
    MLA, 193–194
  parenthetical documentation
    APA, 189
    MLA, 186

Multiple sources, APA parenthetical documentation, 190
Multiple volumes
  bibliography style
    APA, 205
    MLA, 194
  parenthetical documentation, MLA, 187
Music, 110–111
Music, ownership of
  copyright, 212–213
  importance, 213
*Music Dangers and the Case for Control* (Taruskin), 219–225
Myers, Mike, 74–75

## N

Napster, 215
*Narratio*, 126
Narrowing topic, 163
*The Nation*, 249
National Rifle Association, 320
Nation of Islam, 305
Nations, integrating, 350
Nebuchadnezzar, 304
Negotiating
  differences through argument, 6
  ethos, importance of, 75
  as purpose of argument, 18–21
Neibuhr, Reinhold, 301
Neuharth, Al, 72
Neutrality, language, 19
Newdow, Michael, 27
Newsgroup
  described, 97–98
  MLA bibliography style, 199
Newspaper article
  APA bibliography style, 202–203, 205
  researching, 170
Newspapers. *See also* letters to the editor
  editorial tone, 72
  MLA bibliography style, 196
  online versions, 167
  titles, underlining versus italicizing, 190
New Towns movement, 291
*The New York Times*, 320
Nike shoes advertisement, 93–94
*1984* (Orwell), 319
*"'No'" Is the Right Answer* (Martin), 242–244
NoLogo.org, 86
*Non sequitur*, 40
Nonviolence, 300

Norberg-Hodge, Helena (*The March of the Monoculture*), 356–363
Note cards, 160
Notes, taking, 159–160, 180

## O

Objectivity, 24
O'Connor, Paul (*Getting the Message*), 337
Ogbar, Jeffrey O.G. (*Black Is Back*), 227–230
OLLC FirstSearch, 167–170
Ollman, Bertell (*Why So Many Exams? A Marxist Response*), 262–268
*Once There Were Greenfields: How Urban Sprawl is Undermining America's Environment, Economy and Social Fabric* (Benfield, Raimi, and Chen), 279
Ong, Walter ("The Writer's Audience Is Always a Fiction"), 56
Online databases, 203
Online discussion forums, 4–5, 97–98, 105–110
Online journals
  bibliography style
    APA, 206
    MLA, 197–198
  researching, 167
Online media, 175
Online sources
  editorial support, 165
  MLA bibliography style, 192–193, 198
Opinion
  expert, claims supported by, 32
  leading to good arguments, 116
Opponent, audience not as, 118
Opportune moment, 65
Opposing view, summary of, 127
Oral argument, 71
O'Reilly, Bill, 45–46
Organizing
  bibliography, 190–207
  sources for research paper, 180–181
  synthesis, 158–159
Orr, David (*Ecological Literacy*), 79–80
Orwell, George, 319
Outlining
  research paper, 180–181
  synthesis, 159
Ownership
  of music, 212–237
*Oxford English Dictionary*, 124

## P

Padilla, Jose, 312–313
Page, Clarence, 45
Painting, 89–90
Palestine Liberation Front, 223
Paper-selling services, 161
Paragraphs
  average length, previewing, 154
  writers, linking through, 159
Paraphrasing
  benefits, 155, 157
  plagiarism, 162
  quoting versus, 182
  summarizing versus, 157
Parenthetical documentation
  APA style, 185, 188–190
  MLA style, 185
*Partitio*, 126
Partner, audience as, 118
Patriotism, 66
*Peroratio*, 126
Personal digital assistants, 160
Personal experience, 78–79
Personality, writer's. *See* ethos
Persuasion, 4, 88
Philosophy, school of (utilitarianism), 341
Photograph
  as argument, 89, 96
  placement, 87
  text, reinforcing, 94–95
Pity, appeals to, 36
Placement
  photograph, 87
  text, 87–88
Plagiarism
  avoiding, 161–163
  Usenet discussion about, 106–108
Pledge of Allegiance articles, 27–28, 35
Plotz, David (*A Suburb Grown Up and All Paved Over*), 274–276
Politics
  arguments to dominate, 16
  attacks when can't win, 10–11
  character in, 44–45
  classical rhetoric, 127
  direct participation through Internet, 97–98
  guilt by association, attributing, 38
  ignoring questions, 39
Popular discussions, 4–5
Population, 278–280

Position
  changing while examining topic, 15–16
  statement in Rogerian argument, 127–128
Posters
  French State Railways, 90–91
  World War II, 92–93
Post hoc reasoning, 38
Postrel, Virginia (*Misplacing the Blame for Our Troubles on 'Flat, Not Tall' Spaces*), 278–280
Poverty level, U.S., 276
Prashad, Vijay (*Black Is Back*), 227–230
Prayer in school, 10
Preface, MLA bibliography style, 194
Prejudice, appeals to, 36
Preliminary bibliography, 180
Premise
  begging the question, 38–39
  deductive reasoning, 134, 135
  defined, 27
  reliance on fundamental values or beliefs, 28
Previewing
  books through catalog listing, 175
  reading critically, 153–154
Printing press, history of, 14–15
Print media
  editorial support, 165
  ethos, 73–75
  evidence, appraising, 76–80
  reading critically, 70–73
  Web sites republishing, 99
Privacy, survey respondents, 177
Problems
  considering those encountered by others, 2
  negotiating, importance of ethos, 75
  solving through argument, 6
Professional journals, 169–170, 171
Progress, globalization and
  individual action, 374–376
  Living Democracy movement, 365–372
  local culture, destruction of, 356–363
  The Marshall Plan, 351
  nations, integrating, 350
Proof, 126
Proposition, 126
Publisher, 154, 175

Purpose of argument
    to assert, 11–13
    circumstances, sample, 10–11
    to dominate, 16–18
    ethics of, 9
    to inquire, 13–16
    to negotiate and reconcile, 18–21
Pyramid schemes, 286

**Q**

Quarrels, 4, 98
*A Queer Geography* (Browning), 64–65
Question mark, simple annotating, 155
Questions
    cultural attitude toward, 60–61
    ignoring, 39
    structure, 125
Quintillian, 44
Quotation
    integrating, 181–182
    paraphrasing versus, 182
    parenthetical documentation style
        APA, 183
        MLA, 183, 187–188
Quotation marks
    plagiarism, avoiding, 161–163
    titles, bibliography style, 191
Qureshi, Aisam ul-Haq, 46–48

**R**

Racial background. *See* culture
Radio, 5, 97, 110–111
Radio stations, 232–236
Raleigh, Duane, 72–73
Ralph Lauren advertisements, 83–85
Rap music, 227–230
Rather, Dan, 75
*Readers' Guide to Periodical Literature*,
    167–170
Reading critically
    annotating, 154–155
    key points, identifying, 152
    previewing, 153–154
    summarizing, 155, 157
    synthesizing, 157–159
*A Reasonable Approach to Gay Adoption*
    (Guetter), 129–132
Reasons, 134–135
Reconciling, 18–21

Recording Industry Association of America
    (RIAA), 215
Red Cross, 328
Red herring, 315
Reference books, 124
References, in letter, 144
Refutation, 126
Regional planning, 289
Religious groups, 219–225
Religious upbringing. *See* culture
Report of the Committee of Ten, 1892, 241
Researching
    abstracting services, 173
    books, finding, 173–175
    on Internet, 164–167
    interviews, 175–176
    newspaper articles, 170, 172–173
    notes, taking, 159–160
    plagiarism, 161–163
    reading critically, 152–159
    relevant material, finding, 163–175
    selective, avoiding, 164
    surveys, 176–177
Retirement benefits assessment, 11
Revised edition. *See* editions subsequent to
    first, in bibliographies
Rhetoric
    arguments, constructing, 114
    audience, 55–58
    claims and warrants, 35
    culture and, 58–65
    strategies for argument, 23–24
*Rhetoric* (Aristotle), 44, 145
RIAA. *See* Recording Industry Association
    of America (RIAA)
Rivedal, Karen, 119–124
Robinette, J.J., 331
Rogerian argument, 19–21, 127–132
Rogers, Carl, 19, 127

**S**

School desegregation, 303
School issues
    book ban, 146–147
    buying school supplies, 88–89
    early starting dates for school year, 72
    prayer, 10
    skipping classes, 119–124
    teacher salaries, 77–78
    vouchers, 49
Scientific research, 26

Search engines
    described, 165–166
    narrowing searching with Boolean
        operators, 168–169
Security versus privacy, 314–316
Selective research, avoiding, 164
"Sensation" exhibit, 222
"The Sense of Place" (Stegner), 338
Sentences, 40
September 11, 2001, attitudes following,
    311
    appropriateness of topics, 65–66
    economic globalization, 368
    government Web sites, censorship, 33–34
    patriotic spending, 326–330
    Red Cross, money-handling by, 329
    reference to in Pledge of Allegiance
        article, 35
    towards George W. Bush, 65–66
    visual media, use of, 82–84
Sexual orientation, 61, 64–65
Shenk, Joshua Wolf, 50
Shields, Jeanne, 41–42
Shiva, Vandana (*The Living Democracy
    Movement: Alternatives to the
    Bankruptcy of Globalisation*),
    365–372
Simile, 147–148
Simmons, Russell, 230
Singer, Peter (*The Singer Solution to World
    Poverty*), 340–345
*Singing for the Global Community* (Claesen),
    374–376
Single author
    bibliography style
        APA, 199–200, 203
        MLA, 193
    parenthetical documentation
        APA, 188–189
        MLA, 186
Situation, influence on audience, 57–58
Skepticism, 118
Skimming material, 154
Slatalla, Michelle ("The Seductive Call of
    School Supplies"), 88–89
Slippery slope, 40–41
Sloan, Allan, 56–57
Slouka, Mark, 98
Social class. *See* culture
Social problem, essays on, 38
*Social Sciences Abstracts*, 169–170, 171
Social sciences sources, citing. *See* APA

Solomon, Norman (*Mixed Messages Call for Healthy Skepticism*), 336–339
Songs, popular, 110–111
Sound, 110–111
Sources
    documenting, 179–208
    drawing too heavily upon, 161–163
    footnotes and content notes, 184–185
    organizing research paper, 180–181
    parenthetical documentation, 185–190
    researching, 151–177
Soviet Union, action in Hungary, 304
*So What Can We Do — Really Do — About Sprawl* (Meadows), 282–286
Sprawl, 282–286
St. Lawrence Cement advertisement, 94–97
Statement, logical
    of background, 126
    of benefits, 128
    of contexts, 128
    cultural attitude towards, 60–61
    of understanding, 127
    of your position, 127–128
Statistics
    adequacy of claim and, 77–78
    establishing writer's knowledge, 75
Stegner, Wallace, 338
Stein, Clarence, 289
Stereotyping, 64
Strategies
    character-based, 43–51
    emotional, 41–43
    fallacies, 35–41
    logical, 24–35
    rhetoric, 23–24
Straw man, opposing, 39–40
Structure
    classical arrangement, 126–127
    logical arrangements, 132–144
    questions determining, 125
    Rogerian argument, 127–132
Student essays, sample
    argument against eating meat, 135–138
    "A Reasonable Approach to Gay Adoption," 129–132
    skipping classes, 119–124
Student issues. *See* school issues
Style. *See also* APA style; MLA style
    language, effective use of, 145–146
Style manuals, commonly used, 183
Subconscious plagiarism, 163

Subject, 115
Subordinate clause, 40
Subtitles, 154
*A Suburb Grown Up and All Paid Over* (Plotz), 274–276
Sullivan, R. Mark, 77–78
Summarizing
    bias, 157
    of current articles, 173
    method, suggested, 158
    opposing views in Rogerian argument, 127
    paraphrasing versus, 157
    quoting versus, 182
    reading critically, 155
    topic sentence, 155
Superstitions, 38
Supreme Court decisions
    copyright, 212–213
    school desegregation, 303
Surveys, 176–177
Sustainability, 125
Sweeney, Camille, 63–64
Syllogism
    deductive reasoning, 28–29
    faulty reasoning, 29–30
    relying on two parts (enthymeme), 30
    Toulmin model's advantages over, 32
Symmetry, 87
Synchronous online forums, 109–110
Synthesis, 157–159

**T**

Taliban, 219–225
Talk shows, 5
Tape recorder, 176
Taruskin, Richard (*Music Dangers and the Case for Control*), 219–225
Taste, opinions as matter of, 116
Technical language, 58
Technology, copying music, 217
Telecommunications Act of 1996, 233, 235
Television
    adversarial arguments, 5
    advertising, integrating text, 93–94
    commentator Bill O'Reilly, 45–46
    described, 97, 110–111
    sound, 111
Terms, defining, 124–125
Terrorist attacks. *See* September 11, 2001, attitudes following

Testing systems, 242–244
*Tests, Tracking, and Derailment* (Williams), 246–249
Text
    documentation within (*See* parenthetical documentation)
    marking with notes (*See* annotating)
    photograph reinforcing, 94–95
    placement, 87–88
    visual media integrating, 93–97
Theology of end of the world or humankind, 250
*Theory of the Leisure Class* (Veblen), 325
Thoreau, Henry David, 148
Threads, 109–110
Tibet, 359
*Tigers in the Snow* (Matthiessen), 96
Title
    bibliography style
        APA, 199
        MLA, 191
    italics, 190
    underlining, 190
    of work, previewing, 153
Tommasini, Anthony, 224
*TomPaine.com* article opposing Bush tax refund, 76–77
Tone
    audience, 148
    ethos, 75
    newspapers, 72
Toomey, Jenny (*Empire of the Air*), 232–236
Topic
    defining, 115–116
    narrowing or broadening during research, 163
    sentence summarizing material, 155
Toulmin, Stephen, 31
Toulmin model, 31–35, 138–144
Trade barriers, relaxing, 367
Tradition, appeals to, 37
Translations, in bibliographies
    APA style, 204
    MLA style, 194
Triangle metaphor, defining rhetorical situation, 54–55
Truth
    argument as means of discovering, 2, 5–6
    deductive reasoning, 27
    fallacies, guarding against, 35
2002 World Cup article, 42–43
Typing, manuscript form, 208

## U

Underlining titles, 190
UNESCO. *See* United Nations Educational, Scientific, and Cultural Organization
UNICEF. *See* United Nations International Children's Emergency Fund
*Unintended Consequences of High Stakes Testing* (Cizek), 250–260
Unionization, 11
United Nations Educational, Scientific, and Cultural Organization (UNESCO), 229
United Nations International Children's Emergency Fund (UNICEF), 342
University of North Carolina policy on reading the Koran, 45
Updike, John, 288
U.S. *See also* American national identity
   GDP, 353
   government posters, 92–93
   household credit card debt, 327
   income, relative share of, 332
   money spent on eating out, 343
   population density, 280
   poverty rate, 276
   Web site censorship article, 33–34
U.S. Constitution, 303
U.S. Department of Health and Human Services, 168
Utilitarianism, 341

## V

Vague language. *See* equivocating
Values
   claims supported by, 32
   evidence, 80–81
   prejudice, appeals to, 36
   reliance on fundamental, 28
Veblen, Thorstein (*Theory of the Leisure Class*), 325
Vehicle, average fuel economy, 333
Virtual communities, 98
Visual media
   art as argument, 89–93

design and color, 87–89
evidence, presenting, 81–82
power of, 82–85
text, integrating, 93–97
Web sites, embedding, 103
Volumes
   bibliography style
      APA, 205
      MLA, 194
   MLA parenthetical documentation, 187

## W

Wagner, Richard, 222
Warrant
   elements of, 33
   evaluating, 33–35
   legal principle, invoking, 34
   rhetorical context, 35
   Toulmin model, 31, 138, 139–140
   World War II posters, 92
Web sites
   as arguments, 103–105
   censorship, article on, 33–34
   documentation notes, 180
   hypertextual, 99–103
   MLA bibliography style, 198
   online forums, 4–5
   print arguments, online versions, 99, 100
   searching, 165, 168
Web sites, addresses listed
   classical music, 225
   Clean Clothes Campaign, 375
   education news, 259
   Fairness and Accuracy in Reporting (FAIR), 339
   Recording Industry Association of America (RIAA), 215
White
   painting as visual argument, 90
   persuasive power, 88
*Why Fear National ID Cards?* (Dershowitz), 318–320
*Why So Many Exams? A Marxist Response* (Ollman), 262–268
Wile, Joan (*TomPaine.com* article opposing Bush tax refund), 76–77

Will, George, 69–70
Williams, Patricia (*Tests, Tracking, and Derailment*), 246–249
Wilson, Robert (*Enough Snickering. Suburbia Is More Complicated Than We Think*), 288–291
Winning
   dominating, 16
   misconception about argument, 2
Word processing programs
   documentation notes, 180
   graphics, incorporating, 82
   note taking, 160
Words
   ethos, establishing, 75
   powerful associations in emotional appeals, 43
World trade, 352–354
World Trade Organization (WTO), 365–372
World War II posters, 92–93
World Wide Web. *See* Web
Wright, Frank Lloyd, 289
   (*A Beautiful Place Made Ugly*), 273
Writers. *See also* authors
   linking within paragraphs in synthesis, 159
   success through learning to write effective arguments, 6–7
"The Writer's Audience Is Always a Fiction" (Ong), 56
*Writing Space* (Bolter), 14–15
WTO. *See* World Trade Organization

## Y

Yergin, Daniel (*Giving Aid to World Trade*), 352–354

## Z

*Z Magazine*, 268
Zoellick, Robert, 368

KeRfueim